ESSAYS

IN

BIOGRAPHY AND CRITICISM.

BY

PETER BAYNE, M. A.

AUTHOR OF "THE CHRISTIAN LIFE, SOCIAL AND INDIVIDUAL," ETC.

FIRST SERIES.

BOSTON:
GOULD AND LINCOLN,
59 WASHINGTON STREET.
NEW YORK: SHELDON AND COMPANY.
CINCINNATI: GEO. S. BLANCHARD.
1860.

PRINTED BY
GEORGE C. RAND & AVERY.

G. J. STILES,
ELECTRO-STEREOTYPER,
BOSTON.

PREFACE.*

THE papers here published consist in part of contributions to an Edinburgh Magazine, and in part of compositions which have not previously appeared. Of the former, some have undergone only a slight revision; others have been so modified as to be materially changed in character; while several, though, save in a single instance, retaining their original titles, may be considered altogether new. The series from which the republished articles are selected was entered upon about the commencement of the author's twenty-second year, during the prosecution of theological studies in Edinburgh; the occasion of the step being an inaptitude and distaste for private tuition, and a facility and pleasure, experienced from an early age, in literary composition. The selected essays were published, with one or two exceptions, in the two succeeding years.

* The remarks in this preface are intended to apply both to the contents of the present volume, and also to those of a SECOND SERIES, the publication of which will immediately follow.

An apology may be deemed requisite for offering to the public a work, of which even the germ is found in pieces composed at so early an age. Two considrations chiefly weighed with the writer in permitting the publication. He could not let slip the opportunity offered of bringing together that portion of his early performances, to which, however sensible of their defects, he could yet deliberately append his signature, setting them apart from that far larger portion which he would now altogether cast behind him, as mere confusions of a too much wasted youth. And still more powerfully was he influenced by the reflection, which has for a long time had a firm hold on his mind, that, where a reading public is so extended as that of America, capacities of literary enjoyment, and susceptibilities to instruction, will vary so much, both in kind and degree, that it is by no means easy, if possible, to judge, within certain limits, from the abstract character of a book, whether it will or will not prove useless: and that, therefore, an author, abdicating, in great measure, the right to decide as to the worthiness or unworthiness of his compositions, ought to bow to the unsought expression of public will. Such an expression seemed to be found in the offer of American publishers to issue these volumes: and the author screens himself against all attack, by the plain declaration, that they would not now, perhaps would never, have appeared, but for the enterprise and generosity of Messrs. GOULD AND LINCOLN.

The general contents of these Essays, apart from

their inherent qualities, is such as affords some countenance to the belief that they may not altogether fail in usefulness. They partake largely of the character of an introduction, in successive chapters, to the works of great authors living or deceased. Sir Archibald Alison has testified to the correctness of the view given of his political theories; and it may be added that Mr. De Quincey expressed a very favorable opinion of the essay to which his name is appended. It must not be thought that the writer affirms on every occasion the views he endeavors to define: but to open the way, though defectively, to an intelligence of any mind exercising a powerful influence upon the age, must always be a task of importance.

The papers on Mrs. Barrett Browning, on Mr. Tennyson, and on Mr. Ruskin are, with several others, now first published. To these more weight is attached than to the earliest essays. It struck the author, in glancing over his paper on Mr. Ruskin, that the very strength of his convictions had impeded him in exhibiting their grounds, that his feeling of the total powerlessness of his opponents had made him careless in the use of his weapons. There are things too ghostly to stand the blow of an argumentative club; it passes through them as through air; and so profound is his belief that a large proportion of the critical accusations brought against Ruskin are of this sort, that he was unconsciously heedless in his assault upon them. It may be added that he fell into a mistake as to the identity of one of the reviewers whom he attacks; a mistake, however, which he hardly regrets and does not alter, since no man is better entitled to bear blows intended for the real, than the supposed, reviewer.

The writer cannot refrain, before letting fall his pen, from expressing in one word his sense of the manner in which the American press treated his former appearance before the American public. Frankness, cordiality, unmerited and exaggerated generosity characterized the welcome received by one totally unknown, the native of another land. The thought of this will be ever among his most proud and sacred recollections: and has added one other to those manifold and profound considerations, which had formerly drawn him, in admiration and affection, accompanied, he ventures to think, by a more deep and manly intelligence than is common in Great Britain, towards the American people. If the present publication is received less favorably than the last, if even it draws on itself decided disapproval and rebuke, he will be liable to no mistake as to the reason of the change.

BERLIN, April 18th, 1857.

CONTENTS.

I.

II.

III.

IV.

V.

VI.

VII.

VIII.

ESSAYS

IN

BIOGRAPHY AND CRITICISM.

I.

THOMAS DE QUINCEY AND HIS WORKS.

On entering upon the study of De Quincey's writings, the first thing with which we are impressed is a certain air of perfect ease, and as it were relaxation, which breathes around. "The river glideth at his own sweet will;" now lingering to dally with the water lilies, now wandering into green nooks to reflect the gray rock and silvery birch, now rolling in stately silence through the rich, smooth meadow, now leaping amid a thousand rainbows into the echoing chasm, while the spray rises upwards in a wavering and painted column. Mildness, or majesty, or wild Titanic strength may be displayed, but the river is ever at the same perfect ease, all unconscious of the spectator. "My way of writing is rather to think aloud, and follow my own humors, than much to consider who is listening to me;" — these words, used with express reference to the mode in which he composed the "Confessions," may be taken as characterizing, in a degree more or less eminent, De

Quincey's universal manner. The goal, indeed, is always kept in view; however circuitous the wandering may be, there is always a return to the subject; the river's course is always seawards: but there are no fixed embankments, between which, in straight, purpose-like course, the stream is compelled to flow: you are led aside in the most wayward, unaccountable manner, and though you must allow that every individual bay and wooded creek is in itself beautiful, yet, being a Briton, accustomed to feed on facts, like the alligators whom the old naturalists asserted to live upon stones, and thinking it right to walk to the purpose of a book with that firm step and by that nearest road which conduct you to your office, you are soon ready to exclaim that this is trifling, and that you wish the author could speak to the point. But there is some witchery which still detains you; the trifling seems to be flavored by some indefinable essence, which spreads an irresistible charm around; you recollect that nature has innumerable freaks, and may present, in one quarter of a mile, the giant rock and the quivering blue-bell, the defiant oak and the trodden lichen, the almost stagnant pool and the surging cataract: at length the thought dawns upon you, that this author is great because he cannot help it; that he is a force in the hand of nature; that, whether you smile, or frown, or weep, or wonder, he goes on with the same absolute ease, speaking with pure spontaneity the thoughts that arise within him. Then your trust becomes deeper, your earnestness of study redoubles; you are profoundly convinced that here is no pretence, no unnatural effort; your murmuring turns to astonishment at the complexity, richness, and strangely blended variety of nature's effects. If your experience is the same as ours most honestly was, you will proceed from a certain pleasurable titillation, produced by what you deem twaddle, though twaddle deliciously spiced by genius, to the conviction that, however hampered, however open to objection, here is an intellect, in all the great faculties of analysis, combination, and reception, of a power and range which you are at a loss to measure or define. We must take into account, in judging of the powers of De Quincey, the fact that his life has been shadowed by one great cloud, which would have fatally obscured any ordinary intellect; that he has seen the stars through a vail, and that we have to mete the power of that vision which could pierce such an obstruction. It must be remembered, too, that the mind of De Quincey is, on all hands, allowed to be one of a very singular and original kind. It is pre-eminently characterized by two qualities, which are partially regarded with suspicion by hard thinkers, and tend to lower the expectation of the reader who is in search of substantial intellectual sustenance: we mean humor, and what we can only call mysticism. De Quincey is essentially and always a humorist; a humorist of a very rare and delicate order, but whose very delicacy is mistaken by hard minds for feebleness or silly trifling. He is also, to some extent, an intellectual mystic. We use this word in no disparaging sense; nor do we lay emphasis upon the fact, that he has devoted years of study to the works of express mystics. We indeed think that this last is not of material importance in estimating his writings; the influence of these writers was not, it appears to us, of sufficient power materially to color his originality. By the quality of mysticism, as attaching to the mind of De Quincey, we mean rather a certain affinity, so to speak, for the mysterious, — a strange idiosyncrasy, in which associations of terror, of gladness, or of gloom, link themselves with certain seasons and places. Voices of sympathy awaken for him, where no sound falls on the general ear; sorrows, from which the common mail of custom and coarseness, or even active practical occupation, defends other men, affect him with poignant anguish; and joys which are far too delicate and aerial to approach the hard man of the world, float over his soul like spiritual music. He has a sure footing in dim and distant regions, where phantasy piles her towers, and raises her colonnades, and wraps all in her weird and wondrous drapery. He tells us that, "like Sir Thomas Brown, his mind almost demanded mysteries in so mysterious a system of relations as those which connect us with another world;" and we cannot hesitate to use the hint for the explication of much to which he does not, in that connection, intend it to apply. We are met by expressions of sentiment, regarding summer, and death, and solitude, which may appear strange or far fetched, and told of woes which our duller imaginations and less tremulous sympathies almost compel us to deem fantastic. Altogether, to the matter of fact English reader, the phenomena presented by these works are astonishing and alarming; and it is well for him, if his hasty practicality does not prompt him to close them at once, deciding that here is no real metal for life's highway, but only such airy materials as might be used by some Macadam of the clouds. Yet we are confident that De Quincey has performed intellectual service for the age, which could be shown to be practically substantial to the most rigorously practical mind. We would specially urge, moreover, that it is quite possible that writings may be of the highest value, although one cannot trace their association with any department of economic affairs. We are practical enough, and make no pretension to having "wings for the ether." But let it at once be said, that the world is not a manufactory. There are regions where the spirit of man can expatiate above the corn field or the counter; it is lawful for the immortal principle to rise for a time out of the atmosphere of the labor curse; the universe is really wonderful, and it is not well to forget the fact; nay, finally, it is well for a man, perhaps at times it is best for him, to spread the wings of his mind for regions positively removed from, antipodal to, practice, if haply he may gain glimpses of habitations higher than earth, and destinies nobler than those of time. Bold as the assertion looks, we should question the power of any man to be a docile and accurate disciple of the Comte school of philosophy, who found the highest enjoyment of understanding and sympathy in the works of De Quincey!

When, beneath all its drapery of cloud and rainbow, the grand physiognomic outlines of De Quincey's mind reveal themselves to the reader, his primary observation will probably be, that it is marked by an extraordinary analytic faculty. De Quincey's own opinion declares this to be the principal power in his mind; and though we should not deem this in itself conclusive, we cannot but think it strongly confirmatory of the general evidence gathered from other quarters. "My proper vocation," these are his words, "as I well knew, was the exercise of the analytic understanding." The more we know of De Quincey's writings, the more are we driven to the conviction, that his mind is, in this regard, of an extremely high order. His intensely clear perception of the relation between ideas, the delight with which he expatiates in regions of pure abstraction, where no light lives but that of the "inevitable eye" of the mind, the ease with which he unravels and winds off what appears a mere skein of cloud streamers, too closely twined to be taken apart, and too delicate not to rend asunder, afford irresistible evidence of rare analytic power. That our words may be seen to be no rhetorical painting of our own fancies, but a feeble attempt to indicate a fact, we shall glance cursorily at one or two of those portions of De Quincey's works which give attestation of this power.

The science of political economy is remarkable as one of those in which the abstract and the concrete are seen most clearly in their mutual relations. Beginning with mere abstractions, or what appear such, with factors which must be dealt with algebraically, and seem absolutely independent of practice, it proceeds onwards until it embraces every complexity of our social existence, until every mathematical line is turned into an actual, visible extension, and every ideal form has to take what shape it can amid the jostling and scrambling of life. It is thus, in our opinion, perhaps the very best study in which a man can engage for the culture of his argumentative nature. For, as we say, it has every stage: it demands mathematical accuracy in one part, and lays down rigidly the ideal law; it brings you on till you are in the field and workshop, till you have to calculate the strength of varied desires, the probable upshot of complicated chances, the modifications produced by a thousand nameless influences. From the mathematical diagram to the table of statistics, from the academy to the street, from the closet of the philosopher to the world of the statesman, political economy conducts the student. Whatever the practical value of the science to the merchant, legislator, moralist, or philanthropist, — and we have no leisure to demonstrate, as we think is posssible, its practical value to each, — it scarcely admits of a doubt, that, as an instrument of mental culture, it is invaluable. But this remark is incidental: we have glanced at the general nature of the science of political economy, in order that we may exhibit clearly the particular department in which De Quincey is distinguished. This, of course, is the abstract portion. The fundamental laws of the science, or rather the one fundamental law on which it is all built, furnished his mind with occupation. This one fundamental law is the law of value. It determines what is, viewed abstractly, the grand cause which fixes the relative value of articles, — how much of any one will exchange for so much of any other. Once this is found, you know whence all deviations depart, you know how each modifying element will act, you have, so to speak, formed your theory of the seasons, although you cannot tell what showers may fall, what winds may blow, what ripening weeks of sunshine may usher in the harvest. "He," says De Quincey, "who is fully master of the subject of value, is already a good political economist." We agree with him, and think that political economy first and forever became an established science, when the theory of value was perfected. The honor of having published the demonstration belongs to David Ricardo; but De Quincey, as has so often happened, found himself anticipated with the public. He had arrived at the same results; but little remained for him to do, save to silence a few objectors who long continued to oppose Ricardo. This he did in the "Templars' Dialogues," in a manner so clear and conclusive, that assent may be said to have become synonymous with comprehension. It is difficult to convey any idea of these papers to one who has not read them. To quote any passage were an improvement upon the brick sample of the house, for it would be to offer a stone as sample of an arch; to abridge is out of the question, for they are models of terseness. Considered as pieces of reasoning, they are truly masterly. There is an artistic perfection about them. The beauty of precision, of clearness, of absolute performance of the thing required, is the only beauty admissible. Accordingly, there is not an illustration which is not there simply because it speaks more clearly than words; there are no flourishes of rhetoric; all is quiet, orderly, conclusive, like the British line advancing to the charge, and with the same result. It is true that, even in them, De Quincey could not be dull, and so there is the slightest infusion of humor, which adds a raciness to the whole, and is thus promotive of the general effect. Mr. M'Culloch, a man not given to enthusiasm, says of these papers, that they "are unequalled, perhaps, for brevity, pungency, and force."

De Quincey's introduction to political economy was characteristic, and illustrates remarkably the nature of his powers. He took to it as an amusement, when debility had caused the cessation of severer studies. About the year 1811, he became acquainted with a great many books and pamphlets on the subject; but it seems that what had employed the concentrated, protracted, and healthful energies of men for about a couple of centuries, could not for a moment bide the scrutiny of his languishing eye. Thus politely and composedly does he indicate his general impression of what books, pamphlets, speeches, and other compositions bearing on political economy had come in his way:—"I saw that these were generally the very dregs and rinsings of the human intellect; and that any man of sound head, and practised in wielding logic with a scholastic adroitness, might take up the whole academy of modern economists, and throttle them between heaven and earth with his finger and thumb, or bray their fungus heads to powder with a lady's fan." Such sudden and amazing proficiency, we presume, scientific professors would not extremely desire. However, this surprising pupil was soon to meet the master:—"At length," he proceeds, "in 1819, a friend in Edinburgh sent me down Mr. Ricardo's book; and, recurring to my own prophetic anticipation of the advent of some legislator for this science, I said, before I had finished the first chapter, 'Thou art the man!' Wonder and curiosity were emotions that had long been dead in me. Yet I wondered once more: I wondered at myself, that I could once again be stimulated to the effort of reading; and, much more, I wondered at the book. Had this profound book been really written in England during the nineteenth century? * * * * Could it be that an Englishman, and he not in academic bowers, but oppressed by mercantile and senatorial* cares, had accomplished what all the universities of Europe, and a century of thought, had failed to advance even by one hair's breadth? All other writers had been crushed and overlaid by the enormous weight of facts and documents; Mr. Ricardo had deduced *à priori*, from the understanding itself, laws which first gave a ray of light into the unwieldy chaos of materials, and had constructed what had been but a collection of tentative discussions into a science of regular proportions, now first standing on an eternal basis."

Are our readers acquainted with the "Principles of Political Economy and Taxation," by David Ricardo? If not, they will hardly appreciate De Quincey's enthusiasm, or understand what it implies. Butler and Edwards are by no means drawing-room authors, yet the perusal of their works seems to us to approach the nature of an intellectual recreation, compared with that of this book of Ricardo's. We consider it that volume which, of all we know, requires the highest tension and effort of intellect. It has a thousand

* "Senatorial:"—this is a mistake. Ricardo entered the House of Commons in 1819; his work was published in 1817.

times been charged with obscurity, and a filmy subtlety of speculation; yet its difficulty consists principally in that it is the production of a mind so exceedingly clear, that it could completely master and fully embrace a subject, by seeing its great leading points of illumination, without tracing the path from the one to the other. Thus the reader is, as it were, carried from eminence to eminence by the writer, without being shown the way he travels; and having reached each, not by the usual step by step method, he is moved to question the reality of his progress, and to object to the extraordinary new method of instruction, in which he must ever and anon commit himself to the strong arm or wing of the preceptor, to be carried to a higher station. He feels that too large a demand is made on his faith; he wishes to walk a little by sight. Ricardo coolly sets him down, with the assurance that his progress has been real, and that now he stands on a higher platform than he ever occupied before; but with the declaration, that he must find some other to explain pedagogically the mode of advancement, since there are further heights to which his guide must forthwith ascend. Now, De Quincey had the supreme satisfaction of going side by side with Ricardo in his aërial voyagings; he knew well whither he was going, and the absolute certainty that it was onwards; he could look down, with a satisfied, half-sneering smile, upon the strugglers below, who jogged honestly but slowly along, proclaiming their distrust in all aërial carriages. In those "Templars' Dialogues" he seems to sit in the chariot with Ricardo, laughing at Malthus and other disbelievers, and calling to them to look up, and see that all their difficulty of apprehension lies in the fact, that the one path is through the air, straight as an arrow's flight, while the other is along the ground, amid sand heaps and tangled jungles. De

Quincey himself has admirably described the nature of Ricardo's obscurity, by saying that, if it can be fairly alleged against him at all, it can arise only from "too keen a perception of the truth, which may have seduced him at times into too elliptic a development of his opinions, and made him impatient of the tardy and continuous steps which are best adapted to the purposes of the teacher. For," he adds, "the fact is, that the *laborers of the Mine* (as I am accustomed to call them), or those who dig up the metal of truth, are seldom fitted to be also *laborers of the Mint*, —that is, to work up the metal for current use." "Seed corn," says Goethe, "should not be ground." Such were the difficulty and the obscurity of Ricardo. Now, we certainly should found no claim to an extraordinary analytic faculty on the mere power to comprehend any author; but the fact of keen enjoyment, of free, exulting pleasure being derived from the perusal of a book, is always conclusive proof of an affinity with the powers it exhibits; and the instant recognition with which De Quincey welcomed Ricardo's discoveries, as well as the perfect comprehension, nay, light and graceful, and absolutely commanding mastery, with which he ever after used and expounded them, may be regarded, even independently of his own words, as sufficient evidence that he himself had trodden the same high path, that the same laws unfolded themselves, almost contemporaneously, to the analytic intellects of De Quincey and Ricardo. We claim not for the former any honor which the succession of the years denied him; but when the question is not of the honor of a discovery, but the possession of a faculty, our argument is irresistible. We think, therefore, that in the mere power of analysis, leaving all else out of account, an equality may be vindicated for De Quincey with the great legislator in political economy,

More than this we do not claim; but no one who has any acquaintance with the works of Ricardo, will require a further proof that the English Opium Eater is a writer whose works deserve earnest study from all who love clear and far seeing thought.

Leaving political economy, and entering the wider field of history, professing also no longer to abide with psychological correctness by the faculty of analysis, but seeking the traces of general power and clearness of intellect, we would advance the general proposition, That De Quincey has looked over the course of humanity with such a searching, philosophic glance, that, desultory though his teaching has been, he has discerned and embodied in his works certain truths of the last importance. They are of that sort which may be called illuminative; they are rays of light which go along the whole course of time, revealing and harmonizing; their value can be fully appreciated only when one traverses history, carrying them as lamps in his hand, and observing how, in their light, the confused becomes orderly, the dark becomes bright.

We cannot find a better instance than in his ideas regarding war. These furnish, indeed, a remarkable case, and that with which we have been most struck; we think it of itself sufficient to justify what we have above advanced. We had long been of opinion that the ideas regarding war, which not only floated in the public mind, but found countenance from men of high and unquestionable powers, were singularly superficial and unsound; from Foster and Carlyle to John Bright, we heard no word on the subject with which we could agree. It was the first general glance, and that alone, which was taken; the observations on which the arguments were based, were such as every child must again and again have made, — that war was accompanied with great effusion of blood, that in its scowl the face of the world gathered blackness as of death, that there was no enmity or personal quarrel between the individual combatants, and the like. Foster we found unable to thrill to the ardors of the "Iliad;" or, if he did experience a rising sense of its glories, we saw him shrinking as from sin, and likening the poem to a beautiful but deadly knife. Carlyle, with a satire whose intense cleverness made cool examination of the philosophic value of his words almost impossible, resolved our French wars into the aimless volleys by which the peaceful inhabitants of two far-separated French and English villages of "Dumbdrudge" exterminated each other. We found no clear conception of the function, in the evolution of human civilization, of agencies in themselves calamitous: no philosophic conception of war in its real nature, as the most direful yet indispensable of the effects of reason acting under the curse of labor and the obscuration of sin, — the sublimely fearful yet necessary lightning, which has flashed in the night of human history. Such were our notions, when we happened to fall in with an article by De Quincey, in which he treated of war. A glance was sufficient. The germs of a whole philosophy of war were before us; every lingering doubt was dissipated. And it was a consoling assurance that our views were not, as they looked, peculiarly savage, to find that De Quincey, whose womanly tenderness is, to our knowledge, unexampled in literature, yet sympathized, with calmest deliberation and profound intensity, in those feelings to which men have ever attached sublimity, from the shouts of Marathon to the thunders of Trafalgar. But could we have imagined a linguistic garb like that in which his reasonings were arrayed? How perfect was the mastery with which the whole theme was grasped! He played with his subject; he touched it with his magician wand, and it took what colors he chose. Whatever of dimness had attached to our ideas, was dissipated as mist by sunlight; all was boldly, clearly, definitely evolved. The thoughts leaped forth in the mail of logic and the plumes of poetry.

This paper on war we would cite as, on the whole, singularly characteristic of De Quincey. Here, most emphatically, is there attested the danger of trusting to first appearances and impressions. Philosophy and fun so intermingle their parts, that one is astonished and startled. Now all seems mirth and jollity; the writer is intent on proving that the ancients pilfered jokes on a large scale from the moderns; that it must have been the former and not the latter, is plain, from the fact, that those were "heathens, infidels, pagan dogs." Then you have a long detail respecting a fund which is to be commenced by a half-crown legacy of De Quincey's, and which is to be put into requisition when the Peace Congress has prevailed, and war vanishes from human history. The fund may accumulate at any interest; ere required, it will, under any circumstances, have reached to the moon; therefore the man in the moon is named a trustee. The destination of the fund is the support of all those to be put out of employment when armies and fleets are disbanded; and the trustees are eloquently and earnestly charged to deal handsomely, nor bring disgrace on the testator's memory by niggardliness. And all this giggling alternates with flashes of revealing intuition, which rectify your every idea of human history, with truths which open up to you the vista of the past, and enable you to define the position of humanity in the present. It is an intermingled dance of northern lights, and far-illumining gleams of precious radiance. The writer is as one sitting in a chariot at a Roman carnival, and flinging, from the same hand, crackers, and sugar plums, and lumps of pure gold. Ill is it for him who sees the crackers and sugar plums, and thinks there can be no gold! The remark applies more or less to the whole range of De Quincey's writings. No man can fail to perceive the jocularity of the paper we have been describing; but if it is important or indicative of high powers to see beneath all the superficial phenomena of war, and discern its true function in human history, if it is a proof of profundity, that a clear, indubitable light is cast into regions where Foster and Carlyle stumbled about as if blindfold, then we can appeal to the same article as a triumphant vindication of the sterling value of De Quincey's intellectual powers. And how strongly does this confirm what we have said respecting the perfect ease, the absolute want of effort, the free, careless naturalness with which he writes.

De Quincey has devoted several papers to an attempted proof that the sect of Essenes, mentioned by Josephus, were none other than the early Christians. The series is distinguished by great acuteness of argument, and possesses that fascination of style which characterizes every production of the author. The whole logic of the case is brought out in a figure, so simple, so precise, and yet so graceful, that we may quote it:—"If, in an ancient palace, reopened after it had been shut up for centuries, you were to find a hundred golden shafts or pillars, for which nobody could suggest a place or a use; and if, in some other quarter of the palace, far remote, you were afterwards to find a hundred golden sockets fixed in the floor,—first of all, pillars which nobody could apply to any purpose, or refer to any place; secondly, sockets which nobody could fill,—probably even 'wicked Will Whiston' might be capable of a glimmering suspicion that the hundred golden shafts belonged to the hundred golden sockets. And if it should turn out that each several shaft screwed into its own peculiar socket, why, in such a case, not 'Whiston, Ditton, and Co.' could resist the evidence, that each enigma had brought a key to the other; and that by means of two mysteries there had ceased even to be one mystery." The unoccupied sockets are the several heads in the description of the Essenes by Josephus; the missing pillars, the early Christians. Thus is the whole argument seen at a glance. But we cannot say that we have been convinced. We indeed think it remarkably probable that the early Christians and the Essenes were one and the same; but we cannot bring ourselves to regard Mr. De Quincey's manner of accounting for the name satisfactory. We cannot admit the theory of an assumed disguise on the part of the Christians. The plain command to confess Christ before men; the almost excessive valor of the early Christians, prompting them to court martyrdom; the contrariety of such a method of defence to the whole genius of the opposition by the true religion of all that is false in every age, which has always been to unsheathe the sword in the face of the foe, to fling away the scabbard, and to defy him in the name of the Lord; the scarcely conceivable possibility of Christians suddenly, as it were, ducking their heads before the wave of persecution, and emerging again, unrecognized, as Essenes;—these and similar considerations close the avenues of our mind to the most plausible array of proofs which could be adduced against them. But not only are these papers marked by high ingenuity; they contain striking gleams of insight into the whole course of the development of Christianity. We think, for instance, that the following remark is not more daring than it is important: — "In strict philosophic truth, Christianity did not reach its mature period, even of infancy, until the days of the Protestant Reformation." This casts a light before and after. And it is a sublime idea to which it leads; — the idea of the whole human race, through long millenniums, gazing upon the handwriting of God, and only in the slow course of centuries spelling it out. There is also, in the articles before us, an exactness of conception as to what Christianity really is, which sets De Quincey at a quite immeasurable distance from your general Christian litterateur. He does not confound it with "virtue," or any conceivable ethical theory; he does not, with a mouth homage which is but disguised atheism, lay artistic hands on Christianity, and take it, like any old mythology, to play a part, or to act as a background, in an art novel; he recognizes the perennial, supernatural element inextricably involved in its very idea, the continual action from age to age of the Spirit of God on the mind of man. In various parts of his works, indeed, De Quincey exhibits a profound insight into the spirit and nature of Christianity, — its essential distinction from Paganism, as a system of doctrines and morals, and not a mere ritual, and its absolute agreement with what is darkest and deepest in the human heart and history.

We have lingered perhaps too long on the subject of De Quincey's strictly intellectual powers; but we regret the less having done so, because it is here that our remarks may be of the greatest practical value. All men acknowledge De Quincey's genius; all men appreciate, more or less, the grandeur and the delicacy of his imagination; all own the supremacy of his command over the English tongue. But we think it is not so generally conceded, that he is a substantially valuable thinker; that there is not only treasure of intellectual amusement, that there are not only master-pieces of style, within the compass of his works, but that there is much also of that intellectual stuff with which one might build up his system of opinion, or on which he might nourish his highest powers. Even this we have not so much proved, as indicated the means of proving. We might have enlarged on the vast stores of his learning, and still more on the perfect command he has over them all; how with the true poetic might he can fling a subject into the furnace of his genius, shapeless, rugged, and drossy as it may be, and show us it again flowing out in the purity and brightness of molten gold; how at eleven he was a brilliant Latin scholar, and at fifteen could talk Greek, with such fluency and correctness, that his master said he could address an Athenian mob better than his instructor an English; how he studied mathematics, and metaphysics, and theology, and scholastic logic, and all which could give exercise to his soul in the herculean youth of its powers. But we say no more. We think we have said enough to make good our point. We differ from De Quincey in several respects: we fear that, in theology, we march nearer to the standard of Calvin than he would approve; we have already intimated our discontent with certain of his arguments on the identity of the early Christians and Essenes; we think he has under-rated John Foster, and he has certainly outstripped our charity in the case of Judas: but yet we esteem him, and we think our readers will agree with us in esteeming him, a really powerful thinker, whose criticism upon human knowl-edge, and whose direct contributions to its stores, are worthy of being eagerly seized and earnestly scrutinized by thoughtful minds.

We have spoken hitherto of what may be figured as the skeleton or bare framework of De Quincey's mind. We have found him here comparable with Ricardo. But now we pass to a different delineation. We leave Ricardo and all dry algebraists, geometricians, metaphysicians, and scholastics behind. We come to look upon the glorious garment of sympathy in which De Quincey's mind is robed, and his grand imaginative eye, whose glance can clothe every algebraic formula in light as of the stars. He himself speaks of the "two hemispheres, as it were, that compose the total world of human power, — mathematics on the one hand, poetry on the other;" and we must think that he can expatiate in both. It is our belief, indeed, that every mind of a very high order can. It is of beneficent arrangement that men in general are furnished with distinct tendencies and powers: it is well that each man does his own work best, and even has a certain suppressed feeling that his special work is the most important in this world. But it is a positive and confounding error to apply the general rule to the few individual minds which rise far above the common level. Of these minds we think no assertion can be made with less of hesitancy or qualification, than that their powers and sympathies are diverse. We can trace the smothered gleams of a burning imagination through the works of Jonathan Edwards, like volcanic fires kept under by the solid ground, and towered cities, and stable mountains, of some Italy or Trinacria. Plato was the greatest prose poet that ever lived; the softening radiance of poetic light which played over the massive intellect of Luther gave it a beauty which will never fade; and we have no doubt that imaginative fire burned in the unwavering, far-searching eye of Calvin. To borrow a suggestion from those words of De Quincey regarding the hemispheres, we would say, that all great men have an intellectual night and an intellectual day: in the still, vast night, when no color rests on the earth, and the stars in their courses are treading the fields of immensity, they look up calm and abstracted, to learn, by pure, unimpassioned thought, the laws of nature and of truth; in the blaze of day's sunlight, when the world is arrayed in its robe of many colors, and clouds, waves, and forests are rejoicing in beauty, they also share the joy, and take of the glories of nature to clothe the thoughts revealed to them in the silent night.

We are not prepared to say that what De Quincey has actually accomplished will prove sufficient to vindicate for him a place among the mighty ones of bygone ages, among the few who occupy the intellectual thrones of the world; but we do say, that there are unmistakeable traces that his natural endowment was of this royal order, that, in the two great forms of intellect — the imaginative and the abstractive — he was magnificently gifted. The reader has seen how he was affected by Ricardo's political economy, — it was a case of positive, rapturous delight. But now hear this:— "A little before that time (1799), Wordsworth had published the first edition (in a single volume) of the 'Lyrical Ballads;' and into this had been introduced Mr. Coleridge's poem of the 'Ancient Mariner,' as the contribution of an anonymous friend. It would be directing the reader's attention too much to myself, if I were to linger upon this, the greatest event in the unfolding of my own mind. Let me say, in one word, that, at a period when neither the one nor the other writer was valued by the public, — both having a long warfare to accomplish of contumely and ridicule, before they could rise into their present estimation, — I found in their poems 'the ray of a new morning,' and an absolute revelation of untrodden worlds, teeming with power and beauty as yet unsuspected among men." These are the words of De Quincey. Now, we think it a very remarkable fact, and one to which, in forming any estimate of the author of whom we treat, great importance is to be attached, that he was the first, or among the first, to hail the rising, in quarters of the literary heaven so widely apart, and with such an antithetic diversity of radiance of two such stars as Wordsworth and Ricardo. The light of Ricardo is perhaps, in every sense, good and bad, the driest in English literature; the general intellect even of practical England turns away from it. Wordsworth is, of all poets, the furthest removed from the practical world: he is the listener to the voice of woods, the watcher of the wreathing of the clouds; he can drink a tender and intense pleasure from the waving of the little flower, from the form of its star-shaped shadow; he can even enter, by inexpressible delicacy of poetic sympathy, into the feelings which his own creative power imparts, and wish that little flower

"Conscious of half the pleasure that it gives:"

from him, too, the general intellect of practical England, as proved in the case of Arnold, turns away dissatisfied. In the range of De Quincey's sympathies — and the sympathies are the voices or the ministers of the powers, the leaves by which the plant drinks in the air of heaven — there was compass for both.

It is no fable of poetry or dream of a fevered brain, that the human mind is a macrocosm of nature; it is a fact to which even physiological science is now according her assent, and which a psychological comparison of the intellects of the great and the small in all ages would irresistibly demonstrate. Weakness of intellect and littleness of intellect are found, when well examined, to mean narrowness of intellect: trace men, through all their grades, from those humble forms of the "world school," where sit the artisan, the husbandman, and the private soldier, until you reach that august region where human history and all time seem to be spread out, one imperial domain, beneath the sky-like dome of the mind of Shakspeare; you will find every increase of greatness accompanied by, we had almost said synonymous with, expansion of range. And we certainly know of nothing in modern literary history so boldly and strikingly demonstrative of a superb natural endowment, as the delight, which his own words show to have been rapturous, with which De Quincey watched, on the one hand, the unimpassioned Ricardo threading with his safety-lamp the unexplored labyrinths of political economy; and gazed, on the other, on nature in the dewy light cast over it by Wordsworth, and marked, yet again, the magician Coleridge, as he blended the glories of chaos and creation in one wondrous phantasmagoria round his spectral ship and his spectral mariner. I am a man, and nothing human do I deem foreign to me: the sentiment is too true to grow old; and the more human I am, the nearer I approach to what a man may be, the less is there, in all that can be seen or heard, thought or imagined, in air, earth, or ocean, in literature, science, or art, in all this universe, which will be foreign to me.

And since the sympathies are, as we said, but the ministers of the powers, since sympathy is the reconciling, and winning, and gathering invitation, at whose voice all that there is of beauty in stars, and clouds, and dew drops, and the golden leaflets with which summer fringes her robe of green, comes obsequiously to the imagination which can marshal them in a new order, or bid a new creation arise from their combination, the question here presses itself upon us — What has De Quincey himself done, and what field of truth has he opened up, what great poetic structure has he built? The answer is one which can be easily rendered, but which must create sad reflections. We unhesitatingly say De Quincey has done much, but we profoundly and sorrowfully feel that he might have done much, incalculably much, more. Coleridge rose gloriously sunward in his mighty youth, sweeping at once into fields of the poetic heaven which had not been entered since the days of Milton. But, as if some maddening or bewildering enchantment had fallen on him, it was seen that the aërial poise of his wings became unsteady, he seemed to stagger in the sky, and never again, however grand his convulsive flappings, however determined his efforts to sustain his upward flight, did he sail with aught of the Miltonic strength or the Miltonic majesty. That maddening enchantment was opium. Under its tremendous sway fell also De Quincey. The English tongue seems somewhat too practically framed to serve well the purpose of lamenting; it affects rather the battle melody, or the song of the worker; and whatever its powers may be in this direction, we shall not here tune it to elegaic murmurings. It is a truly British sentiment which Carlyle expresses, when he says: —

> "'Tis a thriftless thing to be sad, sad;
> 'Tis a thriftless thing to be sad."

We shall abandon then the language of regret, and endeavor rather to find cause of rejoicing in what has actually been realized for us by De Quincey. And truly, if it may appear startling or absurd to speak of the English language as inexpressive of sorrow, when it is the language in which De Quincey has written, while yet what we allege remains true,—since it is a noble, an elevating sorrow, a sorrow which makes us weep no weak or ignoble tears, and is immeasurably removed from whining, to which De Quincey has given expression, — we may say that the sorrow with which we regard the influence exerted over De Quincey by opium, is one which is unusually and wondrously chequered by gleams of gladness. We confess that sorrow is, on the whole, the prevailing emotion in our minds, when we regard the total phenomenon; for we are convinced that nature in perfect health will always work more grandly than nature in any conceivable state of disease, and we doubt not that all the beauty which we now admire in the writings of De Quincey, had been secured and enhanced had he never known the delirious joys or sorrows of opium. Yet who that has looked in wondering admiration at what he has actually done, can pretend to say that he can know, by any effort of conceptive sight, and not solely by faith, what potentialities of grander performance De Quincey did possess? Are we sure that, had there been no opium in the case, such efforts had been suggested, or that a canvass would have been found for such picturings?

We suppose it will be agreed that there is nothing in our language to be compared with De Quincey's dreams; nay, to speak of comparison is inadmissible, for they are absolutely alone; all other authors who have ventured on visionary delineations — and of these there are enough — would grant that their dreams were generically different from his. In Germany, there have been two writers who can be put in comparison with him, — Richter and Novalis. His own translations and Carlyle's have made us familiar with the terrors and the glories of Jean Paul's dreams. The "Dream upon the Universe," which De Quincey rendered into English in the "London Magazine," and various others which are widely known, enable us to form a definite opinion regarding his general manner; and we record it as our decided impression, that it may be maintained as a general truth, that there reigns over De Quincey's dream creations a taste more austerely classic, more chaste, more majestic, than ruled those of Richter. The "Suspiria" have been much lauded; we acknowledge their surpassing power; but it is to the "Dream Fugue," founded on the "Vision of Sudden Death," that we point, with calmest assurance, as illustrating our general remark, and demonstrating the superiority of De Quincey over Jean Paul. In the visions of the latter there is a certain barbaric splendor, a chaotic wildness, a bewildering accumulation of fearful or of gorgeous images, suggestive rather of the fury and might of the tempest than of the strength of light. The supremacy of order seems, as it were, questioned or questionable. The picture is hidden by its own drapery; the melody scarce traceable in the immeasurable volume of sound. Right or wrong, the British intellect cannot tolerate indistinctness. Now, in that succession of dreams which we have mentioned, and which seems to us to constitute De Quincey's masterpiece, there is, over all the splendor and terror, a clear serenity of light which belongs to the very highest style of poetic beauty. The conceptions are very daring, but each form of spurious originality is absent, — the fantastic and the grotesque; there is the mystery of the land of dreams, yet so powerful is the imagination which strikes the whole into being, that the wondrous picture has the vividness and truth of reality; while, with every change of scene and emotion, the language changes too — now rich, glowing, and bold, when the idea is free, sunny joyousness — now melting into a gentle, spiritual melody of more than Æolian softness — and now rising to a Homeric swell, that echoes the everlasting gallop of the steeds which drag that triumphal car. This "Dream Fugue" is of no great compass, but we think that it would alone have been sufficient to secure a literary immortality. Taken in connection with the incident which was its occasion; considered as a poetic idealization of reality, and an effort of linguistic power; tried by the severe rules of art, as demanding the very highest manifestation of order and harmony possible by man, we think we could maintain against all comers that this is, for its size, the noblest production in English prose. And we cannot but think that nothing so perfect ever rose before the imagination of Jean Paul Richter. The little we know of the dream paintings of Novalis leads us to think that there is a closer similarity between his manner and De Quincey's, than subsists in the case we have mentioned. The delicacy, the mildness, and the powerful imagination of Novalis, remind us strongly of De Quincey; but we do not know enough of his writings to draw a detailed parallel.

We are utterly unable to justify to our readers the above opinion respecting the "Dream Fugue;" and we have a certain reluctance to associate any description we could give with the impressions which the original is fitted to produce. But we feel it necessary to give at least something like positive proof that our words are not those of extravagance; and therefore we compel ourselves to attempt to extract one or two such pieces from the "gorgeous mosaic" of this dream, as may, though faintly, suggest an idea of the whole.

During the French war, De Quincey used to come down annually on the mail-coach from London to Lancashire. It was the office of the mail to spread the news of the great victories. On one occasion, he came down after a great battle. An incident which occurred on the way was the occasion of the "Dream Fugue." It was a night which De Quincey alone was capable of describing:—

"Obliquely we were nearing the sea upon our left, which

also must, under the present circumstances, be repeating the general state of halcyon repose. The sea, the atmosphere, the light, bore an orchestral part in this universal lull. Moonlight and the first timid tremblings of the dawn were now blending; and the blendings were brought into a still more exquisite state of unity by a slight silvery mist, motionless and dreamy, that covered the woods and fields; but with a vail of equable transparency. * * * * * Still, in the confidence of children that tread without fear *every* chamber in their father's house, and to whom no door is closed, we, in that sabbatic vision which sometimes is revealed for an hour upon nights like this, ascend with easy steps from the sorrow-stricken fields of earth upwards to the sandals of God. Suddenly from thoughts like these I was awakened to a sullen sound, as of some motion on the distant road. It stole upon the air for a moment; I listened in awe; but then it died away."

The coachman was fast asleep, and could not be awaked; the horses were going at a fearful pace; the mail was heavy. It was on the wrong side of the road. Any living thing, or any vehicle containing such, which came across its path, must go to shivers. All this and more De Quincey comprehended at one intuitive glance. "Ah, reader! what a sullen mystery of fear, what a sigh of woe, seemed to steal upon the air, as again the far off sound of a wheel was heard!" On they dashed; every effort he made in the way of remedy was vain; at last the horses, by this time at fiery speed, swept round an angle of the road, and all was revealed. "Before us lay an avenue, straight as an arrow, six hundred yards, perhaps, in length; and the umbrageous trees which rose in a regular line from either side, meeting high overhead, gave to it the character of a cathedral aisle. These trees lent a deeper solemnity to the

4*

early light; but there was still light enough to perceive, at the further end of this Gothic aisle, a light, reedy gig, in which were seated a young man, and by his side a young lady." These are either married, or in the highest state of love; for a reason which De Quincey and we do not understand, the young man "carries his lips forward to hers." "The little carriage is creeping on at one mile an hour; and the parties within it being thus tenderly engaged, are naturally bending down their heads. Between them and eternity, to all human calculation, there is but a minute and a half." De Quincey shouts; at the second shout the young man takes the alarm. He has just time to raise his horse's fore feet by a strain on the reins, and pull him round, and make him take one leap forward, when the mail tears past. In its way, it gives a stroke to the little gig, which makes it shiver as a thing alive; those who sit there all but taste the agony of death, yet are safe. "The blow, from the fury of our passage, resounded terrifically. I rose in horror, to look upon the ruins we might have caused. From my elevated station I looked down, and looked back upon the scene, which in a moment told its tale, and wrote all its records on my heart forever.

* * * * * * * * *

"But the lady——! Oh, heavens! will that spectacle ever depart from my dreams, as she rose and sank upon her seat, sank and rose, threw up her arms wildly to heaven, clutched at some visionary object in the air, fainting, praying, raving, despairing! Figure to yourself, reader, the elements of the case; suffer me to recall before your mind the circumstances of the unparalleled situation. From the silence and deep peace of this saintly summer night,—from the pathetic blendings of this sweet moonlight, dawn-light, dream-light,—from the manly tenderness of this flattering, whispering, murmuring love, — suddenly as from the woods and fields, — suddenly as from the chambers of the air, opening in revelation, — suddenly as from the ground yawning at her feet, leaped upon her, with the flashing of cataracts, Death, the crowned phantom, with all the equipage of his terrors, and the tiger roar of his voice.

"The moments were numbered. In the twinkling of an eye, our flying horses had carried us to the termination of the umbrageous aisle; at right angles, we wheeled into our former direction; the turn of the road carried the scene out of my eyes in an instant, and swept it into my dreams forever."

The elements with which the writer works in the "Dream Fugue" are now before the reader: the coach at an unusual pace, and laurelled with the tokens of victory, the umbrageous avenue like a cathedral aisle, the narrow escape of the lady. These reappear in the "Fugue" in various forms, and transfigured by the light of an imagination which creatively remodels, recombines, and illumes the whole. The mail-coach becomes a triumphal car, on whose path all nations attend, and which carries to all peoples, in letters of mystic light, the tidings of a victory which has broken the bonds of the world; over the heads of the horses the tidings go, embodied in this legend, which casts around a golden light, "Waterloo and Recovered Christendom." The gates of cities fly open; rivers are silent, as the car, in its tremendous gallop, dashes across them; "the infinite forests" shiver in homage to the word. The umbrageous avenue becomes an immeasurable cathedral aisle, along which the tireless steeds sweep onwards in almost viewless speed. In the far distance is seen a vast necropolis, "a city of sepulchres, built within the saintly cathedral for the warrior dead that rested from their feuds on earth." "Of purple granite was the necropolis; yet, in the first minute, it lay like a purple stain upon the horizon, — so mighty was the distance. In the second minute it trembled through many changes, growing into terraces and towers of wondrous altitude, so mighty was the pace. In the third minute, already, with our dreadful gallop, we were entering its suburbs. Vast sarcophagi rose on every side, having towers and turrets that, upon the limits of the central aisle, strode forward with haughty intrusion, that ran back with mighty shadows into answering recesses. Every sarcophagus showed many bas-reliefs, — bas-reliefs of battles, bas-reliefs of battle fields; of battles from forgotten ages, — of battles from yesterday, — of battle fields that, long since, nature had healed and reconciled to herself with the sweet oblivion of flowers, — of battle fields that were yet angry and crimson with carnage." And the lady, — what has become of her? Does she still occupy a place in the wondrous pageant? Yes: her transformation is the most strange, and yet, in its beauty, the most perfect of all. Look again: — "And now had we reached the last sarcophagus, now were we abreast of the last bas-relief, already had we recovered the arrow-like flight of the illimitable central aisle, when, coming up this aisle to meet us, we beheld a female infant that rode in a carriage as frail as flowers. The mists which went before hid the fawns that drew her, but could not hide the shells and tropic flowers with which she played, — but could not hide the lovely smiles by which she uttered her trust in the mighty cathedral, and in the cherubim that looked down upon her from the topmost shafts of its pillars. Face to face she was meeting us; face to face she rode, as if danger there were none. 'Oh, baby!' I exclaimed, 'shalt thou be the ransom for Waterloo? Must we, that carry tidings of great joy to every people, be messengers of ruin to thee?'" By sudden and magnificent changes in the dream pageantry the baby is delivered; and perhaps the boldest yet finest effort of imagination in the whole occurs soon after these sentences. But we can quote no more, and, save quotation, we have no resource in such a case. We have given the outline of only one of the visions. We find, in the others, the original elements variously transformed; we have the coach changed into a stately vessel, the avenue into towering cathedral aisles grouped from the mists of the sea, the lady into one who sits in a fairy pinnace on the ocean. The dangers and the splendors are always such as are accordant with the situation.

But we pause; we think we have already vindicated all our assertions. And now will our readers be prepared to estimate the difficulty which attends a decision of the question, whether, on the whole, it is to be regretted that De Quincey fell under the influence of opium? Our own feeling we have already expressed. We think De Quincey was naturally fitted to take his station among the great systematic thinkers of the olden time, and something unique in literature might have been achieved by the combined operation of such a piercing intellect and so imperial an imagination on the pedestal of the nineteenth century. When his arms, in the strength of manhood, and with all their gigantic powers untrammeled, might have been piling mountain upon mountain, he had still to wrestle in mortal agony with a serpent of deadlier venom and more overwhelming power than ever coiled around an ancient hero. No man has more than a certain force allotted him by nature; it may be greater or less, but it is measured; and it cannot be expended twice. Consider the intellectual might necessary to vanquish opium in the three fearful assaults of which De Quincey informs us, and then decide concerning the powers of him whose works, wondrous as they are, were all accomplished in the breathing spaces between paroxysms of convulsive warfare. It may, of course, be alleged, that without the opium we never should have had those writings which are most closely associated with the name of De Quincey. But it is our decided opinion that the dreams produced by opium were but the occasion of the visions wherewith the opium eater has amazed the world. These are strictly works of imagination, and may be tried by the same tests as the dreams of Richter and Novalis. We concede that much of their terrific coloring is traceable to opium; but De Quincey's imagination, we are assured, would have worked under any conditions.

We have done little more than glance at the extraordinary man and the extraordinary works of which we have been treating. We have left ourselves no space to speak of his *taste*, which yet so well deserves notice. We merely remind our readers of his account of the little heroine of Easedale and her infant brothers and sisters, and bid them think of the perfect simplicity of the narrative, of the absence of all rhetoric, of the tender delicacy of the feeling. We merely ask them to consider the grace and ease, the softened glow without glitter, the chastely arranged flower wreaths from which every gaudy weed is instinctively bidden away, in one word, the peace and moderation, which everywhere meet us in the writings of De Quincey. Nor can we speak of him further *as a humorist*, although this is perhaps his most important and prevailing aspect. Often his humor is merely an exquisite flavor of drollery, a half hidden smile, a something which fills you with a certain quiet comfort, but does not make you laugh outright; sometimes it is broad farce, when you do laugh, and cannot but laugh, were it only at the imperturbable gravity of the comic actor; sometimes it is downright horse play, as when old "Toad in the hole" is kicked out, by universal consent of the company and of readers, "despite his silvery hairs and his angelic smile." Sometimes, although very rarely, De Quincey's humor intrudes into places where its presence is utterly indefensible. We shall instance one; by far the most striking. We think it were difficult to match in our late literature, if indeed in our whole literature, the pathetic effect realized in his paper on the Maid of Orleans. De Quincey has there enabled us to define, clearly and conclusively, the function which such as she have, even in their death, performed for mankind. We have so much to harden us in this world, so stern is the struggle of existence, so sadly do the morning dew drops and the early flowers vanish or wither in life's hot day, that you actually confer a precious boon and benefit on a man, when you make him shed a noble tear. No man ever wept with Cordelia by the bed of her stricken father, no man ever saddened at the tale of Margaret's sorrows in the "Excursion," no man ever hung over the dying bed of a true friend, without being a better and a gentler man. And who does not see that, besides all else of instruction and of consolation which arises from the pyres of the martyrs of Christianity, besides the deathless lessons of courage, of devotion, of purest holiness, which they convey, there is this also in the legacy of the fathers to the human race, that, by sympathizing sorrow over their woes, each generation is elevated, and humanized, and ennobled. This great lesson De Quincey has embodied, with an almost unexampled felicity, in his paper on Joan of Arc. But what must we say to the fact that even here humor is permitted to intrude, that even here there is the sacrilegious play of wit and fun? We must not approach that awful and beautiful spectacle, round which angels were weeping, through a porch painted with satyrs and bacchanals; no "insulting light" must "glimmer on our tears;" we must approach through an avenue of cypress, under whose shade we may weep alone. We can pardon the gambolings of an irrepressible humor when the matter is argumentative, but the heavens must be hung with sackcloth around the pyre of Joan of Arc.

The time has probably not yet arrived to attempt a final portraiture of De Quincey, to estimate the value of his works, and to ascertain their rightful place among English classics. The public mind has yet, in great measure, to be introduced to these works, and a few introductory remarks, a few almost colloquial hints, are all we have here offered. It will, indeed, whensoever attempted, be a task of no common difficulty to portray, in its complete and united proportions, the extraordinary mind of which these multiform and many-tinted writings are the production and manifestation. We must not attempt it here. To speak of separate characteristics is, indeed, easy, whether they be those of the author or his compositions. One may mark the indications of a gigantic receptive faculty, seizing, hundred-handed, and gathering into one storehouse, from all lands and centuries, what intellectual treasures it chooses to make its own; proof may be adduced of that power of original thought, which penetrates into untrodden regions, but dimly pointed towards before, and of that creative, imaginative glance which gives form and life to what therefore was airy nothing; special attention may be called to a sympathy resembling a musical instrument of unmeasured range, which can distil a melody more tender than the tear of childhood, but has yet chords to voice the roar of ocean or the thunders of war; and you may enlarge indefinitely on the style, on that astonishing mastery over tho English language, by which, in swiftly changing variation, you are startled, animated, melted, terrified, amused, and which at times attains a softness, a beauty, an aërial glow, to be claimed as peculiarly De Quincey's, and which compel the describer, sensible of his weakness, to borrow the colors of the master himself, and liken them to the timid tremblings of the dawn, or the blending of moon-light, dawn-light, dream-light. But these are at best scattered traits, —individual instances; it is their union which is the wonder and the peculiarity, and of this union we present no theory at present.

II.

TENNYSON AND HIS TEACHERS.

Men seem by universal consent to have associated the genius of Scott with something of magic and enchantment; not enchantment of a stern or gloomy character, but of a gay, glittering, Arabian sort. A peculiar and natural fitness appears to have been recognized in that household phrase, The Wizard of Waverley. And I cannot but believe that the general sense has in this instance been specially felicitous. How can we better represent Scott in our imagination, than as a kindly magician, surrounded by groups of eager and delighted children, before whose eyes he evokes group after group, in endless procession, in that broad, clear, wondrous mirror of his; himself smiling the while, as he half reclines on his well-padded seat, less in complacency at the power of his enchantments, than in pleasure, mingled with mild surprise, at the ecstacies of wonder and joy into which, by every waving of his wand, he throws the children around him? Swiftly, gracefully, beautifully, that long procession moves, the scene ever changing into new forms of loveliness, while an airy music, now rapid and shrill as the sound of clanging arms, now faintly, slowly sinking into mournful cadence, now swelling and glowing into the richer harmony of love, is breathed around. The scene is now the courtly hall, and jewelled figures move stately through the dance. These sweep past and there float into the mirror's magic deeps the grand forms of a mountain land; the cataract leaping to music from the precipice, river hastening to meet river with bridal kiss, and the lake, bearing on its bosom bright island gems, lying placid beneath the crag. Presently, at a sudden turn of the mountain path, there emerges the knight of chivalry, pride and dauntlessness on his brow, a smile of kingly gentleness on his lip. Startled by the sound of his huntsman's horn, the Lady of the Lake, fair as a vision, glides in her skiff, from the glassy deep, into some silvery cove. The scene swims gradually away, and thick clouds, rolling slow before the blast, gather on the moorland, to hang their dim curtains round opposing armies. The battle commences. The pomp and circumstance of feudal war, the plumes, the pennons, the mail-clad steeds, are before us, every form lifted into full, distinct light, and the war cries ringing round. Thus we truly represent to ourselves the poetry of Scott: where all is clear, vivid, instinct with life and motion; where there floats not one cloud of dishonest obscurity, not one film of affected sensibility; where a thousand tints of loveliness glance and gleam before our eyes, like dew drops in clear dawn, or sunbeams on wavering foliage; where the nice definition of form, the elaborate refinement and richness of color, the studied and perfect symmetry, pertaining to the ideal of Greece and of Goethe, are indeed wanting, but where sympathy and love, rejoicing in dewy copse and sparkling flower, in golden corn and smiling meadow, in bounding stream and purple mountain, have become the unconscious ministers of a high artistic perfection, but shed over all a vivacity, an airy sprightliness, a smiling grace, such as were perhaps never won by the more conscious efforts of Art.

Remove from the poetry of Scott the vail of remoteness and enchantment; for that softly glittering morning light, substitute a fierce red glare; let the spirit of the modern time be breathed in its utmost intensity over every scene and into every character; let skilful narrative give place to grand lyric bursts, and sympathetic memory, exhaustless in its stores, to the poetic imagination in its highest might: and for the poetry of Scott you have the poetry of Byron. Passionate, vivid, excitable, sensitive, Byron was the ideal embodiment of lyric poetry. His personality was too intense to permit him to separate himself from his poetic characters, so as to represent them in the whole breadth and symmetry of their relations, in the fashion of a Shakspeare or a Scott. He has himself incidentally informed us that he regarded poetry from the lyrical point of view. "No poetry," he says, in a letter to Murray, "is *generally* good, — only by fits and starts, — and you are lucky to get a sparkle here and there." Like the lyric poet, he concentrated his powers upon particular passages; like the lyric poet, his own emotion colored all he saw; and, like the lyric poet, his dearest theme was passion. When he describes nature, he always, if his genius is in its strength, bathes it in a transforming light, robes it in a grandeur not its own. Herein it is that his essential superiority to Scott, in regard of strict poetic power, is demonstrated. Scott is opulent in detail, and has nature's sweet changefulness, freshness, and variety. But in all the poetry of Scott, there is no such description as Byron's thunder-storm in the Alps. Besides that accurate realism, that broad, natural truth, which it might well have had from Scott, that description burns with a poetic personification such as Scott could never have imparted. The live thunder leaps from crag to crag. The mountains have the hearts of men, and exult to each other in the commotion they produce. Scott describes a battle. We know precisely how the divisions were commanded, and when and where they charged. But where, in all the pages of Scott, do we find a line like this, —

> "Red Battle stamped his foot, and nations felt the shock?"

And if the eye of Byron rolled in that fine lyric frenzy which spreads over nature the hues of human emotion and thought, no less was he a lyrist, and no less was he powerful in the delineation of passion. Since the days of Shakspeare, the burning heart of passion had not been so laid bare. The Corsairs, the Laras, the Gulnares, the Medoras of Byron, perfectly absurd as actual personages, are admirable mouthpieces of lyric emotion, of uncontrollable passion. Totally inadequate to body forth the spirit and tenor of a life, they represent with great effect the feelings of individual exceptional periods. There are such periods in life; volcanic epochs, brief but terrible, when sky and earth are mingled in wild fire-lit commotion, and the peaceful vineyards, ripening in the calm light of long summer days, as yet are not. The emotions of such times, in their burning intensity, in their ethereal tenderness, in the rapture of their joy and the agony of their sorrow, are depicted by Byron with surpassing power. It is when we consider the pure might of imagination exhibited in the individual passages, of which, with a cement of versified prose, the larger poems of Byron have been truly declared by Macaulay to consist, — and the marvellous truth and power with which human passion is everywhere depicted, — that we feel constrained to rank

Byron among the master intellects of mankind, and almost to agree with Goethe that his genius was incommensurable.

But not even in considering the excellence and enduring popularity of literary effort, is it permissible, if it is possible, to abstract any part of the whole life and character. The poetry of Byron is inseparably connected with his life and character. Through the latter there was a fatal flaw; and the former is pervaded by a moral taint, which, as the eye of humanity becomes purer and purer in the lapse of ages, will more and more endanger its literary immortality. The spectacle presented by Byron, in his life and death, is one of which the mysterious sadness may be called infinite. By all we can reverentially assume as to the intentions of the Almighty, and by all the analogy of nature and history, greatness of intellect ought to be one of the forces to keep the soul stable, to preserve a calmness and completeness in the life. So it seems radically to have been with the Platos and Ciceros, the Dantes and Luthers, the Miltons and Leibnitzes, the Pascals and Berkeleys of history. Diverse as the genius of such might be, its power tended to steady them, not to set them rocking like pillars shaken of earthquake. Never for a moment have such faltered in their deliberate assent and submission to the infinite rightness, beauty, and power of moral law. Not even in Swift's case do we find a strict parallel to the phenomenon, so tragically common in these days, of passion conquering genius, and quenching the heaven-soaring flame in its own foul ashes. Mirabeau, Burns, and Byron, to go no further, seem to me to present a spectacle new under the sun. These all had iron constitutions. Physically speaking, they were good for the whole of the threescore years and ten. Yet all three were laid in the dust in the prime of their years; and whatever the palliations we may admit, or the qualifications we may make, it remains a simple fact that they were, in too literal a sense, their own murderers. No cowardly feebleness, no false humility, no "haunting admiration of the grandeur of disordered power," no accursed "hero-worship," ought to be permitted to stifle in us the still small voice which proclaims the awful magnitude of this sin. God and nature affirm the declaration of that still small voice; affirm it in the fevered frame, the burning brow, the early grave: and we are weak, blind, or rebellious, if we do not acknowledge the fact and learn the lesson.

An allusion to the moral taint which pervades the poetry of Byron brings us naturally to the poetry of Wordsworth; which forms the third great school of this opulent period. It is my profound conviction that it was rather to the moral elevation of his poetry, than to his intellectual or æsthetic capacities, that Wordsworth owed the fame and influence he acquired. As you yielded yourself to his guidance, you passed into a region removed alike from that in which the genius of Scott, and that in which the genius of Byron, loved to expatiate. You left behind that joyous land of faery, ringing with the voice of streams and birds, bright with flower and foam, in which you wandered with the border minstrel. You passed beyond the troubled atmosphere where the cloudy grandeurs of the Byronic poetry were unfolded. You stood on the mountain's brow. There at last was the still, unfathomable azure, seeming to look, with calm, eternal smile, on the wild glittering, far below, of the lightnings of passion. The mind of man, the crowning wonder of nature, is in no way more surprising than in its power of sympathy and response. It is easy to cast a spell over it. Any sort of syren chiming allures and subdues it. But its nobler sympathies, inextinguishable though deeply slumbering, have only to be awakened by the tones of a holier melody, when it arises, like a child that has fallen asleep in an unknown land, and looks round, in wistful surprise, listening for that strain which sounded so strangely of home. So it was with the generation that had thrilled to the notes of Scott and Byron. The unchanging verities of faith in God and love to man, proclaimed in their simple majesty, asserted once more the supremacy of their greatness. The still, genial light, diffused in mild and equable radiance through the atmosphere, and gradually whitening the fields into harvest, was recognized as more nobly beautiful than the wild gleaming of volcanic fires. As men stood with Wordsworth on that mountain's brow, they seemed to feel around them the waving of angels' wings, and they looked upon his face as if it were the face of an angel.

And what was it that Wordsworth told his listeners? He told them the world-old truth, that earth's greatest joy and beauty are centred in home; and he turned their eyes once more to that future of immortality, towards which the inarticulate yearning of the human spirit is stronger even than the yearning of passion. Over the natural world, in all the range and richness of its phenomena, he shed a sympathy, more loving, tender, thoughtful, saintly, than had ever been cast over it by any poet. He showed the heaven-light clothing the flowers of earth. With the love of a poet, and the reverence of a high priest, he looked upon the clouds until they smiled down on him unutterable love, and upon the little flowers until they woke in him thoughts too deep for tears. When he looked upon humanity it was rather to pity than to admire the beating of its mighty heart; and the materialism of his age shrunk abashed from the majesty of his disdain.

If this is true, it is not surprising, nor in any way to be regretted, that Wordsworth attained a lofty eminence of fame, and that he exercised an influence of vast potency over his age. But it would be highly absurd to permit it to blind us to the obvious, radical, and demonstrable defects of Wordsworth's poetry. His mind was irremediably wanting in all those qualities which give keenness and intensity to emotion, rapidity and practical force to thought, terseness and brilliancy to style. The absence from his mental composition of any sense of wit or humor was, in its completeness, scarcely human. If one may be pardoned the expression, his soul wanted crystalizing. Had you cleared his eye by one flash of that critical penetration which dwelt in the eye of Pope, had you edged his glance with one ray of that quick, piercing, caustic fire which belonged to Byron, how you would have enriched him! The value of wit, and of the critical faculty, is perhaps not so great to the world at large, as to their own possessor. They warn him, by silent, instinctive monitions, from the ridiculous, the childish, the inane. Such things as *The Seven Sisters* and *Ellen Irwin* are purely, perfectly, unapproachably bad. Parody is cheated by anticipation. We involuntarily exclaim, Every poet his own satirist! If a boy of nine had written *Ellen Irwin*, and died, it would hardly have been pardonable in his mother to publish it. No theory is here of any avail; no arguing can make feebleness impressive, or render art synonymous with commonplace. But for original defect of mind, no theory could have blinded Wordsworth himself to the absurdity of such rigmarole. But not only was the want of wit, humor, and the critical faculty deplorably manifest in Wordsworth. An honest and searching criticism must explicitly allow that he possessed neither the penetrative and grasping imagination which seizes passion, nor the kindling, creative imagination, which gives life and personification. Of this last power, which I believe to be the reflection in man, as the image of God, of the Divine creative energy, and to which can therefore, with no lack of reverence, be applied the term which, immediately, could be applied to God alone, there is scarcely an instance, if there is one, in the whole range of Wordsworth's poetry.

Scott, Byron, and Wordsworth will mainly represent to posterity the great schools of British poetry which shed lustre over the earlier part of the nineteenth century. But these were not alone, nor is it certain that they produced the finest poetical pieces of the time. It would not be easy to make even the slightest descriptive reference to each of the men whose poetical genius, in its full vigor at that period, made their country and their age illustrious. A separate critique might well be devoted to the incomparable battle songs of Campbell, or to the stern, truthful, melodious wailings of Crabbe, or to the ornate erudition of Southey, or to the tuneful tenderness and brilliancy of Moore, or to the delicate, sportive, many-tinted fancies of Hogg, or even to the occasional vigor and intermittent glow of Wilson. Such, however, is here impossible.

But there are three poets to whom special allusion must be made, if not for their transcendant merits, at least for their influence on the poetry which is at present our particular object. I mean Coleridge, Keats, and Shelley. Although the collected poetry of Coleridge does not make a large volume, yet it may be asserted that in few if any more voluminous collections would a systematic critic find more instances of the exercise of genuine poetical genius, wherewith to illustrate his canons. In the Odes of Coleridge, in his *Religious Musings*, and scattered through other pieces, are to be found personifications, which have never been surpassed, and which it defies conception to improve. If I were asked what to me individually appears the most sublime piece of poetical description with which I ever met, in any writer, ancient or modern, British or foreign, I should point to these lines in *The Rime of the Ancient Mariner*: —

> " Still as a slave before his lord,
> The ocean hath no blast;
> *His great bright eye most silently*
> *Up to the moon is cast.*"

No purely realistic description could be conceived, comparable, in power and sublimity, to this. The silent, lorn, appealing look of the eye, is perhaps the most pathetic of all human expressions. In the mere transference of the wearied, despairing gaze of human agony to the ocean, there is an idea conveyed of solitude, dreariness, and woe, which concentrates the descriptions of a thousand calms. Whole poems are gathered up in this marvellous effort of the pure imagination. From the *Religious Musings* I might quote several instances of personification worthy of being compared with the above; but it is needless. It is sufficient to add that in rich and delicate melodiousness, in deep "inwoven harmony," in aërial glow of coloring, there are passages in the poetry of Coleridge which defy description, and turn all praise to shame. There are touches in *Christabel* and *Genevieve* of a pure loveliness, dewy and roseate as the dawn, spirit-like, ethereal, indescribable.

Mr. Carlyle has in one of his essays incidentally characterized the genius of Keats as mere sensibility and random tunefulness of nature. The passage will remain perhaps the most remarkable illustration in literature of the danger, even in the case of writers of great power and general caution, that lies in incidental expression of opinion on important points. Keats sunk into his grave ere he had attained the fulness of his years, pierced by the arrows of cruel mediocrity and withered by disease. Yet there is in his case no necessity to demand an arrest of judgment, on the plea that his genius was undeveloped. *Endymion*, indeed, was a youthful effort, and with all its delicate luxuriance of fancy, is not unmarked by boyish diffuseness, or even, perhaps, by boyish affectation. But *The Eve of St. Agnes* is no youthful effort: it may challenge comparison with anything of its kind ever written. There is a mellow yet transparent glow in its coloring, a finish and melody in its versification, a perfection of form and proportion in its whole execution, which belong exclusively to consummate skill. And what shall we say of *Hyperion?* Is that a youthful effort? Is that characterized only by sensibility and random tunefulness? Even in its present state it is one of the grandest things ever accomplished by the human intellect; and I hold it to be demonstrable that, if it had been finished as it was commenced, it would have found its place among the solitary masterpieces of the world, the greatest philosophical poem that exists. It is well that the central idea of the poem is so clearly indicated in the fragment we have, and that the general plan of the poetic treatment of this idea contemplated by the author is so distinctly suggested, that criticism can view the poem as it must have presented itself to the mind of the poet. The central idea is expressed in these words:—

> "'T is the eternal law,
> That first in beauty shall be first in might;"

and the plan of Keats manifestly was, to exhibit the illustration of this idea afforded by the mythology of Greece. He intended to portray the procession of beauty, from mythology to mythology, and might have brought his whole poem to a glorious close with the transfiguration of all material loveliness in the spiritual beauty of Christianity. It is perhaps impossible to exaggerate the excellence of this idea or of this plan, whether philosophic depth or poetic capability be the ground of estimate. Of all the nations who have passed along the stage of time, the ancient Greeks are most closely associated with all that relates to beauty. In the practical working of the human mind, there never yet was bodied forth any manifestation of the Beautiful, to be for a moment compared, in the chasteness yet grandeur of its perfection, with the mythology of Greece. So intensely perceptive of the Beautiful were the Hellenic race, that it may be considered a philosophic and historical certainty, that it was the fact of their more chastened and delicate loveliness which secured to the Olympians, in preference to the Titans, the homage of the Greek mind. Keats had therefore chosen the very best means afforded him by human history, for setting forth the whole doctrine of the Beautiful in its own garb of beauty. This choice alone demonstrates the master mind. But the execution was, so far as it went, if possible, still more amazing. The colossal vigor of Michael Angelo, and the ethereal delicacy and sense of beauty of Raphael, unite in the wondrous delineations of *Hyperion*.

"Look up, and tell me if this feeble shape
Is Saturn's; tell me, if thou hear'st the voice
Of Saturn; tell me, if this wrinkling brow,

Naked and bare of its great diadem,
Peers like the front of Saturn. Who had power
To make me desolate? Whence came the strength?
How was it nurtured to such bursting forth,
While Fate seemed strangled in my nervous grasp?"

Is it absurd to say that we have here a terseness as of Shakspeare, and a majesty as of Milton? Or to believe that, if the genius of Keats had fully developed in the direction in which it was unmistakeably tending, it might have won him an undisputed eminence, above all the poets who have arisen in Great Britain since the age of Milton?

"Creüs was one; his ponderous iron mace
Lay by him, and a shatter'd rib of rock
Told of his rage, ere he thus sank and pined.
Iapetus another; in his grasp,
A serpent's plashy neck; its barbed tongue
Squeezed from the gorge, and all its uncurl'd length
Dead; and because the creature could not spit
Its poison in the eyes of conquering Jove.
Next Cottus: prone he lay, chin uppermost,
As though in pain; for still upon the flint
He ground severe his skull, with open mouth
And eyes at horrid working."

Is that not a group which might have come from the chisel of Michael Angelo?

"Have ye beheld the young god of the seas,
My dispossessor? Have ye seen his face?
Have ye beheld his chariot, foamed along
By noble winged creatures he hath made?
I saw him on the calmed waters scud,
With such a glow of beauty in his eyes,
That it enforced me to bid sad farewell
To all my empire."

Are there not here touches worthy of the pencil of Raphael?

Consider also the might of the poetic imagination which devised, as the place of meeting for the fallen Titans, a scene like this: —

"It was a den where no insulting light
Could glimmer on their tears; where their own groans
They felt, but heard not, for the solid roar
Of thunderous waterfalls and torrents hoarse,
Pouring a constant bulk, uncertain where.
Crag jutting forth to crag, and rocks that seemed
Ever as if just rising from a sleep,
Forehead to forehead held their monstrous horns."

But does the thought — for thought must at times reveal itself in all poetry — which is to be found in *Hyperion*, partake of juvenile excitement or feeble enthusiasm? The poem, to make use of an expression in itself, is throughout stubborned with the iron of most massive and manly thought.

"Be thou therefore in the van
Of circumstance; yea, seize the arrow's barb
Before the tense string murmur.

* * * * * *

In thy face
I see, astonied, *that severe content*
Which comes of thought and musing.

* * * * * *

Now comes the pain of truth, to whom 't is pain;
O folly! for to bear all naked truths,
And to envisage circumstance, all calm,
That is the top of sovereignty."

These and similar expressions have the true Shakspearean compactness, shrewdness, practicality, and strength. They embody the maxims on which the great silent workers of human history have proceeded. They amply demonstrate that the genius of Keats was no particular development, no mere sentimental rapture, thrilling in melodious flute-notes at sight of the Beautiful, but that his mind was at once mighty in its strength and symmetrical in its proportions; the two sides of the intellectual arch, reason and imagination, supporting and balancing each other. When Keats died at twenty-four, the grave closed over one of the greatest *men* of his time.

Keats died in 1820, aged twenty-four. Two years afterwards, a pale corpse was washed ashore in the Bay of Spezzia, with an open volume of the poetry of Keats in one of the pockets of its dress. It was the body of Percy Bysshe Shelley. His life had been six years longer than that of Keats, and his writings were far more extensive. But he died at thirty; and, in his case too, the rush and roll of the rising waters had not given place to the reposing strength of the full tide.

One is tempted, if but for a moment, to resign himself to that enthusiasm, which a first contemplation of the genius and history of Shelley so mightily awakens. Glowing with Platonic enthusiasms, confident that love burned in the heart of humanity, though to him it presented only a bosom cold as marble, moved by external loveliness to irrepressible, weeping ecstacy, the beautiful, gentle-hearted boy took up his lyre, and shook from it floods of wild, thrilling, ethereal melody. If it were at all safe or permissible to consider poetry a thing apart from the general life and the broad sympathies of mankind; if we could regard beauty in pure and remote abstraction, as a blending of prismatic hues on the central azure, where eye never looked and breath was never drawn; if it were not the instinctive declaration of every manly breast, echoed by all that is soundest in criticism, that what is most human is greatest; we might set the poems of Shelley above all the poetical productions of his time. But we are imperatively forbidden to yield to the impulse. Gazing, in finest frenzy, over the world, Shelley could not think that what he saw was a vision; he could not see that the film in his own eye softened the rugged features of men, and vailed the rocky sternness of the world in enchantment: but we dare not forget these facts. The human eye, accustomed to look upon clear, golden corn fields, and loving the simple, unvailed beauty of garden flowers, will ever behold, in much of Shelley's poetry, no more than the wavering and unhealthful scenery of dreams, or than "the pageantry of mist on an autumnal stream." Marvellous as is the wreathing of that mist, gorgeous as are the hues of its trailing draperies, men will continue to prefer the steady rainbow on the summer shower, and healthful criticism will not forget that mildew and pestilence may lurk behind those lighted folds.

The Revolt of Islam, Shelley's most extended and perhaps most elaborate work, must always be regarded as a wonderful achievement of genius. Its human groundwork is, indeed, supremely weak and puerile. A nation is set free, a great revolution is accomplished, by a promising young gentleman, somewhat mealy-mouthed, and a sentimental young lady, both promoters of the vegetarian movement. But considered as a mere allegory or idealization, in which light, Shelley, no doubt, wished it to be chiefly regarded, the poem loses much of its absurdity, and is seen to partake, in many places, of an epic grandeur.

What is very remarkable, it contains some of the strongest realistic word-painting in the language. Its descriptions of the plague turn the most terrible passages of Wilson's poetic drama on the same subject into infantile lisping.

The Cenci may be taken to mark an epoch in the development of Shelley's genius, in some respects corresponding to that marked by *Hyperion* in the case of Keats. It is, indeed, extremely improbable, that a mind, so superbly gifted in one set of faculties as Shelley's, should have proved ultimately and essentially defective in the stabler elements of intellectual power. However this may be, the severe majesty of *Hyperion* is hardly further removed from the loose-flowing exuberance of *Endymion*, than the human strength of *The Cenci* is from the gorgeous dreaming of *The Revolt of Islam.*

But I am inclined to think that, on the whole, the most perfect, and perhaps the most nobly characteristic, of the poems of Shelley, is the *Adonais.* It is an elegaic poem on the death of Keats. It is not, indeed, wholly undefaced by Shelley's peculiar dreaminess of fancy. But the theme is one capable of commanding universal sympathy, and its treatment is not such as to repel any mind gifted with a real sense of the Beautiful. The poem is no less classic in its symmetry and unity, than superb in its imagery. The dead poet lies under the blue Italian sky, the fitting charnel house for such an one as he. Nature mourns around him.

"All he had loved and moulded into thought,
From shape, and hue, and odor, and sweet sound,
Lamented Adonais. Morning sought
Her eastern watch-tower, and her hair unbound,
Wet with the tears which should adorn the ground,

> Dimmed the aërial eyes that kindle day;
> Pale ocean in unquiet slumber lay,
> And the wild winds flew around, sobbing in their dismay."

If absolute perfection could be predicated of any human thing, I should call that stanza perfect; utterly faultless, at once in feeling, imagery, diction, and rhythm. The description of the poets who come to join their lamentations with those of nature is of corresponding excellence. The close is very sublime. In its majestic sadness, the stately Spenserian stanza reaches a swell and grandeur, perhaps unequalled in any passage in which it has ever been used.

> "The breath whose might I have invoked in song
> Descends on me; my spirit's bark is driven
> Far from the shore, far from the trembling throng
> Whose sails were never to the tempest given;
> The massy earth and sphered skies are riven!
> I am borne darkly, fearfully afar;
> Whilst burning through the inmost vail of heaven
> The soul of Adonais, like a star,
> Beacons from the abode where the Eternal are."

And words from the pen of Keats were probably the last which ever passed through the lips of Shelley!

The last tones of the grand old music had died away. Scott and Byron, Campbell and Coleridge, Keats and Shelley, had ceased to cast abroad their vocal spells; and when men thought of Wordsworth, they thought less of an actually living man than of a marble bust, already in its niche of fame, the lips closed in majestic silence, never more deigning to solicit their applause. The heart of the British nation had ceased to throb with the excitement of the war. Napoleon had died amid the wail of the far Atlantic, his sceptre wrested from his grasp, and only the gleam of his vanished armies to flit before his eye as it flickered in the last delirium. The death of Napoleon was the termination of the great historical drama, whose first act opened in the Hall of the States General at Versailles in 1789. A period of greater stillness, particularly in Great Britain, succeeded; a period marked by no poetic fertility, and in which poetry ceased to take the lead in popular literature, but one in which many influences were working towards undefined issues, and which brought to light, in various quarters, more piercing and delicate thought, a deeper reflectiveness, and a more refined culture, than had been apparent in the stirring time which went before. In the province of philosophy, the essays of Hamilton marked the introduction of a profounder erudition and a more searching analysis. Carlyle's essay on Burns may be considered the first of a series of biographical studies by that author, which must accomplish a revolution in our mode of viewing man, and, by consequence, in our mode of writing history: a revolution in the course of which the whole theory of man and his ways, accepted from French philosophism, and illustrated in such writings, marvellous in many respects, as the history of Gibbon, cannot fail to be crumpled up like a faded map and flung aside. Mainly, also, through the labors of Mr. Carlyle, the influence of the last great outburst of German poetry and philosophy entered, more deeply than it had previously done, into the agencies by which the most powerful young minds of Great Britain were directed. But as yet there was no poetic voice in which the blended influences of the time combined in cunning harmony, and which expressed the most delicate result of its refined and reflective culture. For such a voice, the nation waited.

In 1830 and 1832 there issued successively, from the

publishing establishment of Mr. Moxon of London, two poetical volumes. The critics of the olden time looked at them, sniffed lightly, uttered a few words of angry contempt, and passed on. Here and there an eye glistened, as at the streaks of a new dawn. Here and there an ear hearkened, as to the sound of a new and trancing melody. But the great body, even of the cultivated portion of the people, was unmoved. Year after year went on. Gradually, imperceptibly, surely, a change was wrought. The light which had touched the highest intellectual mountain-tops crept slowly but certainly down towards the lower grounds. The fact at length dawned broadly upon the intellect of the nation that an eye had once more been opened on the Beautiful, that a fresh revelation of loveliness was being made, that a great poet had arisen. That poet was Alfred Tennyson. After all that philosophers have said, the essentially correct definition of poetry in the concrete is, The Beautiful in sight wedded to the Beautiful in sound. Alfred Tennyson, it was perceived, was gifted with an original perception of the Beautiful in man and in nature, and with an original power of melody by which to constrain men to gaze upon his visions. It was found, too, that, under whatever strange and new conditions, the new poet shared the sympathies of his time. His poetry was, as that of every great poet more or less is, reflexive of the feelings and characteristics of his age; not necessarily of the most common or even the strongest, but certainly of some and those distinctive. A movement may be traced in the literary public of Great Britain of that period. The vast body of readers which had found intellectual enjoyment in the poetry of Scott and of Byron had divided into two great portions. The one, and by far the larger, ceasing to discover in the poetry of the day that passionate excitement which had been found in the poetry of Scott and Byron, had betaken itself to prose, mainly to the works of Dickens and his brother novelists. The other, educated by such influences as those at which we have glanced, and with literary tastes refined by a familiar and meditative acquaintance with the poetry of the previous period, sought after a more exquisite and costly intellectual pleasure than could be yielded by such writers as Dickens. Such a pleasure was afforded in the poetry of Tennyson. That poetry reflects the most delicate civilization of the second quarter of the nineteenth century; its dainty elegance, its critical fastidiousness, its reflective musing, its slumbering might. The time, as I said, was one less of new emotion or aspiration, than of musing upon emotions and aspirations which had entered the world of mental influence in the preceding years; and in the poetry of Tennyson, to use an image furnished by itself, all those thunder-clouds of doubt, fear, and ambition, which had long been roofing the European world, were still visible, only they floated in an evening atmosphere, and had grown golden all about the sky.

The poetical schools of Great Britain during the first part of this century have passed cursorily before us; and I think the glimpses we had of them enables us, with sufficient decision, to trace the outline of Tennyson's poetical training. We can picture him first, in the enthusiasm of boyhood, hanging enraptured over the page of Scott or Byron. The solemn music of Wordsworth would then woo him to a loftier region and awaken him to a more spiritual enjoyment, the works of the two most popular poets of the age ceasing to satisfy the highest cravings of his nature. Coleridge, Keats, and Shelley would afford that nourishment and that delight to his strictly poetical taste, of which he was in quest. The great poets of a former age, Shakspeare, Milton, and whoever were greatest among their predecessors and successors, would not, of course, have escaped his studious attention.

It may be said that these remarks are superfluous, since, in an age of culture, every poet may be concluded to have made himself master of the poetic wealth of his country. But I am impressed with the idea that an altogether peculiar relation subsists between the poetry of Tennyson and that of the great masters by whom he was preceded, more especially of those near his own time. The spirit of former schools appears to me to have passed into his poetry, determining its character though undergoing perfect transformation. If, to change the figure, I might imagine the great poets of the language pouring the contributions of their genius into one golden chalice, I should call the poetry of Tennyson a delicately tinted, exquisitely refined foam, mantling on the top. This comparison, I need hardly say, does not necessarily assign to Tennyson a higher place than belongs to any of the poets who preceded him. You may excel any number of masters in single effects, yet be, on the whole, inferior to them all. On this point I do not speak. Nor does the figure impugn the essential originality of Tennyson's genius. Originality is to be judged by the result: so long as the hues of the flower are blended in the unity of life and nature, and compel you to feel the magic and freshness of their beauty, you cannot affect its essential newness by naming its scientific elements, or by telling how the soil was dressed in which it grew. But bearing these things in mind, it is an interesting and quickening application of the critical faculty, to trace, in the poetry of Tennyson, the effects of that complex influence under which his genius developed. His figures are more definite in form and more finished in detail than those of Scott: but in the bright, wandering gleams from the days of chivalry, which flit across the page of Tennyson, may we not detect the influence of the great romancer of Scotland? In his occasional bursts of passion, may we not, though dubiously, suffer ourselves to be reminded of Byron? The spirit of Wordsworth is ever near, as a mild, pervading presence; breathing not only in the high and unsullied morality, but perceptible at times, in idyllic passages of liquid sweetness, in a whispered suggestion of Wordsworthian childishness. The influence of Coleridge and Shelley we can hardly err in discovering in the delicate harmony and inwoven richness of the versification, perhaps, also, in the choice of imagery. Nor must we fail to recollect those foreign influences to which allusions has been made, as playing an important part in moulding the ideas of the most cultivated minds in the period of Tennyson's education. The poetry of Dante became then the object of very careful study, and the manner of Dante, the sternest of poetical realists, is perpetually exhibited in the poems of Tennyson. That intense realization too, of the idea of art, which was represented by Goethe, and that absolute elaboration which his works exhibit, had beyond question left an ineffaceable impression on the mind of Tennyson. But of all the teachers of Tennyson, there was none with whose genius his own was more strictly consonant, or whom he has, or appears to have more diligently studied, than John Keats. So close, indeed, is the affinity between the poetical genius of Tennyson and that of Keats, that the mention of the latter conducts us naturally to what must be the central problem in a critique on any poet, the question as to what is the particular quality and order of his imagination.

A truce to philosophers. If we once permitted ourselves to dive into the subterranean regions of discussion, analysis, and definition, we should emerge into the fair fields and open skies of objective poetry, only with jaded limbs and exhausted patience. Whether there is an essential difference between fancy and imagination, in what exact sense imagination can be pronounced creative, whether its operation is of the nature of that of the reason, conscious and deliberate, or of the nature of dreams, involuntary and hardly conscious, are questions on which I may have a decided opinion or not, but which I beg leave not to discuss at present. Our object will be attained with equal completeness, and far greater comfort, by considering merely two modes, broadly discriminated and perhaps all-embracing, in which different poets produce their effects, or in which the same poets write on different occasions.

The first of these modes might be styled that of the imagination stimulative: the second that of the imagination delineative. The one deals in bold, dashing, single strokes. It casts a flash of light over a wide surface of country, causing every mountain ridge, every valley stream, every castled crag, to gleam for a moment on the eye, but revealing no geographical details. It evokes the imagination of the reader, by striking but comparatively indefinite epithets. It says a face was lovely, a storm terrible, a lake beautiful; but it does not dwell on the "snow-and-rose-bloom" in the maiden's face, it does not particularize the terrors of the storm, it does not speak of every cloud that wandered over the lake, or mention the flowers that glassed themselves in its mirror. It runs with wizard hand over a thousand cords of association, sympathy, affection, touching the string but trusting to nature for the vibration. Not so with imagination in her other mood. She then seems to draw near to the painter, that she may imitate the definiteness of his colors, to the sculptor, that she may reach the perfection of his forms. She exhausts her subject. She deals in measurement and detail. Her aim is not to arouse but to satisfy, not to stimulate but to delineate; or if both to rouse and stimulate, then by the effect of minute and elaborate painting.

But old Hume reminds me that criticism will not be of much use until it deals in abundant instance and illustration. I shall attempt, therefore, to make good my position, respecting the modes of imaginative operation which I have defined, and to afford illustration of those modes, by one or two references and citations. I premise that, as there is no such thing as a mathematical line in nature, neither have we here an exact boundary line. No poet has ever exhibited either of the imaginative modes to the complete exclusion of the other. Some poets exhibit both in proportions difficult to define. But certain poets lean so manifestly towards the one, and others so generally to the other, that the fact affords a satisfactory means of classification.

Of imagination stimulative, I suppose Homer would be cited as having furnished examples hardly to be surpassed. The old man is of course garrulous and minute, but he is fond also of the single flash, of the daring sweep, of the word that kindles a whole dawn, of the comparison which evokes a whole shadowy host of thoughts, sympathies, imaginings. His heroes are so often lion-like! His many sounding sea draws on our imagination so endlessly! Stentor bawls as loud as fifty; a great indefinite bellow, only beyond the reach of any dozen of ordinary mortals. Achilles wanders by the surf, looking unutterable things, but the curtains of his sublime sorrow are not drawn. Milton, with all his austerity, and though his rhythm is as the measured and martial music of angelic armies, is one of the greatest masters of this from of imagination. Generation after generation will ponder his immortal words, and every new form of apprehension, distress, dismay, terror, or the reverse, that the ages exhibit, will be compelled by his irresistible imagination to minister to its ends. The eyes of men will ever peer into that "darkness visible," and never will they cease to discover in it

> "sights of woe,
> Regions of sorrow, doleful shades, where peace
> And rest can never dwell."

Celestial music ever new in tone, celestial fragrance never to be exhausted, breathe round his Raphaels and Uriels; and the deep scars of thunder, sublimely indefinite, will never cease to be gazed at, with awe and terror, on the brow of the fallen Angel. But the finest example of this form of imagination in existence is beyond question the description of the horse in Job. "Hast thou given the horse strength? hast thou clothed his neck with thunder? canst thou make him afraid as a grasshopper? the glory of his nostrils is terrible. He paweth in the valley, and rejoiceth in his strength: he goeth on to meet the armed men. He mocketh at fear, and is not affrighted; neither turneth he back from the sword. The quiver rattleth against him, the glittering spear and the shield. He swalloweth the ground with fierceness and rage; neither believeth he that it is the sound of the trumpet. He saith among the trumpets, Ha, ha! and he smelleth the battle afar off, the thunder of the captains and the shouting." There is, under all this description, a stern and accurate realism. The abstract qualities of the horse, his strength, courage, and the majesty of his movements, are discerned with unerring truth. But what words can express the wonder with which we silently look upon the final picture! If the impressions of a thousand differently constituted minds could be recorded after surveying the marvellous portraiture, each set of impressions would prove different, yet every mind, if capable of being moved at all, would have been stirred to its depths. By the very freedom which is accorded to the impressions of the individual beholder, imagination is laid under a spell which will make it work in all climes and countries forever.

Dante and Spenser belong to the class of imaginative *delineators* perhaps as obviously as any poets of the whole past. Mr. Macaulay has contrasted Milton and Dante on essentially the same grounds as those on which we are at present dividing poets into two classes. The poet of Florence, whose face we see in his portraits, staring on there, as if, with unblenching earnestness, it would look through the very sky, seems to have disdained the ministry of the imagination of his fellows. Cold, stern, determined, he graved, with a pen of iron, to the last line, and then left his writing in the rock forever. Spenser is equally minute, but there is no sternness in Spenser. Dante finishes, because his proud austerity will leave no touch to be added by any other finger, because he scorns toil and pain, and yearns after hard actual truth. Spenser finishes because he loves, or because his genial all-embracing humor makes him never tire of any figure, however grotesque or monstrous, which he has once evoked. He will not lose one of the smiles of Una. He loves every tree of the forest, and gives you the name of each. If he stands on a heaven-kissing hill, he is so enraptured with the beauty of earth and heaven, that he must needs tell you of every cloud in the sky and every flower in the meadow. Even when he yokes unsightly creatures in hideous cars, he does not get angry with them: he looks and lingers, and describes, laughing, perhaps, a quiet laugh.

Shakspeare will afford, wherever we choose to open, admirable examples of both our forms of imaginative exertion.

> "Ay, every inch a king:
> When I do stare, see how the subject quakes!"

These words of Lear are a magnificent example of the imagination that awakens and stimulates. There is nothing of kingly dignity, of imposing presence, of majesty to awe, and power to terrify, which you cannot associate with that line and a half. The description of Dover Cliff, almost immediately preceding, is a specimen, though not so pure, in the other kind. The suggestive imagination insinuates its voice in a whisper; but the closeness of detail is sufficient for illustration.

> "How fearful
> And dizzy 't is, to cast one's eyes so low!
> The crows, and choughs, that wing the midway air,
> Show scarce so gross as beetles: half way down
> Hangs one that gathers samphire; dreadful trade!
> Methinks he seems no bigger than his head.
> The fishermen, that walk upon the beach,
> Appear like mice; and yon tall anchoring bark,
> Diminished to her cock; her cock, a buoy
> Almost too small for sight: the murmuring surge,
> That on the unnumbered idle pebbles chafes,
> Cannot be heard so high:—I 'll look no more;
> Lest my brain turn, and the deficient sight
> Topple down headlong."

Of all the poets of the commencement of this century, John Keats exhibited, most distinctively and with the greatest success, the second form of imaginative description. His intimacy with Leigh Hunt perhaps influenced him to adopt this style. The *Story of Rimini* by the former is a very fine specimen of rich, warm, detailed coloring. But *The Eve of St. Agnes* not merely casts the work of Hunt into utter eclipse but is one of the very finest examples of the style in existence. The opening stanza at once reveals imagination in her lingering, loving, particularizing mood.

> " St. Agnes' Eve — Ah, bitter chill it was!
> The owl, for all his feathers, was a-cold;
> The hare limp'd trembling through the frozen grass,
> And silent was the flock in woolly fold:
> Numb were the Beadsman's fingers while he told
> His rosary, and while his frosted breath,
> Like pious incense from a censer old,
> Seem'd taking flight for heaven without a death,
> Past the sweet Virgin's picture, while his prayer he saith."

But I need not scruple to quote once more the most wonderful passage in this wonderful poem, a passage which perhaps no poet but Keats could ever have written, which in the closeness of its detail is a perfectly distinctive example of the delineative imagination, and which, in the perfect loveliness of every tint, exhibits how rich a poetic effect can be produced by the imagination that so works.

> " A casement high and triple-arch'd there was,
> All garlanded with carven imageries
> Of fruits, and flowers, and bunches of knot-grass,
> And diamonded with panes of quaint device,
> Innumerable of stains and splendid dyes,
> As are the tiger-moth's deep-damask'd wings;
> And in the midst, 'mong thousand heraldries,

And twilight saints, and dim emblazonings,
A shielded scutcheon blush'd with blood of queens and kings.

Full on this casement shone the wintry moon,
And threw warm gules on Madeline's fair breast,
As down she knelt for heaven's grace and boon;
Rose bloom fell on her hands, together prest,
And on her hair a glory, like a saint:
She seem'd a splendid angel, newly drest,
Save wings, for heaven:—Porphyro grew faint:
She knelt, so pure a thing, so free from mortal taint.

Anon his heart revives: her vespers done,
Of all its wreathed pearls her hair she frees;
Unclasps her warmèd jewels one by one;
Loosens her fragrant boddice; by degrees
Her rich attire creeps rustling to her knees:
Half hidden, like a mermaid in sea weed,
Pensive a while she dreams awake, and sees,
In fancy, fair St. Agnes in her bed,
But does not look behind or all the charm is fled."

I must repeat that no poet of great genius belongs exclusively to either of the classes I have endeavored to discriminate. The general manner is, in *The Eve of St. Agnes*, unmistakeably marked: yet there might be cited from its stanzas example after example of those far-illumining words and burning metaphors, which belong specially to the first kind of imaginative action. In turning to Tennyson, we must not expect a uniformity not to be found elsewhere, and perhaps inconsistent with powerful genius. But the order of his imagination is marked with a distinctness not admitting of doubt. It delights in detail, delineation, finish. Herein is found the key to a critical appreciation of the poet; the point of view from which, surveying all he has done, his true station among masters in the same kind may be discovered. Broad as are the flashes of light which he casts at times across his page, exhaustless as is the suggestion which lurks in many of his metaphors, belonging as some of his entire poems do to the other class, it is side by side with Dante, Spenser, and Keats that he takes his stand. It was just about the time when his poetical genius was first growing into consciousness of its might, and in all probability looking earnestly for any aids, in the way of model or advice, to help its expansion, that Great Britain was awaking to a sense of the loss sustained in the death of Keats, and when that criticism, which had killed by its loud and indiscriminate censure, was hasting to mock by its loud and indiscriminate applause. I cannot but think, therefore, that Tennyson must have devoted to the works of Keats a close, deliberate, and emulous attention; nor do I know a better introduction to the poetry of the former than a familiar acquaintance with that of the latter. One might shrink from the comparison of Tennyson with the three great poets with whom I have classed him. My idea of his poetry, as an abstract of the perfections of other schools wrapped in the light of a new idealization, tends to repel even the suggestion of such a comparison. But I do not hesitate to say that in the works of our great living poet, there are traces of the supreme excellences of Dante, of Keats, and Spenser: the austere grandeur and painful finish of the Florentine, the classic taste and intellectual strength exhibited in *Hyperion*, and the mellowed splendor, the golden glow, the lavish opulence, of Spenser.

A glance, however cursory, at certain of the poems of Tennyson, is sufficient to prove and illustrate the preceding statements.

The *Recollections of the Arabian Nights*, one of the

most remarkable pieces in Tennyson's first volume, reminds one strongly of the *Lamia* of Keats. In that poem, the latter shrinks not from the most minute detail. He describes his hall of banquet with the accuracy of an inventory. You know how the flowers festoon from pillar to pillar, how every capital is wreathed, whether the vases are fluted or plain, where the light falls from every lamp. The youthful Tennyson, in the poem I first named, dreams himself away to a scene in the far East, when the Sultan is in the full blush of his glory, and gazes entranced on the floral and festal magnificence by which he finds himself surrounded. Dauntless in its consciousness of power, his imagination does not say *how* beautiful or grand was the eastern garden scenery; it tells precisely *what* that scenery was, it details each of its particular appearances. We may think it beautiful or not as we please: the poet merely tells us what he saw. No sooner is he afloat on the Tigris than we find that the gold of the shrines of Bagdat was fretted, and that the gardens were high walled. His shallop rustles through foliage that is low and covered with bloom, and the shadows, falling over the fragrant, glistening water, are not general, indiscriminate shadows, but the particular ones cast from the citron trees. When he passes from the river into the canal, he finds the outlet guarded by platans; the pillared palms make a vault above him as he glides along, and the sweet odors which attempt to climb heavenward are stayed beneath the dome of hollow boughs; the canal is rounded to a lake, and the silver-chiming music of the rills, that fall into the water from the green rivage above, seems to shake the sparkling flints beneath his prow; on either side of the lake are fluted vases and brazen urns, duly occupied by flowers, of which some drop low their crimson bells, while others are studded with disks and tiaras;

and the bulbul sings in the coverture of the lemon grove. Getting ashore and leaving his boat hanging by its silver anchor, he is led on towards the pavilion of the Caliphat. The doors are of cedar, and are carved; they are flung inward over spangled floors; broad flights of stairs run up, and the balustrade is of gold; there are fourscore windows, which are lighted. At last he looks upon the great Sultan himself, and the author of the Court Circular, published next morning in Bagdat, could not have described more faithfully the *tout ensemble* of his Majesty.

> " Six columns, three on either side,
> Pure silver, underpropt a rich
> Throne of the massive ore, from which
> Down-droop'd, in many a floating fold,
> Engarlanded and diaper'd
> With inwrought flowers, a cloth of gold.
> Thereon, his deep eye laughter-stirr'd
> With merriment of kingly pride,
>   Sole star of all that place and time,
>   I saw him in his golden prime,
>   The GOOD HAROUN ALRASCHID!"

The Lady of Shallott, *Ænone*, *Mariana in the Moated Grange*, and *Mariana in the South* need only to be named in order to recall the detail of their finishing. It is the hand of a pre-Raphaelite that draws the lines and brings out the tints. But it is needless to multiply examples. I choose one which will, I think, prove ample, and may be conclusive.

The Palace of Art is one of Tennyson's most characteristic and marvellous works. If all his other poems were lost, I am persuaded that, from this alone could be defined the essential quality and order of his genius. Of its value in philosophy, of the profundity or practical worth of the thought it embodies, I do not now speak. It is as an exhibition of Tennyson's mode of imaginative operation, that I regard it. But it is impossible to proceed except by quotation, since no summary could convey an adequate idea of its architectural detail. I begin, therefore, by citing the passage in which the erection of the Palace is described.

"A huge crag platform, smooth as burnish'd brass,
I chose. The ranged ramparts bright
From level meadow-bases of deep grass
Suddenly scaled the light.

Thereon I built it firm. Of ledge or shelf
The rock rose clear, or winding stair.
* * * * * *
* * * * * *

Four courts I made, east, west and south and north,
In each a squared lawn, wherefrom
The golden gorge of dragons spouted forth
A flood of fountain-foam.

And round the cool green courts there ran a row
Of cloisters, branched like mighty woods,
Echoing all night to that sonorous flow
Of spouted fountain-floods.

And round the roofs a gilded gallery,
That lent broad verge to distant lands,
Far as the wild swan wings, to where the sky
Dipt down to sea and sands.

From those four jets four currents in one swell
Across the mountain streamed below
In misty folds, that, floating as they fell,
Lit up a torrent-bow.

And high on every peak a statue seem'd
To hang on tiptoe, tossing up
A cloud of incense, of all odor steam'd
From out a golden cup.

So that she thought, 'And who shall gaze upon
My palace with unblinded eyes,
While this great bow will waver in the sun,
And that sweet incense rise?'

For that sweet incense rose and never fail'd,
And, while day sank or mounted higher,
The light, aërial gallery, golden rail'd,
Burnt like a fringe of fire.

Likewise the deep-set windows, stain'd and traced,
Would seem slow-flaming crimson fires
From shadow'd grots of arches interlaced,
And tipt with frost-like spires."

The structure, it must be seen, is conceived as a whole. It has the massiveness of architecture, its proportion, and its completeness. Roberts could not have rendered more minutely the aërial gallery, the statues on the top, or the Gothic windows with their frost-like spires. Contrast with Tennyson's description the following by Edgar Poe.

"In the greenest of our valleys,
By good angels tenanted,
Once a fair and stately palace,
Radiant palace, reared its head.

In the monarch Thought's dominion,
It stood there;
Never seraph spread a pinion
Over fabric half so fair.

Banners yellow, glorious, golden,
On the roof did float and flow."

With the respective merits of these delineations we have nothing to do. But how different they are! The great American poet awakens your imagination by the mention of radiant lights and floating banners. His palace is ideal, shadowy, touched with new hues by every imagination. Painters for many generations might attempt to portray it, and each canvass would exhibit an edifice bearing no traceable resemblance to any of the others. But Tennyson will have none of your palace: he builds you his own. If you paint it, you must be careful; if you painted it a hundred times, you would be constrained to make the great features the same. A crag platform, rising four-square from a plain of grass; a stream pouring over the face of the crag; a roof with peaks, on each of which stands a statue bearing incense; a bartizan faced by a golden railing:—these must enter into every attempt to paint the Palace of Art. We find, then, that the characteristic of Tennyson's delineation is extreme accuracy, minute architectural clearness. Yet the passage I have quoted would in general be pronounced obscure, and it is precisely in such passages that the difficulty of Tennyson's style is exhibited. I feel assured that the lines of Poe would, by the majority of readers, be pronounced the clearer of the two. How is this? The answer can be rendered with perfect decision. The general imagination is far more distinguished by excitability, than by definiteness of vision. The eye glances along the page, securing the mental impression, not realizing the separate pictures. This impression is what the stimulative imagination aims at, and the most popular poetry of all ages has therefore been the work of the stimulative imagination. But it is quite impossible for the same sort of perusal to suit both the modes of imagination. In the one case, the single word or metaphor produces its own effect, and there an end. In the other case, word must find its word, stanza must be, swiftly or slowly, collated with stanza. If all the limbs and features of the body, in a human delineation, are specified in their true forms and colors; if all the parts of an edifice architecturally correspond; the scattered members can unite into one living frame, the separate courts and galleries into one palace. But if the delineative poet has, in the course of his perilous enumeration, put an arch where there should be a pillar, or a battlement where there should be a rampart, his edifice is strictly a heap of disjointed rubbish. If the reader's imagination refuses to follow the poet in meek obedience, the whole becomes, whether correct in itself or no, an unintelligible mass of confusion, or an unimpressive blank. The descriptions of Spenser, Keats, and Tennyson are literally too clear to be instantly comprehended; dark with excess of light. Only be silent and listen to such poets and they will tell you far more than that their mansions are stately, their forests rich in light and shade, their maidens sweet and rosy. The indefinite, flickering light of your own imagination is sternly shorn away: but by degrees the creation of the poet, resting calm as against the sky of dawn, every crystal spire unchangeably fixed, every golden pillar standing immovable, rises before you and remains forever.

It is a tempting question, which of these orders of delineation demands the greater power and is essentially the greater. Perhaps they are co-ordinate. I confess that, though the delight I have received from such descriptions as those of Spenser, Keats, and Tennyson, has been inexpressibly intense, I am inclined to yield to the voice of humanity, which has, in all ages, accorded supreme popularity to the poets of the first class. From Homer to Byron, those poets have exercised the most potent influence over the mass of men, whose touch has been sweeping, who have delighted in broad masses of shade and sunshine, who have scattered imaginative spells rather than finished imaginative pictures. Viewed abstractly, however, the case on the other side is exceedingly strong. If imagination works perfectly in every detail, and yet unites her whole composition in living harmony, is it fair to impugn the supremacy of her might, because the human eye, dazzled, it may be, by false glories, turbid through ignoble admirations, and incapable of a long, calm gaze, fails to take in the magnificent sweep of her lines, to perceive the elaborate correspondence of her colors? Beyond question, the higher the scale of culture, the higher is the pleasure found in the work perfect in its minuteness as well as in its majesty; beyond question, too, the poets who have delighted in such work, Dante perhaps excepted, have depended more, for their power of fascination, on their pure sense of beauty, than on the breadth of their human sympathies or power of general interest. The sense of abstract loveliness was possessed by Spenser and Keats as strongly and as exquisitely as by any men that ever lived. It might be urged, too, that, in this form of imaginative exertion, the sister Arts, poetry and painting, meet, while the indefinite imagination affords no forms or colors which the painter can follow. The ideal end of painting as an Art, and that of the Spenserian imagination, — to reveal beauty in perfect form and color, — are identical. Of all painters, in landscape at all events, Turner, on a great scale, and old David Cox on a less, have alone, so far as I can remember, attempted in form and color the suggestiveness and mystery of the stimulative imagination. But here, it is to be feared, Poetry might step in, arrayed in her most gorgeous robes, and declare, with a smile of haughty disdain, that Turner and Cox merely struggled into her empyreal freedom above the constraints of the inferior Art, and that the imagination, which catches a gleam from the infinite, and transcends any definite form of color to be rendered by human hand, is, after all, the grander of the two.

The description of the palace in the poem we have been contemplating, is perhaps sufficient for our purpose. But every stanza is of the same order. A few of them I cannot forbear from quoting.

"Full of great rooms and small the palace stood,
All various, each a perfect whole
From living Nature, fit for every mood
And change of my still soul.

For some were hung with arras green and blue,
Showing a gaudy summer-morn,
Where with puff'd cheek the belted hunter blew
His wreathed bugle-horn.

One seem'd all dark and red — a tract of sand,
And some one pacing there alone,
Who paced forever in a glimmering land,
Lit with a low, large moon.

One show'd an iron coast and angry waves,
You seem'd to hear them climb and fall,
And roar rock-thwarted under bellowing caves,
Beneath the windy wall.

And one, a full-fed river winding slow
  By herds upon an endless plain,
The ragged rims of thunder brooding low,
  With shadow-streaks of rain.

And one, the reapers at their sultry toil.
  In front they bound the sheaves. Behind
Were realms of upland, prodigal in oil,
  And hoary to the wind.

And one, a foreground black with stones and slags,
  Beyond, a line of heights, and higher
All barr'd with long white cloud the scornful crags,
  And highest, snow and fire.

And one, an English home—gray twilight pour'd
  On dewy pastures, dewy trees,
Softer than sleep—all things in order stored,
  A haunt of ancient Peace.

* * * * *

* * * *

Or sweet Europa's mantle blew unclasp'd,
  From off her shoulder backward borne:
From one hand droop'd a crocus: one hand grasp'd
  The mild bull's golden horn.

Or else flush'd Ganymede, his rosy thigh
  Half-buried in the Eagle's down,
Sole as a flying star shot through the sky
  Above the pillar'd town."

I doubt whether it is within the limit of possibility to bestow too high a commendation upon these delineations, unsurpassed as they are in the whole range of art. Each stanza is a poem. Each stanza exhibits a strength and calmness of imaginative vision, a sense of symmetry and proportion, in one word a capacity to see and delineate the Beautiful, which would render it, if found separately, as infallibly demonstrative of supreme poetic genius. A single gem, of unparalleled loveliness, tells of the one mine in all the world where it can have been dug. Of the mastery of the English language which concentrated so many complete pictures into such frames it is needless to speak. But how distinctly traceable in every line is the hand of the finishing imagination! What can you add to that figure of Europa? Her mantle is unclasped and borne backward from her shoulder. The crocus droops from one hand; the other grasps the horn of the bull, the horn being golden and the bull mild. The one epithet which might be regarded as a signal of freedom to the imagination, "sweet," hardly releases you here, for you can imagine only a quiet, contented, hoping smile. This little picture has always seemed to me to reveal the genius of Tennyson to the very life, — Tennyson, his mark.

It would be a very delightful but is not a necessary task, to trace the imaginative action, of which I have said so much, through all the poems of Tennyson, whether his earlier or his later. For the present I confine myself to the former, and even of these I can in this connection say but a few words. Observe how the poet always gazes face to face upon what he portrays, how distinctly he hears every word falling from the lips of his characters. He never slurs, he never generalizes. Is he in his idyllic mood, wandering by the brook or among the hay-cocks? He sees the apple-blossom as it sails on the rill; the garden walk is bordered with lilac; the green wicket is in a privet hedge. He lets you hear the very words of the simple, kindly rustics, and you see the flowers plucked for the wreath to bind the brow of the little child. Is it of affection or passion, in the depth of their tenderness or the might of their burning, that he speaks? He shows you the eyelid of the mother quivering, and every little flutter, of love and doubt, in the breast of the village bride. Or the irresistible emotion reddens over cheek and brow, like a northern morning, and the inmost secrets of the spirit dawn out in the dark of the hazel eye. He seems to track the blood in the veins as it courses from the heart to the cheek. The bride in *The Lord of Burleigh* has just heard the announcement, that the landscape painter whom she had loved is a great and wealthy noble. Tennyson does not say how she was impressed. He merely looks at her and reads off the signs on her face.

> "All at once the color flushes
>   Her sweet face from brow to chin:
> As it were with shame she blushes,
>   And her spirit changed within.
>
> Then her countenance all over
>   Pale again as death did prove."

This is all. You hear, in a little, how she strove against her weakness, and addressed herself to her wifely duties, but of her feelings at the time you hear nothing. The characters in which nature wrote those feelings are set before the eye; and how vivid, how profound their portraiture, how delicate and deep their pathos!

Tennyson's diction and melody are in perfect harmony with his imaginative faculty. To describe his command of language, by any ordinary terms, expressive of fluency or force, would be to convey an idea both inadequate and erroneous. It is not only that he knows every word in the language suited to express his every idea; he can select with the ease of magic the word that of all others is best for his purpose: nor is it that he can at once summon to his aid the best word the language affords; with an art which Shakspeare never scrupled to apply, though in our day it is apt to be counted mere Germanism and pronounced contrary to the genius of the language, he combines old words into new epithets, he daringly mingles old colors to bring out new tints that never were on sea or shore. His words gleam like pearls and opals, like rubies and emeralds. He yokes the stern vocables of the English tongue to the chariot of his imagination, and they become gracefully brilliant as the leopards of Bacchus, or soft as the Cytherean doves. He must have been born with an ear for verbal sounds, an instinctive appreciation of the beautiful and delicate in words, hardly ever equalled. His earliest poems are festoons of verbal beauty, which he seems to shake sportively, as if he loved to see jewel and agate and almondine glittering amid tropic flowers. He was very young when he published the *Recollections of the Arabian Nights;* yet that piece displays a familiarity with the most remote and costly stores of the English language not exceeded in the same space by Spenser. If these expressions seem to any extravagant, I would beg to suggest a study of two poems; —I might name twenty. Consider *Eleanore* and *The Lotos Eaters.* Both these poems are every way characteristic of Tennyson, and illustrate admirably his imaginative method. I regard them, in respect of diction, as not only justifying every word I have said, but as putting utterly to shame my attempts to convey an adequate impression of Tennyson's power over words. Here I cannot quote single verses; for there are no degrees in perfection; and the most minute acquaintance with these poems leaves me deliberately unable to point to a line in either, of which the diction is not absolutely perfect. In the case of *Eleanore* I can just imagine it objected, that the ambition of the diction overleaps itself and falls on the other side, that the skill of the poet, like the inimitable finish of Lewis on the dress of an uninteresting woman, is expended so lavishly on robes and jewelry, that the serene imperial Eleanore fails to concentrate our regard. But of *The Lotòs Eaters*, this cannot be even argued. As you read that poem, you are so steeped in its golden langor, you are so overpowered by the trance-like joy of its calm, that you cannot think even of the spell that binds you. The force of language could no further go.

Tennyson's choice of measure, and general sense of rhythm and melody, correspond accurately with the order of his imagination, and the pearly delicacy of his diction. It, too, generally requires, for its full appreciation, an ear that will listen carefully, and even permit itself to be tuned to the melody. There is rarely that instantaneous attractiveness, which a well known measure, handled with any novelty or skill, is sure to possess; an attractiveness to be deemed analogous to that superficial beauty, which clearness and elegance impart to prints in annuals, and soft, well contrasted lights and shades to pictures generally. There is no reliance on antithesis, as is so common in the smaller lyrics of Byron. There is no courting of anapestic buoyancy, or voluptuous sweetness, as in the lyrics of Moore. In almost every case, the radical metrical foot is the iambus, that most deeply consistent with the genius of the English tongue, but that, also, affording the poet the least resource in dashing turns or sounding cadences, and forcing him to trust most exclusively to his real power, to the gold seen gleaming beneath the pellucid current of his verse. *Locksley Hall* is a magnificent exception to Tennyson's general habit, its trochaic measure being superbly adapted for the expression of passion, and itself being incomparably the finest of trochaic melody in the language. But though Tennyson's measures are generally iambic, he breathes into them a melodiousness which is new, and gives them forms of his own. The stanza of *The Palace of Art* is quite new, and it is only by degrees that its exquisite adaptation to the style and thought of the poem is perceived. The ear instinctively demands, in the second and fourth lines, a body of sound not much less than that of the first and third; but in Tennyson's stanza, the fall is complete; the body of sound in the second and fourth lines is not nearly sufficient to balance that in the first and third; and the consequence is, that the ear dwells on the alternate lines, especially on the fourth, stopping there to listen to the whole verse, to gather up its whole sound and sense. I do not know whether Tennyson ever contemplated scientifically the effect of this. I should think it far more likely, and indicative of far higher genius, that he did not. But it appears to me that no means could be conceived for setting forth, to such advantage, those separate pictures, "each a perfect whole," which constitute so great a portion of the poem. Wherever the picture to be drawn is spread over several stanzas, or the same precise strain of feeling is kept up for so long, the form of the verse is felt to be by no means equally suitable, and the ear, accustomed to the deep rest of the full stop after the short line, will hardly consent merely to stop a moment at a comma, and then hasten to the succeeding verse. But it is a poor business analyzing verse like this, or attempting to reduce it to scientific rules. It is like trying to convey an idea of a flower, by enumerating its stamens and tissues, or by presenting it, dried and shrivelled, with its name beside it, in some adust herbarium: instead of holding it up to the living eye, arrayed in that dress of purple, or blue, or scarlet, which God taught it to weave for itself from the sunbeams, or inhaling that fragrance, which eludes, like a spirit, the rude touch of science. Better is it, in thinking of the melodiousness of Tennyson's poetry, to recall those hours, so intensely, so serenely happy, when gradually the ear came under its spell: when the miller's daughters, and gardener's daughters, first glided into the field of vision, to tender, mildly cheerful music; when the *Dream of Fair Women*, and *The Lotos Eaters*, and *The Palace of Art*, almost hushed the beatings of the heart, at the flute-like softness and dreamy calm of their melody; when the tropic lightnings of passion first flashed amid the thunder of *Locksley Hall;* or when the great autumnal sorrow of *In Memoriam*, voiced itself in a rhythm, solemn and majestic as the roll of the melancholy main. The melody of Tennyson's poems is perhaps more peculiarly his own even than his other characteristics; it is still more difficult than in the case of these, to find its prototype in preceding English poetry.

We have hitherto, strictly speaking, considered only the methods and appliances of Tennyson's genius. His form of imaginative exertion, his diction, and his melody, are perfectly separable, in critical consideration, from the emotions he portrays, the thought he utters, or the new aspects of nature's beauty to which he opens our eyes. Expression is, in a sense, everything in poetry, as painting is in a sense everything in the pictorial Art: in the sense, namely, that, whatever thought and feeling may be exhibited, without metrical expression, in the one, or pictorial expression, in the other, loses the distinctive characteristic, however much it may retain of the general character, of either. Yet expression can never be all in all, whether in painting or in poetry. Some association, however we may define it, with the world of human thought and feeling, is indispensable. The perfect tones of a prism will never be to man as the imperfect tones of a picture; and the pure notes of music are vacant of influence, until, by combination into melodies, they attain the power of touching the mystic chords of association. Whatever the conditions prescribed by the nature of each Art, there is no Art in which it is not necessary that there be a something related to its expression as substance is related to form. Here again, the genius of metaphysics beckons us to answer a few stiff and ancient questions, touching the nature of those truths, of experience, of feeling, of reason, which may be pronounced necessary in poetry. What, asks that menacing presence, is the connection between the Good, the Beautiful, and the True? Are Science and Poetry one, or are they different, and how? Happily Poetry has not the unreasonable habit of that beautiful but whimsical lady, the Sphynx. Poetry does not insist upon our explaining the riddle of the nature, or any other riddle, before enjoying the benignity of her smile. But our present business is criticism, and a word or two, as to the relations of Poetry and Science, may render us important assistance as we proceed.

Professor Wilson pronounced Poetry to be "the true exhibition, in musical and metrical speech, of the thoughts of humanity when colored by the feelings, throughout the whole range of the physical, moral, intellectual, and spiritual regions of being." As a definition of poetry, this might be open to objection, but as a definition of poetry by Professor Wilson, it is of value. Wilson's scientific capacity was perhaps as feeble as his dramatic. But he was the greatest sympathetic critic that ever used the English language, the man most thoroughly capable, through delicacy, power, and range of sympathy, to discover and appreciate poetic excellence. Nor was he ever tempted, by over-refinement of sensibility, or sickly admiration for any particular mannerism, to abandon the broad canons of criticism which base themselves on deep and universal laws of human nature. He is pre-eminently fitted to represent the cultivated but healthy human mind, as affected by poetry. Viewing him in this capacity, importance must be attached to his words. When thought is contrasted with feeling, as he contrasts it, it must have reference to truth. Thoughts without any substantial basis of truth are valueless or inconceivable. And Professor Wilson's words clearly indicate that, in regarding poetry, he experienced an instinctive craving for this substantial truth, whether as recorded in experience or construed to reason.

The view of Goethe and his school in Germany, adopted by Mr. Carlyle, touching the relation between the True and the Beautiful, between Poetry and Science, I understand to be, that Poetry, in its true essence and noblest realization, presents the truths of reason in the forms of sense. The mere expression of such an opinion indicates the necessity felt by such thinkers as Goethe and Carlyle to discover, in the last resort, some intimate, indissoluble alliance between the True and the Beautiful.

But it is unnecessary to make any parade of authorities on this point. The right doctrine can be reached without any painful consultation of Aristotle, Bacon, and the rest. When understood in its proper sense, it will be universally conceded as an axiom, that truth is inseparable from every sound form of composition. But what is truth? of what does it consist? It may all be classed under two categories, each containing two divisions: —

1. (a) *What* is; (b) *What* may supposably, in change of time or condition, be.

2. (a) *How* what exists is; (b) *How* the supposably existent would be.

All Art has, as its subject matter, truth of the first category: all Science truth of the second.

There is nothing here in the slightest degree obscure, or difficult of comprehension. Goethe and Carlyle, in recognizing the essential connection between poetry and form, lend us really their support; their antithesis between truth of reason and form of sense can alone be rightly interpreted, in accordance with our categories; only I think that, by fairly recognizing truth as equally independent of poetry and science, we are secured from certain errors, into which a definition of poetry simply as the truths of reason in the forms of sense might lead us. It would be erroneous to give any countenance to the idea that poetry receives certain truths from reason, attained by the method of logic, and proceeds to clothe them in the forms of sense. We should thus find ourselves identifying Art with allegory; a peril not altogether escaped in the poetry of Schiller, and surely affecting the rugged truthfulness of *Wilhelm Meister*. I shall not, however, enter here into any debate. Concluding that the antithesis suggested by Mr. Carlyle is the key to the whole subject, and professing merely to interpret and formally apply it, we shall find the division I have made sufficient for the classification of all Art and all Science, whether real or ideal.

Art, then, always deals with what is, or with what may be. Its postulate is that nothing is, or may be imaginatively represented, which is not worthy of observation. It is divided into realistic and ideal. Realistic Art concerns itself with what is; its subject matter is the now existent universe: ideal Art concerns itself with the world of imagination; its subject matter is all that the imaginative faculty calls up in vision, looks forward to in hope, or combines into new creations. The ultimate attainment of realistic Art would be, by all-embracing, all-potent observation, by all-penetrating, all-compelling imagination, to body forth, in form, motion, color, the existent universe, animate and inanimate. The last achievement of ideal Art would be, to represent, not in theory but in fact, a perfect universe. It would set before us, with Plato, the world of the idea, with the idea at last perfectly expressed in form; it would show us that "type of perfect in the mind," for which Tennyson looked in vain in nature; in an expressly Christian scheme of things, it would exhibit humanity re-adorned in its paradisal garments, in a world fitted to such a race, or robed in a purer whiteness than that of Paradise, on the plains of heaven. The province of Art is thus shown to be commensurate with the powers of the human intellect, and the regions of the finite.

Turning to Science, there is no more difficulty in discriminating between real and ideal Science, than between real and ideal Art. The utmost conceivable perfection of realistic Science would be formally to construct, from its elements, the whole material universe, of nature and of man, — to trace, in all their operations, the laws by which it consists. Ideal Science is not so familiar to our conceptions as ideal poetry. But if we do concede it a sphere, its ultimate achievement is definable as the exhibition, in its forming and sustaining laws, of possible perfection. A perfect *theory* of Plato's ideal world, a perfect *theory* of man and nature renewed by Christianity, would precisely answer to this.

The grand antithesis between Art and Science is that of

form and law, of result and cause, of representation and dialectic, of the visible and invisible. Art looks; her guide, from star to star, is the cherub contemplation: Science investigates. Art depicts; Science records.

This distinction is available for important practical purposes.

It enables us, to begin with, to perceive how and why it is that Art is associated inseparably with the Beautiful, while Science has no essential connection with beauty whatever. Science deals with what nature does not *show*. She lifts the green turf of the mountain, to investigate the strata; she divides the ray of light, to examine its separate filaments; she lays open the cheek of beauty, to trace the course of the arteries. She is entirely conversant with those processes and those forms, by contrast with which nature produces her final effects of beauty. Science, therefore, save in the work of discovering and classifying perfected forms hitherto unobserved, has no office whatever in connection with the Beautiful. But Art has to do only with what is *seen*, whether by the eye of sense or of imagination. She gazes enraptured on the dress of nature, intended to be admired: that garment, woven by the hand of God, ineffable in its beauty, in which the purple of night, dark against the star-fires, the green of earth, touched with crimson and gold, the blue of ocean wreathed with tinted foam, the azure of the sky, flushed with dawn and even, and hung with broidered vails of cloud, combine in one picture of sublimity and loveliness, over which the angels clap their hands, and on which we of the earth can never gaze with sufficient wonder and earnestness. All that Art can see of the untainted workmanship of God is beautiful. Wherever the shadow of sin has come, a blight has passed over beauty. In humanity, in world-history, Art does not find all beautiful. But beauty is bound up in the purpose of the ages; the Good, the True, the Beautiful struggle on together, to celestial music, through the night of time; with every new throb of the heart of mankind towards a higher life and a loftier nobleness, a fresh glory and loveliness passes, as it were a blush, along its countenance. At the meridian splendor of this loveliness, ideal Art guesses and gazes from afar. And thus Art's function, whether in the real or the ideal, is ever with the Beautiful.

But, next, does not our antithesis explain the fact that, in all ages, pleasure has been associated with Art, that the poetic nature finds delight in external nature, and that a magnificent, rapturous ease is the mood deemed appropriate to poetic composition? The forms of God's universe are fitted, with sublime beneficence, to impart joy. God willed that whatsoever countenance, of man or angel, unstained by sin, looked upon his world, should break into a smile. God said let there be light; and morning drawing aside the vail of night will ever continue the emblem of joy, because it shows us, once more, that world which then flashed into visibility and beauty. The fact that the contemplation of external loveliness is productive of joy cannot be called in question; and we may view it either as a proof that the Creator of the universe is good, or as a proof that the God of Christianity is the God of Nature. I am perfectly assured that whosoever has spoken of the exercise of the poetic faculty, whether in the case of Milton, Dante, or Goethe, as something arduous, difficult, painful, has erred. To all earnest and honest labor a joy is annexed; there is pleasure, if not in the preliminary toil, at least in the ultimate discovery, of science: but in true poetic composition, the joy approaches rapture. The fine frenzy that Shakspeare saw in the eye of the poet was unquestionably a frenzy of joy. De Quincey, in his own fashion of flinging abroad, with princely recklessness, hints that lighten over wide regions of thought, remarks that the life of poetic enthusiasm, which Coleridge led during his youth, unfitted him for the sternness of life and made him an easy victim to opium. He required, says De Quincey, finer bread than was baked with wheat. The observation is pointedly true in the case of Coleridge: and doubtless the irregular lives of poets, and their inability in general to grapple steadily with the difficulties of life, are to a great extent traceable to the insipidity with which every day realities must present themselves, after the rapturous excitement of imaginative vision.

Truth then, to return, is of the essence of poetry as well as of science. But in the one case, the truth is always enveloped in form; in the other it is eliminated from form. Science gives you truth in algebraic formula; poetry gives you truth in the dance of the stars. A Newton is mighty in the exposition of law, a Shakspeare in the exhibition of fact, of human and physical nature as actually existing or as seen under the revealing idealization of his imaginative genius. An Aristotle applies a powerful analysis to the laws of morals; a Milton exhibits those grand revolutions, in human and angelic existence, in which the might and grandeur of moral law have been displayed.

But it is necessary to guard here against a misapprehension. We are so apt to associate everything with inference and lesson, that when we talk of truth in Science or Art, we almost irresistibly think of some expressly didactic moral. But it hardly admits of question, that neither Science nor Art is by nature bound to acknowledge the justice of the claim thus implied. Truth in visibility is all Art professes to give: truth in law all we can require of

Science. Science may investigate the laws of cookery, or those of the heavenly bodies: and her dignity, no doubt, increases as she ascends. Art may delineate the wayside weeds, or pencil out the lightest bodyings of fancy, — the reveries of the child, the dance of the fairies; she may represent also the mountains that steady the earth, the armies that have shaken the plains of heaven: and her greatness, too, increases as her subjects are ennobled. But as to express moralizing, Science may be dumb as the pyramids, and Art silent as the dew.

It is necessary, also, once more to recollect that neither is there here a mathematical line of demarcation. Art and science, realism and idealism, perpetually mingle in the concrete example.

Tennyson's right to a place among the really great poets of the human race is vindicated by this fact, That he has looked, as a great man might, upon what is most distinctive in the age in which he writes, and that he has bodied forth the result with marvellous poetic realization. This I proceed briefly to establish.

One good example may at times convey, expressly or by implication, a whole argument. I choose here one illustration of Tennyson's truth-grasping power, which seems to me to necessitate the conclusion that he is a great poet, in the sense of seeing and poetically embodying great truths. It is the same as that I selected as a perfectly satisfactory illustration of his peculiar imaginative mothod, *The Palace of Art.* When we contemplate this poem, what do we behold? We see a human being, represented by the soul of the poet, separating from the rest of the world, and going to dwell in a palace apart. This palace is gorgeously constructed. Its roofs gleam with gold. Its courts echo with fountains. A torrent-bow is lit up from the edge of the crag on which it is built. The interior is adorned with the most rich, refined, and elaborate magnificence. The eye can rest on no spot from which there does not come an answering beam of beauty. In the towers are great bells, moving of themselves with silver sound. Through the painted windows, stream the lights, rose, amber, emerald, blue. Between the shining Oriels, the royal dais is placed, hung round with the paintings of wise men, and there the inmate takes her throne, to sing her songs in solitary beatitude.

"No nightingale delighteth to prolong
Her low preamble all alone,
More than my soul to hear her echo'd song
Throb through the ribbed stone;

Singing and murmuring in her feastful mirth,
Joying to feel herself alive,
Lord over Nature, Lord of the visible earth,
Lord of the senses five ;

Communing with herself: 'All these are mine,
And let the world have peace or wars,
'T is one to me.' She — when young night divi[illegible]
Crown'd dying day with stars,

Making sweet close of his delicious toils —
Lit light in wreaths and anadems,
And pure quintessences of precious oils
In hollow'd moons of gems,

To mimic heaven; and clapt her hands and crie[illegible],
'I marvel if my still delight
In this great house so royal-rich and wide,
Be flatter'd to the height.

O, all things fair to sate my various eyes!
  O, shapes and hues that please me well!
O, silent faces of the Great and Wise,
  My Gods with whom I dwell!

O, God-like isolation which art mine,
  I can but count thee perfect gain,
What time I watch the darkening droves of swine
  That range on yonder plain!

In filthy sloughs they roll a prurient skin,
  They graze and wallow, breed and sleep;
And oft some brainless devil enters in,
  And drives them to the deep.'

Then of the moral instinct would she prate,
  And of the rising from the dead,
As hers by right of full-accomplished Fate;
  And at the last she said:

'I take possession of man's mind and deed.
  I care not what the sects may brawl.
I sit as God, holding no form of creed,
  But contemplating all.'" *

Thus it continues for three years. Then, suddenly, all is changed. The proud soul is smitten from the height of her glory into sore despair. A darkness and a pestilence pass over the beauty with which she is surrounded. She cannot comprehend how the woe has come, but her palace is now an abode of loathing and ghastliness.

"'What! is not this my place of strength,' she said,
  'My spacious mansion built for me,
Whereof the strong foundation stones were laid
  Since my first memory?'

* Quoted from the tenth edition.

But in dark corners of her palace stood
  Uncertain shapes; and unawares
On white-eyed phantasms weeping tears of blood,
  And horrible nightmares,

And hollow shades enclosing hearts of flame,
  And, with dim fretted foreheads all,
On corpses three months old at noon she came,
  That stood against the wall.

Back on herself her serpent pride had curl'd.
  'No voice,' she shrieked in that lone hall,
'No voice breaks through the stillness of the world:
  One deep, deep silence all!'"

At last the end comes:—

"She howl'd aloud, 'I am on fire within.
  There comes no murmur of reply.
What is it that will take away my sin,
  And save me lest I die?'

So when four years were wholly finished,
  She threw her royal robes away.
'Make me a cottage in the vale,' she said,
  'Where I may mourn and pray.'"

In all this—in the whole of the poem,—with its perfect symmetry, and that elaborate fullness of beauty which isolated quotations so defectively represent—it is just possible that certain persons may not find any great truth revealed. Stated in so many words, the poem does not contain a single didactic lesson. The poet-nature of Tennyson, instinct with an unconscious appreciation of the essence of Art, prevented the possibility of there being any such. But taking the poem in the noble characters of its breathing form, is there any difficulty in knowing what it means? Even had those lines, in which the poet explicitly announces his design, been absent, the significance would have been perfectly clear. But those introductory lines, and the name of the poem, leave one and only one possibility open for mistake, — incapacity to comprehend or estimate the truth embodied. That truth is very ancient, if not in didactic expression, at least in historical manifestation: but as proclaimed by Tennyson, it may lay claim to a high originality. The right is always original; if we embrace in the term right, seasonableness of occasion, verity of doctrine, and perfect execution. The truth embodied in *The Palace of Art* has the infallible mark of originality, that it was specially called forth by the requirements of the time. In itself, besides, it is of so refined and exalted a nature, that it never can become commonplace. It is simply this, That Art can never be religion, that man can never live nobly all for himself, that the supremacy of intellectual culture, ministered to by all the beauty and intelligence of the world, is not so excellent as the lowly self-sacrifice of daily life. It is, that there are abysmal deeps of personality, in which slumber earthquakes, to convulse the soul despite of all the azure smiling of beauty; and that all the lamps which man can kindle here, to make a heaven for himself, will be but a vain mimicry of real felicity. When we consider that Tennyson's poems generally, and this poem in particular, teem with unmistakeable evidence that he has drunk, perhaps more deeply than any other poet, at the fountains of Art; when we reflect that the influence of Goethe upon the development of his genius has been profound and pervasive; and when we remember that the most refined and plausible delusion of the age, presented in many forms, is radically this of putting culture for godliness, we are shut up to the conclusion that the writer is original and powerful, and that the truth he practically proclaims is substantial and important. I should hold it, too, in the highest degree dishonoring to Tennyson, to imagine, that he exhibited this truth merely as a poetical artist, that he chose it for its literary capabilities. In no case does our great poet protrude his religion; but his moral tone is as pure as Milton's; and *In Memoriam* contains numerous passages, indicative of a deep and meditative acquaintance with the highest questions of religion, and revealing the heaven-light of Christianity plainly irradiating the moralities of earth. In *The Palace of Art*, let it not be questioned, Tennyson's grand intent was, to exhibit the ghastly isolation of mere individual culture, the hollowness of self-worship (or that reflected self-worship which in "the Great and Wise" finds "Gods,") in contrast, not didactically unfolded but poetically suggested, with the household sanctities, the simple joys, the home-love, the heaven-love, the ancient, motherly smile, of Christianity. Of the imaginative power with which the great truth of the poem is exhibited, it is unnecessary, after what has been said, to make any remark. Suffice it to say, that, after having as it were kept this poem before my mind's eye for many years, I still gaze in fresh wonder on its marvellous poetical perfections, combining towards the enforcement of one great truth.

Only a great poet could have composed *The Palace of Art*. I do not, therefore, deem it absolutely necessary to cite any other instance, from the poems of Tennyson, of the combination of strictly intellectual with strictly poetic power. But I cannot forbear making a reference to *The*

Two Voices. This poem is perhaps unique. It is in the highest sense philosophic, nay, metaphysical, throughout: yet no lyrical trill of undiluted melody, no lilt sung by village maiden, was ever more purely and entirely poetical. The subject of the piece is that riddle of the painful earth, of which we hear in *The Palace of Art.* The argument on the one side is, that it were better to curse God and die; on the other, that it were better not to do so. The force and acuteness of the reasoning would be sufficient to fit out a powerful and original dissertation in metaphysics. But does the poet stumble on syllogism, or glide out of the form of poetic Art, into the analysis of metrical Science? By no means. The poem is a study of the richest poetry, from the consistency with which nature sustains the argument on either side. If sorrow is expressed, it is less in human accents than in the tears of nature; morning weeping in her still place, and the daisy fading away in death. If joy is described, it is written in the calm light of a Sabbath morn, and in the flowers hiding the grass. If doubt, disappointed hope, vain aspiration, are shadowed forth, they are emblemed by the mist of the hills, and the crags momentarily seen and then hidden behind its wreathing folds. If courage and resolution are the theme, we see the flashing of the battle in the distance, and mark the gleam on the face of the dying warrior as he watches the last victorious charge. Such knowledge of nature's language, so true, so deep, so varied, never belonged but to the born, the master poet. Readers who are novices in this language, who have not sympathetically studied in the mighty volume of nature, find the poem obscure. The express declarations of didactic composition, the exposed links of science, they miss. Such the poetic instinct sternly denies them. But when the poem is read poetically, it beams with light.

Truth, says the scientific skeptic, is unattainable. That is a simple fact, simply stated, and its accompaniment may be either irony or whatever else of a prosaic nature will suit. The poet-skeptic states the same fact, and likewise accompanies it with delicate irony. But you have a series of views, intelligible or unintelligible, instead of a statement:—

"Cry, faint not: either Truth is born
Beyond the polar gleam forlorn,
Or in the gateways of the morn.

Cry, faint not, climb: the summits slope
Beyond the furthest flights of hope,
Wrapt in dense clouds from base to cope.

Sometimes a little corner shines,
As over rainy mist inclines
A gleaming crag with belts of pines.

I will go forward, sayest thou,
I shall not fail to find her now.
Look up, the fold is on her brow.

If straight thy track, or if oblique,
Thou know'st not. Shadows thou dost strike,
Embracing cloud, Ixion-like."

Truth, answers the scientific believer, may be difficult to define in the abstract; but I must credit the nobleness of the great believers and actors of human history. The poet-believer answers thus:—

"I cannot hide that some have striven,
Achieving calm, to whom was given
The joy that mixes man with heaven·

Who, rowing hard against the stream,
Saw distant gates of Eden gleam,
And did not dream it was a dream,

But heard, by secret transport led,
Even in the charnels of the dead,
The murmur of the fountain-head —

Which did accomplish their desire,
Bore and forbore, and did not tire,
Like Stephen, an unquenched fire.

He heeded not reviling tones,
Nor sold his heart to idle moans,
Though cursed and scorned, and bruised with stones:

But looking upward, full of grace,
He pray'd, and from a happy place,
God's glory smote him on the face."

The conclusion of the poem is remarkable, both for the perfection of its poetical form and for the depth of its significance. The argument had not taken a wide range. The first voice had sunk into silence, merely from its inability to prove a universal negative. No recourse had been had, in opposing it, to the promised glories of Christianity. But now the light of dawn breaks ruddy along the whole horizon. It is the Sabbath morn, and men wend to the house of God, passing by the graves without a sigh. The hidden hope of the world, the millennial and celestial expectations of mankind, are emblemed in that house into which they enter. Great in thought and marvellous in poetry, this piece might alone sustain a reputation.

So much for separate poems. Tennyson is great likewise in isolated gleams of thought.

I said that the real and the ideal are not always separated

by any poet. I may add that the poetic and the scientific modes of thought and expression are not always kept distinct. Tennyson, however, remains singularly true to the character of a poet, seeming to have truth revealed to him in figure and impersonation while others reach it only by the chain of logical sequence. And there are verses of his which compress into their limits the essential characteristics of the national life of Europe for a hundred years.

> "The people here, a beast of burden slow,
> Toil'd onward, prick'd with goads and stings,
> Here play'd a tiger, rolling to and fro
> The heads and crowns of kings;
>
> Here rose an athlete, strong to break or bind
> All force in bonds that might endure,
> And here once more like some sick man declined
> And trusted any cure."

Could Count de Montalembert convey, in any number of volumes, a more accurate account of "the state of society in France," before and during the first Revolution, than is contained in that first verse?

> Slowly comes a hungry people, as a lion, creeping nigher,
> Glares at one that nods and winks behind a slowly-dying fire."

What a picture is this of Feudalism settling to its last sleep, with Freedom advancing upon it! Or of aristocracies, that nod and wink in the waning light of their heraldic honors, with the grand roar of the democracy beginning to be heard!

> "All the past of Time reveals
> A bridal dawn of thunder-peals,
> Whenever Thought hath wedded Fact."

This is a magnificent poetic embodiment of one of the most important and mysterious facts in philosophic history. But it would be absurd to attempt an exhibition of such passages as might, even with approximate completeness, illustrate Tennyson's power as a poetic thinker. The perplexities, the longings, the fitful gleams of hope, the tendency to lapse into ennui or despair, characteristic of the time, are all sympathetically reflected in his verse, shadowed or brightened by his supreme imagination. In *The Lotos Eaters*, there are glimpses into the mysteries of human destiny, penetrating perhaps as far as human eye can go. I confess I could have wished, although I consider the poem to possess a perfection defying any attempt at estimate, to have seen the atmosphere of Epicurean repose over the heads of the Lotos Eaters shaken by the thunder of some higher truth, — by the tumult of passionate, acting men, by the roar of battle; and I am assured that Tennyson could have effected this, without any serious damage to the preceding impression. But it has been hinted that the poet's sympathy with the joy of calm is somewhat more than healthy; and he has certainly succeeded in setting before us a trance of intellectual and sensuous peace, in comparison of which all other paintings of calm, whether with pen or brush, pass at once out of calculation.

I might enlarge indefinitely upon the order of subjects which Tennyson delights to handle, but a critique need not be an inventory, and I must hasten to a conclusion. One word, however, of those idyllic picturings, which form so remarkable a portion of his works. These have no parallels in the language, if in any language. The pastorals of the Pope and Dryden school are not to be named beside them. Wordsworth's "solemn-thoughted idyl," as Mrs. Barrett Browning, with a sincerity of compliment which from her mind at least dismissed all idea of suppressed irony, bears the comparison better, yet not well. Tennyson's coloring is of a mellowness and glow, of which Wordsworth never gives a suggestion. Tennyson depicts passion with a pencil of fire, vivid, tender, true, as life: Wordsworth knew only the loves of the flowers, and even Wilson, in his elaborate apology, concedes that he wanted strength and vividness of diction. One finds himself utterly at a loss for expressions to convey the idea of sylvan loveliness, of tender, vernal gaiety, of gentleness in emotion and simplicity in thought, derived from such idyls as *The Gardener's Daughter* or *The Brook.* They make you think of sunbeams wandering among roses and lilies, of light streaming silently through delicate foliage, turning all its green to gold, of the prattling of children by sunny rills, of the tears and smiles of whispering lovers. They, too, are, of course, ideal; though in a very different way from the old pastoral. The miller's daughter must have had her gleaming beauty somewhat dimmed by the adhesion of that floating meal to her hair and dress, and there can be no reasonable doubt that, when Eustace and his friend visited the real gardener's daughter, they found her seated on the back-log peeling potatoes. If the shepherdesses of the old pastoral were court ladies or Grecian Nymphs, the peasant girls of Tennyson are exquisitely refined English ladies. But this does not affect the inner truth of the portraiture, — since village girls and titled ladies love very much alike, — or do more than pleasantly enhance our sympathy with the emotions delineated.

As the poet of a period of unparalleled civilization, Tennyson occasionally reflects a mood, differing, in a peculiar and remarkable way, from any of the moods of passion. Not a few of his poems suggest a time of wearied emotion and jaded sympathy, when passion, as it throbs in human breasts, is looked upon for its artistic effects, and contemplated in unparticipating, unimpassioned admiration. Civilization lies languid on her noonday couch, oppressed with the weight of her own crown, faint in the sun of her own prosperity. To a biographer of Tennyson, this characteristic of his poetry would be very suggestive, and it must have struck Mrs. Barrett Browning as distinctive when she described that poetry in the words "enchanted reverie." I could scarce define the cause, but *The Day Dream* is always associated in my mind with this general impression.

The greatest poem, all things considered, that Tennyson ever wrote, is *In Memoriam*. Its name indicates one of the most difficult efforts which can be made in literature. It aims at embalming a private sorrow for everlasting remembrance, at rendering a personal grief generally and immortally interesting. The set eye and marble brow of stoicism would cast back human sympathy; the broken accents and convulsive weeping of individual affliction would awaken no nobler emotion than mere pity: it was sorrow in a calm and stately attitude, robed in angel-like beauty, though retaining a look of earnest, endless sadness, that would draw generation after generation to the house of mourning. No poet, save one possessed not only of commanding genius but of peculiar qualifications for the task, could have attempted to delineate a sorrow like this. The genius of Tennyson found in the work its precise and most congenial employment; and the result is surely the finest elegaic poem in the world.

In whatever aspect we view it, by whatever test we try it, this poem is great, is wonderful. Very absurdly did those critics talk, who spoke of the grief it contained as not very strong, perhaps not quite sincere, because it was so elaborately sung, and dwelt upon so long. They utterly misconceived the nature of that grief. They applied a general and commonplace rule to an altogether exceptional instance; an instance which might give new canons to criticism, but which might well perplex the old critics. The shadow of death had fallen between two spirits, knit together in close and noble friendship. That friendship had depended for its endurance on the community of lofty and immortal sympathies, of great thoughts, of pure and earnest affections. It was beyond the power of death to bring it to a termination. Death could only cast a vail of shadow between the two friends, and leave the one still on the earthward side to endeavor to pierce its obscurity, to hope for the day of its removal. It was rather a solemnity, a stillness, a composed and majestic mournfulness, that was cast over the life of Tennyson, than a darkening, overpowering distress. It was the silence and sadness of Autumn enveloping all the glories of summer; it was the melancholy of that aspect of nature, perhaps the loveliest of all, when the year first knows the approach of winter, and welcomes it with a resigned yet mournful smile. The shadow fell everywhere. Amid all the groups of living men, amid all the forms of external nature, there was still its presence, and into all the regions of thought and feeling it came. Everywhere it brought its solemn sadness: only, on the skies of the future, like the shadow of the earth cast up towards immensity, it seemed to kindle brighter lights as it were stars. The maiden combing her golden hair, in expectation of her lover, whose steps will not be heard that evening, or at all again, at the door, the bride leaving her father's house, the wife whose husband lives apart from her sympathy, in high and remote regions of thought, the boy friends of the village green whose paths in after life lie far asunder, — these all move in the procession of the poem, passing through the shadow of its sorrow. Nature, too, must mourn with the poet, as Shelley saw her mourning by the bier of Adonais. The ocean must sink into calm around the coming corpse; the gorgeous gloom of evening must shroud it; and all the tears of morning must fall over it. Into the world of thought and meditation, the same solemn influence comes. The greatest questions on which the human mind can be engaged, questions relating to the being of God, to the immortality of the soul, to the limits of knowledge, to the nature and conditions of future existence, all of which arise naturally before a mind ever looking beyond the bourne for the face of a friend, present themselves to the mourner, if perchance he may find any solace or enlightenment in them. From the simplest scenes of domestic life Tennyson has ascended into the rare atmosphere of metaphysics, and from those heights of contemplation where he so well can tread, sees the shadow of his sorrow falling over the filmy clouds. Nor is this all. The shadow of that sorrow fell everywhere, but, as the poet himself tells us, it was a shadow glory-crowned. Death at times takes up the harp of life, as love did in one of Tennyson's earlier poems, and draws from it grand and inspiring music. The mighty hopes that make us men, the future glories of humanity, the social joys and tendernesses which even on earth shed a softening radiance over settled sorrow, the encouragement which a noble heart finds in dwelling on a life honorably finished, in listening to the earnest voices of the dead, all mingle in the lofty strain. So perfect is the unity, so mighty the sweep of this poem: what more could elegaic poetry be?

The measure adopted by Tennyson for *In Memoriam*

was almost new to the English language, and it has none of that sweetness or ring which at first take the ear. But, for its subject, it is perfectly adapted. The melancholy of the poet seeks no sudden changes or excitements; it is deep, solemn, still; and the sameliness of the melody, its majestic uniformity, its calm Æolian flow, correspond exactly with the theme. Yet amid its stately uniformity, there is sufficient variation to prevent any disagreeable monotony. Now, in its calm, dream-like harmony, it seems, as it were, to give voice to the silent gaze with which we look into the eyes of Mary looking upon Christ; now it is deep, solemn, organ-toned, "Æonian music" measuring out the steps of Time — the shocks of Chance — the blows of Death; and yet again it takes up a trumpet note, and our hearts leap as it bids the wild bells ring out to the wild sky.

It will be fitting to add a few passages from *In Memoriam*, illustrative of the varying subjects which the poet treats, and the mode in which he adapts his delineation and his harmony to each. Let us glance, first, into one or two of those domestic scenes into which falls the light of sorrowing love.

"Could we forget the widow'd hour
  And look on spirits breathed away,
  As on a maiden in the day
When first she wears her orange flower!

When crown'd with blessing she doth rise
  To take her latest leave of home,
  And hopes and light regrets that come
Make April of her tender eyes;

And doubtful joys the father move,
  And tears are on the mother's face,
  As parting with a long embrace
She enters other realms of love;

Her office there to rear, to teach,
  Becoming as is meet and fit
  A link among the days, to knit
The generations each with each;

And, doubtless, unto thee is given
  A life that bears immortal fruit
In such great offices as suit
  The full-grown energies of heaven.

Ay me, the difference I discern!
  How often shall her old fireside
  Be cheered with tidings of the bride,
How often she herself return,

And tell them all they would have told,
  And bring her babe, and make her boast,
  Till even those that miss'd her most,
Shall count new things as dear as old?

But thou and I have shaken hands,
  Till growing winters lay me low;
  My paths are in the fields I know,
And thine in undiscover'd lands."

Of a somewhat different kind, but from the same class of incident, is the following:—

"Dost thou look back on what hath been,
  As some divinely gifted man,
  Whose life in low estate began
And on a simple village green;

Who breaks his birth's invidious bar,
  And grasps the skirts of happy chance,
  And breasts the blows of circumstance,
And grapples with his evil star;

Who makes by force his merit known,
  And lives to clutch the golden keys,
  To mould a mighty state's decrees,
And shape the whisper of the throne;

And moving up from high to higher,
  Becomes on Fortune's crowning slope
  The pillar of a people's hope,
The centre of a world's desire;

Yet feels, as in a pensive dream,
  When all his active powers are still,
  A distant dearness in the hill,
A sacred sweetness in the stream,

The limit of his narrower fate,
  While yet beside its vocal springs
  He play'd at counsellors and kings,
With one that was his earliest mate;

Who ploughs with pain his native lea,
  And reaps the labor of his hands,
  Or, in the furrow musing stands;
'Does my old friend remember me?'"

Once more:—

"Two partners of a married life—
  I looked on these and thought of thee
  In vastness and in mystery,
And of my spirit as of a wife.

These two—they dwelt with eye on eye,
  Their hearts of old have beat in tune,
  Their meetings made December June,
Their every parting was to die.

Their love has never past away;
  The days she never can forget
  Are earnest that he loves her yet,
Whate'er the faithless people say.

Her life is lone, he sits apart,
  He loves her yet, she will not weep
  Though rapt in matters dark and deep
He seems to slight her simple heart.

He thrids the labyrinth of the mind,
  He reads the secret of the star,
  He seems so near and yet so far,
He looks so cold: she thinks him kind.

She keeps the gift of years before,
  A wither'd violet is her bliss;
  She knows not what his greatness is;
For that, for all, she loves him more.

For him she plays, to him she sings
  Of early faith and plighted vows;
  She knows but matters of the house,
And he, he knows a thousand things.

Her faith is fixt and cannot move,
  She darkly feels him great and wise,
  She dwells on him with faithful eyes,
'I cannot understand: I love.'"

Sometimes the delineation is of feeling still deeper and more hallowed, as in this picture of Mary, when Lazarus has returned from the grave:—

"Her eyes are homes of silent prayer,
  Nor other thought her mind admits
  But, he was dead, and there he sits,
And He that brought him back is there.

Then one deep love doth supersede
 All other, when her ardent gaze
 Roves from the living brother's face,
And rests upon the Life indeed.

All subtle thought, all curious fears,
 Borne down by gladness so complete,
 She bows, she bathes the Saviour's feet
With costly spikenard and with tears.

Thrice blest whose lives are faithful prayers,
 Whose loves in higher love endure;
 What souls possess themselves so pure,
Or is there blessedness like theirs?"

Of the aspect of nature, with the great shadow falling over it, as represented by the poet, the following superb piece of imaginative description may enable us to form some conception.

"Calm is the morn without a sound,
 Calm as to suit a calmer grief,
 And only through the faded leaf
The chestnut pattering to the ground:

Calm and deep peace on this high wold,
 And on these dews that drench the furze,
 And all the silvery gossamers
That twinkle into green and gold:

Calm and still light on yon great plain
 That sweeps with all its autumn bowers,
 And crowded farms and lessening towers,
To mingle with the bounding main:

Calm and deep peace in this wide air,
 These leaves that redden to the fall;
 And in my heart, if calm at all,
If any calm, a calm despair:

Calm on the seas, and silver sleep,
  And waves that sway themselves in rest,
  And dead calm in that noble breast
Which heaves but with the heaving deep."

Again:—

"Sweet after showers, ambrosial air,
  That rollest from the gorgeous gloom
  Of evening over brake and bloom
And meadow, slowly breathing bare

The round of space, and rapt below
  Through all the dewy-tassell'd wood,
  And shadowing down the horned flood
In ripples, fan my brows and blow

The fever from my cheek, and sigh
  The full new life that feeds thy breath
  Throughout my frame, till Doubt and Death,
Ill brethren, let the fancy fly

From belt to belt of crimson seas
  On leagues of odor streaming far,
  To where in yonder orient star
A hundred spirits whisper 'Peace.'"

From these we turn naturally to the more meditative and metaphysical parts of the poem. The hope that crowns the shadow with glory dawns here, though somewhat faintly:—

"Oh yet we trust that somehow good
  Will be the final goal of ill!
  To pangs of nature, sins of will,
Defects of doubt, and taints of blood:

That nothing walks with aimless feet;
  That not one life shall be destroy'd
  Or cast as rubbish to the void
When God hath made the pile complete;

That not a worm is cloven in vain;
  That not a moth with vain desire
  Is shrivel'd in a fruitless fire,
Or but subserves another's gain.

Behold, we know not anything;
  I can but trust that good shall fall
  At last—far off—at last, to all,
And every winter change to spring.

So runs my dream: but what am I?
  An infant crying in the night:
  An infant crying for the light:
And with no language but a cry."

In the next, the spirit of man rises up indignant against the idea that nature's grandest piece of work will be crumbled into nothingness by death.

* * * "And he, shall he,
Man, her last work, who seem'd so fair,
  Such splendid purpose in his eyes,
  Who roll'd the psalm to wintry skies,
Who built him fanes of fruitless prayer,

Who trusted God was love indeed
  And love Creation's final law—
  Though Nature, red in tooth and claw
With ravine, shriek'd against his creed—

Who loved, who suffer'd countless ills,
  Who battled for the True, the Just,
  Be blown about the desert dust,
Or seal'd within the iron hills?

No more? A monster, then, a dream,
  A discord. Dragons of the prime,
  That tare each other in their slime,
Were mellow music matched with him.

O, life as futile, then, as frail!
  O, for thy voice to soothe and bless!
  What hope of answer or redress?
Behind the vail, behind the vail."

In the following, the last I can quote, there is involved a whole philosophy of human history.

"Contemplate all this work of Time,
  The giant laboring in his youth;
  Nor dream of human love and truth,
As dying Nature's earth and lime;

But trust that those we call the dead,
  Are breathers of an ampler day
  For ever nobler ends. They say,
The solid earth whereon we tread

In tracts of fluent heat began,
  And grew to seeming-random forms,
  The seeming prey of cyclic storms,
Till at the last arose the man;

Who throve and branch'd from clime to clime,
  The herald of a higher race,
  And of himself in higher place,
If so he type this work of time

Within himself, from more to more;
  And, crown'd with attributes of woe
  Like glories, move his course, and show
That life is not as idle ore,

But iron, dug from central gloom,
  And heated hot with burning fears,
  And dipt in baths of hissing tears,
And batter'd with the shocks of doom

To shape and use. Arise and fly
  The reeling Faun, the sensual feast;
  Move upward, working out the beast,
And let the ape and tiger die."

I have hitherto used solely the language of commendation. It is perhaps not too presumptuous to say, that I have exhibited some little capacity at least for the enjoyment of Tennyson's poetry. I consider what I have adduced to be matter of simple and conclusive demonstration; and I believe it to be sufficient to vindicate for Tennyson the highest place among the British poets of his day. He will henceforth, beyond question, be

"A star among the stars of mortal night:"

the brightest in that galaxy of poetic genius, containing Bailey, Elizabeth Barrett Browning, and Alexander Smith, which illustrates the brave days of the Mother Queen,

"And like one constellation bright,
  Moves round Victoria."

But now I am brought to a stand still. I should certainly feel that my estimate of Tennyson's genius and achievement was little worth, if I could apply such terms as I have hitherto made use of to one of his recent poems. With precisely the same decision as I affirmed of *In Memoriam*, that in every aspect and by every test it is great and marvellous, do I affirm of *Maud* that it is a failure.

The grounds of defence adopted by the esoteric few

who are daring enough to profess admiration both for *Maud* and for Tennyson shift and vary. Is it demonstrated that the feeling of the poem — its love-story and passionate delineation — is, by every possible definition, commonplace? You are assured that *Maud* is a grand ethical composition, in which sublime truths, concentrated in the bolts of satire, are hurled at a degenerate nation. Is it proved that the thought, the truth, the doctrine, of the poem, are, in a similar sense and degree, hackneyed, and, though hackneyed, by no means profoundly or unquestionably true? You are informed that the description of passion is exquisite and exact. Is it shown that there is here no artistic perfection, that, in one word, *Maud* is not beautiful? You are met with knowing and oracular hints about truth to nature and dramatic force, and asked whether, beautiful or no, the characters and incidents of *Maud* are not exhibited in the actual world, and peculiarly at the present time. Thus do these select persons change their position, able to make a final and definite stand nowhere. If the mere fact that certain aspects of feeling are not incorrectly rendered, and the circumstance that here and there the melody is exquisite and the color glowing, are sufficient to make a poem worthy of comparison with those of the poet of *In Memoriam*, it may be conceded that *Maud* ranks with the other efforts of Tennyson. But whatever the position assigned it, the following points appear to me to be literally and irresistibly demonstrable: that its thought is commonplace and superficial; that its central idea, in respect of plot and passion, is in no possible sense original; and that no consideration of dramatic fitness is of the least avail to redeem its essential defect as a work of Art, its want of beauty.

What is the tale, what the argument of *Maud?* The

poem cannot be seriously charged with obscureness. It is so short that, after one or two perusals, its plan becomes perfectly clear, and the most deplorable of pedants finds himself unable to pretend that it contains mysterious truths patent to him alone. A certain person, lying under circumstances of misfortune, which he believes traceable to lust of gold, and, if you will, to the evil character of the times, indulges in long and fierce soliloquies on the social morality of Great Britain. He falls in love. His affection is reciprocated. The whole world beams and brightens around him. The grass has a fresher green, the flowers a sweeter fragrance; and he asks the stars whether the whole world has gone nearer to their light that they shine so softly brilliant. Suddenly his heavens are overcast. He kills the brother of the loved one, escapes to the continent, falls into a disordered state of mind, is haunted by the phantom of Maud, and at last, having returned to his native land, is comforted and tranquillized by the information, imparted by the ghost, that there is "a hope for the world in the coming wars," of which the Russian war is the commencement. That is all. The only originality about which I care to dispute is the right thing in the right place. The high argument by which the sanative influence of war in human history can be made out, by which carnage can be proved to be the daughter of God, would have been amply sufficient, if invested with poetic form in a manner worthy of the imagination before which arose *The Palace of Art*, to have vindicated for the poem a true originality. But do we not pause in astonishment when we learn that there are persons who are not sensible of an incongruity and absurdity, nay who profess to find a magnificent poetic fitness, in the proclamation of this great truth by means of the machinery of a private love affair, the hero of which is on all hands allowed to be a weakling! The author of *Locksley Hall* and *The Palace of Art* demands our assent to a mighty truth, by letting us hear a jargoning, ill-conditioned misanthrope declare that a tailor, dishonest in peace, would be brave in war; and by introducing the ghost of a pretty girl, informing her distracted lover, that the Russian war will be a good beginning of the end! Scott has been blamed for warning Fitz-James by means of a mad girl, but his device is unobjectionable compared with this. Putting together the importance of the intelligence and the weight of the authority, one is reminded, by Mr. Tennyson's climax, only of the person, somewhat crazed, who convoked, it is said, the inhabitants of Edinburgh for the purpose of announcing some momentous fact, and declared, to the assembled Athenians, that he was about to assert his title to the throne of Great Britain, seeing that his mother's ghost had informed him, on the Broomielaw of Glasgow, that he was the Prince of Wales. It needs more than a ghost to tell us some things! To descend more to detail, the gloomy descriptions of the age blustered forth by our hero can be accurately paralleled from any one of Mr. Carlyle's books, written after the period at which that author abandoned reasoning and resolved to confine himself to denunciation. Selected passages from the *Latter Day Pamphlets*, very scantily softened by the form of verse, would fairly outdo, in downright jagged scolding, all the rant of this uncouth lover. There is nothing now more utterly commonplace than indiscriminate and unmeasured denunciation. Tennyson was surely not the man to follow in the wake of Mr. Kingsley in mimicking the worst parts of Carlyle. The love-story, again, apart from the ethical truth it so artistically embodies, is as commonplace as the denunciation. It is true that happy love spreads a blessed illumination over the face of things, and unhappy love a blasting gloom. But there can be no originality in describing, for a second or a fiftieth time, what you have yourself described before, or what has been elsewhere described much better. The harp of life, struck by the hand of love, was heard in *Locksley Hall* discoursing new and most eloquent music; the moorland was there found to be dreary, and the shore barren, when the light of love was withdrawn. The influence of happy affection and the reverse was told once and forever in *Locksley Hall.* It is deeply to be deplored that Mr. Tennyson returned to a theme which the might of his own genius had exhausted. But not only will the author's own volumes deprive the delineations of feeling in *Maud* of originality. We must assert its claim to that characteristic, if we insist in so doing, in face of all the circulating libraries. In *Jane Eyre*, in *Shirley*, in *Villette*, in the loves of Jane and Rochester, of Shirley and Moore, of John and Polly, the not very recondite truth that the birds do n't sing sweetly when the heart is weary and filled with care, is proclaimed and illustrated. Here, in fact, lay the chief strength of one of the most powerful female intellects which ever existed; and it is no insult to Tennyson to say that, if in *Locksley Hall* he showed love in joy and in sorrow, with an epic power beyond any emulation of the novelist, he has, in *Maud*, fallen immeasurably behind Charlotte Bronte.

I have named *Locksley Hall* as exhibiting in some respects a resemblance to *Maud.* But the two poems do not, on the whole, admit of comparison. *Locksley Hall*, though, rhythmically considered, an exception to Tennyson's previous poems, is of its sort an absolute masterpiece. No lyre ever voiced the wild yet melodious raptures of passion more deeply or powerfully. But what is the melody of *Maud?* It is neither the rapid, glancing lilt of Scott, the fervid rush of Byron, nor the rich inwoven harmony, of lute and harp and organ, to which our ear had been tuned by Tennyson. Its music is the music of kettle drums at a recruits' ball. Sometimes, indeed, a wandering strain from the old music, seeming to rise magically from the far distance, takes us with the old delight:—

"Alas for her that met me,
That heard me softly call,
Came glimmering through the laurels
At the quiet evenfall,
In the garden by the turrets
Of the old manorial hall."

In the love song of the garden, too, the lyric harmony and glowing joyousness are truly refreshing and delightful. But as for the poem in general, it will never be recognized as tuneful by any human ear, unless hopelessly stuffed with pedantic cotton. One cannot help imagining it sung by skeletons, to the accompaniment of rattling bones.

I am perfectly aware, dear pedantic critic, — who have had the misfortune to study yourself out of all human sympathy, and think nothing worth discovering unless it *is n't* there, — that you will affirm both the flitting feverish style of narrative, and the jerking, jingling melody, adapted to the general character of *Maud*, and on that account right. I answer that the person, into whose mouth the whole is put, must be supposed to utter it after his madness is over; and that an enveloping calm, which Tennyson knows so well how to combine with power of expression, would have had a far finer artistic effect than this atmosphere of wildness and raving. It is, besides, a fatal objection to any work of Art, even though it be descriptive of madness, that there does not dwell in it some fascination, making you contemplate it with a certain pleasure. In the case of poetical Art, this pleasure is inseparably connected with tune, and were it only that the ear acknowledges no fascination in *Maud*, it would be proved artistically and poetically wrong. An all important distinction is here to be made, between the effect on our feelings, produced by the scenes or characters of the artist in themselves, and the charm by which he constrains us to look upon them. We loathe Iago and detest Shylock, yet, while delineating them, Shakspeare enthrals us with a mighty fascination. We shrink in horror from Haley or Legree, and almost shriek when old Tom is lashed to death: yet to the repulsiveness of Haley and Legree, and the death of the Negro, much of the popularity of *Uncle Tom's Cabin* is to be imputed. The power, in fact, of the artist's genius is displayed mainly in the spell by which he fixes our gaze when he chooses. With Crabbe, we tire not in looking upon the jabbering maniac; with Tennyson, we calmly behold the ancient dragons tearing each other in their slime. Art paints you the sea shore, but it does not spatter you with the sand and surf. In *Maud* all this is forgotten. We are charmed by no sense of appropriateness, lured by no perception of means converging to an end, to sympathize with or suffer the unmelodious ranter. It is as if Mrs. Stowe had at once broken on us with the screams of Uncle Tom; as if Crabbe had merely jotted down the ravings of his maniac; as if Shakspeare had simply, accurately, and by themselves, echoed the chatterings of Lear. I argue, of course, on the supposition that unmelodiousness is conceded in *Maud* and defended on the ground of appropriateness.

The mere play of the sympathies of the reader is not

secured in this poem. The heroine may pass. She can sing. But why does she love this remarkable hero? He is a sour, shabby, purposeless soliloquizer. By all physiological and physiognomical reasons, he is sallow, squalid, with his skin hanging loose on his bones, with matted hair, shuffling, conceited, probably squint-eyed, demonstrably a sloven. Why does she love him? He hates her kindred and all men and women. He is moody, idle, given to night walking. Worst of all, he writes such verse as

> "I kissed her slender hand,
> She took the kiss sedately,
> Maud is not seventeen,
> But she is tall and stately."

It is a scientific fact, deserving, for the honor of the fair, all due prominence, that no woman of the Anglo-Saxon race *could* love a man capable of such maundering. Why does Maud love him? He goes about with an aggrieved, injured-looking, gingerly expression, which makes you expect he is going to knock you down. Poe's raven is the only hero in literature his precise counterpart; but the raven had some dignity, and was not so intensely egotistical, so profoundly selfish, as this ungainly, gaunt, and ominous radical. And Maud, with aristocracy in every line of her face, loves him! Nay, she seems to be attracted by his personal appearance, perhaps by his bright and benignant look when he first makes up his mind that she has neither savor nor salt. She smiles him on without any meetings that we hear of, without any attractions on his part that we can conceive. What great Apollo will render us the reason of this?

The Princess, though inferior to the general run of

Tennyson's earlier poems, on the one hand, and to the single magnificent effort of *In Memoriam*, on the other, contains much exquisite poetry, and can hardly fail to maintain its place as a classic. It will stand higher than the *Story of Rimini*, though not, I think, in a different class.

It is my strong conviction that neither *Maud* nor *The Princess* was the result of very deep or natural feeling on the part of Tennyson. Let it not be imagined that I bring here any charge of mere affectation against the poet, or for a moment sanction the idea that he deliberately set himself to sing about what he cared nothing for. This superficial affectation is rare indeed with men of real genius. But it is competent to criticism, nay it is one of the most important tasks of a criticism aiming at philosophic accuracy, to penetrate the sources of feeling in the case of poetic production, to determine whether it dwelt really in the deepest nature of the poet, commanding all his powers, or whether it was, more or less decidedly, more or less unconsciously, assumed. It can hardly be alleged that the feeling in Byron's Tales is not, in a sense, strong and sincere: yet there are few who would now declare that the central affection of Byron's nature, a nature, as Moore declared, at bottom essentially practical and *English*, was awakened by those scowling Giaours and tragical Gulnares. The genius of Tennyson, I must be permitted to consider, is radically of a far rarer kind than Byron's; and being of a rarer kind, it admits less of any compulsion, however subtle, it acts with more pure unconsciousness. Byron was to a remarkable extent a made poet; he knew well whence he drew his stores and who were his masters; he could at any time write about equally well on any subject. He did a set of Hebrew Melodies, we might almost say, to order, and did them incomparably; he had acquired the Art of

Poetry as Landseer has acquired the Art of Painting. But Tennyson is not thus master of his capacities; their very rareness, costliness, dewy delicacy, prevent his being so. It is said that, before accepting the Laureateship, he stipulated that he should not have to compose birthday odes by tale; and the fact would merely indicate his own consciousness of the glorious impotence of genius. Now, in the case both of his earlier poems and of *In Memoriam*, the impulse to poetical production was natural, spontaneous, and mighty. In the former it was the first youthful enthusiasm for the Beautiful, the pure outgoing of uncontrollable radiance from the poet's soul, coloring all nature, and, wherever it fell, coming straight from the centre. In the latter, the impulse was one which affected the whole life; a deep, genuine, though noble and manly sorrow, constrained all the powers to minister to it. But in the case both of *The Princess* and *Maud*, I am assured that Tennyson felt himself expected to write, that he more or less *looked out* for a subject. In almost every other case, his subject was not sought for, but came of its own accord. The poem in which it bloomed out in fadeless beauty expanded spontaneously like a rose amid the dews and sunbeams. In *Maud* and *The Princess* it is Tennyson that works: in the others his mind is but the Æolian harp from which the cunning hand of nature draws ethereal music.

There are scattered over certain of the larger poems of Tennyson, and there are found separately among his earlier pieces, short lyrics of a highly remarkable character. They combine an elaboration that reminds one of the odes of Keats, with a rapidity and sweep not altogether unworthy of Campbell. Amid the beauty of Tennyson's general poetry, such lyrics shine out conspicuously beautiful, like diamonds in gold fields. I cannot do better, in drawing towards a conclusion, than take up a few of these gems, and string them together, as it were, into a diamond necklace.

The first shall be taken from *The Miller's Daughter*. That poem is one of the finest emotional poems in the language; true in its originality, tenderly beautiful in its imagery, life itself in its feeling. The poetry of married life is there expressed perhaps for the first time, and so well that it might be the last. The very spirit and essence of connubial felicity breathe through the piece, and its supremacy, in the deep rest and peacefulness of its joy, to the fiery thrillings of passion, is triumphantly asserted.

> " True wife,
> Round my true heart thine arms entwine;
> My other dearer life in life,
> Look through my very soul with thine!
>
> * * * * *
>
> The kiss,
> The woven arms, seem but to be
> Weak symbols of the settled bliss,
> The comfort, I have found in thee."

But I digress. It is not with *The Miller's Daughter* we have at present to do; it is with one of those trills of lyric melody, which so charmingly interrupt its general flow; a little love song, given by the bridegroom to the bride on their wedding day. The ideas are simple, and their suggestion probably as old as Anacreon, but the birds in the hedges, as the young pair passed along, could not have carolled more gaily or tenderly.

"It is the miller's daughter,
And she is grown so dear, so dear,
That I would be the jewel
That trembles at her ear;
For, hid in ringlets day and night,
I 'd touch her cheek so warm and white.

And I would be the girdle
About her dainty, dainty waist,
And her heart would beat against me
In sorrow and in rest;
And I should know if it beat right,
I 'd clasp it round so close and tight.

And I would be the necklace,
And all day long to fall and rise
Upon her balmy bosom,
With her laughter or her sighs,
And I would lie so light, so light,
I scarce should be unclasp'd at night."

The next is a higher effort. It may, without any hesitation, be pronounced one of the most successful efforts ever made in lyric poetry. Except perhaps the appropriation of "the vision of the world and all the glory that shall be," as the song of the poet, there is in it no originality of idea. The feat of Orpheus was essentially that here recorded. But where, in the compass of sixteen lines, can we find such a description, of that sudden amazement and rapture, with which the voice of human song was from of old said to take the ear of nature? The delineation is as clear as it is condensed. Every touch is laid on as with a pencil of light; and Homer never was more graphic. In the melody there is a blending of buoyancy and stateliness beyond all praise.

THE POET'S SONG.

"The rain had fallen, the poet arose,
He pass'd by the town and out of the street;
A light wind blew from the gates of the sun,
And waves of shadow went over the wheat;
And he sat him down in a lonely place,
And chanted a melody loud and sweet,
That made the wild swan pause in her cloud,
And the lark drop down at his feet.

The swallow stopt as he hunted the bee,
The snake slipt under a spray,
The wild hawk stood with the down on his beak,
And stared, with his foot on the prey,
And the nightingale thought, 'I have sung many songs,
But never a one so gay,
For he sings of what the world will be
When the years have passed away.'"

The following is in a strain equally exalted: perhaps more so. The vision swept grandly before the poet's eye, and he shed out on it a light of immortality.

"Of old sat Freedom on the heights,
The thunders breaking at her feet:
Above her shook the starry lights:
She heard the torrents meet.

There in her place she did rejoice,
Self-gather'd in her prophet-mind,
But fragments of her mighty voice
Came rolling on the wind.

Then stept she down through town and field
To mingle with the human race,
And part by part to men reveal'd
The fullness of her face —

Grave mother of majestic works,
  From her isle-altar gazing down,
Who, God-like, grasps the triple forks,
  And, King-like, wears the crown;

Her open eyes desire the truth.
  The wisdom of a thousand years
Is in them. May perpetual youth
  Keep dry their light from tears;

That her fair form may stand and shine,
  Make bright our days and light our dreams,
Turning to scorn with lips divine
  The falsehood of extremes!"

Our next is of a lowlier order and a milder tone, but in its way is exceedingly fine. Tennyson is a great master of pathos; knows the very tones that go to the heart; can arrest every one of those looks of upbraiding or appeal, by which human woe brings the tear into the human eye. In the few simple verses that follow, the pathos is purely realistic. Trusting to the mighty simplicity of nature, the poet has so completely divested the lines of all meretricious adornment, nay of all the coloring which even a chaste imagination can cast over fact, that they at first appear somewhat hard and bare. But only look long enough upon that simple fact: those tears, tenderest of all, that mingle joy with sorrow, can hardly fail to come.

"Home they brought her warrior dead:
  She nor swoon'd, nor utter'd cry;
All her maidens, watching, said,
  'She must weep, or she will die.'

Then they praised him, soft and low,
  Call'd him worthy to be loved,
Truest friend and noblest foe;
  Yet she neither spoke nor moved.

Stole a maiden from her place,
  Lightly to the warrior stept,
Took the face-cloth from the face;
  Yet she neither moved nor wept.

Rose a nurse of ninety years,
  Set his child upon her knee;
Like summer tempest came her tears—
  'Sweet my child, I live for thee.'"

There is far more than mere realism in the next. Imagination in her highest mood strikes the harp, and marshals the stately imagery. The pathos here too is deep, but it is the majesty not the prostration of grief.

"Tears, idle tears, I know not what they mean,
Tears from the depths of some divine despair
Rise in the heart and gather to the eyes,
In looking on the happy autumn-fields,
And thinking of the days that are no more.

Fresh as the first beam glittering on a sail,
That brings our friends up from the under world,
Sad as the last which reddens over one
That sinks with all we love below the verge
So sad, so fresh, the days that are no more.

Ah, sad and strange as in dark summer dawns
The earliest pipe of half-awaken'd birds
To dying ears, when unto dying eyes
The casement slowly grows a glimmering square;
So sad, so strange, the days that are no more.

Dear as remember'd kisses after death,
And sweet as those by hopeless fancy feign'd
On lips that are for others; deep as love,
Deep as first love, and wild with all regret;
O death in life, the days that are no more."

It has been said that the whole of *In Memoriam* is in the following; and the expression is not absurd.

"Break, break, break,
On thy cold gray stones, oh Sea!
And I would that my tongue could utter
The thoughts that arise in me.

O well for the fisherman's boy,
That he shouts with his sister at play!
O well for the sailor lad,
That he sings in his boat on the bay.

And the stately ships go on
To the haven under the hill;
But oh for the touch of a vanish'd hand,
And the sound of a voice that is still!

Break, break, break,
At the foot of thy crags, oh Sea!
But the tender grace of a day that is dead
Will never come back to me."

The two pieces preceding the last are from *The Princess*. So is the next. The heroine of that poem is represented standing on the roof of her palace, a golden circlet round her hair and a babe in her arms, and uplifting, "like that great dame of Lapidoth," the martial strain. It is uttered in exultation over the defeat of her enemies by her selected champions.

Our enemies have fall'n, have fall'n: the seed,
The little seed they laugh'd at in the dark,
Has risen and cleft the soil, and grown a bulk
Of spanless girth, that lays on every side
A thousand arms, and rushes to the sun.

Our enemies have fall'n, have fall'n: they came;
The leaves were wet with women's tears: they heard
A noise of songs they would not understand:
They mark'd it with the red cross to the fall,
And would have strewn it, and are fall'n themselves.

Our enemies have fall'n, have fall'n: they came,
The woodmen with their axes: lo the tree!
But we will make it faggots for the hearth,
And shape it plank and beam for roof and floor,
And boats and bridges for the use of men.

Our enemies have fall'n, have fall'n: they struck;
With their own blows they hurt themselves, nor knew
There dwelt an iron nature in the grain:
The glittering axe was broken in their arms,
Their arms were shatter'd to the shoulder blade.

Our enemies have fall'n, but this shall grow
A night of Summer from the heat, a breadth
Of Autumn, dropping fruits of power; and roll'd
With music in the growing breeze of Time,
The tops shall strike from star to star, the fangs
Shall move the stony bases of the world."

I add only that singular, mysterious, yet strangely fascinating lyric, a play of wild fantastic melody, and flashing, foam-like color, which was composed, I believe, to the Killarney bugle music. The descriptive touches in the first verse are superb.

"The splendor falls on castle walls
 And snowy summits old in story;
The long light shakes across the lakes,
 And the wild cataract leaps in glory.
Blow, bugle, blow, set the wild echoes flying:
Blow, bugle; answer, echoes, dying, dying, dying.

O hark! O hear! how thin and clear,
 And thinner, clearer, further going!
O sweet and far from cliff and scar,
 The horns of Elfland faintly blowing!
Blow, let us hear the purple glens replying:
Blow, bugle; answer, echoes, dying, dying, dying.

O love, they die in yon rich sky,
 They faint on hill or field or river:
Our echoes roll from soul to soul,
 And grow forever and forever.
Blow, bugle, blow, set the wild echoes flying.
And answer, echoes, answer, dying, dying, dying."

Historical parallels are not always or entirely to be relied on; for time never accurately repeats itself, and external resemblances may divert attention from essential though deep-lying differences. The British world of to-day is altogether different from that of the commencement of last century. Yet I cannot but perceive, if not a parallel, at least a correspondence, between the poetry of Tennyson and that of the Pope and Dryden school. Since the Puritan era, there had been in Great Britain no period of excitement so deep and general, as that of the end of last century and the commencement of the present. In the former period, the minds of men were shaken in religious and civil revolutions; in the latter, though religion had receded into the background, the convulsive strugglings of democracy, and the magnificent war-drama with all Europe for a stage, had awakened every energy and every enthusiasm that slumbers in the human breast. These two periods seem to answer each other with their rolling thunders, silencing all intermediate noises. Each had a poetical literature. That of the Puritan age was concentrated in one man, John Milton. He was a literature in himself, an ample, a magnificent literature. The earnestness of that heroic time, of which throbbings may yet be detected both in Britain and America, will burn, through the night of all ages, in his sublimest epic. The poetic literature of the modern period is represented in Great Britain by a multitude of names, Scott, Byron, Wordsworth, and the rest; men endowed with a poetic genius so true and so powerful, that they plainly tower above all who had preceded them since the Puritan era: but whose highest applause it must be, that their united voice wakes an echo worthy to reply to the single harp of Milton. After the Puritan poetry, came the poetry of Dryden and Pope. This was calmer, smoother, smaller. Neatness and elegance succeeded to rugged strength, appropriate thoughts neatly expressed, balanced sentences trimly versified, to great ideas chafing in the harness of diction, and burdened sentences rolling on in stern majestic rhythm. Dryden is a versifier but no poet, said Milton: the Puritan poet would probably have considered inconsistent with the poetic character that power of dexterous manipulation, that capacity of delicate chiselling, by which the poets of the new school set so much store. To the poetry of the modern revolutionary time, succeeded the poetry of Tennyson. It contrasted with that immediately preceding, in the perfection of its finish, and in its deeper, more delicate harmony. It was also, on the whole, more calm and reflective. So far it may correspond to the poetry of Pope and his compeers. But the parallel cannot be carried further. The poetry of Tennyson is pervaded by an intense realism, by a deep unvarying truth, which sets it altogether apart from that of the school of Pope. Here all passion, from the panting ecstacy of first love to the satisfied, smiling happiness of connubial affection, is voiced with pure veracity. Here the deepest thoughts that can occupy the human mind are earnestly grappled with, and every shred of conventionality is flung aside. The very finish, the polish and delicacy, are not the result of deliberate manipulation, but the natural mode in which a poet, endowed with marvellous powers of expression, and accustomed to wander through all the Muses' walk, clothes his ideas and emotions. Such a poet cannot soon be popular with the million; but as the last and most exquisite culture of educated minds, as the ultimate sublimation of thought and beauty, as the most refined expression of the most refined civilization that ever dawned upon the world, his works must continue to exercise a mighty influence upon the leading intellects of those nations which lead the world.

III.

MRS. BARRETT BROWNING.

There are two things, for which, I think, the world has especially to rejoice, in contemplating the position and circumstances of Shakspeare. The first is, that he was not technically a scholar, that between him and the great ancient hearts whose secrets he was to read, there intervened, not the frosty twilight of antiquarian lore, but only the unpretentious dimness of translation and tradition. How well that, in great Julius, the greater Shakspeare had to recognize the heart only of a brother! How well that the thaumaturgic hand had not to clip, and measure, and adjust, amid moth-eaten cerements and rusty helmets, in order to fashion forth the old Roman exterior and shell of Julius, but only to cast asunder the gates of the human heart that those deathless notes might be heard, which are the undertone of human emotion in all ages, and to show us Julius himself! How well that he, who was to give to the Anglo-Saxon tongue that tune it was never to lose, whose language, exhaustless in range, in delicacy, in force, in variety, taking every hue of thought and feeling as the sky takes shade or sunshine, as the forest takes breeze or calm, was to remain forever the emblem of the multitudinous life and lightly moved and all-conceiving spirit of the modern time, as contrasted with the grave uniformity and petrified aristocratism of antiquity, was tempted, by no familiarity with ancient writings, to any formal rotundity of diction or obscure involution of sentence! How dreadful the thought that he, whose hall of audience, increasing with civilization, is the world, he who has moved a broader stratum of human sympathy than any other man, might have passed into that narrow chamber, narrowing with every generation, in which Gray, Collins, and such erudite minstrels receive frost-bitten compliments from critics and pedants. But it is wronging Shakspeare to suppose, even for a moment, that the temptation of learning could have overcome him. He, of all men, would have been least apt to prefer the poor glitter of learned paint to God's sunlight of living smiles, the classic drops of Naiad's well or Castalian fountain to the sacred dew of human tears. He, of all men, would have been least apt to set the icy guerdon of a pedant's approbation above the sight of simple emotion, welling irresistibly from the heart of a peasant. Only, when one thinks how much learning has done to veil genius which it is not absurd to name along with Shakspeare's, and reflects that the throne of Milton, though of the loftiest, was never raised, on its classic pedestal, to the height of Shakspeare's, it is impossible to suppress a sense of satisfaction that the greatest author of mankind was not learned.

The next thing for which, perhaps still more expressly, we may be thankful in the case of Shakspeare, is the complex fact, that he never attained to consciousness of his powers, that he heard not the voice of his fame, and that he was never surrounded by a circle of admirers. Healthy, whole-hearted, it perhaps never occurred to him to ask, what precise position he, Shakspeare, might occupy, in relation to other writers. His chief life-work, he may have, on the whole, concluded, was the realization of a comfortable living in his native Stratford: one can imagine him staggering in bewildered incredulity, if the eyes of all coming generations, hailing *him* as the mightiest of mere men, had gleamed suddenly in vision before him. Gruff Ben Jonson, too, wishing he had "blotted a hundred" words of his dramas instead of boasting that he never made an erasure, and the other brave spirits of the Mermaid Tavern "whistling him down," when, though, indeed, clever, he was becoming something of a rattle, were not likely to permit Shakspeare to dote over his faults, to coax him into a belief that what the general common sense disliked in his poetry was its peculiar excellence, to make him imagine that any veil filming his genius was greater than his genius itself. Hero-worship is twice cursed; in the hero who is befooled, and in the zanies who befool him. The one is bewildered into extravagance, like, shall we say, Mahomet, or enervated by conceit, like, shall we say, Wordsworth: the other brings himself to rejoice in any feast of shells, if only it is laid out by his hero. The grand evil which hero-worship brings upon the literary hero is confirmation in his mannerism, instead of being left, like Shakspeare, and with nature always assisting him, more and more to cast off his mannerism in the broad light of truth. Living so near Wordsworth as this generation does, and recalling many phenomena allied to that presented by him, his hero-worshippers, and their mutual relation, one is tempted to say that the peculiar danger to which literature is in these days exposed is that of having mannerisms extolled into models. At all events, must we not rejoice that the subtlest of all poisons was never mingled in Shakspeare's cup, that he was all unconscious of his praises, perhaps even of his powers, that, like a great cataract, he rolled heedless down "the dust of continents to be."

The reader may not yet be prepared to sympathize with me in the feelings with which I regard the poems of Mrs. Barrett Browning. I cannot claim instant assent, when, though allowing that between her and Shakspeare, as well as many other men, there can be instituted no comparison, I yet deliberately assign her the same place among women as Shakspeare occupies among men. To show ground for this opinion will be, more or less, the object of all the following remarks. But it must at present be allowed me to declare, that no circumstance to which reference could be made, in connection with the genius of Mrs. Barrett Browning, is to me more evident or distressing, than the fact that it is prevented, by certain vailing clouds of esoteric culture and repelling mannerism, from casting abroad, with full, sunlike charms, the rich magnificence of its power. If it were the homage of a second rate applause that were challenged for this poetess, — if it was to be mentioned in honor of *her*, that she could translate from Bion and Æschylus, and talk of gnomons, zodiacs, and apogees, — it would be absurd to regret that certain characteristics of her poetry withhold it from the many and confine it to the few. But it is the very highest distinction that can be claimed for her; it is that mysterious power, to be communicated by no culture, and related to learning as the living flower, rich in green leaf and tinted petal, is related to the wooden framework over which it climbs, which she possesses. The power of stirring the inmost fountains of laughter and tears, of bringing music from the rough metal of every day life, of kindling those lights in human eyes, which glance from scholar to rustic, from peasant to king, with the gleam of recognition, reconcilement, and relationship, is hers. To this, all learning is a very small matter. And believing that Mrs. Barrett Browning is gifted with this, I cannot but deeply regret that it is impeded in its way to that over which such power exerts its noblest sway, the general heart. Why, you cannot but ask, should the words of this woman, burning in their tenderness, penetrating in their truth, so broadly and deeply human in their application, not reach the strongly pulsing heart of common humanity? Why should not the cottage mother thrill with the expression she has given to maternal ecstacy? Why should not the mourner at the village grave see a beam falling from heaven on the sod, at the recollection of her words? Why should not the peasant Christian, who rejoices to trace, with Bunyan, the path of the Pilgrim from the city of destruction to the celestial gate, glow with a still loftier emotion, as this great Christian singer casts for him rays of revealing light, far and deep into the night of history, over the most mysterious sublimities of human destiny? That all this does not happen, that Mrs. Browning's readers are what is called select, and that they are students rather than listeners, is a well known fact. The cause can be easily discovered, — a certain obscurity, an excessive demand on the reader;— and I cannot help thinking that this cause came to operate, partly through her learning, (occasioning un-English involution of style,) and partly, however unconscious she may have been of the influence, through some hero-worshipping bray, proclaiming in her ears that her obscurities were her beauties. We are all, geniuses and common persons, subject to weakness. As one hears Mrs. Browning talking of apogees, and addressing Lucifer as Heosphoros, and marks the involved and sonorous Latinity of her style, he can hardly repel the suggestion, that the weapon which, probably with considerable toil, she acquired, with the aid of her fellow-men, for herself, was by her deemed of greater value, than those weapons which it cost her no trouble to attain or wield, and which not man but God had given her. Her womanly humility even, her virgin modesty, may have hidden from her the fact that *she* could afford to thrust all learning into the background! As to the other influence, the applause of defects by cultivated pedants, I am far from asserting that Mrs. Barrett Browning ever indulged in any weak, Wordsworthian self-canonization; but in *Casa Guidi Windows*, one of her latest poems, I find the same sources of obscurity as in her earliest, and such as seemed at one stage to be clearing themselves away; and I cannot but think that the literary dilettantism of the age, with its execrable inversion of criticism, with its commendation of what the common heart does *not* feel, and of what the unsophisticated mind will *not* comprehend, has, to some extent, cast its enchantment over her.

It were a mistake to infer, from anything I have said, an ignorance, on my part, of the fact, that there is a legitimate obscurity attaching to certain kinds of composition, and attendant upon certain moods of genius. The strong surge of passion, bearing a writer along, may render him incapable of attending to the small niceties of composition, and putting in those little links, on which clearness depends. Shakspeare, his heart and brain throbbing with the passion and the thought of a *Hamlet*, cannot point and round his sentences with such nice discrimination, or even keep his ideas in such lucid sequence, as is easy for a Pope. A Tacitus will not write so clearly as a Macaulay. The theme, too, may be so remote from the beaten tracks of thought, the ideas may so far underlie the general growth and efflorescence of practical thinking, that effort, beyond what all readers will give, is necessary to their intelligence. To these considerations I would give full weight in proceeding to survey one or two of Mrs. Browning's most remarkable poems; but this can be done in perfect consistency with what has been said.

The *Drama of Exile* is of itself sufficient at once to justify and to illustrate all I have advanced. Many, I doubt not, have cast aside the poem in despair, ere proceeding far in its perusal; and many more, after penetrating to the end, have said, with a feeling of honest regret, that they had been aware of the presence of astonishing genius, that they had met with many fine thoughts, but that the whole seemed to them a wild and wavering phantasmagoria. Yet this may fearlessly be pronounced one of the greatest poems in the language: of a pathos genuine and unfathomable, of sublimity exalted, and in which a resistless imagination casts its lit eye, with a glance swifter than that of logic, far aloft into the regions of intellectual and religious truth. So confident am I of this, and so confident also am I that the *Drama of Exile* is withdrawn from the knowledge and admiration of thousands whom it might instruct and delight, that I feel it an august task to attempt, as I purpose, indeed, to do in relation to Mrs. Browning's poetry in general, to wave aside the cloud-drapery, and loosen forth some of the notes of its mighty music.

The scene—for the form, though but the form, of the poem, is dramatic—is laid on the outer side of the gate of Eden on the evening of the day of the expulsion, and Adam and Eve are seen flying in the distance along the glare of the flaming sword. The first speaker is Lucifer. He opens the poem with a chant of exultation over God and man, and of haughty congratulation to himself and his angels. This chant has, in its first stanza, one of those grotesque rhymes which Mrs. Browning too carelessly permits, and by which, with a fastidiousness perhaps somewhat feeble and excessive, the English reader is apt to allow himself to be prejudiced against a whole performance. One might desiderate, too, somewhat more of the majesty of the Miltonic fiend, to temper the fierce and passionate boasting of Lucifer. But the passage is nevertheless true in conception and magnificent in execution. It is the commencement of the poem, in the essential respect of striking its key note, of providing for its catastrophe or triumph, of folding up the end in the beginning. Lucifer, man's victor, stands upon the earth which he has conquered, calls upon his host to arise through the shaken foundations of the world, and boasts, with an assurance which his very despair seems to crown, that this throne must remain his, since it is evil, and God himself cannot do other than curse it. It is necessary to quote this opening strain, and the reader will do well to permit no slight offences to the ear to turn him aside from pondering it carefully, line by line.

"Rejoice in the clefts of Gehenna,
  My exiled, my host!
Earth has exiles as hopeless as when a
  Heaven's empire was lost.
Through the seams of her shaken foundations,
  Smoke up in great joy!
With the smoke of your fierce exultations
  Deform and destroy!
Smoke up with your lurid revenges,
  And darken the face
Of the white heavens, and taunt them with changes
  From glory and grace.
We, in falling, while destiny strangles,
  Pull down with us all.
Let them look to the rest of their angels!
  Who 's safe from a fall?

HE saves not. Where 's Adam? Can pardon
Requicken that sod?
Unkinged is the King of the Garden,
The image of God
Other exiles are cast out of Eden,—
More curse has been hurled!
Come up, O my locusts, and feed in
The green of the world!
Come up! we have conquered by evil.
Good reigns not alone.
I prevail now! and, angel or devil,
Inherit a throne!"

The pure intellectual might—the strict metaphysical truth—displayed in the *Drama of Exile*, is precisely on a level with its consummate poetry. Satanic motives and emotions may be beyond the reach of human searching, but when we penetrate as far as reason and imagination can carry us, we find nothing deeper than reliance on evil in itself, and a belief, never shaken from old eternity, that the bond between woe and sin cannot be severed by the hand even of the Almighty, that not even God can take from the devil his crown of thorns. Mrs. Browning's fifth stanza, in the piece I have quoted, is a superb expression of this reliance and this belief, and by broadly exhibiting these in the outset, she lays the stablest possible foundation, in metaphysic truth, for her whole poem.

To this chant of Lucifer's there succeeds a dialogue between Gabriel and the fiend. Its tone is at first half Miltonic, half Byronic. The first piece of unmistakable originality it contains is the following remarkable passage. It is by no means entirely unexceptionable, but deserves our best attention from that free strength of imagination, which introduces, in contrast to the tumult of the Miltonic contests between fiend and angel, the truer and more awful idea of the calm potency of light, on the one hand, and blank despair written, by the very calmness of its beam, on the visages of the rebel angels, on the other. The style of delineation, besides, is highly characteristic of the poetess. The occasion of the lines is found in an allusion made by Gabriel to divine and angelic pity.

"*Lucifer.* * * As it is, I know
Something of pity. When I reeled in Heaven,
And my sword grew too heavy for my grasp,
Stabbing through matter which it could not pierce
So much as the first shell of, — toward the throne;
When I fell back, down, — staring up as I fell, —
The lightnings holding open my scathed lids,
And that thought of the infinite of God,
Hurled after to precipitate descent;
When countless angel faces still and stern
Pressed out upon me from the level heavens
Adown the abysmal spaces, and I fell
Trampled down by your stillness, and struck blind
By the sight within your eyes, — 't was then I knew
How ye could pity, my kind angelhood!"

The dialogue between Lucifer and Gabriel ended, and Adam and Eve still seen flying along the sword-glare, a Chorus of the Spirits of Eden sends, from within the walls of Paradise, a chant of melancholy condolence and farewell after the exiles. The idea embodied in the varying music of this chant of the Spirits, is the sorrow, pervading the whole world of Eden, — its streams, its trees, its flowers, — on account of the departure of the human pair. To bring out such a thought, in prominent poetic manifestation, was an evident necessity in any treatment of the subject, and Mrs. Browning performs the task with opulence and delicacy of fancy, with great powers of thought, and with exquisite tenderness of feeling. But the personification is not happy, and the pathos would have trickled with far more deep and dew-like power on the heart, had there been less about songs built up note over note until they "strike the arch of the Infinite" and silence shivering, and shadings off to resonances, and such like touches of gorgeous feebleness, to which Mrs. Browning declines, when learning and criticism turn her from the clear monitions of her own genius, and the simplicity of nature, to make her mock herself.

In the next scene, we emerge more into the kindly blue of pure, plain, human feeling. For the first time, we are made unmistakably aware that our guide is a woman; not from any weakness, not from any sameliness or extravagance, but from the access of elements of pathos and beauty, which no man could have commanded, and belonging only to one, whose womanliness is as intense as her genius is consummate. A broad gleam of softest light, dewy, beautiful, original, like a stream of sunlight falling through a shower on a rugged hill side, is cast over the tragical realities of her theme, from the feminine knowledge and womanly sympathy of Mrs. Browning. Eve, in distress and despair, accuses herself of having brought the great woe upon Adam, and adjures him to bring down at once the curse of death on her, "for so," says she, "perchance, thy God might take thee into grace for scorning me; thy wrath against the sinner giving proof of inward abrogation of the sin."

Adam replies.

* * * * * *

"If God,
Who gave the right and joyaunce of the world
Both unto thee and me, — gave thee to me,

The best gift last, the last sin was the worst,
Which sinned against more complement of gifts
And grace in giving. God! I render back
Strong benediction and perpetual praise
From mortal, feeble lips (as incense-smoke,
Out of a little censer, may fill heaven),
That Thou, in striking my benumbed hands
And forcing them to drop all other boons
Of beauty, and dominion, and delight, —
Hast left this well-beloved Eve — this life
Within life — this best gift — between their palms,
In gracious compensation!"

All can sympathize with *this!* And with this: —

"*Eve.* Is it thy voice?
Or some saluting angel's — calling home
My feet into the garden?

Adam. O my God!
I, standing here between the glory and dark, —
The glory of thy wrath projected forth
From Eden's wall, the dark of our distress
Which settles a step off in that drear world, —
Lift up to Thee the hands from whence hath fallen
Only creation's sceptre, — thanking Thee
That rather Thou hast cast me out with *her*
Than left me lorn of her in Paradise,
With angel looks and angel songs around
To show the absence of her eyes and voice,
And make society full desertness
Without her use in comfort."

The scene, however, soon changes, and the action of the poem becomes of more dark and terrible interest. Lucifer again appears, and the dialogue is sustained between him and the exiled pair. Passages of power and pathos abound in this part.

"*Adam.* Ay, mock me! now I know more than I knew:
Now I know thou art fallen below hope
Of final re-ascent.

Lucifer. Because?

Adam. Because
A spirit who expected to see God
Though at the last point of a million years,
Could dare no mockery of a ruined man
Such as this Adam.

Lucifer. * * * *
* * * * * *
Is it not possible, by sin and grief
(To give the things your names) that spirits should rise
Instead of falling?

Adam. Most impossible.
The Highest being the Holy and the Glad,
Whoever rises must approach delight
And sanctity in the act."

The pathos in the first of these lines is very noble. The thought with which they conclude is an impressive illustration of what has been advanced, touching the intellectual substance of this poem. It is one of the great lights ordained by God perennially to burn in the heaven of truth, dividing moral day from moral night; and its calm, celestial effulgence casts into pale and sickly pining that "worship of sorrow," which, in the hands of Goethe and Carlyle, is but the sublime of sentimentalism, in spite of the grain of living truth, summed up by St. Paul in one verse, which it does contain.

As Lucifer disappears, there is heard a low music, proving to be "The Song of the Morning Star to Lucifer." This is one of those portions of the poem which cannot fail to repel many readers. The song of the star may be as good as the theme rendered possible; but it has no hold on human sympathy, and attains, for beauty, only a cold, unsatisfactory gorgeousness. Perhaps no poet could make you feel for a star, and certainly no person will feel in this instance. The piece plays, as will be seen, an important part in the evolution of the poem, but must in itself be pronounced in no sense felicitous.

The next scene is one of the longest and most important in the poem. The exiles are now far out in the desert, and the night is thickening round them. The farewells of the Eden Spirits have died away. The shadow of the curse is on the face of the world. The change is thus announced.

"*Adam.* How doth the wide and melancholy earth
Gather her hills around us, gray and ghast,
And stare with blank significance of loss
Right in our faces! Is the wind up?

Eve. Nay.

Adam. And yet the cedars and the junipers
Rock slowly through the mist, without a sound;
And shapes which have no certainty of shape
Drift duskly in and out among the pines,
And loom along the edges of the hills,
And lie flat, curdling in the open ground—
Shadows without a body, which contract
And lengthen as we gaze on them."

The meaning of this becomes gradually apparent. We have now the reverse of that soft music, in which the Eden Spirits had bidden adieu to those who were among them the centre of all blessing. To the outer world the man and woman bring a curse, and they are received with the grim welcome of universal execration. The mode in which the poetess has chosen to body forth this detestation of all creatures for those who have brought them sin, is singular rather than happy, and would have gained in effect by gaining in simplicity. The signs of the zodiac become instinct with life, and stand in horrid circle round Adam and Eve. From that circle "of the creatures' cruelty," they cannot escape, and within it the spirits of organic and inorganic nature arise to taunt and curse them.

That this conception is strong and original, it would be hard to deny. But it can be wholly defended neither from the charge of extravagance nor from that of obscurity. The passage abounds in masterly delineation, and the horror and anguish, gradually darkening down like the night upon the human pair, arising from the contempt and hatred of those creatures over which they had been appointed to reign, are very powerfully expressed. I can quote but one stanza. It may convey some idea of the spirit and intent of the whole, but none at all of the execution. The spirit of inorganic nature speaks.

> "I feel your steps, O wandering sinners, strike
> A sense of death to me and undug graves!
> The heart of earth, once calm, is trembling like
> The ragged foam along the ocean-waves:
> The restless earthquakes rock against each other; —
> The elements moan round me — 'Mother, mother' —
> And I wail!"

Lucifer suddenly rises in the circle, but only to increase the anguish of the exiles, now approaching its climax. Lucifer, fierce and remorseless, launches at them this bolt, the more piercing in its agony that it is winged with truth: —

"Your sin is but your grief in the rebound
And cannot expiate for it."

Hardly a line now occurs but might be quoted. The following passage, however, cannot be passed by. It is important, not so much in its bearing on the catastrophe of the poem at the stage at which we have now arrived, as in its peculiar and felicitous exhibition of Mrs. Browning's mode of imaginative conception and handling. The lines in which Lucifer applies to himself the comparison of the lion are too long to quote.

"*Lucifer.* Dost thou remember, Adam, when the curse
Took us in Eden? On a mountain-peak
Half-sheathed in primal woods and glittering
In spasms of awful sunshine, at that hour
A lion couched, — part raised upon his paws,
With his calm, massive face turned full on thine,
And his mane listening. When the ended curse
Left silence in the world, — right suddenly
He sprang up rampant and stood straight and stiff,
As if the new reality of death
Were dashed against his eyes, — and roared so fierce
(Such thick carnivorous passion in his throat
Tearing a passage through the wrath and fear),
And roared so wild, and smote from all the hills
Such fast, keen echoes crumbling down the vales
Precipitately, — that the forest beasts,
One after one, did mutter a response
Of savage and of sorrowful complaint
Which trailed along the gorges. Then, at once,
He fell back, and rolled crashing from the height
Into the dusk of pines.

Adam. It might have been.
I heard the curse alone."

No hand but Mrs. Browning's could have drawn that picture of the lion. The pathos of Adam's last words is sublime; and, so far as I know, original. In *Isobel's Child*, a later poem of Mrs. Browning's, there occur the following words, the person addressed being one of the redeemed, and the time the day of judgment:—

"Thrones and seraphim,
Through the long ranks of their solemnities,
Sunning thee with calm looks of Heaven's surprise—
Thy look alone on *Him*."

This idea has often been expressed, but I do not remember an instance in which the *opposite* note, in the same grand harmony of pathos, is struck. Mrs. Browning has given both.

The attention of the reader is now drawn studiously to Lucifer, as if the poetess had some purpose with him. With strange dauntlessness, does this marvellous woman gaze down into the depths of Satanic misery.

"*Lucifer*. * * * *
I the snake, I the tempter, I the cursed,—
To whom the highest and the lowest alike
Say, Go from us—we have no need of thee,—
Was made by God like others. Good and fair,
He did create me!—ask Him, if not fair!
Ask, if I caught not fair and silverly
His blessing for chief angels on my head
Until it grew there, a crown crystallized!
Ask, if He never called me by my name,
Lucifer—kindly said as 'Gabriel'—
Lucifer—soft as 'Michael!' while serene
I, standing in the glory of the lamps,
Answered 'my Father,' innocent of shame
And of the sense of thunder. * * *

*　　*　　*　　*　　*　　*

Pass along
Your wilderness vain mortals! Puny griefs,
In transitory shapes, be henceforth dwarfed
To your own conscience by the dread extremes
Of what I am and have been. If ye have fallen,
It is but a step's fall, — the whole ground beneath
Strewn woolly soft with promise! if ye have sinned,
Your prayers tread high as angels! if ye have grieved,
Ye are too mortal to be pitiable,
The power to die disproves the right to grieve.

*　　*　　*　　*　　*　　*

*　　*　　Increase and multiply,
Ye and your generations, in all plagues,
Corruptions, melancholies, poverties,
And hideous forms of life and fears of death, —
The thought of death being always eminent,
Immovable and dreadful in your life,
And deafly and dumbly insignificant
Of any hope beyond, — as death itself, —
Whichever of you lieth dead the first, —
Shall seem to the survivor — yet rejoice!
My curse catch at you strongly, body and soul,
And HE find no redemption — nor the wing
Of seraph move your way — and yet rejoice!
Rejoice, — because ye have not set in you
This hate which shall pursue you — this forehate
Which glares without, because it burns within —
Which kills from ashes — this potential hate
Wherein I, angel, in antagonism
To God and His reflex beatitudes,
Moan ever in the central universe
With the great woe of striving against Love —
And gasp for space amid the Infinite —
And toss for rest amid the Desertness —

Self-orphaned by my will, and self-elect
To kingship of resistant agony
Toward the good round me — hating good and love
And willing to hate good and to hate love,
And willing to will on so evermore,
Scorning the Past, and damning the To Come —
Go and rejoice! I curse you!"

Milton never sent a plummet so far down into the depths of Satanic anguish! And if we earnestly ponder, with what amount of scientific precision is possible in the case, wherein that anguish must consist, we shall, I think, arrive at the conclusion of the poetess. Precisely in this necessity of sorrow where there is persistence in ill, — precisely in the inevitable arrangement that the being personifying sin must personify also that pain which is the essence of all its influence subjective and objective, — precisely in being eternally blasted by the rays of Light and Love defied, — must lie the deepest reality of Satanic woe.

After a further elaboration of melancholy circumstance, rather retarding than advancing the action of the poem, the humiliation and despair of the wanderers reaches its climax. Adam and Eve, able to resist no longer, appeal to the Deliverer who has been promised. Then comes the change for which we have been so long prepared. A vision of Christ appears. The circle which had enclosed the human pair "pales before the heavenly light," and the spirits of creation, pouring, until now, their indignation on the head of the man and the woman, give signs of alarm and dismay.

The Saviour thus stills the tumult of the rage and hatred of the creatures.

"*Christ.* Spirits of the earth,
I meet you with rebuke for the reproach

And cruel and unmitigated blame
Ye cast upon your masters. * * *
This regent and sublime Humanity
Though fallen, exceeds you! this shall film your sun,
Shall hunt your lightning to its lair of cloud,
Turn back your rivers, footpath all your seas,
Lay flat your forests, master with a look
Your lion at his fasting, and fetch down
Your eagle flying. * * *
* * * * * *"

Then occurs another of those inimitable passages, in which Mrs. Browning is peculiarly herself; in which she vindicates for her sex the distinction that a woman and not man has written of it *most* nobly. In fitness of conception, in terseness of diction, in loftiness of thought, the following lines have all that the genius of a man could impart: while the thrill of deeper tenderness pervading them tells, in unmistakable accents, of a heart which can throb with wifely emotion, and a breast on which a babe, sleeping in the light of its mother's smile, may rest. In all great poems, there are many lesser poems, complete in themselves; and this passage may be regarded as a poem, on the duties and joys of woman, by Mrs. Browning. It occurs in the form of a blessing, pronounced by Adam, at the command of Christ, on Eve. I regret that it is too long to be quoted entire.

"*Adam.* * * Henceforward, rise, aspire
To all the calms and magnanimities,
The lofty uses and the noble ends,
The sanctified devotion and full work,
To which thou art elect for evermore,
First woman, wife, and mother.

Eve. And first in sin.

Adam. And also the sole bearer of the Seed
Whereby sin dieth! Raise the majesties
Of thy disconsolate brows, O well-beloved,
And front with level eyelids the To Come,
And all the dark o' the world. Rise, woman, rise
To thy peculiar and best altitudes
Of doing good and of enduring ill,—
Of comforting for ill, and teaching good,
And reconciling all that ill and good
Unto the patience of a constant hope,—
Rise with thy daughters! If sin came by thee,
And by sin, death,—the ransom-righteousness,
The heavenly light and compensative rest
Shall come by means of thee. If woe by thee
Had issue to the world, thou shalt go forth
An angel of the woe thou didst achieve,
Found acceptable to the world instead
Of others of that name, of whose bright steps
Thy deed stripped bare the hills. Be satisfied;
Something thou hast to bear through womanhood,
Peculiar suffering answering to the sin,—
Some pang paid down for each new human life,
Some weariness in guarding such a life,
Some coldness from the guarded; some mistrust
From those thou hast too well served; from those beloved
Too loyally, some treason; feebleness
Within thy heart, and cruelty without,
And pressures of an alien tyranny
With its dynastic reasons of larger bones
And stronger sinews. But, go to! Thy love
Shall chant itself its own beatitudes,
After its own life-working. A child's kiss
Set on thy sighing lips shall make thee glad;
A poor man served by thee, shall make thee rich;
A sick man helped by thee, shall make thee strong
Thou shalt be served thyself by every sense
Of service which thou renderest. * * *

* * * * * *

Eve. * * * I accept
For me and for my daughters this high part
Which lowly shall be counted. Noble work
Shall hold me in the place of garden rest,
And in the place of Eden's lost delight
Worthy endurance of permitted pain;
While on my longest patience there shall wait
Death's speechless angel, smiling in the east
Whence cometh the cold wind."

Every sentence here is full of meaning and pathos, meaning which every mind can apprehend, pathos which every heart can feel.

High, however, as has been the flight of the poetess hitherto, she may be said to have yet unfolded but the minor sublimities of her song. Christ, who has until now stood before the exiles in the majesty of his Divine nature, takes the aspect of humanity and suffering, and proceeds to predict for them his own great anguish and the accomplishment of their supreme hope. To execute so daring an attempt on the part of the poetess,—to put words into the mouth of the Saviour foretelling his own humiliation, with perfect preservation of Christian reverence, yet with an energy befitting the theme, and poetic beauty embracing the whole,—was a task of overpowering difficulty. Mrs. Browning has performed it in a way not unworthy of Milton. The Saviour announces first his own crucifixion, and his being forsaken of the Father. This is done in a passion of perhaps overstrained sublimity. To personify eternity would have tasked the genius of Milton and Shakspeare combined, and it is high praise to Mrs. Browning to say that, thus personifying, she has not absolutely failed: but first to personify eternity, and then to represent its silent astonishment at the death of Christ, was surely, in conception at least, as magnificent as daring.

"Eternity stands alway fronting God;
A stern colossal image, with blind eyes
And grand dim lips that murmur evermore
God, God, God! * * *
* * * * * *
Eternity shall wax as dumb as Death,
While a new voice beneath the spheres shall cry,
'God! why hast Thou forsaken me, my God?'
And not a voice in Heaven shall answer it."

From his own sufferings, Christ passes to the blessings of which they are the source to mankind. Only a part of this superb passage can be quoted.

"In my brow
Of kingly whiteness, shall be crowned anew
Your discrowned human nature. Look on me!
As I shall be uplifted on a cross
In darkness of eclipse and anguish dread,
So shall I lift up in my pierced hands,
Not into dark, but light—not unto death,
But life,—beyond the reach of guilt and grief,
The whole creation. Henceforth in my name
Take courage, O thou woman,—man, take hope!
Your grave shall be as smooth as Eden's sward,
Beneath the steps of your prospective thoughts,
And, one step past it, a new Eden gate
Shall open on a hinge of harmony
And let you through to mercy. Ye shall fall
No more, within that Eden, nor pass out
Any more from it. In which hope, move on,
First sinners and first mourners. Live and love,—
Doing both nobly, because lowlily!

Live and work, strongly, — because patiently!
And, for the deed of death, trust it to God
That it be well done, unrepented of,
And not to loss. And thence, with constant prayers
Fasten your souls so high, that constantly
The smile of your heroic cheer may float
Above all floods of earthly agonies,
Purification being the joy of pain!"

Christ departs. The spirits of the earth sing in submission and commiseration. Choruses of angels chant the glories of redemption and the triumphs of the Redeemer.

"When your bodies therefore
Reach the grave their goal,
Softly will we care for
Each enfranchised soul!

* * * * *
* * * *

From the empyrean centre
Heavenly voices shall repeat,
'Souls redeemed and pardoned, enter,
For the chrism on you is sweet.'
And every angel in the place
Lowlily shall bow his face,
Folded fair on softened sounds,
Because upon your hands and feet
He images his Master's wounds!"

"The last enemy," it is written, "that shall be overcome is death." This final conquest shall close the roll of the Saviour's victories. But what hand so bold as attempt the delineation of that crowning triumph? Mrs. Browning, gazing, with her woman's eye, where Michael Angelo's might have blenched, has dared to depict Christ taming the steed of Death. The piece is the last of those poems within this poem, which, never transgressing the grand law of rythmic and imaginative harmony, in obedience to which they all move, have yet a beauty, as of separate stars in a constellation, pertaining to themselves alone. The extracts I have already made occupy so much space that I cannot quote this remarkable passage: but let any one dispassionately, and making allowance for certain extravagances and obscurities, consider its conception and execution, — the descent of Christ into Hades to guide the Death-steed calmly, from amid the moaning and trembling ranks of the lost, — the last journey of the pale horse up through immensity, while the planets become ashen gray and motionless as stones — up towards the crystal ceiling of heaven, through ranks of angels paling at the sight — up straight to the Throne — where the eye of Jehovah, looking out in the light of life essential, strikes upon the phantasm, and, "meek as a lamb at pasture," it staggers, shivers, expires, — and then decide whether there is here a mighty and marvellous imagination, or whether there is not.

But the poem is not yet ended. The full circle of its great unity is not completed. It opened with that exultant song of Lucifer's, in which he boasted over man, and in which the lurid joy of a revenge that could not be balked tinged the darkness of his despair. The jewel in the Creator's crown, which he had blackened and blasted by sin, could not surely be taken from him: the light of God, meeting sin, *must* turn into lightning to afflict and destroy. But now, amid the rejoicing angel voices, is heard a strange cry.

"*First voice.* Gabriel, O Gabriel!

Second voice. What wouldst *thou* with me?

First voice. Is it true, O thou Gabriel, that the crown
Of sorrow, which I claimed, another claims?
That HE claims THAT too?

Second voice. Lost one, it is true.

First voice. That HE will be an exile from His Heaven,
To lead those exiles homeward?

Second voice. It is true.

First voice. That HE will be an exile by His will,
As I by mine election?

Second voice. It is true.

First voice. That I shall stand sole exile finally,—
Made desolate for fruition?

Second voice. It is true.

First voice. Gabriel.

Second voice. I hearken.

First voice. Is it true besides—
Aright true—that mine orient Star will give
Her name of 'Bright and Morning Star' to Him,—
And take the fairness of his virtue back,
To cover loss and sadness?

Second voice. It is true.

First voice. Untrue, untrue! O Morning Star! O MINE,
Who sittest secret in a veil of light
Far up the starry spaces, say—*Untrue!*
Speak but so loud as doth a wasted moon
To Tyrrhene waters! I am Lucifer—
[A pause. Silence in the stars.]
All things grow sadder to me, one by one."

The culminating pathos of Paradise Regained, *had it been completed*, could have been none other than that here expressed. I know not where, out of sacred writ, a pathos more sublime is attained.

I have judged it best to devote particular attention to one of Mrs. Browning's poems, that the reader may have an opportunity of comparing my statements and opinions, with at least a few of the passages on which they are based. If he is acquainted with anything in the range of female poetry, worthy of being set for a moment on a level with what we have seen, I must confess my own ignorance: there seems to me to be enough in this poem alone, to set the poetess at the head of her sex. The imagination it displays is not only fertile in metaphoric brilliancies and lyric bursts, but broad of vision, and mighty to control a thousand elements into one harmony. The intellectual power of the poem is exhibited, not only in the rugged vigor of the style, but in the penetration with which the metaphysic depths of the subject are searched, and in the easy mastery with which great truths, of the sort on which minds of sound sagacity, yet daring speculation, pillar themselves, are set in their due place to support the whole. Two things further appear to be peculiarly characteristic of this poem: beautiful apart, they are still more beautiful in combination. The first is its earnest and essential Christianity: the second its intense and pathetic womanliness. Mrs. Browning is in the highest sense, and always, a Christian poetess. She has drunk more deeply into the spirituality of the gospel, and, it may even be, looked with greater earnestness and amazement upon certain of its most sublime facts, than Milton. The poem before us is, throughout, Christian; not ethically, not sentimentally, not alone in spirit, far less for artistic purposes, but in the strictness and literalness of actual belief. It is true that, in legitimate consistency with her poetic object, — to contrast a mankind that found salvation with an angel host which did not, — she has used the general expressions applied by Scripture in that sense, and which, alone, would imply universalism. But it is not necessary to suppose her declaring her belief that those who, in the most free exercise of their human will, defy the Saviour, and take part with the diabolic tormentors of man in time, will share the *same* futurity with those who *now* commence an eternity of opposition to evil under the banner of the Redeemer. Such a belief introduces elements of fatal weakness into a system of thought, and is inconsistent with any theory of things, in which strength of realism repels fancy and sentimentalism. But interpreting the expressions to which I allude in the sense I have indicated, we find, in the *Drama of Exilè*, all those central truths of Christianity which have been accepted by the mightiest minds of the era, Paul, Augustine, Luther, Calvin, Edwards, Neander; and once more it has been demonstrated that the bare facts of Christianity transcend in sublimity any counterfeit, and more powerfully stimulate a really great imagination than any other theme whatever. The Christianity of Mrs. Browning's poems is far too constant and deep-lying — it enters too pervasively into the warp and woof of her thought and feeling — to be by possibility an affectation or fashion. It is manifestly the life of her life, the breath of immortality at the centre of her being. In the dedication of her first volumes to her father, she appeals, with solemn tenderness, to his knowledge that she holds "over all sense of loss and transiency, one hope by one Name." Her poetry testifies that in so saying she speaks words of truth and soberness. Her genuine womanliness is, in this poem, no less conspicuous. It is characteristic of this century, that in all senses women play a more important part in literature than heretofore. Not only have women of genius commanded universal homage, but the distinctive characteristics of the female nature, have been exhibited with more exquisite analysis and more powerful truth than heretofore. The heart of woman was, I suppose, never laid bare as it has been by Charlotte Bronte and Mrs. Browning. And in the *Drama of Exile*, in such passages as we have seen, the mission of woman to the world — her peculiar glory of sowing blessing with every tear she sheds — her angelic privilege of being the incarnation of peace above conflict, of gentleness mightier than anger, of love stronger than hate — is defined and illustrated, with that bold sweep which pertains to truth, and in those colors which only sympathy can supply. But we must embrace in our view other poems besides the *Drama of Exile* before we apprehend, to the full, the revelation of the female heart, opened to us by this poetess.

And now, since readers may be willing to concede that in this poem there is a sufficiency of simple human emotion, expressed in the mother tongue of noble passion, to thrill all hearts with pleasure, I must once more appeal to them, whether it is not cause of regret, that the elaborate machinery and painful erudition of the poem will indubitably prevent the general mind from penetrating to its inner beauty. The sense reels under the bewildering pageantry of earth spirits, and bird spirits, and river spirits, and zodiacs, and stars, and chorusing angels: the mind is perplexed with gnomons, and apogees, and vibrations, and infinites. One stares on all this as he might on the foam, glorious in its shivered snow and wavering irises, that roars and raves round a coral reef. The vessel draws near the reef, and many an eye looks into that foam, but its beauty fascinates only for a moment, and the sail fills, and the island is left forever. Never, perhaps, is it known, that in the heart of that island, hidden by the torn fringes of tinted foam, there was soft green grass, and a quiet, crystal fountain, and cottages smiling in the light of flowers, and all the home affections offering a welcome.

Of Mrs. Browning's other poems, I shall say, comparatively, but a few words.

The Seraphim is a poem which all ought to study, who would habituate their minds to soaring thought and lofty imagination. It is in conception that it is finest. The poetess depicts the emotions with which the highest of the heavenly host contemplated the crucifixion. How magnificent the daring of this! Nay, rather, let us say how irresistible must have been the afflatus, breathing on the poetess, as she contemplated this, to her, central fact of human story, and bearing her towards the highest heavens, to find hearts strong enough representatively to feel, and tongues fit to express, the emotions she experienced. The speakers are two seraphim, Zerah and Ador. In the following passage, the only one I can quote from the poem, I know not whether the imaginative energy, or the almost startling realism, is the more remarkable; but their union makes up one of the most extraordinary passages in English poetry: —

"*Ador.* The pathos hath the day undone:
The death-look of His eyes
Hath overcome the sun,
And made it sicken in its narrow skies —
Is it to death?

Zerah. *He* dieth. Through the dark,
He still, He only, is discernible —
The naked hands and feet, transfixed stark,
The countenance of patient anguish white
Do make themselves a light
More dreadful than the glooms which round them dwell,
And therein do they shine."

A Vision of Poets can hardly fail to suggest Tennyson. A first and partial acquaintance, indeed, with the works of Mrs. Browning, is apt to prompt the opinion that she may be classed among the pupils and followers of that poet. Both belong to one time, and their thoughts run, not unfrequently, in the same channels. But a more complete knowledge of Mrs. Browning's works puts to flight every imagination of an influence which could do more than stimulate, which could in the slightest degree control, her powers. Her genius is of an order altogether above that which can be permanently or organically affected by any other mind. And,in truth, her whole mode of imaginative action is different from that of Tennyson. The unrivalled finish and strange perfection of the latter, — his unique imaginative faculty, which combines a color more rich than that of Eastern gardens, with a science more austere than that of Greek architecture, — his instinctive and imperious rejection of aught wearing even the semblance of fault or imperfection, requiring that all his marble be polished, and all his gems crystals, — can in no respect or degree be said to characterize Mrs. Browning. Tennyson, more than any English poet of mark, approaches the statue-like calmness of Goethe: Mrs. Browning thrills with every emotion she depicts, whether passion kindles with a smile her own funeral pyre, or earnestness flows rhythmic from the lips of the Pythoness, or irrepressible weeping shakes the breast of the child. Tennyson is the wizard, looking, with unmoved face, into the furnace, whose white heat melts the flint: Mrs. Browning has the furnace in her own bosom, and you *see* its throbbings. Tennyson's imagination treads loftily on cloth of gold, its dainty foot neither wetted with dew nor stained with mire: Mrs. Browning's rushes upwards and onwards, its drapery now streaming in the wind, now draggled in the mountain rivers, making, with impetuous lawlessness, for the goal. Mrs. Browning has scarcely a poem undefaced by palpable error or extravagance: Tennyson's poetry is characterized by that perilous absence of fault, which seems hardly consistent with supreme genius. Between our greatest living poet, therefore, and the greatest of all poetesses, there can be instituted no general comparison. But in *A Vision of Poets*, and in *The Poet's Vow*, there is much to recall Tennyson. In the former, the individual portraits, in the latter, the central thought, point unmistakably to *The Palace of Art*. But even when most like Tennyson, Mrs. Browning is unmistakably herself. If the succession of individual likenesses in *A Vision of Poets* recalls that in *The Palace of Art*, as the melody sometimes suggests that of *The Two Voices*, there is a boldness, a sweeping breadth of touch, in Mrs. Browning's delineations, belonging to herself alone. If the thought of *The Poet's Vow*, — the fatal error and deadly sin of preferring self-culture to human sympathy, — is the same as in *The Palace of Art*, the imagery is totally dissimilar from Tennyson's, and is adapted, but for the intervention of some of Mrs. Browning's tantalizing dimness, to come upon the general heart with more powerful directness than the more elaborate idealization of Tennyson. The poet gave the thought in allegory: the poetess gives it in life. One or two of the portraits of "God's prophets of the Beautiful," from the hand of Mrs. Browning, cannot be passed over. They occur, of course, in *A Vision of Poets*.

> "There, Shakspeare! on whose forehead climb
> The crowns o' the world. Oh, eyes sublime —
> With tears and laughters for all time!
>
> *   *   *   *   *

Here, Milton's eyes strike piercing-dim:
The shapes of suns and stars did swim
Like clouds from them, and granted him

God for sole vision. * * *
* * * * *
And Sappho, with that gloriole

Of ebon hair on calmed brows—
O poet woman! none forgoes
The leap, attaining the repose!
* * * * *
And Burns, with pungent passionings
Set in his eyes * * *"

This is a critique on Burns. When you have said this, you have spoken the one indispensable word concerning him; if you wrote folios on his poetry, you could hardly supplement, however you might illustrate, those "pungent passionings."

"And Shelley, in his white ideal
All statue blind."

That, too, is marvellous: in philosophy profound, in pathos genuine, in poetry perfect. There are few such examples of condensation in the language.

"And visionary Coleridge, who
Did sweep his thoughts as angels do
Their wings with cadence up the Blue."

It is little to say that these lines contain a biography.

"And poor, proud Byron,—sad as grave,
And salt as life: forlornly brave,
And quivering with the dart he drave."

This is very bold, and in almost any case might be pronounced towering presumption. But Mrs. Browning had a right to say it; she whose intellectual and imaginative powers are to the full as great as those of Byron, and who has never stained, by one foul image or impure emotion, the gold and azure of her genius.

The Poet's Vow is one of those poems in which there is exhibited a certain mode or habit of poetic representation, of so frequent occurrence in the pages of Mrs. Browning, that it may be pronounced a principal part of her manner, or mannerism. At first, you are merely astonished and bewildered. You know not who are the actors, what is the subject, at what point the narrative is commenced. But there comes gleam after gleam of backward-falling light; and when finally you open on the full meaning of the poem, and when the cataract of its passion flashes on your eye, the light streams along the whole avenue by which you have approached. To illustrate this peculiarity in detail would occupy too much space; but no better example of it than this poem could be cited. I must content myself, however, with quoting one or two stanzas, not illustrative of this point, though individually remarkable. The poet speaks thus: —

"Hear me forswear man's sympathies,
His pleasant yea and no —
His riot on the piteous earth
Whereon his thistles grow!
His changing love — with stars above!
His pride — with graves below!"

This expresses his determination to put away from him all that can break the serenity of self-culture, to abandon men and seek the grand solitudes of nature. The thought in the two last lines in Goethe's, and has been made familiar to all by the iteration of Mr. Carlyle. But I do not remember a case in which it was more finely applied.

The solitary divides his wealth among his friends, and bids a determined adieu to his brothers who "love him true as brothers do," and to Rosalind, his betrothed, who loves him as no brother can. The following words are spoken by Sir Roland, whom the poet would fain have the accepted lover of his forsaken Rosalind. Both she and Sir Roland, of course, scorn the union, as well as the dower which the poet offers; and Sir Roland addresses him thus:—

"And thou, O distant, sinful heart,
That climbest up so high,
To wrap and blind thee with the snows
That cause to dream and die—
What blessing can, from lips of man,
Approach thee with his sigh?

Ay! what from earth—create for man,
And moaning in his moan?
Ay! what from stars—revealed to man,
And man-named, one by one?
Ay, more! what blessing can be given,
Where the Spirits seven do show in heaven
A MAN upon the Throne?—

A man on earth HE wandered once,
All meek and undefiled:
And those who loved Him, said 'He wept,—
None ever said He smiled,
Yet there might have been a smile unseen,
When He bowed his holy face, I ween,
To bless that happy child."

There is here another illustration of the way in which the

vital Christianity of Mrs. Browning leads her constantly to the purest loveliness and the deepest truth. Tennyson has struck no note so high in *The Palace of Art.*

Rosalind dies of a broken heart, leaving a written scroll, to be put in her coffin, and laid, with her body, at the door of the lonely castle, where her lover dwells apart. At midnight the poet opened his bolted door, to look upon the midnight sky. The stars shine on the face of the corpse. He sees and reads the scroll. The two following verses are part of its contents.

"I have prayed for thee with bitter sobs,
  When passion's course was free!
I have prayed for thee with silent lips,
  In the anguish none could see!
They whispered oft, 'She sleepeth soft'—
  But I only prayed for thee.

* * * * *

I charge thee, by the living's prayer,
  And the dead's silentness,
To wring from out thy soul a cry
  Which God shall hear and bless!
Lest Heaven's own palm droop in my hand,
And pale among the saints I stand,
  A saint companionless."

The victory is won.

"Bow lower down before the throne
  Triumphant Rosalind!
He boweth on thy corpse his face
  And weepeth as the blind.
'T was a dread sight to see them so—
For the senseless corpse rocked to and fro
  With the wail of his living mind.

But dreader sight, could such be seen,
  His inward mind did lie;
Whose long subjected humanness
  Gave out its lion cry,
And fiercely rent its tenement
  In a mortal agony.

I tell you, friends, had you heard his wail,
  'T would haunt you in court and mart,
And in merry feast, until you set
  Your cup down to depart —
That weeping wild of a reckless child
  From a proud man's broken heart.

O broken heart, O broken vow,
  That wore so proud a feature!
God, grasping as a thunderbolt
  The man's rejected nature,
Smote him therewith — i' the presence high
Of his so worshipped earth and sky
That looked on all indifferently —
  A wailing human creature."

You might read that after Shakspeare and Æschylus, and yet pronounce its excellence supreme.

Our inspection of the *Drama of Exile* may have enabled us to form some idea of Mrs. Browning's manner, in the treatment of those sublime themes which are, in a sense, removed from human sympathy. As in a region congenial to her soaring imagination and dauntless intellect, we found her, with steady poise, casting her illumining glance around the abode of the Seraphim, following her high argument above the Aonian Mount and Muse's Hill. We have had one brief look, also, into her mode of handling subjects connected, directly or indirectly, with the principles of her own art. In *A Vision of Poets*, which was specified rather than criticised, her idea of a poet's training is set before us; and *The Poet's Vow* shows that she has not only exhibited unconsciously in her works, but presented consciously to her own mind, the conviction, that the Human is the noblest theme and inspiration of poetry, above all the beauties, enticements, and meanings of physical nature.

There is still at least one other class, demanding separate consideration, among the poems of Mrs. Browning. It consists of those which may be most broadly characterized as poems of personal emotion, and which are more expressly to be described, as delineations of feeling peculiar to the female heart. The passion of love in the maiden heart, the devotion of the wife, and the affection of the mother, are severally and fully portrayed. In each case, the emotion is conceived and exhibited with a power of sympathy, and a dramatic force, of which it is, I believe, but slight applause to say, that they are totally unrivalled. Mrs. Browning has given us the counterpart to all the poetry of chivalry. Troubadour and minstrel sung for ages in homage to woman; knights and monarchs waited for the smile of beauty; the imagination of Europe exhausted itself in devising heroic adventures, by which, penetrating through dark woods, crossing tempestuous seas, fighting giants and monsters, breaking enchantments and prison walls, the bold soldier forced his way to his ladye-love. But the counterpart in this picture, the devotion of the woman to him she loves, was wanting; and we stand in unfeigned astonishment as Mrs. Browning reveals to us what a woman's passion means. This extraordinary writer is always original; but here she had the field almost to herself. We feel her words to be true: they come on us with the authoritative emphasis of nature, coined in the mint of the heart and accepted by the heart at once. Yet none but a woman would have had a *right* to assert, that passion so intense and self-annihilating could be inspired by man in the heart of woman. Ties of relationship, worldly station, riches, life, are cast into the crucible; they are instantly not only melted but dissolved and cast aloft as impalpable vapor. All this happens, and the crucible is still, itself, firm; the heart is yet unbroken: until the passion is unrequited, until the flame is left to eat the heart itself, and then it too dissolves in ashes and death.

In *Isobel's Child*, it is the maternal instinct that is portrayed. The poem suffers greatly from accumulation of useless and distracting machinery. The nurse's dream appears to me simply an incumbrance, and far less ought to have been said about owls and elements. But the beat of the mother's heart falls clear and true amid all this; and when we penetrate far enough to hear it, our own heart cannot but beat in unison. The incident of the poem, stripped of accessories, is very simple. A mother has long watched, in agony of hope and fear, by the sick-bed of her child, for whose recovery she earnestly prays. Her petition is granted, and the child recovers. Her heart is, for a brief hour, filled with pure and unspeakable ecstacy. But, by not very happy imagery, it is revealed to her, that her prayer has deprived her babe of the bliss of present heaven. So she recalls her prayer, yields him up, and herself presently expires. I do not attempt to convey any idea of this composition; but do not the following lines, spoken by Isobel in anticipation of the death of her son, express with strange exactness, yet no less marvellous poetic power, the feeling of a mother looking on the grave of an only child.

"How I shall shiver every day
In thy June sunshine, knowing where
The grave-grass keeps it from his fair

Still cheeks! and feel at every tread
His little body which is dead
And hidden in the turfy fold,
Doth make the whole warm earth a-cold!"

But her love for her babe is stronger than her joy in possessing him. When his corpse lies before her, she speaks thus:—

"I changed the cruel prayer I made,
And bowed my meekened face and prayed
That God would do His will! and thus
He did it, nurse! He parted *us.*
And His sun shows victorious
The dead calm face, — and *I* am calm;
And heaven is hearkening a new psalm."

From many remarkable poems, such as *The Romaunt of the Page*, *Bertha in the Lane*, *Lady Geraldine's Courtship*, and so on, each of which could hardly have failed to make a reputation, I select, for special notice, *The Rhyme of the Duchess May*. This, take it all in all, is, in my opinion, Mrs. Browning's masterpiece. All the exceptions which can possibly be taken to it may be summed up in a single sentence: while it is difficult to say how many specks and flaws might have been covered up from sight, in the broad and steady blaze of its general power. The comparison of an ancient wood, standing "mute adown," to a "full heart having prayed;" such an expression as "the castle seethed in blood," when we hear of but five hundred archers besieging it, and when the besieged have not a score of men killed; the tediousness and apparent triviality of the refrain about the little birds; the monotony of the recurrence of the words "toll slowly," which altogether fail, as any words would have failed, to produce the effect, on the ear or imagination of the reader, which would have been produced by the tolling of a death-knell: — these exhaust the heads of offending, which can be specified, with any show of reason, against the poem. I think each of them is more or less objectionable, and I would totally do away with that weakening and irritating "toll slowly;" but they are worthy of notice not for their importance but their unimportance. Contemplating the piece, which consists of several hundred lines, in its entireness, it is found to be a production, whose rare artistic completeness is only less remarkable than the quality of its detailed drawing and local color. It could have been the work only of one to whom long practice had imparted the skill of consummate art; and no poet could have produced it, save one on whose burning genius consummate art had exercised no constraining power.

In considering this poem, as, indeed, in forming a judgment of any of Mrs. Browning's poems, it is necessary clearly to discriminate two things: the realistic basis, and the imaginative form. Not Byron, not Scott, not Burns was a greater realist than Mrs. Browning: not one of them could take, with surer hand, the lineaments of living passion. But the imaginative drapery in which she clothes her figures is of that sort which we formerly saw, loose-flowing as the mist, perpetually suggesting the supernatural or mysterious, gorgeous, indeed, in coloring, but in effect bewildering. In *The Rhyme of the Duchess May*, the groundwork, laid in with uncompromising realism, is the passion of wifely devotion, triumphing not over but through death. The covering in which imagination wraps this central passion — the outward form of the poem — will strike many as romantic. If it is insisted that the element of romance too much abounds, let it be so: the realistic basis still remains. But I think that if the piece is fairly and deliberately viewed, it will be found that the charge of excessive romance has no force whatever. The central portion of the poem, that to which alone the accusation can apply, is professedly and expressly imaginative. It comes, with its passion and its change, between the stillness before and after, like a meteor between two calm celestial spaces. The poetess sits in a churchyard; there she reads, the church bell tolling deathfully the while, an "ancient rhyme," a tale of life and sin, weird and wondrous, which would contradict all our expectations, if it proved staid and regular, like a modern copy of verses; when the Rhyme is finished, we are again in the churchyard, and a deeper calm is around us than before. Surely, if the delineation of the passion at the heart of the poem is true, there is here no unwarrantable license of imagination.

The description of the churchyard, with which the poem opens, does not long detain the reader. The Rhyme itself soon hurries him into the main current of interest. The Castle of Linteged, the scene of the whole incident, is thus boldly dashed in:—

"Down the sun dropt large and red, on the towers of Linteged,—
Toll slowly.
Lance and spear upon the height, bristling strange in fiery light,
While the castle stood in shade.

There, the castle stood up black, with the red sun at its back,—
Toll slowly.
Like a sullen smouldering pyre, with a top that flickers fire
When the wind is on its track."

To this castle, three months before this time, the Duchess May had come, as the bride of Sir Guy of Linteged. She had been the ward of her uncle, the old Earl of Leigh, who betrothed her in her childhood, for the sake of her inheritance, to his son, Lord Leigh. On coming of age, however, she was rather more than indifferent to the young lord, and haughtily defied both him and his father. The son, as base and avaricious as the father, declares that, let her love him or let her loathe him, let her live or die, marry her he will. Then: —

> "Up she rose with scornful eyes, as her father's child might rise,—
> Toll slowly.
> 'Thy hound's blood, my lord of Leigh, stains thy knightly heel,' quoth she,
> 'And he moans not where he lies.'
>
> 'But a woman's will dies hard, in the hall or on the sward!'—
> Toll slowly.
> 'By that grave, my lords, which made me orphaned girl and dowered lady,
> I deny you wife and ward.'"

This Duchess May is one of the most admirably drawn figures that ever came from the pencil of art. Every line is so definite, every tint so bright and clear. Her whole external existence, her haughtiness, her beauty, her queenliness of mien and manner, are touched in with the airy vividness of Scott: her inmost heart is laid bare, her boundless womanly tenderness, her inflexible womanly pride, her womanly ecstacy of self-sacrifice, — with, I speak deliberately, the power of a Shakspeare. In some respects, she reminds one of a large class of female characters; Scott's Die Vernon, Shakspeare's Beatrice, still more closely, Currer Bell's Shirley. Shirley, indeed, comes exceedingly near; she is the Duchess May in a novel, as the Duchess May is Shirley in an atmosphere of epic grandeur. But, on the whole, the Duchess May must be ranked with the Juliets and Desdemonas, far beyond any flight of Scott or Currer Bell, and perhaps not admitting of being introduced save where tragedy in sceptred pall sweeps by. Beatrice is one of the most charming characters ever portrayed, but she could not have died like Desdemona, to whom it is not the epithet, charming, that we would apply.

The Duchess May bestows her hand upon Sir Guy of Linteged, and the bridal train, pursued by the Leighs, dashes off at midnight, through storm and rain, for the castle among the hills.

"And the bridegroom led the flight on his red-roan steed of might,—
Toll slowly.
And the bride lay on his arm, still, as if she felt no harm,
Smiling out into the night."

This lets us see the essential contrast, which, in its unity, completes the delineation of the lady: defiance of kindred, scorn of all terrors of midnight and storm, dauntless courage and inflexible pride, where love is to be vindicated,—perfect rest, submission, confidence, halcyon repose, as of a child on the breast of its mother, as of a dewdrop in the bosom of a rose, in the encircling arms of love accepted and returned.

Sir Guy and his bride reach the castle in safety, and three happy months pass by. Then the castle is besieged by Lord Leigh, the rejected suitor, and after a fortnight's siege is about to fall into his hands. Ruthless and grovelling, he is still determined to wed the Duchess, though it be over the corpse of her present husband. In this the lady is resolved, through life and death, to foil him. Attired in purple robes, and with her ducal coronet on her brow, she looks down upon him from the wall, withering him with her scorn. Meantime Sir Guy has been superintending operations on the east tower, the highest of all. He perceives that hope is gone, bethinks him that he alone stands between his wife and followers and safety, that resistance at the breach would result simply in the destruction of all, and determines at once to put an end to his life. His wife, he thinks, will soon get over her distress, soothed and entreated by his victorious foes, who made war on her only for his sake:

"'She will weep her woman's tears, she will pray her woman's prayers,'—
Toll slowly.
But her heart is young in pain, and her hopes will spring again
By the suntime of her years.'"

He binds his men by oath not to strike a blow that night. He then demands, of his two most faithful knights, the last service of leading the good steed which he rode on that unforgotten night journey, in full harness, up the turret stair, to the place where he stands. He will leap from the wall and so die on his battle-steed, as a good knight ought. But the Duchess May has a heart as strong as his. She is bound, on the one hand, by her womanly honor, not to wed Lord Leigh: on the other, she will show her husband what lightnings may lurk amid the softness of woman's tears. As the knights are goading the horse up the stair, she comes from her chamber and inquires their errand. They tell her that one half-hour completes the breach, and that her lord, wild with despair, is about to ride the castle wall. For a moment, the thought of love past, and the weight of all this anguish, overcome her: she bows her head, and tear after tear is heard falling to the ground. The knights, gentle in their valor, assay to comfort her:—

"'Get thee in, thou soft ladye!—here, is never a place for thee!'—
Toll slowly.
'Braid thy hair and clasp thy gown, that thy beauty in its moan
May find grace with Leigh of Leigh.'"

In a moment she is herself again: love's pride sets its iron heel on love's tenderness.

"She stood up in bitter case, with a pale yet steady face,
Toll slowly,
Like a statue thunderstruck, which though quivering seems to look
Right against the thunder-place."

These two lines are not alone in Mrs. Browning's poetry: they belong to a considerable class, which might be cited to prove that she has attained the very highest success in the very highest order of poetic effort. This by the way. The Duchess May brushes impatiently aside the well intentioned kindness of her consolers, and takes herself the rein of the good steed. He now needs no goading:

"Soft he neighed to answer her, and then followed up the stair
For the love of her sweet look.

* * * * * * * *

On the east tower, high'st of all,—there, where never a hoof did fall,—
Toll slowly,
Out they swept, a vision steady,—noble steed and lovely lady,
Calm as if in bower or stall."

The passage succeeding this, it would be totally absurd to attempt, by any description, to bring before the reader. The wife has determined that, if her husband leaps over that wall, she will leap over with him. He endeavors frantically to urge the horse over alone. The breach falls in as she pleads, and the crash of wall and window, the shouts of foemen and the shrieks of the dying, rise in one roar around the pair. But love is victor. In vain he wrings her small hands twice and thrice in twain. She clings to him as in a swoon of agonized determination. At last, when the horse, rearing on the verge of the precipitous battlement, could no longer be stopped, "she upsprang, she rose upright," and took her seat beside him :

"And her head was on his breast, where she smiled as one at rest,—
Toll slowly.
'Ring,' she cried, 'O vesper bell, in the beechwood's old chapelle!
But the passing bell rings best.'

They have caught out at the rein, which Sir Guy threw loose — in vain, —
Toll slowly.
For the horse in stark despair, with his front hoofs poised in air,
On the last verge rears amain.

Now he hangs the rocks between — and his nostrils curdle in, —
Toll slowly.
Now he shivers head and hoof — and the flakes of foam fall off;
And his face grows fierce and thin!

And a look of human woe from his staring eyes did go, —
Toll slowly.
And a sharp cry uttered he, in a foretold agony
Of the headlong death below, —

And, 'Ring, ring, thou passing bell,' still she cried, 'i' the old chapelle!'
Toll slowly.
Then back-toppling, crashing back — a dead weight flung out to wrack,
Horse and riders overfell."

Sterner realism than this description cannot be conceived. That horse is frightfully true to fact. Mrs. Browning has once more shown that only on the rugged crags of the real can imagination preen her wings for flight to the regions of the ideal. The passion here, too, doubt it not, is true: Mrs. Browning's heart sympathetically thrilled with it, as she touched that smile on the face of the bride, sinking into the abyss of death in her husband's arms: with all her gentleness, Mrs. Browning could have smiled that smile, and ridden that wall! Woman's love can make of the chariot of death a car of victory; amid the flames of the funeral pyre it can find the softest bed. There is even a strictly practical value in this realization, to our perceptions and sympathies, of transcendent passion. It furnishes us with the key to many singular biographical problems. I consider it a literal fact, that the love of such women as Esther Johnson and Esther Vanhomrigh, for such a man as Swift, which, tried by any ordinary rules, seems simply madness, has been rendered far more clearly intelligible and conceivable, by such delineations of female nature, as have been given us by Charlotte Bronte and Mrs. Browning.

The wild ancient Rhyme having sung itself out, we return to the calm of the churchyard, and are reminded of a serenity enveloping and subduing all passion. The poetess fixes her eye on a little grave beneath a willow tree, on which is engraved an inscription, stating that it is the grave of a child of three years. Mrs. Browning, however she may indulge the play of dramatic sympathy, has far too stable an intellect to waver, for a moment, from the conviction, that passion can never be the *highest.* From her thoughts, too, the essential points of the morality preached from the Mount are never absent; she draws, in her own rapid, inimitable manner, rather suggesting than detailing, a contrast between the passage of the child-soul to heaven, encompassed by star-wheels and angel wings, and the passionate dashing up of those frantic lovers against the thick-bossed shield of God's judgment. And so the poem ends in rest and stillness: leaving us in silent wonder at its artistic symmetry and matchless execution, and gazing up into the celestial blue which overarches all its passion.

Thus has Mrs. Browning poetically realized the feelings of the bride and of the wife: she has depicted with corresponding power and delicacy the feelings of the mother. In *Isobel's Child*, as I have already remarked, it is the maternal instinct which is the central subject of representation. It is, however, in *Aurora Leigh*, that Mrs. Browning's delineation of this affection, in all its tenderness and in all its rapture, attains its highest perfection. To do even approximate justice to the succession of passages in which, in the poem named, Marian Erle and her babe are the objects of portraiture, would demand a separate critique. But were we to embrace all that is revealed in one view to us of woman in the *Drama of Exile*, *The Duchess May*, *Isobel's Child*, and *Aurora Leigh*, not to mention other poems, we should find it difficult to dispute the position that this poetess has sung of her own sex, as no poet or poetess ever did.

Of *Aurora Leigh*, as Mrs. Browning's last and longest poem, it will be proper to speak at somewhat greater length.

Whatever the estimate of this poem, at which we may on the whole arrive, no doubt can be entertained that it is the finest which has appeared in Great Britain since *In Memoriam*. Merely to specify its beauties would occupy an extended space. The descriptions of English scenery in the early books may challenge comparison with anything in the language. Vivid as if resting in the very light of clear English mornings, fresh as if the dew-drops glistened on the page, broad and powerful as is the work of strong imagination, touched everywhere with those more playfully delicate lights which are commonly attributed to fancy, these limnings must make every Englishman proud of a country that can be so described, and of a poetess who can so describe it. To the delineations of Italian scenery, a similar character may be ascribed, the necessary changes being of course made. Even without a personal familiarity with that scenery, the accuracy of such descriptions is instinctively relied on: there is in them an honest minuteness which is its own guarantee. Besides these more general delineations, there are in this poem certain descriptive passages, such as the view of London, and the sail by night along the Sardinian sea-coast towards Italy, which would require a separate and more elaborate characterization. They are among those solitary efforts of genius to which, with scientific precision, we may apply the epithets, magnificent and sublime. Turning to the human figures, Marian Erle is in all respects worthy of Mrs. Browning's genius. The historical existence of Emma Lyon renders it no outrage on poetic probability to suppose such ability and such character as those of Marian Erle in an English girl born in the lowest order of society; nor in the present diffusion of the elements of knowledge, is the mode, in which she is represented as acquiring some considerable culture, by any means strained or unnatural. It must, of course, be permitted to a poet to violate minor probabilities: a reasonable possibility is all that can be demanded. Marian Erle is imbued with true poetic life: we approve, admire, and love her: and so perfectly are we interested and enchained by the tenderness, the loveliness, the inexpressible pathos, of which she is made the centre, that it is only afterwards we reflect on the marvellous genius displayed by the poetess.

It may appear that after such a specification, and with the

clear admission that it might be very greatly extended, no alternative remains but to pronounce *Aurora Leigh*, on the whole, a successful performance, a poetical achievement at once noble and complete. I am compelled to state that, after careful deliberation, my conclusion has been the reverse. In all the other poems by Mrs. Browning, with which I am acquainted, the defects, though sometimes great, are not sufficient to neutralize the excellence: to *Aurora Leigh*, all things considered, the only word to be applied is "failure." The grounds of this opinion will be briefly indicated.

In the first place, nearly all the exceptions which critics have incidentally taken to Mrs. Browning's poems come here into application, and certain of them can be urged with greater force than in any former instance. The style, indeed, is somewhat simplified, and if parenthesis and involution still prevail to a greater extent than is now necessary to any one using the English language, the charge of unintelligibility, or even of decided difficulty, can hardly be brought against the poem. But there is a considerable number of those overstrained and extravagant images, those sublime conceits towards which Mrs. Browning has so often manifested a tendency.

> "Then the bitter sea
> Inexorably pushed between us both,
> *And sweeping up the ship with my despair*
> *Threw us out as a pasture to the stars.*"

Mr. Carlyle has been bold enough to declare that Shakspeare sometimes premeditates the sheerest bombast. It was more probably through momentary negligence that Mrs. Browning permitted this unpardonable passage to escape her pen. At all events, no Homeric bellman, no Ossianic juvenile, ever perpetrated purer nonsense, or more unredeemed bombast. What possible resemblance there can be between a ship and a pasture, why and when stars go out to grass, and wherefore, having so gone out, they should feed on ships and young ladies — these are questions of insoluble mystery, but hardly more mysterious than how Mrs. Browning could crowd so many absurdities into two lines. The lines are enough in themselves seriously to damage a great poem: and though perhaps the worst, they constitute by no means a solitary example of extravagance.

In the next place the melody of *Aurora Leigh* is defective. There are indeed passages in which the thoughts and images fairly float themselves away in the sphere-dance of harmony; wonderful passages, in which it is again demonstrated that true melody in language is but the rhythmic cadence natural to a mood of thought, imagination and expression, sufficiently elevated, calm and mighty. But over wide spaces of the poem the ear finds no delight, and the ear most rightfully demands from the poet what the eye demands from the painter. In a very fair review of *Aurora Leigh*, published in Blackwood's Magazine, a method of estimate was applied to the poem of a sort which Edgar Poe strongly insisted on. Certain passages were given without the form of verse. Has Mrs. Browning read those passages? If she has, and if the impression made on her mind was that conveyed irresistibly to mine, how did she contemplate the fact that her poetry suggested Mr. Kingsley's prose? It is no commendation of Mrs. Browning, and no disparagement to Mr. Kingsley, to say that it could only be in the case of utter, though perhaps temporary, abrogation of her highest qualities, that a production of the former could recall the work of the latter; yet it is so. The crowding, the vehemence, the feverish haste and impatience, which so frequently characterise Mr. Kingsley's novels, can hardly fail to be suggested by such passages as those to which allusion is now made. It cannot be pleaded that these are exceptional. The heroine invariably talks like one of Mr. Kingsley's characters. There is a lack, besides, of tenderer strains to refresh and relieve the ear; the atmosphere wants calm, the landscape wants perspective. Once more, the irreverent or seeming irreverent use of the names of the Persons of the Trinity, which had been formerly objected to Mrs. Browning, is carried further in *Aurora Leigh* than in any of her previous poems. No defence can be offered for this circumstance. It may be perfectly true that Mrs. Browning's irreverence is only seeming, and that it results mainly from a constant habit of reference, in life, to the will of the Deity. But the fact remains, and is indubitable, that the simple and sincere worshippers of God throughout the British islands will be pained at heart by the words of Mrs. Browning. Something called reverence by Goethe and Carlyle may be consistent with a familiarity in the use of Divine names, such as we instinctively shrink from in the case of a sister, a mother, a father, a departed relative, a tenderly beloved friend; but if Mrs. Browning would have her books associated with the Bible, the Pilgrim's Progress, the Christian Year, in the homes and hearts of simple, godly people, she must condescend to a reverence conceivable in itself, and uncontradicted by the whole analogy of nature. The example of Tennyson ought surely to have preserved her from this great and pervading error. Genius need not be ashamed to learn from its equal; and Mrs. Browning would do well to meditate on Tennyson's invariable mode of reference to

> "That which we dare invoke to bless."

These are serious objections; yet they are the least important which can be urged against *Aurora Leigh.* They are the light musketry; the park of artillery has still to open fire.

Aurora Leigh is herself an essentially defective character. We do not love her: we cannot love her. Had Mrs. Browning not instructed us, it might have been otherwise. But since Mrs. Browning, in her Eve and her Duchess May, has shown us what woman can be, what sort of women we ought to love, it is impossible for us to reject and scorn all her teaching, in the single act of accepting Aurora Leigh. The intellectual character of this young lady may pass; she has even a certain bare and masculine sense of justice, and willingness to be kind: but real warmth of heart, true womanly tenderness, she has not. She is generically different from any other female character from the pencil of Mrs. Browning. None other which Mrs. Browning has drawn could have been, on the whole, so cold, hard, heartless, as, on the occasion of the death of her aunt, Aurora Leigh shows herself to be. It is absolutely astonishing that Mrs. Browning has permitted her heroine to exhibit no trace of generous relenting, of natural grief, of mere human tenderness, on the death of one who really loved her. There is no dew-drop in the bosom of this rose.

The heroine is a failure in respect of the intention of the poetess. She must be considered as claiming our admiration and love; and she is not worthy of their being accorded her. But Aurora Leigh is, I think, true to nature: realistically, if not poetically, the portraiture may be correct. What is perhaps the most important of all the charges to be brought against the poem before us still remains to be made. In the portraiture of Romney Leigh, and in the whole treatment of socialism, the necessary realistic basis wholly fails.

Mrs. Browning is in theory a stern realist. She earnestly proclaims that the Homer of his time must always write of the present. Throughout *Aurora Leigh*, she aims at bold, broad, truthful delineation. She takes her reader to the purlieus of St. Giles's, and writes off fearlessly the curse of the ruffian, the slang of the prostitute. So far,—it may be,—good. The truth as to the real and the ideal, the present and the past, in relation to poetical composition, is easily defined. In the real is found the only true mode of ascent to the ideal; the loftiest tree must have its roots in the ground. The present is the subject of all poetry, inasmuch as the substantial frame-work of man's moral and intellectual nature is, in essentials, in all ages, the same. Costume, using the word in its widest sense, varies from age to age; it is a noble work of a perfectly informed imagination to picture forth, in perfect exactness, that worn by any past generation; but the living men whom that costume enveloped, in their essential attributes of reason and passion, can be accurately conceived only by knowledge of the men that think and love in the present. To all objections that her descriptions in *Aurora Leigh* are too realistic, Mrs. Browning will almost glory in the reply that she paints the life. But the objection now urged is that her realism is in the cases mentioned, utterly at fault, and that her realism failing, her idealization becomes of necessity mere vagueness, vapour, nonentity. A single illustration from the poem itself will show Mrs. Browning that it is not in respect of theory or method that the present exception is taken. Her view of London is sufficiently real and grandly ideal. The light of imagination is there, but it falls on a real river, on real spires and palaces. Her Romney Leigh and her view of socialism have no such basis of reality, of fact; they are not the stuff of which the poetic dream can make anything; they are dreams about dreams.

There have, in all ages, been individual enthusiasts; but in no age could an individual enthusiast have been representative; and even as an enthusiast, Romney Leigh is impossible. He is represented as a man of ability, without the smallest trace of intellectual power; he is represented as a man of statistics and of science, while his conception of human regeneration is purely fanciful, and precisely as scientific as the proposition that twice five make out the dozen. He represents the age in a way in which a fifth-monarchy man, of *ne plus ultra* principles, would represent the age of Cromwell. Joe Smith would be considered an inappropriate hero for a poem descriptive of the present time. I am personally of opinion that he might be made the centre of a great poem. But, whether or no, the Mormon leader would represent incomparably more of the present time than is represented by Romney Leigh. Thus delusive as representative of his time, he is in himself unsubstantial. There is no actuality or life in him: He wants bone. Nothing can convince the reader that he walks the solid earth. This circumstance is fatal.

The general conclusion from Mrs. Browning's new poem is, that socialistic schemes are nonsensical. But Mrs. Browning does not exhibit the slightest degree of knowledge of the science of the social system, the special science of the present time. She has studied in the school of Carlyle: the doctrines and methods of which school bear almost precisely the same relation to the social regeneration of peoples, as the scholastic logic bears to the construction of railways. Mrs. Browning has not even skirted the border of that realistic field in which the noblest idealizations of the present time are to be planted. Facts and figures are not poetry, but they may be the materials from which a mighty imagination will build up the noblest poems. Mrs. Browning has such an imagination. But she has no surmise that, in dry statistical tables is to be found the most glorious theme that can invite imagination in these years: she has totally overlooked a factor which is necessary, I say not to the solution, but to the smallest contribution towards a solution, of the great problem, at which, to say the least, she looks. To reiterate abstract maxims, were they elaborated by the combined intellects of Bacon and Goethe, comes here to little; to discover that misery abounds in the world and merely to depict it, in colors however true and striking, is almost equally valueless; to fling abroad vague denunciation upon those who, in good and in bad report, with less light or with more, strive earnestly through long years to benefit their fellow men, is in itself worse than useless, and has now become hopelessly commonplace. Through the whole history of mankind, the world has been a place of sorrow as of sin. The brightest year that ever swept, in kindly change of seasons, over the earth, saw enough of individual distress, to drive a man, were it presented to his imagination with vivid poetic power, raving mad. So surely as the race continues as it is, so surely must this, for many centuries to come, be still the case. The man who cannot deliberately envisage this dread circumstance, who cannot thus look before and after, and yet retain the faith that earth is a place in which to live and work, becomes a rebel against the order of things; in consistence, he ought to commit suicide or accept atheism. But the strong and healthful man will, we shall agree, find it, on the whole, rational and advisable to submit to the conditions of his existence and to believe in God. To enable him to do so, it is necessary not that he should accept any delusive representation of the present or Utopian prediction for the future, but that he should perceive in the history of man *a progress*, that he should be assured that, however slowly, the evil and the sorrowful recede, and the good and the joyful advance. Now there is one fact which the great science of statistics has already proved, in reference at least to that island which is the principal scene of Mrs. Browning's poem; —that crime and misery are on the decline. Amid all the vociferation of Mr. Carlyle and his school, in full view of stupendous individual crimes, with ready admission of multitudinous cases of individual distress, the wise man will calmly and earnestly fix his eye on this fact; on the bare figures in which it is inscribed he will look with unspeakable joy, nay reverence, as if he saw them traced in light by the finger of God. Ahriman, they proclaim, though fighting sternly, does draw back his foot. The ocean rolls darkly beneath a troubled sky, but the sand-grains are being deposited, year by year, which will one day build the broad continent right into the sunlight. The night is still murky, but a rim of light slowly broadens out to dawn. How magnificently, how epically, might Mrs. Browning, with such an imagination as hers, have concluded her poem by showing us this ring of light on the horizon of the world, this aureole which proves that the sorrowful earth is still among the family of God! But except out of realism no true idealization can arise; and the realism which it is necessary to master in this case is to be found in a science, which Mrs. Browning probably despises and of which she is certainly ignorant. The conclusion to which, in *Aurora Leigh*, we *are* conducted, is exceedingly true, and is presented in very beautiful poetry: but, in originality and practical utility, it is not one whit superior to the doctrine preached on the subject, any Sunday in the year, in the churches and chapels of England. Miss Leigh's platonism cannot in the least affect the state of the case: the originality wanted was not to be had by looking across two thousand years, but by accepting the present, not in the philosophy of Plato, but in criminal reports, in the history of free trade, in the works of Grey, MacCulloch and Chalmers, in the letters of Colonel Jebb.

Aurora Leigh, then, despite countless beauties, despite passages sufficient to furnish forth anthology after anthology, despite an exuberant display of that genius which makes Mrs. Browning the greatest poetess in the world, is a failure. Why is it so? It would be tiresome and probably vain to attempt to answer the question at length. But one cause, perhaps a principal cause, seems to lie in that recoil from common men and exoteric doctrines, to which an early reference was made. The influence of Mr. Carlyle upon Mrs. Browning has been very powerful; and it has been evil. To apply to her the words used in a different connection by a thoroughly able writer in the Edinburgh Review, she has more and more learned from Mr. Carlyle what she could not have learned "from Greek philosophy or Holy Writ, a fierce and unenlightened disdain . . . . of the MULTITUDE."

> "Heavens,
> I think I should be almost popular
> If this went on!"

So exclaims Aurora, and though passages might be quoted which seem to point to a different conclusion, this indicates the doctrine of the book. Yet there was ONE of whom his disciples were not ashamed to declare that "the common people heard him gladly."

To refer, save in the most general way, to Mrs. Browning's smaller poems, is now impossible. Some of them, as *The Cry of the Children*, *Cowper's Grave*, *The Cry of the Human*, and *The Sleep*, are absolute masterpieces. The first is one of the greatest of strictly *modern* poems. It demonstrates that a pathos may be got out of cotton fuzz and rattling machinery, to which the woes of Achilles and Hector, and the sublime sorrows of battling goddesses, around windy Troy, were a very poor affair: it shows that, though tragedy on the boards may be looked upon with very dry eyes, the real tragedy is still amongst us. The poem reminds us of Hood. The pathos of Hood is true and piercing; it is the pathos of bare fact, of life; it is the tear of sorrow itself, falling upon the heart. But *The Cry of the Children*, to a realism as literal as Hood's, adds an imaginative gleam such as Hood could not impart. The piece is radiant with poetic fervor. There is perhaps no respect in which it is not a study: in language, in melody, in imagery, in truthfulness.

Cowper's Grave is an outburst of emotion, irrepressible in its earnestness, unspeakable in its tenderness. Some of the thoughts are by no means common, and some of the turns might, from their point and ingenuity, almost suggest the word, conceit: but a passion of tenderness glows so visibly over the whole, that we think no more of premeditation than if we witnessed a paroxysm of weeping.

The Cry of the Human does not omit that word, with out which all denunciation of man's vice and shortcoming, all lamentation over man's misery, must be pronounced aimless fury or maudlin puerility. Mere despair at the sight of sorrow, mere frenzied indignation at the sight of sin, can beseem no man, when we think Who atoned for human sin, and Who shared human suffering.

> "Then, Soul of mine,
> Look up and triumph rather—
> Lo! in the depth of God's Divine,
> The Son adjures the Father—
> Be pitiful, O God!"

The Sleep is one of those poems of Mrs. Browning's, in which not only the inmost thought and feeling are beautiful and simple, but in which no veil intervenes between these and general sympathy. This remark, indeed, extends, more or less, to all the pieces now under notice. In her smaller poems Mrs. Browning seemed to be working fairly clear of what must be called her mannerism. In these she stands before us in no classic adornment, clothed on with the perfect beauty of her own womanliness and truth.

"O earth, so full of dreary noises!
O men, with wailing in your voices!
O delved gold, the wailers heap!
O strife, O curse, that o'er it fall!
God strikes a silence through you all,
'And giveth His beloved sleep.'

His dews drop mutely on the hill,
His cloud above it saileth still,
Though on its slope men sow and reap.
More softly than the dew is shed,
Or cloud is floated overhead,
'He giveth His beloved sleep.'

* * * * *

* * * *

And friends, dear friends,—when it shall be
That this low breath is gone from me,
And round my bier ye come to weep,
Let one, most loving of you all,
Say, 'Not a tear must o'er her fall—
He giveth His beloved sleep.'"

The man who cannot feel this is capable of no poetic feeling at all. Had Mrs. Browning been always so simply herself, her poems might be found on every cottage shelf. And who has more nobly told us that nature's truth is better than art's conventions, than Mrs. Browning herself? *The Dead Pan*, another poem of sustained and consummate excellence, is most of all precious, for its bold modernism, and haughty protest against the cant of classicism.

"Earth outgrows the mythic fancies
Sung beside her in her youth:
And those debonaire romances
Sound but dull beside the truth.
Phœbus' chariot-course is run.
Look up, poets, to the sun!
Pan, Pan is dead.

* * * * *
* * * *

Truth is fair: should we forego it?
Can we sigh right for a wrong?
God Himself is the best Poet,
And the Real is his song.
Sing his Truth out fair and full,
And secure His beautiful.
Let Pan be dead."

These words are worthy of a time of universal reaction towards reality: against all formalism and artifice; a time which has seen unveiled the face of Cromwell, and when Ruskin is flinging open to the *peoples* the gallery of Art.

But it were a bootless task to attempt to refer, even in a word, to all that are peculiarly marked among Mrs. Browning's smaller poems. She touches in them a thousand chords of feeling, and glances into unnumbered spheres of thought. From deep metaphysical musings, and philosophical delineations of the characteristics of the age, to the tenderest limnings of home life, they exhibit every mood of thought and emotion. A deep tone of pathos is very constantly present, its pervading idea being the inextricable blending of joy and sorrow in the lot of man, the necessity that there seems of all joy being *through* sorrow. The smile, the mother smile, comes on a cheek white with an "eight-day weeping," and, says the poetess,

> "All smiles come in such a wise."

"Who," she asks, "can love and rest?" But neither does she ever permit the shadow to fall over *all* man's glory; she knows of a sky, pure and blue, above all plaining.

> "Thy voice is a complaint, O crowned city,
> The blue sky covering thee like God's great pity."

This last is but an instance of a universal characteristic of Mrs. Browning's writings on which one loves to dwell. Somewhat decided language has been applied to the unseemly familiarity with which the Divine names are used in *Aurora Leigh*. But no further qualification is necessary in asserting the pervasive Christianity of Mrs. Browning's works. Over all the domain of her poetry, over its central ranges, its quiet gardened valleys, its tinkling rills, falls a radiance of gospel light. Ever, as her music rises to its noblest cadence, it seems taken up by an angel harp: the highest tone is as the voice of spirits. It would, I cannot doubt, be to their own sincere enjoyment and real profit, if the Christian public pressed boldly into the temple of Mrs. Browning's song. She is a Christian poetess, not in the sense of appreciating, like Carlyle, the loftiness of the Christian type of character, not in the sense of adopting, like Goethe, a Christian machinery for artistic self-worship, not even in the sense of preaching, like Wordsworth, an august but abstract morality, but in the sense of finding, like Cowper, the whole hope of humanity bound up in Christ, and taking all the children of her mind to him, that he may lay his hand on them and bless them. It is well that Mrs. Browning is a Christian. It is difficult, but possible, to bear the reflection, that many great female writers have rejected that gospel which has done more for woman than any other civilizing agency; but it is well that the greatest woman of all looks up, in faith and love, to that Eye which fell on Mary from the cross.

The greatest woman of all! This is my firm and deliberate conviction. I am, of course, not acquainted with the works of all great female writers, perhaps not even of many. But, as you look towards the brow of a towering mountain, rising far over the clouds and crowned with ancient snow, you may have an assurance, even though it rises from a plain, or, if amid lower hills, though you have not actually taken the elevation of each, that in height it is peerless. In the poems of Mrs. Browning are qualities which admit of their being compared with those of the greatest men; touches which *only* the mightiest give. With the few sovereigns of literature, the Homers, Shakspeares, Miltons, she will not rank. But in full recollection of Scott's magical versatility and bright, cheerful glow, of Byron's fervid passion and magnificent description, of Wordsworth's majesty, of Shelley's million-colored fancy, of Coleridge's occasional flights right into the sun-glare, of Bailey's marvellous exuberance, and of Tennyson's golden calm, I yet hold her worthy of being mentioned with any poet of this century. She has the breadth and versatility of a man, no sameliness, no one idea, no type character: our single Shakspearean woman. In this view I am agreed with by the author of *The Raven*, a critic of great acuteness and originality, and who had no moral or religious prepossessions in favor of Mrs. Browning.

"Woman, sister,—" says Thomas De Quincey, "there are some things which you do not execute as well as your brother, man; no, nor ever will. Pardon me, if I doubt whether you will ever produce a great poet from your choirs, or a Mozart, or a Phidias, or a Michael Angelo, or a great philosopher, or a great scholar. By which last is meant—not one who depends simply on an infinite memory, but also on an infinite and electrical power of combination; bringing together from the four winds, like the angel of the resurrection, what else were dust from dead men's bones, into the unity of breathing life. If you *can* create yourselves into any of these great creators, why have you not?"

Mrs. Browning has exalted her sex: this passage *was* true.

IV.

GLIMPSES OF RECENT BRITISH ART.

A DIALOGUE.

* * * Englishmen of pith,
Sixteen named Thomson and nineteen named Smith.—BYRON.

Thomson. Oh — Mr. Smith. How d' ye do? In that good old English salutation everything is included, — wealth, health, and family. — How are you?

Smith. All well. Everything in order at the old place. Crops good, boys and girls well, and wife, I will say, buxom, blithe, and debonair as you could wish an English matron.

Thom. And you have given all your country comforts the go-by to have a look at London?

Smith. Not exactly. Business brought me to town, but to-day I am free. London, you know, is on the race-course, — which it may have to itself for me, —and I have seized the opportunity for a stroll through the rooms of the Academy.

Thom. Indeed. This is fortunate. You know my love of Art? — I, too, had made up my mind to avail myself of the absence of fashion and dilettantism to inspect, with favoring quiet and leisure, the works of the year. Suppose we make a day of it — looking as we talk, and talking as we look?

Smith. Agreed — most heartily. I hold you something of an authority, whereas I know nothing of pictures, and profess no opinion on the subject. I know when I am pleased, and my pleasure is often deep. But there I stop. I have a feeling, even, that I have but a questionable right to the pleasure I experience. I am one of the common crowd, hated and shunned by connoisseurs, and despised by the artists whose pictures they buy. Like the rest I bow to the connoisseurs, and placidly receive what artists condescend to tell me. But with you I am free. Even if you were a connoisseur at all points, which you are not, the indulgence of the friend would vail the terror of the critic. I am a child, of course, but I shan't be startled at the dreadful crest; and you won't hector, will you? I give in, to begin with. I surrender all freedom of judgment, while retaining utmost freedom of impression and remark. I give you a general permission to laugh at me. You may even give me a smart touch with the whip, when I am running fairly off the road. I know nothing of pictures.

Thom. Hm! — All remarkably fine. Your modesty is no counterfeit — that I know; — but let me broadly declare it is a mistake. We shall perhaps contrive to raise you somewhat in your own opinion as a picture critic. In the meantime, what, pray, do you mean by "having no knowledge of painting?" You are fond of Art. You make at least an annual visit to London, to see whatever pictures the year produces. And has not your interest in Art led you to read a little on the subject?

Smith. Well, really, you will do me a service if you teach me to cast myself free of that timorousness with which I now think of any picture. But you must take care that a worse thing come not upon me; I should rather be a coward among critics, than a pretender among dunces.

You ask what I mean by being ignorant of painting. Well, I could not give you a single rule of perspective, or read you off one of the harmonies of color, or define tone or chiaroscuro. In one word, I am ignorant of the technical part of painting. I cannot paint, and I do not know the rules of painting. Besides, — for I shall make a clean breast of it, — I have a lurking preference for pictures that are bright, clear, clean, new; and I fancy I might give my money for a school copy with just as much heartiness as if I bore away the real master. Still worse, I have not nearly the due measure of enthusiasm for the said masters. I sigh over my want of raptures on the subject of Rubens's flesh-tint; and when I catch sight of a number of undressed ladies, even though the catalogue calls them Diana and her Nymphs, and even though it be Titian who draws aside the curtain of—of—decency—I am despicably inclined to get out of the way. In short, you must give me up.

Thom. Not quite yet. Nor have you told me all you have to tell. There is a positive as well as a negative side.

Smith. I have said nearly all that is to the purpose, I think. But you would ask what I have seen and read in connection with Art? There *is* a little to tell in that direction. Plain folks as we are in the Dell, I cannot pretend to a total ignorance of what is said, seen, and written in the world. There is no excuse now-a-days, even among our fern and heather, for complete ignorance. Why, — think of it. I read in the afternoon, at my tea table, the debate of last night in the House. Every rumor which circulates in the London clubs, political, literary, or artistic, finds its way to us in a few hours. I hear to-day of the arrival or production of a new painting: to-morrow I mingle with the throng inspecting it. Half a dozen libraries are ready to supply me with every new work, on Art as on every other subject. I do n't see, therefore, what right I have to be inferior in Art-knowledge to townsmen as such. I imagine that I am not so. For many years I have visited all the principal exhibitions, and have taken pleasure in penetrating, as far as I could, into the truth and meaning of the pictures. What with this, and with reading, I have formed a notion, correct or not, of the distinctive ideas which reigned in particular schools, and of the way in which subjects have been treated by particular masters. But all this is beyond the pale of technical knowledge; all this is outside the studio; and I have nothing to plead in arrest of the verdict of artistic barbarism.

Thom. Very good. But talking threatens to encroach on looking. We must get at the pictures. As you have said all you can for yourself, however, grant me just another minute to see whether I cannot allege something additional in your favor. There is a little matter which you not ungracefully omit, but which I consider of paramount importance. You know nothing, it appears, of color. You are rather hazy in chiaroscuro, and are apt to lose yourself in golden and silvery tones. You never saw, you might have added, the original Venus de Medicis, nor affected rapture over Leonardo's *Supper* at Milan. Very sad, indeed! Now I happen to have visited you in that Dell of yours, so sweetly sinking, with its crag and copse, from the general level of the upland. I well remember a walk with you, one fresh, dewy morning, which would have been dull in town, but which in the country only made everything more rural, quiet, country-like. The sky was of course well filled with broken clouds. No other composition of the sky, if I may steal a term from Art and apply it to nature, gives at once transparency of air, pure richness of color, and fine effects of light and shade. There was a moment when the sunbeams, which had been peeping and peering for an outlet in the clouds all morning, suddenly streamed through a valley opened for them by the gentle wind, and spread themselves in their countless companies along the faint purple of the hill. The gleam of their golden banners shone clear against the shadow which was still lying dark over the greater part of the mountain. The eyes of both of us were at once on the ridge, which had caught the light; and when I looked at yours, shall I tell you what I saw there? If not exactly a tear, at least a glistening which told that the heart required some kind of overflow. Nor have I forgotten that day, when, like a good, respectable Mr. Smith, you drove me to the market-town in your own gig. It was about the end of July. As we passed along, a cornfield lay by the wayside. Through it the hand of autumn had just begun to sprinkle the gold into which melts the green of summer; and, amidst this golden-green, myriads of poppies waved their crimson flames. "These," you exclaimed, casting a glance in the direction of the poppies, "take a pretty penny out of my pocket, but for two reasons I am happy to pay the price; first, because of the pure delight of the color, and second, because that one sight, to leave out a thousand others, and the emotion it excites, are amply sufficient to annihilate, once for all, the theory of beauty professed and defended by Francis Jeffrey."

Smith. Ah, let me interrupt you. Perhaps that was severe on Jeffrey. His dissertation is extremely valuable as a classification of what the beautiful is *not.* It is a monument *ære perennius;* only you must turn it upside down! Go on.

Thom. Now, of whatever precise value it may be, I think I need not prove that in estimating one's capacity for judging in Art, it is at least well to know his power to observe and enjoy the beauty of nature. The instances I have adduced show that, whatever you may say of the landscapes of the former, you are not indifferent to those of the latter. Were I to pass beyond landscape, and inquire in the same way into your fitness to form an opinion on painting of human life, I should find my case still stronger. Nothing human have I ever known which did not, one way or other, interest and attract you. I have seen you look with genial curiosity on the equipages, the dresses, the languid smiles, the artificial flowers, of Hyde Park. I have seen you mark with stronger interest, and sympathy far more ardent, the glowing cheeks and glittering, twinkling eyes of the haymakers in your own fields. I think you would know the mark of human feeling wherever you saw it, in field, in street, or on canvas. But we can put this to the proof at once. Look here. What think you of this picture?

Smith. It impresses and delights me: more I shall not yet venture to say.

Thom. But wherein consists your pleasure? What do you see in the picture? Read me off your impressions as clearly as you can.

Smith. I shall make the attempt. It seems to me, as I look, that there gradually dawns upon me the whole modulated beauty of a lyric poem, written not in alphabetical characters but in soft, sweet, variegated light. There is before me the well stored room, kitchen and sitting-room in one, of a homely yet substantial farmhouse. The wife of the good yeoman is seated on the left, beautiful with the beauty of joy and health, her cheek white and ruddy, her whole face bathed in the tender illumination of that smile, which prosperity never fails to light upon the countenance of a true woman. She is perfectly happy and contented in her babe, lying there in her lap, in rosy, healthy slumber. That woman is a realization of all that is kind, vigilant, comforting, blissful, in the character and office of a mother. The yeoman's boys, stout, hearty little fellows, who spend nine tenths of their time in leaping and shouting in the fields, are seen near their mother. And what boy is that beside them? What child is it, who has glided in through the half-open door, and stands, in his thin rags, his little cap in his hand, looking up, submissively, piteously, into the face of the old grandmother? Why is he so woe-begone, so forlorn, weary-looking, beside the jocund children of the farmer? He is *The Mitherless Bairn!* Look at that babe on its mother's knee, and those boys standing beside. The blessedness of a mother's smile rests on them visibly, reddening on their cheeks, beaming in their eyes. To the right, the brood-hen has come fussing on the floor, followed by one or two chickens. Even these are cared for! But that feeble, trembling child stands alone, — homeless, uncared for, motherless. In all this, there is a felicitous truth, a telling lyrical contrast, such as I might hope for from a Burns, a Crabbe, or a Thom. And the artist has, with a wise tenderness, relieved the mere sadness of his story, by letting me know, in the softened look of the grandmother and the dewy smile of the mother, that the little stranger has this day found a home. These are my impressions of Mr. Faed's picture.

Thom. Exactly. And yet you pretend to be unable to form an opinion touching its merits! Is it not an extreme absurdity that people will stand by such a picture, the very tears in their eyes attesting their power of appreciation, and disclaim all right to have an opinion regarding it?

Smith. Ha! — I trust I have made my first step to the acquisition of that valuable human quality, conceit. But this picture is of the simplest kind, and I suppose I must not attempt to deny that men of natural feeling and ordinary culture may appreciate pictures of that school, of which the great Wilkie and the greater Hogarth are in Britain the legitimate masters. But I should be at a loss if you asked me to criticise the quality of the painting, strictly so called, even in this picture; and I am not sure that I should not be deceived into purchasing a poor copy of it after seeing the original. What have you to say to that?

Thom. We shall see. But you must not imagine that I pronounce extended acquaintance with pictures of no importance, or undervalue any kind of artistic knowledge accessible to people in general. I maintain, merely, that the knowledge which is necessary to the Artist, the entire range of those subjects which relate to the producing methods of Art,—the laws of perspective, of coloring, and so on,—are foreign to the sphere both of the beholder and the critic. This truth,—which I hold to be demonstrable, we may indirectly illustrate in the course of this our dialogue,—which, by the way, will, I hope, be rambling.

Smith. Oh, rambling by all means. You and I, I rather think, are not the men to converse in the linear dialectics of those hard fellows who talked under the Greek plane trees. Fancy, whim, the caprice of the moment, the suggestion of a word or glance, have a place in conversation. I believe that these are not only among the most potent of the elements which make airy, vivacious, sincere, confiding talk one of the supreme pleasures, but that they cast at times such revealing side-gleams upon truth and beauty, as bring out more subtle and pointed intellectual views, and more rare and delicate lights of loveliness, than can be obtained by the elaborate method of study and composition. It has sometimes occurred to me that the best things ever uttered may have been uttered in conversation; and it is my settled conviction that the conversation of men of culture, trained in the expression of their ideas, is very nearly as accurate — even formally and grammatically — as their published writings.

Thom. We shall not confine ourselves, then, to any stated topic, but glance generally round the horizon of Art, tarrying a little wherever an opening into the pure blue may draw our eyes with promise. But another word just now as to this deceivability by copies, which seems to lie so heavily upon you. The danger is neither so great nor so important as you imagine. You must remember, to begin with, that the difference between high, or even the highest truth and beauty, as embodied in a work of Art, and what is commonplace, may be not only not very easily perceptible but actually slight. It may be the dewdrop, scarcely noted by the eye, yet making one rose the fairest of the garden. It may be the inscrutable somewhat, of beauty and music, which renders one poem a household term, a nation's watchword, for ages, while another, in which you can hardly define an inferiority, is a mere fleeting popularity. It may be the nameless, indescribable expression, lending to one face a subduing and incomparable witchery, whose absence from another, with features of even higher order, leaves a countenance insipid and commonplace. The difference of a hair's-breadth in line may be that which sets Phidias and Michael Angelo at the head of sculpture: a diminution, if possible still less, in the ethereal mildness and saintly elegance of Raphael, might have cost him his throne among painters. Now I think the original may be distinguished from the copy, by bearing well in mind this last and exquisite difference, not to be defined in words. The master has rested on his work. There is in it a patient intensity of care. Its tints blend more delicately, more elusively, than in the copy. Its lines have either the sweep or the accuracy that belonged to but one hand. An artist, familiar with the operations of drawing and painting, may have peculiar skill in detecting a certain quality of lines as lines, or of colors as colors; and here the man devoid of technical knowledge is at a disadvantage. But a master is to be distinguished by his effect as well as his means, by the result as well as the processes by which it has been attained; — a certain depth and clearness of sky, neither more nor less, a certain truth of feeling, a certain approximation to the softness and the color of a living face. And on these points, a thorough acquaintance, on the one hand with nature, and on the other with this master's power of approaching her, is all that is required in order to ability to discriminate his work from a counterfeit. All this, I need not say, is distinct from technical power of hand or eye. Your knowledge must be accurate, your practice great, but neither the knowledge nor the practice demands any acquaintance with artistic methods. Have you not found this so? Do you not, after all, believe in your liability to be deceived, more because the connoisseurs tell you that it must attach to you, than from positive experience?

Smith. I am bound to confess that there is some truth in your words. And, in fact, for that matter, both artists and connoisseurs fall into error on the subject of originals and copies, to all appearance about as readily as ordinary mortals.

Thom. Of course. What is still more, this of distinguishing between copies and originals, though made very much of, is not of the first importance, after all. Art will never be much worth as an influence on the public mind, until we learn to respect work for its own sake, and not for the name it bears. The craftsman can never be an artist; the copyist does not necessarily share one spark of the genius of the master: but while I have the thought, the feeling, the truth of the artist conveyed to me by a copy, I shall prize the picture, just as I should the book, which, by means of types arranged by a nameless printer, transmits to me the thoughts of a Plato or a Luther. But we are again forgetting the pictures around us. You must allow me to throw the rein right over the neck of my enthusiasm as I look upon Mr. Faed's principal work of the year,—*Highland Mary*. This is one of those pictures for which I am ready to thank and bless an artist: so deep, so delicate, so pure is the pleasure it imparts; so beautiful and unsullied are the emotions it awakens; so sweetly attractive, so airy, so endless the imaginings it evokes; so thickly-crowding, so noble, so natural, the thoughts and associations it suggests. Highland Mary is on her way back from Ayrshire, and has already reached the mountains of native Argyllshire. She rests by the wayside. Around her are mountain flowers,—the fox-glove, the heath-bell. In the distance the view is closed in by the blue and gray of the hills. With one hand she draws closer round her her plaid of tartan. Her other rests on the little scarlet bundle in her lap. Her hair is bound by a simple blue braid, and the blue, gray, and russet of her dress combine into a pleasing harmony of color. Everything breathes a subdued but tender loveliness; not the loveliness of Greece, not the loveliness of Italy; not the loveliness of regal purple or queenly jewels; but that which lurks in the sequestered dell or about heathery braes, and which peeps out here and there from the cottage and the dress of the peasant. But this is not all. There is a picture within the picture. There is a central beauty, to which

19*

all the rest of the loveliness ministers, and up to which it leads. This is the face of the figure; that face of Highland Mary which beams on you from the hill side, holding you with its pensive beauty, so faultless yet so Scottish. The full, ripe lips are closed in silent kindliness and love, no Paphian curve expressing the consciousness or pride of beauty. On the cheek rests the color of the mountain rose, that indivisible blending of the dawn-red and the snow-white, which is nature's highest effort in hue. The eye, soft, deep blue, looks out in maiden purity beneath the unwrinkled maiden brow. Spread over the whole face, breathing through its every feature, what thought is that which is its life and spirit? Ah, we can guess it well! Highland Mary is dreaming of that strange Ayrshire youth from whom she lately parted; that swarthy youth with the glittering eye, in whose words dwelt so potent, so perilous a fascination. She thinks of Robert Burns. A thousand fancies and questions, of virgin pride, of womanly ambition, of glad, loving surmise, are whirling in summer tempest, spanned by its rainbow, through her breast. Further than this the poet-painter does not reveal: but who can hinder imagination from looking somewhat beyond, and seeing the lowly headstone in the highland churchyard, beneath which so soon were laid all the earthly hopes and loves of Highland Mary!

Smith. Permit me to express my decided hope that your Pegasean enthusiasm has finished its flight, and to congratulate you both on the emptiness of the rooms and the patience of your one listener. But Mr. Faed's is no doubt a beautiful picture, a work of unquestionable genius. Have you reflected on the seeming difficulty of painting a really beautiful female face? No manifestation of beauty exercises so entrancing a power over man. The grace of the forest, the color of the garden, the evening on the sea, the morning on the mountains,—all these possess but a feeble enchantment compared with that of the countenance of a lovely woman. I must add that the power to bring this beauty upon canvas is very rare among artists. Faed is one of the few painters who has an unerring eye for female beauty; among living painters he seems to be without an equal in this department. I trust that nothing may induce him to desert the manifest walk of his genius.

This picture pleases me, also, because it supports a little theory of mine, which, countryman as I am, has been discussed more than once at my fireside. In perception of what may be called typal loveliness, in capacity to apprehend abstract and, so to speak, geometrical beauty, particularly of the human face and form, the Greeks surpassed all nations. In the very accuracy of their perceptions here, might lie, partially at least, the cause of that restriction of their sympathy for the beautiful, which contrasts with the expansiveness of the Gothic spirit. Grant that there was a certain meagreness, a sameliness, a too scrupulous elegance, in their sense of beauty; grant that they bound the zone of Venus a little too tightly; yet I think you will find that with them lay the discovery of those essential, geometrical forms, of which all beauty in lines must be a modification. This face in Mr. Faed's picture is perfectly Scotch. The brown hair verging to golden, the cheek somewhat round and full, the general tendency to depart from the perfect oval,—these all abandon the Aphrodite model. Yet the Greek type is discernible. It is seen in the proportion and unity of the features, in the chiselling of the brow, in the delicate straightness of the nose. It is the Greek ideal of female loveliness, only not shaped from Ægean foam, or breathed on by Ægean breezes. It grew amid the mountain heather, and its cheek was visited by the rough wind of Scotland.

Thom. It is unpleasant to hint an objection to such a picture, and while Mr. Faed gives us such beauty, I for one have not the heart to bid him venture on any modification of his system. But what do you think of that background?

Smith. The mountains are certainly generalized. I cannot say I like generalization; but you know the connoisseurs are very terrifying on that subject.

Thom. We must be too severe neither with Mr. Faed nor with the connoisseurs. That the background of this picture is generalized, there can be no doubt. The painter evidently concentrated his power upon his figure, and left the trees and hills in great measure to the brush. Yet the generalization is not extreme. The mountains, you observe, are by no means strictly conventional, — in form at least. They are bold and serrated, true to the general type of the Argyllshire mica schists. Mr. Faed has evidently looked on these mountains, and that with a penetrating, mindful eye. So much on his behalf. To the connoisseurs it must be conceded, that their theory of generalization, if not true, is an apology for and aim at truth, — and finds its analogue in nature. What is that theory? It is that every picture should have one central interest, idea, object; that everything ought to be subordinated to this; and that, therefore, the painter should fling in his backgrounds in broad, general, conventional masses, lest the minute perfection of their painting arrest the attention of the beholder, and diminish the power of the central idea. Now, it is unquestionably true that nature teaches and pleases by single effects, keeping in view particular objects in particular cases, to the marked, though not entire, exclusion of others. The carolling of the birds in temperate climates, the songs of the linnet, the lark, the blackbird, are plainly intended to be delightful to man, and poets in all ages have testified to the completeness of success with which the intention has been carried out. It is equally manifest that the colors of tropical birds — the most brilliant of nature's colors, though inferior, in all qualities save brilliancy, to the color of flowers and precious stones — are intended to be a source of joy. I do not mean, of course, to assert that everything on earth is meant exclusively for man. The manifestation of his own glory and perfection is an all-sufficing end to the Creator. Yet is it true that man, in virtue of his Divine origin and relationship, has had his eye so far opened to the mystery of nature, that the mode in which he is affected by any natural phenomenon may lead him on by gentle hints to the intention of nature in the case. In the contrasted instances I have quoted, the unmistakable effect aimed at, in the one, was of sound, in the other, of color. And what I would have specially observed, is the singleness of the effect in either case. The plumage of the nightingale does not divert your attention from her note: you listen in vain for anything beyond an unmusical screech, from the bird that glances with dazzling flash through the gloom of southern forests. Look, again, to the vegetable world. Take the two great families, discriminated for Art, not for Science, of the flowers and the trees. Of all the ministers of beauty, pure and simple, flowers are the best accredited: their office in creation it is impossible to mistake. "What is the use of flowers?" This question, in its generally received implication, is one of the most foolish and ignoble which can be put. Economic use they have none. They are nature's living antithesis to economic use. They exist to be admired, looked at, loved. They are chalices of Divine workmanship, of purple, and scarlet, and liquid gold, from which man is to drink the pure joy of beauty. But remark that the whole attention of nature is concentrated on what is specifically and exclusively the flower, — on the part that blooms into color and breathes fragrance, — in cutting its petals, and touching them with pure and perfect hues. Whether you will or no, your attention is fixed on the colored part; you think not of the rest of the plant; it furnishes merely the stalk, it finds its sole merit in supporting the flower. That a rose is intended to glorify God in its color is to me as evident a truth as that man is intended to glorify Him in worship. When we turn to the trees, there is a broad, an unmistakable difference. Through all the kingdoms of inanimate nature, trees are peerless in form. The shape of the wave is beautiful, but it is samely. The forms of the clouds are beautiful and of utmost variety, but their beauty is vast and grand, not coming quickly home to the human mind, and not unfrequently stretching into long straight lines, or losing itself in shapeless hugeness. But the forms of forest foliage have a variety, whispering of nature's infinitude; they are precisely of a size, and are precisely so placed as to render them obvious to the eye; and, in their chastened, regulated, consummate beauty, they never fail. The birch, with nodding plumes as of the forest queen, and waving tresses as of the woodland maiden; the elm, with its imperial drapery, and majestic yet graceful port, a "Queen Elizabeth" among trees; the elastic, defiant, soaring beech, its boughs seeming to leap into the sky:—these, and how many others, present the finest compositions in abstract form presented in the whole range of inanimate nature. But here again a central purpose is unmistakably traceable. There are no flowers now to draw the eye from the arching of the leaves and the grouping of the boughs;

no local intensity, no concentration of color, prevents it from resting calmly on the broad sweeps of green which robe but conceal not the majesty of the form. Among trees themselves, a manifestation of the same law of unity — or rather a thousand manifestations — may be found. The fruit tree has no fineness of form, nor is it valuable as timber; but what it wants in form and timber, it makes up in flower and fruit. Its wood is valueless compared with that of the oak, its form paltry compared with that of the elm: but no tree of the forest can boast of apple-bloom in spring, and the golden and roseate offerings of many an autumn atone for the worthlessness of the fallen trunk.

To conclude this whole matter, so far as nature is concerned, — the provinces of creation, in the illimitable variegation of their beauties, are filled with separate unities, with accomplished individual aims, not with one vast uniformity. Nature is always perfect; but perfect in her wholes; part is related to part, and the less beautiful has given the oil of its own waning lamp to kindle the greater flame of loveliness.

I should transgress all bounds if I attempted to inquire at length into the manner in which Art embodies and reflects the laws of nature. But I think we shall agree in not entertaining a doubt as to the general principle, that nature's laws of beauty reappear in human sympathy with beauty. The universal law I have noted has in all ages found its counterpart, its echo, in the universal and importunate demand made by the human instinct in every department of Art for unity. In all poetry, from the epigram to the epic, unity is indispensable. Whether in the single glimpse of thought, the momentary thrill of feeling, or in describing the ruin of planets and the procession of creations, there must always be the restraining, governing, unifying law. The thought may be sharpened into a single epigrammatic dagger: then it must not be beaten into length or breadth, or overladen with jewelry; and it must have no rust to dim its keen glittering, or to eat off its invisible edge. The feeling may be one pulse of emotion to dance, like a gush of summer lightning, along the veins: then it must be poured forth in one lyric swell, every word a note of music, every line a gleam of light. Or an immeasurable variety both of thought and emotion may have to be portrayed; philosophy, religion, love, may pass and repass on the page: but here too, every episode must be governed by one central law; and the most uncultured taste will be offended, in profound unconsciousness as to the reason why, if a single incident, a single sentiment, a single thought, is knit to the central purpose by no traceable affinity, catches no gleam of an all-suffusing light. In the case of painting it is emphatically true that there is no departure from this universal law of Art. Take the most unsophisticated man you can find; place him before a canvas in which there is a multitude of figures, each exquisitely painted, but engaged neither in any one pursuit interesting them all, nor in a variety of pursuits coalescing in one general idea (as in a fair); let the soldier be seen in this corner, burnishing his arms to attack no foe, the merchant in that, erecting his booth on the sea-shore; let there be a specimen from every order of craftsmen, each separate from all the rest and each engaged in objectless labor:—how will he be affected? He will declare that it is a collection of pictures within a single frame, or a stupid agglomeration and no picture at all. The necessity of a single aim and interest is most obvious in the case of human subjects; but the law holds good also in landscape. Now it is just an attempt to carry out this law of nature and of Art which has resulted in the academic canon of generalization. Your central idea, it is argued, must be prominent, must arrest and rivet attention; therefore, in painting your picture, all the skill you can command must, in human subjects, be devoted to your most important figure, and in landscape to your most prominent object. The argument and aim were right: of the inference from the argument, of the mode of attaining the aim, I have something to say not by any means of a complimentary nature.

Smith. Well, well: — this last remark is to the point. Grant that the object had in view in the accepted method of generalization is a correct one, will that avail you much in defending the connoisseurs? Have not errors always, or almost always, lain in methods? Have not aims generally been right? The method of imparting unity of idea and interest to a picture, by putting in a false background, I assert to be utterly and in every way wrong, — unnatural, pernicious, preposterous. It is unnatural: for nature has attained her object in a way perfectly different, a way which may be defined in one word as, The establishment of a relation of more and less, among incidents, forms, colors, in their own excellence, and in their power over human sympathy. Thus, at the head of all interest, nature places human interest: the grandest scenery, of precipice and cloud and forest, never attracted a lover as the smile in his loved one's eye. In other provinces of creation, her most delicate form and her richest color are relieved by forms and colors which are in themselves not so exquisite or so pure. Her finish is always the same; the rose leaf is finished as the rose petal; but the pink and white has a natural, an inherent supremacy over the plain green. The distinction between nature's plan and that of the generalizer is exceeding broad, and of the last importance in Art; it has an appearance of subtlety, but it is really obvious if we give it fair and earnest consideration. The generalizers precisely evade the problem proposed and worked out by nature ; and by so doing, spread a vail between themselves and all the regions of the Beautiful. Nature gives all her forms and colors fair play ; but so *arranges* them that your eye, while gazing impartially over her prospect, is drawn by a sweet, mild, unconscious, but irresistible compulsion, to what is intrinsically noblest in form and hue. The academic generalizer finds it extremely difficult to discover the truly natural subordination of thought to thought, emotion to emotion, form to form, color to color. This demands long and searching observation and deep reflection. He cannot trust to *his* lovers for an interest greater than that of the oak under which they whisper ; he cannot trust to *his* cataract for an interest greater than the copse by its side. So he turns his oak into broad splashes of green, and his copse into broad daubs of brown. Thus his method is unnatural. It is pernicious: for, by its legalized blunder, it altogether turns away the artist from the right path of natural study. It prevents him from catching sight of nature's chief Art-secret, from learning her cunning method of unity. It accustoms him to all manner of degrading and enfeebling slovenliness. It causes him, as a true bungler, to say aloud, *this* I want you to observe, *this* mountain I specially painted, *this* rose I elaborately handled: whereas nature is always majestically silent, leading the eye to the mountain by the soft smile of its own blue, and not plucking off or misshaping her leaves that the eye may rest on her roses. Thus his method is pernicious. It is preposterous, for, when Art-culture has made the slightest progress, it certainly defeats itself. At whatever prospect we look, whether a picture or no, the eye can, at any one moment, rest only on one point. This is a physiological law, unvarying and indisputable. In looking over a natural landscape, I am, suppose, attracted by a group of human figures. That group alone, I, for the moment, see. All other things are in a certain indistinct light around it. But I am not physically able to look long on any one point. I naturally cast my eye around. What then happens? The scene becomes definite. I discover no interference with the general aspect of nature; clouds, hills, houses, are all in their proper places and in their perfect forms. Looking upon these, my eye is rested; my attention gently relaxes; probably without any conscious emotion whatever, I turn again to the centralizing group. How is it in the picture of the academic generalizer? While the eye rests exclusively on the one portion which he has ventured to paint correctly, all may be so far well. But in a moment it wanders over the other parts of the picture. Then it is startled, disturbed, pained, by meeting an impossibility, a wild agglomeration of forms that form have none, and hues unknown to nature. It is deluded of the repose it seeks. It is not softly conducted from the pinnacle to the plain. It is called, instead, to contemplate something new in this world. The hills, the trees, the clouds, are no longer hills, trees, or clouds. The hills have permitted themselves to be pounded into dust; the trees have been mashed up for the sake of their green and brown; the clouds have kindly had themselves condensed, to yield a liquid medium for the æsthetic amalgam; and the result is a surprising and afflicting phantasmagoria, suggesting only some hideous and unprecedented convulsion in all the elements.

Thom. To all that I must assent. It is indeed difficult to exaggerate the pernicious influence of this theory of generalization. By rightly using the backgrounds of nature, an incalculable accession of power might accrue to a picture. The pale moon setting beyond the white wave, lends only a deeper sadness to the human sorrow which Burns breathes through his poem. Let us really see a few sufferers clinging in despair to a wreck that tosses in mid ocean, far from any shore; and the sun setting behind them in blood, and casting a burning glare over the cruel sea, will but enhance our feeling of the human anguish. Every aspect, phenomenon, and mood of nature takes a light from human sympathy; "ours is the wedding garment, ours the shroud;" the poet-painter might bring unnumbered voices of dewdrop and sunbeam, of wild wave and lightning gleam, to blend their silent but expressive accents with the main thought or emotion of his picture.

Smith. Talking of generalization, and of the methods of nature, what do you think of the pre-Raphaelite pictures?

Thom. I am inclined to venture on the paradoxical looking answer, that there are no pre-Raphaelite pictures.

Smith. No pre-Raphaelite pictures! Either argue me out of my eyesight, or explain.

Thom. I mean that pre-Raphaelitism has hitherto done little or nothing. I recognize the principle; I have little faith in the men.

Smith. O,—and you like to be antithetic;—well, go on.

Thom. I see many things in pre-Raphaelitism, but this first and best of all: a new earnestness in Art taking the right direction. I shall not separate the direction from the earnestness, because I like to believe that there was an original and causal connection between the two. An intense and lofty devotion to Art arose among certain students; it at once sent them to nature: in nature their earnestness found its fitting and fostering aliment. One cannot but experience a glow of sympathy with those young men of "stubborn instincts," who rebelled against the stepmother academy, and rushed to the bosom of the mighty mother herself. Seldom has a pursuit led to no great results, never has it failed to lay a giant grasp on the heart of man, when followed in the spirit which sent Holman Hunt from the luxury and adulation of a London season to take up his station with the vultures in the white blaze of a desert sun, by the wan glare of an accursed sea, merely in order that the look of lorn and lonely despair with which it lies swooning under its pestilential atmosphere, might be brought to his canvas. Such resolution and courage I shall honor, though as yet their achievement is slight.

Smith. Very good. But neither earnestness of application nor nobleness of devotion ensure exemption from radical error; and radical error at the commencement will turn into mockery all hopes of subsequent excellence. Bear this, if you please, in mind.

Thom. Do n't be alarmed; grant me, also, a few minutes all to myself, even though I seem to forget the fundamental law of conversation, — that there be no engrossing. The doctrine of pre-Raphaelitism I take to be, that whatever is painted should be done as well as the artist can, and that nature is the great educator. It would not be far wrong to say that pre-Raphaelitism is a rebellion against the false theory of generalization; that, in its true interpretation, as given, for instance, in the works of Ruskin, it is a proclamation of the great Art-law of unity. Since this is the chief organic law, the Magna Charta, of Art, there is no dishonor, but much honor, due to pre-Raphaelitism in thus defining it. In speaking of the new school, therefore, I shall, in some sense, carry out what we have already said on the express subject of generalization.

Not contending for absolute accuracy, and bearing always in mind that there are no geometrical lines, no museum cases, in nature, we find all painters divide themselves into three broad classes. Of course they are mingled and modified in all sorts of ways, but never mind that. The first is the class of the simple narrators; the second that of the selectors; the third that of the inventors, the color-*poets.*

Painters belonging to the first of these orders engage in the mere express delineation of whatever is characteristic of the general life of their generation; its interiors, its costume, its architecture. Such delineation must ever continue an honorable and important occupation. The human mind, striving with an earnestness proportioned to its general nobleness and capacity, to make itself at home in all centuries, must prize whatever enables it to effect, with vividness and certainty, this domestication. What would we give to have such representations of Greek and Roman, or, still more precious, of Jewish interiors, at the time, say, of the spread of Christianity, distinct and accurate as the Flemish interiors of Jan Steen and Ostade? All portrait-painting might be claimed for this class, and if we once concede the claim, how high in honor and estimation does it rise! If, however, the claim were exclusive, it could not on any account be acknowledged: and it is unnecessary to press it, since it is quite certain that painters simply of what is seen, in its bare actual realization, will always be popular in their own generation, and esteemed by those which follow. In the popular mind, it is probable, the love of imitation is as powerful as any of the instincts gratified in Art, and to this instinct the painters in question are the declared and perpetual ministers. Interest in the past is also undying, and on it these painters may depend for their estimation in succeeding times. But it is undeniable that paintings of things as they are, indiscriminatingly taken, if belonging to Art at all, and not exclusively to artisanship, occupy the lowest rank. The reason of this is distinct and conclusive; — that the power they demand is purely mechanical, that of hand and eye, and that they afford no sphere to the free will, to the originating or altering capacity of man.

The next great class of painters, I have called the selectors. Their reliance is not placed upon any mere power of imitation, although power of imitation is indispensably necessary. What is ordinary, they pass by. They look for the rare, the exceptional, the excelling, and it they paint. I speak of their choice of whole subjects, not of their mode of securing interest in individual pictures. They select: I do not say they generalize. Academic generalization is always wrong: selection rightly performed is always right. In every landscape nature subordinates form to form, working every form perfectly out: but nature has some landscapes more beautiful than others. It is true that there is beauty in all. But this is a dangerous commonplace, and I rather imagine that those who very much use it — there are exceptions, of course — have no very delicate sense of beauty in any case. All loveliness, as presented to the human mind, influences by degree, and displays itself by contrast. The dripping, cheerless clouds, with but a few touches of livid blue breaking their monotony of ashy gray, are not so beautiful, and were not intended by nature to be thought so beautiful, as those same clouds, when the wind has gently waved them into valleys and avenues, and the bounteous sun has flung abroad upon them his varied light, here clustering into roses, there gleaming into gold. The broad, blunted features of the clodhopper, the dim, relaxed features of the sluggard, are not to be called beautiful beside the delicately cut features, the mantling color, the radiant expression, of such a face as one may see once in a year or a lifetime. The dreary, drizzling, colorless day sets off the azure and vermilion of its evening. The heavy, ill-proportioned features, the blunt lines and torpid expression, of a thousand faces, contribute power to the one face of dazzling beauty. And in the case of beauty, as elsewhere, nature is most bountiful to him who appreciates her gifts, and who, by long, resolute, concentrated study, makes them his own. Were that vague, monotonous loveliness a characteristic of nature, man might cast on the world a heedless and wandering gaze. Its beauty would not vanish; there would be nothing to unvail, nothing to be discovered. But now the choicest natural beauties are momentary glances, evanescent as glorious; nature's smiles have to be watched and waited for; the eye must train itself to see, the mind to remember. Doubt it not, the most worthy student of nature, he who shows for the works of God the most pure and reasonable reverence, is not he who pays to the beauty of the world a general, indiscriminate admiration, but he who has listened well to nature's voice, who has learned to distinguish her degrees of beauty, who has been handed from the lichen to the daisy, from the daisy to the heather-bell, from the heather-bell to the lily, from the lily to the rose, until, passing from loveliness to loveliness, he has at last attained to such glimpses of the purest, highest beauty, as might touch the eye of an angel with rapturous fire. Here, of course, one man is originally gifted more exquisitely than another: and he who, to a peculiar sensibility to beauty, adds a rare perseverance in its culture, is the man who will excel as a painter of the second class. He is the commissioned of his fellow-men to be a spy upon nature: to visit her in her solitudes; to steal upon her at eventide when she is shedding her faintest, tenderest purples into the mountain valleys; to mark the streaming of the light over unseen mists in the gorges of remote hills; to trace the glittering cloud edges, as they break into white fire in the glance of the lightning. If he deals with human subjects, it is his to note the manifestation of mighty and noble passion; to arrest forever the gleam of strange, flitting light which glances along the features, when a sudden throb of uncontrollable emotion strikes the heart. He goes, too, into the paths of common life, looking there for what is honorable, and lovely, and of good report. Whatever he deems worthy of choice, he paints. But he is not original save in the exercise of choice. Once give him his subject, and he paints it with literal exactness.

Whole schools of painting belong to this second class, — conspicuous among them, the Dutch and Flemish. Ruysdael and Cuyp are admirable examples. Mr. Ruskin speaks of the works of Ruysdael as furniture pictures, void of all the higher attributes of Art. Neither for Cuyp has he any great affection. Were it not that profound stupidity has no tendency to modesty, this fact might have made it impossible for *critics* of Mr. Ruskin to tell the world that all he cares for is finish, and that for its own sake. But this by the way. Be the pictures of Ruysdael and Cuyp what they may, they have been long, widely, and profoundly popular; and while adducing them as examples of their class, I would point to them also as incontestably proving our second class of painters fitted to exercise a very powerful influence upon the human mind. It seems impossible for an unsophisticated mind not to be arrested and delighted by the works of Ruysdael. Yet wherefore is it so? Wherein lies their charm? If you wandered bodily by that wood beside the moor, with the sparse sunbeams struggling here and there through its foliage — if your eye rested on that moorland, bleak and brown, as it actually presented itself to the eye of Ruysdael, with its bit of black road, and its one pool so dead and murky — would you not hurry on, glancing carelessly at the whole scene, uninduced even by that ruin, seen by the struggling sunlight through the trees, to linger for a moment? Or if you stood by the original of this torrent, in another picture, with one or two uninteresting cottages on the hill side above, a few larches, somewhat tattered looking, on the river bank, and a broken stem or two lying across the current, would you think the scene, though perhaps deserving a look, worthy of being long and heedfully observed? Surely not. Yet here you are enchained. If not enraptured, you at least experience an intense pleasure. Why, I say, is this? Is it not because a touch of nature makes the whole world kin, and here nature is rendered in all the plainness of her truth? The slightest effort of imagination bears you away to Ruysdael's moorland, spreading bleak and brown under those sullen, lowering clouds. His earth has the very look of nature's surfaces — not glazed, not rolled out in smooth uniformity, the green all enamel, the black all jet, but rough and fretted, as nature's surface always is, with its millions of points, singly invisible, of grass-blade, reed, and heather. His clouds have the mass and depth, the light and shade, of cumulous clouds, and that look of laggard dreariness, which those clouds wear on a chill, gloomy day, threatening rain. His torrent, though it takes from the dull gray of the sky a dissatisfying bluish dimness, where you looked for bright, leaping spray, is yet true under its own sky, and you feel that those larches actually grow by that grumbling northern stream. Limited as Ruysdael's range may be, you cannot but see that what landscapes he selected he painted, so far as bare truth was concerned, with consummate power. If you find, as I do, any fascination in the particular scenes he depicts, he will appear to you to have done no mean work.

For Cuyp, too, let me speak a word. He must, indeed, have been, in some sense, a dull man. If nature could be consulted, she would surely declare the man who could see and love but one of her aspects, who was contented to paint during his whole life one of her innumerable phases, a votary not worth having. I do not remember any picture of Cuyp's, and pictures by Cuyp are to be found in every collection, in which there was not a broad yellow light streaming from the left. Always, I think, that light touched, with a faint copper color, the tops of stately cumulous clouds, piled up, their domes towards sunset, in the repose of evening. Yet Cuyp's monotony has not deprived him of popularity, nor ought it entirely to have done so. There was a power in his dullness. He set himself to paint his one effect with unflagging assiduity; and he painted it, as it appears to me, with consummate success.

This second class of painters is the widest of any. It embraces all the men of unquestionable talent, but not high genius. I hold them in great honor. In their inability to paint more than one effect variously modified, I find an attestation of the infinitude by which the works of God excel the works of man. Their endowment is certainly beyond the common; their perseverance is indomitable; yet they spend their whole lives in attempting to trace and imitate one touch of the Divine finger! There are of course many living painters who belong to this class. Cooper, Lee, Cooke, and others without end, able, meritorious artists, are men possessing, so to speak, one piece of knowledge. You can tell precisely what each sees in nature. Lee paints everything as if it had been "washed, just washed, in a shower." He takes his palette to the fields in the intervals of the showers that drift before the west winds of June. Green, gray, blue, — these are his colors. Cooper is as fond of yellow sunlight as Cuyp, whom, indeed, he seems to have closely studied. His cows are of the color of tortoise-shell, and you may be sure of the dreamy yellow of afternoon on his skies and streams. Cooke keeps to nearly the same color as Cooper, with the modification enforced by the nature of his marine views. A pale yellow illumination is about all his skies and clouds, — now and then, perhaps, fading into gray.

Smith. Allow me to interrupt you for a moment. I once happened to look at a landscape in this Academy, by which I was not a little puzzled. The sky, the clouds, the trees, were certainly the painting of Lee. But where had Lee got those yellow lights, those broad pale gleams, changing the tone of the whole picture? The cattle, on the other hand, the yellow tones here and there, were Cooper's, but how had Cooper stolen a march upon Lee, whence had he got the west wind shower to wash up his picture? A glance at the catalogue resolved the mystery. The landscape was Lee's: the cattle were Cooper's.

Thom. Thank you. The case is precisely in point. I have only to add, as to this class of painters, that all which has been said of them as landscapists applies to them, with obvious modification, as painters of life. Caravaggio's gamblers answer precisely to Cuyp's evenings and Cooper's cows.

There is a third class of painters, the inventors, the poets. It is an inalienable attribute of man that he can modify, recombine, adorn nature. He casts a gleam from his crown as king of the world. To recur to Coleridge's matchless thought, he breathes over earth the music of his bridals, and compels its melodies to take a tone from his funeral wails. Raphael's Madonna did not altogether grow amid the Italian mountains. The most skilful daguerreotypist of our nineteenth century could not bring a Madonna like Raphael's from any valley of the Appenines or any plain of Italy. The angelic mildness of the eye, looking in satisfied, unchanging gaze of love and adoration on the face of that Child in her arms, — the saintliness and hallowed purity of all around the still group, — the sweet and tender loveliness of the maid-mother's face,—these were Raphael's own. And in the case of every painter among the mightiest, there is this something added, which gives its last glory to the picture. To expatiate upon this highest class of artists is needless, since its existence will be disputed in no criticism worth opposition, and its works cannot be easily mistaken.

Smith. Have you forgotten that this is all an introduction to your answer to my question about pre-Raphaelitism? May I ask whether the length of the reply is to be inferred from its introductory exercitation?

Thom. Do n't be impatient. I have not lost my reckoning. What I have been saying is not exclusively, or even strictly, an introduction; and so far as it is, be so good as to compare it to a winding avenue, that opens upon a country mansion. You take some time to thread the approach; but once you reach its end, you embrace the house in one brief glance. Now for that glance.

Apply the grand pre-Raphaelite principle, that whatever is painted should be painted as well as the painter can, in each of the provinces of Art that we have been surveying. Since I must take it for granted that the academic theory of generalization has been demolished, it is unnecessary to inquire whether this is the only true principle for the guidance of painters of the first two classes. The question is of the third class. Does not pre-Raphaelitism of necessity cabin, crib, confine the greatest minds? Rightly understood, it does not so, by any means. Perhaps, in its most important aspect, it is an educational principle; and as such, its main value lies in *destroying* erroneous and pernicious principles of Art-education. There has been from time immemorial, in the schools of Art, a fatal confusion between two kinds or divisions of training; that which is mechanical and reducible to rules, and that which relates to things not mechanical, and which cannot be done by rule. There is a certain amount of intellectual culture, a certain attainment in intellectual excellence, which one generation can transmit to another with precisely the same ease and certainty as a method of ploughing or an improved system of rotation in crops. But there is a province in human affairs, in which teaching, whatever it may do, can never get the length of prescribing rules; in which the influence of education must be indirect and informal. This province is that of the poetic, the creative imagination, answering to that of the inventive intellect. It is specially the province of Art as distinguished from any sort of artisanship. As well appoint rules for invention in manufactures, as draw up canons by which *great* pictures may be produced. In other provinces of exertion this great principle is recognized. The fallacy which from time immemorial has covered our exhibition walls with *Deluges*, and *Lears*, and *Orpheuses*, which has kept ordinary men, age after age, attempting to puff themselves into genius, has never drawn breath in healthier atmospheres, where no dilettantism turned aside the searching but salubrious influence of the popular gale. The human mind has always, in the might of its unsophisticated instincts, spurned the idea of a *poem* written by rule. Fancy a lyric constructed upon scientific principles! Fancy a lark instructed out of Whewell how to flap his wings, or a nightingale conning the theory of music! Might not an epic be put together in an age when mechanical invention has got so far? "For your tempest, take Eurus, Zephyr, Auster, and Boreas, and cast them together in one verse; add to them, of rain, lightning, and thunder (the loudest you can), *quantum sufficit.* Mix your clouds and billows well together till they foam, and thicken your description here and there with a quicksand. Brew your tempest well in your head, before you set it a blowing. For a battle, pick a large quantity of images and descriptions from Homer's Iliad, with a spice or two of Virgil, and if there remain any overplus, you may lay them by for a skirmish. Season it well with similes, and it will make an excellent battle." You remember Swift's exquisite humor. And will not all men laugh with him at the absurdity involved in this "Recipe for an Epic?" But Art has ever yet been the possession of comparatively a few; and in painting, it is quite possible, by adherence to certain rules, of composition in form, and harmony in color, to produce pictures pleasing the eye and satisfying a mediocre taste. Hence your regular crop of mock sublimities from year to year: hence the oversight of that axiom of all Art-criticism and Art-education, that the distinguishing character and very essence of genius lies in the impossibility of attaining its results by rule, in the vanity of all attempts to steal its celestial fire and set it to burn in the cast-iron grates of mediocrity. The word, "conventionality," is very much in use at present, and I have no doubt that very little meaning is in many cases attached to it: but I consider all conventionality, so far as it is evil, to consist simply in the accumulation of methods by which genius may be mimicked. Now true pre-Raphaelitism—the pre-Raphaelitism of Ruskin — appeals from the hoary conventionalism of Art-teaching to nature, declares that rules can never produce great pictures, and maintains that the one infallible method of securing sound work — plain, valuable artisanship if the worker is but an artisan, the invaluable fruits of genius if he is a born artist — is to hold to nature, and paint what is seen. Is not this a principle, "which to look at is to love?"

Smith. True, true; but do you not at least imply an oversight of part of the truth? Can you dissociate past effort from present study? Will you assert that I can derive no benefit from knowing how my fellow-men of past generations looked on the face of nature? Will you pronounce *present* knowledge of natural phenomena, *present* discovery of more excellent Art-methods, of the highest importance, yet tacitly affirm that neither fact nor principle can be so assuredly ascertained, as to be transmitted to posterity? Nature, with all her demand for labor, has a grand motherly habit of thrift, by which she encourages, rewards, dignifies toil. Newton sets his foot easily, for a second ascent, upon the principle, to discover which was a long and painful task for Archimedes. Watt does not re-invent steam before he invents the steam engine. Can you wholly exclude this law from the province of Art?

Thom. By no means; and allow me to say that I think I have already said enough to indicate how far and in what sense it is either admitted or excluded. No sort of Art-education, pre-Raphaelite or other, can confer the creative capacity of genius: Archimedes did not tell Newton *how* he had discovered; Milton, schoolmaster as he was, could teach no pupil to write a *Paradise Lost.* But this prevents not that a thousand ordinary mathematicians, between Archimedes and Newton, apply to useful purposes the discoveries of the former. Now it is impossible wholly to dissever Art from mere workmanship; the pure spirit must dwell in a temple of clay: and the greatest genius, if he had to paint a house or a man, would act absurdly by attempting to re-invent all his processes and rules. Only, if his province is that of real Art, he can breathe the new life into the old form, and to do that no rules will avail him.

Smith. Well: but will study of nature enable him to do this either?

Thom. You think that a clincher. I answer without any hesitation, No. By learning accurately to paint all the earth and all the sky, a man would learn to produce painted landscapes capable of affording great pleasure and information to his fellow-men; but he would never necessarily learn to produce a work of Art. I might find it difficult to establish this proposition, but for the stores of instance afforded me by the history of painting. With these I can have no difficulty. The Dutch painters have shown the world what workmanship can attain without genius. The daguerreotype has shown it still better. These give nature, but not the poetry of nature. Turner's *Temple of Minerva Sunias* gives nature and the poetry of nature also; it is a work of Art. By study of the works of bygone artists, encouragement, suggestion, awakening, may be found for genius; therefore such study is good: only it must be remembered that nature is the great check upon human influence, that she furnishes the test of accepted truth, and is the source of every truth that is new.

Smith. Now what would you say if I pronounced you at your conclusion a little further off than you were at your commencement? You seem to have left very little of distinctive character to your pre-Raphaelitism.

Thom. Why, if you so pronounced, I should simply say you are not so shrewd a man as I take you for. You are very well aware that the two things invariably and essentially opposed to truth are novelty and paradox. Ruskin and the pre-Raphaelites cannot be accused of having propounded any new-fangled, unheard of idea. They proclaim an ancient and substantial truth; and it is as representing and promoting a reaction towards this truth, that they can claim a position of their own. A conventionalism, piled fold after fold for centuries, had stiffened and benumbed the limbs of Art. This fact must be borne in mind in contemplating the whole phenomenon of pre-Raphaelitism. Had not Mr. Ruskin opened the eyes of all who will see to its certainty, the fact of established conventionalism might take long to prove. But it is now preposterous to call it in question. Surely, surely, in all reason and honesty, it must be admitted that the old traditions and admirations retarded Art, lowered and deadened the general sense of artistic truth, produced pictures without number whose greatness was a sham, and evoked applause without end which was an hypocrisy. The Claudes, the Salvators, the Poussins sat on their hero-thrones, their sceptres, whether leaden or golden, stretched out to protect placid absurdities, with their scholars, surrounded by all their ghastly paraphernalia of extinct classicism, manufacturing "great" pictures at their feet. Only conceive the power of that moral and intellectual narcotic, through which men came not only to tolerate but to praise those landscapes, for instance, which the said masters called after Scripture subjects? The picture was called *The Marriage of Isaac and Rebecca*, *The Sacrifice of Isaac*, *The Departure of the Queen of Sheba to visit Solomon*, or by some such name. The painter put in his modern villas, harbors, and trees, and when he had finished, you had to search the picture over and over, until you lighted on a miserable figure or two in a corner, in some trivial or despicable attitude, representing the artist's conception of some one or other of the most solemn and interesting incidents in human story. I have seen a picture by Salvator Rosa called *Paul preaching in the Wilderness*. The apostle has precisely the look of a vulgar, crusty, petulant monk, and he points to a couple of crossed sticks in his hand, representing a rude cross. The scene is a rocky gorge after the manner of Salvator, and such as might have existed in the country of the Galatians. Imagine Paul addressing those same Galatians with a cross in his hand by way of illustrating his doctrine! Read his letter to those mountaineers, and inquire into the truth, say rather the complicated, outrageous falsehood, of Salvator's picture. Now I do not of course blame the painters for such things as these. The civilization of their time admitted and encouraged such falsities. Nor do I forget that there are abstract qualities of hue and line. But was there not need for a reaction, when men, on the intellectual level of the nineteenth century, were told to take such men as infallible models, and when imitations of their manner were set apart in a specially great school? The Art of Great Britain is passing through a transition period. It experienced of old, more or less, the paralyzing effect of an excessive conventionalism. The truth and beauty which former masters had perceived and exhibited was not estimated in itself or valued for its own sake. Instead of this, the reverence for authority, for men, for names, entered in.

Painting surrendered its freedom and its originality in a species of hero-worship. But Ruskin and the pre-Raphaelites sent artists back to the fountains of nature. They proclaimed again that all truly great, all nobly ideal Art must arise out of the real; that over the gaunt skeleton of material fact must the elastic muscle, the trembling nerve, the vital blood, the mantling bloom, of artistic creation lie. Re-invigorated by converse with nature, Art may again turn to the old masters; not now to worship, but to examine, to see, to know, to admire, to learn. It will watch the first efforts of Cimabue, the dawning glory of Giotto, the softened splendor, surely a noonday splendor, of Raphael. It will mark Claude as he "sets the sun in heaven," and follow to the fields the hardy workers of Holland. It will watch the hand of every great and honest man who ever painted.

It can hardly be conceived that the simultaneous appearance of Ruskinism, pre-Raphaelitism, and photography is not destined to yield some great result. That simultaneousness may reverently be held to have been providential. All three send Art in the same direction, — to nature. Photography is gradually becoming perfect in the rendering, not only of faces, trees, and buildings, but of the great forms of landscape. The eye finds so much delight in color, that it is not in the least surprising that the brown and white of large photographs should not be generally admired or liked, or that they should be unable at first to enter the lists of popularity against pictures. But as the eye accustoms itself to dispense with the charm of color, and learns to dwell on the abstract forms revealed by the photographer, the beholder experiences a profound delight. I have been myself positively surprised at the increasing sense of beauty, grandeur, majesty, with which I have looked upon Alpine photographs. The silent, stable masses, resting in their colossal strength on the foundations of the world, — the faint, diffused shade, drawing me on into the depths of solemn valleys, — the rich variety of the pine foliage on the lower reaches of the hills; — these have come by degrees to afford me an exquisite pleasure. This is nature in her own majesty. She is disrobed of the mantle of Art; and methinks it is hardly flattering to one's human pride to find how well the human drapery can be dispensed with. It may be that the universal presence, in prints and pictures, of *some* added element —whether the imperfection of incompetency, the mistake of conventionalism, or, if you will, the poetry of genius — gives a special zest to representations in which this is wanting. It may even be that the literal forms of nature have in themselves an august beauty which man has as yet, generally speaking, failed not only to improve but to equal. But however it is, I confess I find more nourishment for eye and soul, in a few good photographs of Swiss scenery, than in a similar number of prints or pictures. Depend upon it, as the public eye becomes, by means of pre-Raphaelite paintings, of photographic views, and, let me add, of modern facilities in beholding the hills and rivers of nature, accustomed to fact, the craving for more truth in the works of artists will become too general and too intense to be resisted. The old ideal of landscape will be unable to maintain itself. It must either pass away or learn to embody all the fresh knowledge of the time. That there is a possibility of this being done, even of a grandeur being added to all that nature can display, I have no doubt whatever. A future of unexampled glory *may* await Art.

Smith. Let me add a word as to the dangers to which pre-Raphaelitism is peculiarly exposed. Of the mistake of offering or accepting correct studies as pictures, and of that of drawing not only feature but expression from models, I cannot speak. These have simply to be mentioned, as indefensible and fatal. But there is a subtler and more comprehensive error than these, of which pre-Raphaelites would do well to beware. I mean the error of dishonoring the creative imagination, confounding it with a mere combination of accuracy of memory and power of eye and hand. Memory and imagination are essentially distinct. The one is indeed the handmaid of the other, the serviceable, the indispensable handmaid; but the handmaid cannot change places with the mistress. Memory brings the materials and lays them out; it may be in systematic arrangement, it may be in chaotic disorder; imagination looks upon them, and they are grouped into unity or spring to life. Mere mechanical order becomes living harmony, and disorder subsides into a world. All those lights of natural beauty, all those truths of symmetry and form, which the Greek imagination embodied in Aphrodite, could be catalogued and counted over by memory. The bend of the sea-wave, the white foam, mantling, in the sunlight, into rose-bloom, the laughing light that danced in a thousand smiles over the broad front of ocean, might all have been chronicled and remembered, yet remained forever dead and apart. But imagination comes upon the scene. Lo! the bending wave is a moving arm; the snow of the foam and the tints of its rainbows blend in a living cheek; the many-twinkling laughter of the sea is gathered into the witching eye of Aphrodite. Take another example. A most powerful and touching description could be drawn out in detail of the horrors of popular commotion, of anarchic revolution. The poverty occasioned by the obstruction of steady industry might be depicted; the number of the slain might be specified, and the miserable manner of their death described; the destruction of ancient dynasties, the conflagration of opulent cities, the blackening of fertile provinces, might be dwelt on in all the ghastliness of their coloring and all the minuteness of their detail. In all this, memory alone might have been at work. A totally different faculty is in operation when Coleridge annihilates, by one stroke of consummate perfection, all descriptions of popular madness, in these brief words:—

> "Lo! the giant Frenzy,
> Uprooting empires with his whirlwind arm,
> Mocketh high heaven."

To say how, precisely, this faculty works is what no critic ought to attempt, and what he who possesses it most might be of all least able to do. But as to its radical difference from memory, no question can be entertained. Pre-Raphaelitism, rightly understood, does not endanger the distinction. By recognizing it in all its force, Mr. Ruskin has both exhibited to those willing or able—which you like—to follow him, the completeness and symmetry of his system, and set whole nests of hornet-critics, whose characteristic is that they can fasten upon but one point at once, buzzing about his ears. He hailed pre-Raphaelitism as mighty, because it companied with truth; he gazed wondering upon the imaginative "dream," as it bodied itself out under the pencil of Turner. "Why," buzzed the hornets, "this man, this Turner, is among the mists on the mountain's brow; these pre-Raphaelites have stuck their palettes among the weeds at its foot, and paint as with microscopes: how can any one pretend to admire and approve of both?" Ruskin, with the eye of true critical genius, embraced the whole mountain from brow to base. Turner he saw far up among the mists, which turned to glory round him: between his station and that of the pre-Raphaelites lay many a wreath of cloud, hiding the pathway up: but on the same pathway were both, — the pathway of loving submission to nature, of earnest devotion to truth. Pre-Raphaelitism is the surest path — though, recollect, no path can be guaranteed—to the capacities and achievements of creative genius; and whatever it positively ensures, it has the grand negative advantage of producing no utterly abortive work. When, therefore, I look to the works of Ruskin and consider his estimate of Turner, I fear no misconception of pre-Raphaelitism. But it is not equally so, when I look at the works of Millais and recollect Ruskin's estimate of them. I should be sorry to say anything implying disrespect for the powers of Mr. Millais. However much certain of his works may fall short or offend, the man who has looked upon nature with his earnestness is deserving of honor. No man but one very peculiarly gifted could have given so mighty a realization of the deep, dark amethyst of the autumn hill, as Millais has given in his *Autumn Leaves.* But with all his realizing power, I cannot believe that this artist has any real imaginative force. You may test the fact simply but infallibly. Attempt to take his pictures to pieces. Endeavor to trace the process of their composition. To do so in the case of imaginative genius may be pronounced impossible. The touch there is invisible as the conception was instantaneous. The mode of working is subtle as life. Coleridge could not have told you how that giant sprung to life in his soul. A mechanical mind, considering characteristics and adopting traits for a century, could not have produced the impersonation. But whenever Millais attempts imaginative work, he lets his hand be seen. You know how idea after idea struck him, and was taken up, and fitted to its place, and put in. In his large picture, *Peace Concluded*, for instance, who cannot perceive that triviality after triviality, about the cock, the bear, the turkey, the lion, suggested itself to his mind, and was mechanically suited to his purpose? You can put the colons and full stops into the long-winded pointless tale. Mr. Ruskin may continue to admire Millais, but he will never persuade more than a coterie that his favorite possesses a fine sympathy or a high imagination. It would be a dreary consummation if pre-Raphaelitism, aftre toiling long in the mines of truth, laid its stores, not at the foot of some wizard imagination, capable of evoking perfections of loveliness undreamed of in the world, but before mere memory, gigantic indeed in its powers, but mechanical and manufacturing after all.

Thom. Whether Millais has true imagination or no, he has produced one great picture. *The Rescue* appears to me by far his finest painting as yet, — there are one or two of his, by the way, that I have not seen. The *Autumn Leaves* gives perhaps greater promise, but the children in it are so intolerably ugly, and their gestures so strained and artificial, that the picture seems to me destroyed. *The Rescue* pointedly exhibits the possibility of mere faithful rendering of nature yielding noble pictures. Learn to depict her faithfully, and when you come upon her in a grand mood, you produce a grand picture. The story of *The Rescue* is simple. A fireman brings three children in safety from a burning house. The mother awaits him, kneeling at the foot of the stair. One of the children she receives from his hands; the two others still cling to him. He stands upon the creaking staircase, in the full red blaze reflected from the conflagration. The figure of the mother has generally been regarded as the principal one in the picture; but, in spite of the depth of tenderness, mingled with love and gratitude, in the expression of her face, I cannot say that it fully satisfies me. The fireman is certainly good: resolute, manly, strong as iron, like one accustomed to pass through the fire. But the central figure in the picture, its climax, if I may so speak, is the boy on the fireman's shoulder. That child's eye is the grandest thing Millais ever did. The little fellow has just been snatched from a fearful death, and the fierce flame yet glares on him its burning crimson. But it is not terror that reigns in his face. He does not, like the younger children, stretch and shriek towards his mother. That mighty glare has caught him, not with its terror but with its sublimity. He gazes on it, in awe and wonder, fascinated by its maddened beauty. The soul of the man, with all its regal supremacy over nature, is in his lit eye; that supremacy, in virtue of which man can abstract every phenomenon from its effects, and behold it in itself; causing the tempest to play before him like a beautiful wild beast, and gazing into the eye of the lightning until he has mastered the secret of its beauty. The younger children will forget the whole incident in a few months or years: but when that boy's eye is dim, and the snows of eighty years are gathering over that fair brow, his grand-children will learn from his lips, in minute detail, every circumstance and every aspect of that tremendous fire. If there is nothing but realism in this picture of Mr. Millais, it is realism of a very valuable sort.

But let us now bid farewell to the pre-Raphaelites. There are one or two young men, who work upon principles closely allied to those of the brotherhood, — if not, indeed, identical with these, — but whose genius seems to me, in certain important respects, higher, and whose pictures are totally free of crudity, affectation, or singularity. At the head of these, I set the young Scotch painter, Noel Paton. Very high in their ranks are Mr. Wallis and Mr. J. C. Hook. The two former paint with an accuracy and universality strictly pre-Raphaelite; but their sense of beauty is so exquisite that when you behold its results you feel constrained to ask whether Mr. Millais has a special sense of ugliness. If the old theory of generalization receives a support it by no means merits, from the frequent lack of power, among the pre-Raphaelites expressly so called, to impart to their pictures any centralizing interest, it is irrecoverably overthrown by the absolute and uniform finish, combined with perfect unity, of Paton and Wallis. *Home* by Paton is the chief poem-picture called forth by the Russian war. It has the beauty of truth, that beauty which, when reached, seems so plain, obvious, easy of attainment, but which, even in so simple a case as this, demands, if not strict imaginative intuition, yet so rare a variety and harmony of powers, so delicately yet accurately attuned a sympathy with human emotion, so true a sense of pathos, so exquisite a capacity for perceiving the line, invisible to a thousand eyes, which marks off, on all sides, the tender, the graceful, the beautiful, from everything coarse, forced, or glaring, that it is difficult to name it otherwise than with the name of genius. The soldier has arrived in the heat of the day, wounded, weary, footsore, has walked into his little cottage, and sunk on a chair. His wife had been sitting beside the cradle of her child, engaged partly in sewing, partly in inspecting certain letters, preserved in that casket, the most precious, doubt it not, in the dwelling, which stands upon the table. She had been musing once more upon him who was away, her eye now filling in anxious solicitude, now brightening in delicious hope, now resting in connubial joy and pride on the letter in her hand; — and he was far away. Then, suddenly, he entered and sank upon the chair. She spake not a word, but, kneeling down, laid her head on his breast and strained him to her heart of hearts. His mother meanwhile, resigning him to his wife, had drooped her head over his chair, her face unseen, but the tears falling. The soldier gazed downward on the face of his wife, in a silent rapture of manly tenderness, of perfect love. Such was the story the painter chose to tell, and this the moment which, as the most impressive, he fixed upon to reveal the whole. Every heart acknowledges his power.

Smith. Is not the expression on the face of the wife too negative, too sleep-like? You do not see any emotion through her eyelids, though she has closed them over balls throbbing like fire.

Thom. I agree with you. I think that, in any case of emotion so powerful, the face would needs show more vivid trace of it. But I have heard it maintained that the slumbering look of the face is accurately true, expressive of a feeling which is satisfied, which no longer goes outward, but gathers itself up in the heart. Perhaps this is the more delicately penetrative criticism, but I cannot repel a suspicion that Mr. Paton told his lay figure to close her eyes, and forgot himself into painting what he saw. Millais in the same way painted a girl with her eyes shut for a blind girl, giving that equable radiance of expression over the whole face which belongs only to the entire complement of the senses, and of course not painting a blind girl at all. This is one of the minor dangers of pre-Raphaelitism, but one into which such painters ought surely not to have fallen.

You have seen Paton's *Quarrel* and *Reconciliation* of Oberon and Titania from Midsummer Night's Dream?

Smith. Yes. They are characterized by great spirit and vivacity, delightful in fancy, masterly in execution, but not comparable for a moment with the bit of real life at which we have been looking. He has on one occasion failed, — ambitiously, powerfully, as only a strong man fails, yet indubitably. His far-famed picture, *The Pursuit of Pleasure*, is a failure. The subject was one of surpassing difficulty, to be successfully treated only by the highest imaginative energy, and it does not perceptibly detract from the promise of a young artist that it baffled him. The idea on which the picture is founded is the commonplace, that all men follow after pleasure, each seeking it in some particular manner, and each finding it a delusion. The triteness of the thought did not in the least affect the possibility of original treatment. It is a commonplace truth that war is replete with horrors and that peace brings joy and plenty; but the picture by Rubens, in which this truth is embodied, is by no means commonplace. Treatment will redeem any subject. But Mr. Paton's treatment is irredeemably bad. In the immediate foreground you behold a motley group of pleasure seekers, — the warrior, the miser, the rake, and so on, women mingling in the throng. Each of these, let it be granted, is finely conceived and painted. Before the group, there floats in the air, life-size or nearly so, rich in color, and with a leering expression, a golden-haired female figure, almost entirely nude. Lured by her witching smile, that motley group follows on heedless towards dark spaces of ocean. Over the whole, afar in the sky, is seen the Shadow of Death, cloud-like and ghastly, — a powerful thought, suggested, I should think, perhaps unconsciously, by the

22*

genius of David Scott. Omitting all consideration of detail, the question as to whether the picture is a failure or not resolves itself into this other, Has the painter succeeded in bodying forth the unity in variety, and the variety in unity, of the universal pursuit of pleasure? Has he, on his canvas, given local habitation and name to that mystic something, which allures all yet seems different to each? To this question I answer, He has not. To ninety-nine out of every hundred, for one thing, his figure of pleasure would suggest only sensual pleasure; and the power of that figure to allure the gambler and miser would be simply a negation or a puzzle. But even this fact is not necessary to my case. Be it that sensual pleasure is not solely indicated by the alluring maiden. If *any* characteristic can be named, in virtue of which her influence upon her followers can vary in each case, the painter has, I acknowledge, attained his end. But after the most candid and careful exercise of judgment, I cannot discover any kind of varying identity in the figure; and I am absolutely satisfied that none such exists. Therefore the painting is an explicit failure.

Thom. How could the idea have been better embodied?

Smith. You are very well aware that such a question, if intended to invalidate an adverse criticism, is weak and futile. The critic does not profess to be a painter or a poet; the question he has first of all to discuss is how the thing is done, not wherefore the artist has failed in doing it. But I do not scruple to assert that, in the present instance, certain sources of suggestion are patent to all, by duly availing ourselves of which, we may secure one or two important hints as to how Mr. Paton might have modified his treatment. The idea is one which has been from the earliest times familiar to the intellect and imagination of the race. Poetry has variously shadowed it forth. How did the ancients represent it? I cannot but wonder that Mr. Paton did not find a suggestion in the marvellously true yet marvellously beautiful myth of the Syrens. The sisters sat at the mouth of their sea-side cave, half hidden in its twilight shade, clearly discernible by the eye of no traveller. There they sung their witching song. It was heard on the ocean by the voyager, mingling its deep tone with the waves, mystic, indefinable, irresistible. To every listener, that music told a different tale. The lover heard in it the voice of his mistress. To the warrior, it was the promise of glory and fame. To the miser, it brought visions of treasures untold. To all it came with irresistible potency. Turning at once to our own times, do we not naturally picture to ourselves the allurement of fancied joy in some vague, half-defined manner, the enchantment of distance, the shadows of mystery, entering into the conception? "The curtain of existence," says Carlyle, speaking of Burns, "was slowly rising before him in many-colored splendor and gloom." Do not the words superbly express the idea generally formed of those wavering, varying tints, which lure every one on in the name of happiness? Or are we not apt to think of promised joy as a vague illumination on the horizon, seeming to grow on the sight, yet ever receding, ever disappointing? Or, once more, is not pleasure thought of as a rainbow, followed by children, never yet caught by any child? In one word, *indefiniteness* is the never-failing characteristic of all attempts naturally made to represent the attraction of pleasure. Had we caught sight, dimly through veiling clouds and in the distance, of some fair maiden, striking a harp; or had some indistinct, mysterious illumination been seen gleaming over the further waves; we could have sympathized with each figure in Mr. Paton's eager group. But his Syren has come to look us in the face, and by so doing her spell has been forever broken.

Thom. The public sentiment coincided with your view of *The Pursuit of Pleasure.* I earnestly hope, for the sake both of Mr. Paton and his country, that he will not learn to despise public opinion on such matters. His *Home* has awakened no feeling of disappointment in the multitude, who, be assured, differ from connoisseurs in this, as much as in other things, that they like better to praise than to censure. If, moreover, they are not apt to censure, still less likely are they to fawn or flatter, which a coterie of friends and of friendly connoisseurs always do. Were I a poet or painter, I might not wish for new imagination, melodiousness, or success: but I should wish and pray that I might not fall under the enervating, the humiliating influence of a circle of blinded admirers. The poet or painter who knows the grand secret that man's honor and blessedness here below consist not in being praised for his powers but in getting that work out of them, to the utmost, which God has fitted them to perform, will desire to go out, as far as is possible, a mere voice or presence, into the wide atmosphere of the world, with its bracing winds, its ready thunders, and its benignant glory of calm.

Smith. As I have spoken of what, as an express and demonstrable failure, may be pronounced with some confidence one of Mr. Paton's worst pictures, I shall now turn to what may with equal confidence be pronounced his best. The picture to which I refer might be variously named. A lady has just expired. A watcher bends over that face from which the majesty of death has not yet obliterated the smile of womanly farewell. The corpse lies by an open casement, and, beyond, is the saintly calm of a summer night. From the dim mountain-horizon streams upwards silently towards the zenith, that suffusion of fair, faint radiance, which is, through the whole summer night, a prophecy of summer dawn. Never painter, one had almost said never poet, blended so many great silences into one ecstacy of repose. Night, death, and sorrow make up the awful calm. A star twinkling in that sky would break the perfect rest. The moon must not walk in brightness there. That veil of faint dawn-radiance shuts out the gaze of moon and stars, and only the eyes of human love look on the face of the dead. The lamp has gone out in the chamber; its last pale smoke-wreath curls gently upward in the still air. — I shall not say of the painter of such a picture that there is nothing in the highest province of poetic painting which he may not attempt; it were a superfluous remark in reference to a man who has already produced a masterpiece in the very highest department of Art. No theme is more august or sublime than that of death. Around it gathers all that is darkest in human woe, and brightest in human hope. It is a cipher of the mystery of human existence. And Mr. Paton has spread over it the solemnity of night, and touched it with the glory of dawn, falling on it from afar. In the bowed form of the watcher beside the pale corpse, we see that human weakness which faints under the mighty shadow; but yonder radiance reminds us of a victory beyond death, of the breaking of a resurrection morn, of the angels now welcoming the human spirit which has fled.

Thom. To offer advice to a painter like Mr. Paton, to declare dogmatically in what province he may best exercise his genius, would be presumptuous. But one may be pardoned for saying how, with his own bounded means of judging, he would *like* to see Mr. Paton exerting his powers. It seems, then, to me, that he might find a peculiarly suitable sphere in certain departments of religious painting. The highest note of a man's fame is not generally struck until he has himself passed away. It is in the far distance that the great mind "orbs into the perfect star." It would probably be thought incomparably absurd to name the genius of Paton along with that of Raphael. Yet I cannot but feel that, allowing for any difference in degree, the powers of the former are in some sense akin to those of the latter. I am strongly impressed with the conviction, that no living painter is so well qualified as Paton to realize for us, if human skill can in any measure realize, those moments in the history of our Saviour, when the mildness, the tenderness, the sorrow, of the human hearts and faces round him, were so touched and irradiated by his presence, that the whole scene seems to appertain to some region, if not all of heaven, yet surely not solely of earth. If any man could paint for us the eyes of Mary, "homes of silent prayer," resting on Him who had called Lazarus from the grave, I think it could be done by Mr. Paton. If any man could bring to canvas even a faint suggestion of that Divine tenderness, with which the dying Lord committed his earthly mother to the care of John, I believe it would be he. Only I am by no means prepared to maintain that such subjects could possibly be so treated in painting as not to disturb and degrade the ideal of them which dwells in the imagination of the devout Christian.

Smith. I also might be well pleased to see Paton taking the shoes from his feet and entering such holy ground. Meantime it is well that his genius frequents such lowly paths, as, while leading, perhaps best of all, to the highest ideal, secure his mind perfectly from extravagance and affectation. Let him paint such pure and perfect color-lyrics as *Home*, let him breathe into simple joys and sorrows, over peasant faces and into cottage interiors, the immortality of beauty, and not only will he touch chords to which the heart of humanity must vibrate, but will find for his own genius a wholesome and precious aliment.

Thom. Have you remarked how completely Paton's paintings refute that old generalization theory? Is there a generalized hair's-breadth in his picture of Death and Night? Is not the casement painted to its last stone? Has not the brush lingered on each filament in that faint, dying wreath of lamp-smoke? Yet has not the artist proved himself capable of dispensing with the base ministry of imperfection and slovenliness? Have not, on the contrary, all the details of the picture been compelled to do service and homage to that mighty thought, to that mastering emotion, which his genius set in its central and undisputed throne? Perfect unity and perfect finish.

Smith. If that miserable fallacy required one other death-blow, it would receive it in this picture by Mr. Wallis — who stands, I suppose, next to Paton among those who act on the pre-Raphaelite principle, without falling into the pre-Raphaelite grotesqueness, mawkishness, or affectation. *The Death of Chatterton* is a subject worthy of the highest ambition, and requiring commanding powers. Mr. Wallis has attempted it and not failed. Chatterton lies before us on his humble truckle-bed, in his squalid garret. The first glimpse of dawn sheds a drear and slumbrous light, of faint cowslip-yellow and fainter rose, over the distant dome of St. Paul's. The window is half open, and on the sill is one rose-bush. A rose, a solitary one, had burst suddenly into full bloom, but then broke its slender stalk, and now hangs its head, the petals falling one by one. Chatterton lies on the bed, his full auburn locks falling over the coverlid, his relaxed arm holding the phial drooped to the floor, his face pale and rigid in death. His form and posture express simply the awfulness, the silence, the might of death. There is in the face no triumph over the last enemy; nor is there lingering anguish as of the final conflict; nor do fear and horror cast their shadow over it. It is the calm surrender of despair: "Death, thou hast conquered!"

Thom. Mr. Wallis has produced a noble picture; deserving, it may be, of Mr. Ruskin's expression of applause, "faultless and marvellous."[1] But there was one thing which transcended even this picture, indubitably, immeasurably transcended it;—the bare fact itself. There is in the work of Art before us a certain beauty on which the eye can rest with pleasure. Part of the dress of Chatterton is of a rich, lovely purple; and other touches of color about the picture complete the sweet harmony of which this is the central chord. Mr. Wallis has permitted himself a certain idealizing license; he has paid a modicum of deference to the taste of the public, to the delicacy of fastidious eyes. But when death smiled from beneath his grisly crown upon the dead Chatterton, there was no dallying with cultured sensibilities, no tender refinement of idealization. The boy staggered upstairs that evening, haggard, squalid, hunger-stricken. Had Mr. Wallis dared to give the rugged fact, we should have seen those cheeks sunken and livid, that flesh clinging to the bones with the clasp of starvation. In all England, that evening, there was no boy of seventeen dowered with faculties so princely as those of Chatterton. And he knew it! Yes: that was the most searching element in his agony. His critical capacity was developed as fully as his poetical. He knew not only his right to literary distinction, but his power, if he were but once known, infallibly to secure it. He longed, he yearned, to live. But a week or two before, he had written a boastful letter to his mother and sister, full of hope and courage. He had sent them also a few cheap presents, confident that they would be followed by others of a very different sort. But hunger overtook him: sheer starvation dug a grave before his eyes. He did not need much. One loaf per week, bought stale that it might last the longer, was, with water, all he needed. But that was denied him. So, in the strength of despair and madness, he ended his torment, preferring instant rest within the jaws of darkness, to that agonized flutter by which he strove vainly to resist the deadly fascination. No soft, sweet colors met the eyes that first looked upon him next morning; only threadbare ghastliness and squalor. Death, that night, was in his coarsest mood, and had arranged no picturesque effects. Read the simple detail of Chatterton's life and death as given in his biography by Mr. David Masson, and you will, I think, allow that, whatever Mr. Wallis has attained, he has not realized the stern fact.

Smith. But we have wandered from the circumstance which first attracted us to this picture. Observe how minute the painting is. You have the wavering of the light on the rose-petals, you have every crease in the bed-cover, every chink in the garret wall. Would we have felt more for Chatterton if the dome of St. Paul's had been a blot of black paint and the walls of the cottage random sweeps of brown?

Thom. J. C. Hook is worthy to be mentioned with Wallis and Paton. Of him much may be expected, for he is one of those men who have really a great deal to say. His *Finding of Moses* is a beautiful and original picture. Perhaps for the first time in the history of Art the true key-note in that incident, the strongest, purest, noblest tone of human emotion it affords, is struck. It was no doubt a grand sight, for any eyes which that morning beheld it, to see the Princess of Egypt, in glitter of jewels and stateliness of fine linen, surrounded by her maidens, proceeding to the river to bathe, or looking down upon the babe found among the bulrushes. But there was a heart near, whose palpitations expressed an emotion, to which any feeling in the breast of Pharaoh's daughter was a faint, fleeting tenderness, a slight womanly interest. A mother's heart was beating near, the heart of the mother of that child. And since the destinies of mankind hung upon the fate of that little boy, since Christendom lay folded in that frail cradle, a Divine hand led a little girl, standing by, up to Pharaoh's daughter, to offer to fetch a nurse for the child. The mother came. She took her boy into her arms, crushing down in her breast the tears of joy which forced themselves to her eyes with the importunity of anguish. Then she turned from the king's daughter, and clasping her babe to her breast, uplifted her streaming eyes to the God of Abraham, in gratitude unutterable. At that moment, the sublimity of the incident reached its climax; and that is the moment fixed upon by Mr. Hook. You see the mother in the foreground in the attitude described. In the background, not unseen but occupying only their natural station of importance, are the Princess and her maidens. The mind in which this picture originated must be gifted with no ordinary measure of power, emotional and intellectual.

Smith. Mr. Hook has not, to my knowledge, painted any other picture comparable to this. His more ordinary walk is quiet, homely life. In this department his feeling is so true that had he adopted the medium of words instead of colors, he could not have failed to secure an abiding if not a sounding popularity, as a poet of the affections. Observe this simple picture. Had you passed the cottage and happened to note the little incident Mr. Hook records, it would probably have had power, slight as it is, to bring a tear into your eye. The boat has arrived, and the tired fisherman goes up the steep stone steps, leading from the beach to his dwelling. His wife has come out to meet and greet him. And how does her womanly, wifely instinct instruct her to give him the welcome that most will warm his heart? She brings out *their* child, just beginning, as the Scotch say, to "toddle," and pushes it gently before her on the steps. The little fellow has a timorous look, as if never before trusted so far from his mother's arms. The eyes of father and mother meet on him in one harmony of love. All this is doubtless very plain, very ordinary. Yet does not your heart bear witness to the power of the picture? Such men as Mr. Hook and Calcott Horsley — whose feeling is at times, I think, still more exquisite — must exercise a genial, salutary influence, at a time when Art is beginning really to lay a finger on the public heart.

Thom. By the bye, are we to omit *Burd Helen* by W. L. Windus? He is, indeed, an express pre-Raphaelite, and we have bidden adieu to such; but the laws of conversation permit us to double on our steps, and if any pre-Raphaelite is worth turning back for, he is Mr. Windus. The lines from the old Scotch ballad by which the painter explains his picture tell its story touchingly and well.

"Lord John he rode, Burd Helen ran,
A live-lang simmer's day;
Until they cam' to Clyde water,
Was filled frae bank to brae.

'Seest thou yon water, Helen,' said he,
'That flows from bank to brim?'
'I trust to God, Lord John,' she said,
'You ne'er will see me swim.'"

The girl clings to the stirrup leather with one hand, pressing the other to her side with a look of utter weariness and desolation. Lord Ronald looks down in stony heartlessness. The river flows before, and the ashy gray of an evening sky roofs the lone moorland. There is a fringe of ghostly trees on the sky-line. All this is true, and deeply imaginative. But I cannot think that the fearful character of the incident is brought out with perfectly sufficing power. At that time of the evening, the flanks of the horse would have been flecked with foam; all the jaunty pride, with which he pranced and curvetted in the morning, would have been broken with fatigue: but here he steps daintily along, as if setting out on his journey, no suggestion of weakness or weariness about him. In the face of the rider, too, it may at least be asked whether there is the determination necessary for the deed. Must not such cruelty have been "stubborned with iron?" This man looks piqued, provoked, petulant. His features, though blunt and base, are small. He is the image of spite, of meanness, of petty malevolence, not of such fiendish and inflexible cruelty as seems necessary for deeds like his or Iago's. We shall not, however, be dogmatic on this point. I am not sure that attainment in crime, that mastership in iniquity, writes itself even in a clouded form of those big bones and massive brows which denote strength of character. It is perhaps with feebleness of character, with incapacity to resist any suggestion of the flesh or the devil, with total and enervating absence of sympathy with good, that colossal ability to commit cruelty best consists. It may be that we gratuitously postulate, in the soul of the utter villain, some such powers and feelings as, in our own, would have struggled with advancing depravity and gone down only after a fierce wrestle. It would have required a giant strength of will in most men never to have winced during the protracted agonies of Cook the victim of Palmer, — never to have flinched through the whole execution of that diabolic purpose. Yet the face of Palmer gave no indication of natural strength of character. It had no strong, noble bones. It was suffused with a foul dinginess of sensuality, and had no look even of dogged resolution. It had, now that I think of it, a distant generic resemblance to the face of Lord John in Mr. Windus's picture. Perhaps, therefore, the deliberate choice of the artist was truer than my hasty impression.

Smith. The day is westering, and yet we have even glanced at very little in the wide kingdom of Art. I fear we must leave the greater part, until that promised day, when we are to have you at the old place, and you and I shall have another chat on our favorite subject, with mountains, clouds, and brooks for reference.

Thom. That is a pleasant prospect; we have indeed much to talk of. Only a few artists have passed in review before us. But we have not altogether erred in fixing our regards mainly on the prospective phases of Art, on the youthful and the promising. It is more important to know and hail the new than to linger about the old, whether to build over it a mausoleum or to pronounce on it a solemn anathema. We need not part, however, without saying a word or two about some of those painters who bulk more largely in the world's eye than those we have mentioned, and whom general consent would set at the head of the contemporary British school.

In the treatment of marine subjects, as was allowed even by the somewhat ungenerous savans of the French Exposition, we stand supreme; and the first of living marine painters is Clarkson Stanfield. *The Abandoned* is a good example of his work. The scene is the "deep mid-ocean," no shore, no rock in sight. The wearied, mastless vessel has lain down like a spent animal after the shock of the last sea, when she is met by another fierce, massy buffet, the furious billow dashing once more over her timbers in wild, flying, filmy foam. The sky is broken in the midst, and a burst of white light streams down, pouring along the trough of the sea, and whitening every tossing wavelet, on the broad backs of the swells. That light will soon pass away; for to windward, a cloud, still blacker than those around the vessel, comes drifting swiftly on. Beneath the edges of that cloud, the livid waves spring, and writhe, and dance, in the mad music of the wind. Soon the canopy of a new storm will shroud the doomed ship in deeper night; and away she will roll, tossed from valley to valley by the might of the sea, borne into the remote solitudes of ocean never to return. The picture is one of genius and power. Stanfield is your true man to paint a wave. He knows it in all its freaks of motion, in all its wild play of glistening, wavering, flashing light. He has watched it in the fair, racing breeze, in the vexed chopping sea, where tides and winds contend, and under the murky tempest, when it gathers itself into a huge billow, fronting the blast like an angry brow, corrugated in agony and rage.

Smith. The genius of Collins seems to have been more pensive, and it may be less daring, than that of Stanfield.

In the rendering of far, faint horizons, and bleak, sandy flats of shore, I suppose he stands wholly unequalled. I could name no paintings which bear you so completely to the scenes they represent. The salt breeze cools your forehead; you shiver sympathetically with the fisherman, toiling along between wave and bent.

Cooke must surely be a substantial, hearty man, enjoying life, and going at his work with a will. His most generally chosen subjects, indeed, are rather of a quiet than a stirring character. He loves to paint boats with sails faintly flapping over slumbering seas, above which his clouds, permeated with that soft pale-yellow radiance of his, are a true and fitting drapery. But he can paint a strong gale, as well as a glassy sea. Observe this scene on the Adriatic; *Chioggian fishing vessels, &c., running into the lagune of Venice, on the approach of a borasco or violent squall.* You remark Cooke's characteristic orange on the broad sail of that big, bright boat, bounding like a sea-monster in front. How the thing of life leaps into that wave, laving her shoulders with the sheeted foam as the sea comes galloping like a race-horse from the left! She positively stands out from the sky amid the storm clouds. It was a sweeping and strong hand, I think, too, a joyous one, which painted that boat. The picture makes you hold your breath.

Thom. Sir Edwin Landseer is the most popular living painter. His subjects are not the highest, yet I cannot find it in my heart to grudge him his pre-eminence. He stands apart from all animal painters. If Turner can be alleged to have differed from other landscapists, by embracing in the comprehensiveness of his love and power all the moods of nature, while they dwelt on particular aspects, still more expressly may it be said of Landseer that he differs from all animal painters, in having imparted to his own subject a breadth and dignity absolutely unexampled. He has thrown over the animal world the light of human association, a task hard to perform, but which he has accomplished with incomparable felicity. In bare realism, there may be one or two departments in which he has been equalled, I shall not say surpassed; but wherever his supremacy as an animal painter may be disputed by another, the disputed glory is not, I think, worth contending for. The ferocity, terror, rage, and pain, of animal life, were perhaps never conveyed as by Snyders. But his pictures can be profitable only in such a manner as gladiatorial shows or prize fights might be profitable; and can be vindicated only by such fallacies as might be urged in order to screen these from a just condemnation. I cannot look upon a group of bears and dogs rending each other, from the hand of Snyders, without being sensible that the man possessed observation to pierce, memory to seize, and a conquering power of execution. Grant that I find a certain lesson in the earnestness with which he must have devoted himself to his task, a certain encouragement in his marvellous success. As much as this can be said in favor of the moral advantage derived from him who, after his fight of an hour and twenty minutes, his one remaining eye starting bloodshot from his head, scarcely, for utter exhaustion, hears the shouts that hail his victory. The didactic uses of Snyders are perhaps as great as those of Ben Caunt or Harry Broom. But the sin of palliating the misuse of power by the very circumstance which lends that sin its aggravation, by the excellence of the gifts debased, has prevailed too widely in these hero-worshipping days. The time, I trust, will soon arrive, when Art shall disclaim, indignantly and forever, the base privilege of perpetuating what ought to be forgotten, and bringing into light what decent nature vails in darkness. Complete and happy sympathy with what there is of idea or feeling in the pictures of Snyders would imply a gross, a ferocious, a brutish nature; and, since distempered tastes are known to grow by what they feed on, all such pictures ought to be rejected unmercifully and with scorn. Let it be mentioned to Landseer's real honor, that he cannot dispute with Snyders his tarnished crown. A total exemption from blame cannot, indeed, be claimed for him. Once or twice he has fallen into the error of painting the base and revolting in animal life. No humane man could for a moment look upon the writhings of a transfixed otter, without pity, shame, horror; and no painter ought to have pandered to the degraded tastes which could enjoy such a spectacle. But that was almost a solitary instance. The sound feeling of the multitude, which conferred popularity upon Landseer, warned him that such pictures were essentially wrong. In the overwhelming majority of cases, he has fallen into no such error. On the contrary, he has, as I said, shed over animal life an exquisite and novel illumination, poetical in a high sense, and partaking of countless delicate elements of humor, of pathos, of vivacity, of mirthfulness. I do n't know whether any pictorial critic, of the small, nibbling, pedantic order, has ever happened to lay down the limits of motive and expression, within which the animal painter ought to confine himself. It would be pleasant to compare the result with what Landseer has done, to note how and how often genius had overleaped the stakes of mediocrity. Landseer's animals are, with the possible exception I have noted, more like nature's animals than any ever painted. Yet he contrives, while painting them, to touch with cunning hand a thousand chords of human sympathy, glancing with delicate satire at human foible, and gracefully suggesting the more deep and tender human emotions. Since, moreover, he is professedly an animal painter, no more would have been strictly demanded in his backgrounds than is given in those of Snyders or Hondekoeter. But he has scorned to avail himself of any such indulgence. He has given the solitude of the Arctic night, the sweep of the sea-horizon, and, above all, effects of mountain mist, in a manner which entitle him to high consideration among landscape painters. In power and range of expression, once more, while still strictly within his own province, he has surpassed not only all animal painters, but all prose and poetic fabulists. I remember no exception to the rule, that when writers have desired to draw any lesson from animal life, they have assumed a jocular, serio-comic tone. But Landseer's *Night* and *Morning* create no trivial emotions, make no appeal to the risible faculties.

The drear moonlight shivers through the storm, drifting along the lake, and all the mountains are wrapped in gloom. In the foreground, you see two stags in contest. Landseer's utmost power is here displayed; in the knotted sinews, entangled horns, and bloodshot eyes, of the animals, you have perfect expression of a rage stronger than anguish or death. This is *Night*. Turn to the companion picture. Morning has brought perfect peace. The lake, still as glass, watches for the first cloud to rise like a smile on the fair face of the sky. The mountains stand silent and beautiful, in the ruddy dawn. The noble stags are rigid in death, their limbs in the unyielding posture of their last grapple. And, see there, creeping up the hill, now almost touching the booty, with a look of archness, of cunning, of pure, approving satisfaction, which Landseer alone could have painted, the hill fox approaches his prey. The mountain eagle, too, is winging his way across the lake, snuffing the feast. And thus the monarchs of the waste have ended their mortal duel! Never, in prose or rhyme, was the story so grandly told. It is fable become epic.

Consider, again, his *Highland Nurses*, dedicated to Miss Nightingale. This is the second poem-picture called forth by the Russian War. The wounded stag has retired to die on the highest and loneliest crag, curtained by the mist. Two hinds bend over him and lick his wound. On the rock beside, are one or two mountain birds. Such a scene is probably impossible in animal life, yet who will say where the superadded expression, separating them from the animal world, becomes visible in those life-like hinds? The pathos of the picture cannot but be felt.

It will be as an animal painter that Landseer is remembered. Yet I am assured that he would have succeeded if he had devoted himself exclusively to such high ideal painting as he has once or twice attempted. His *Peace* and *War* might alone support a reputation in this kind. *War* is all narrowness, gloom, horror. The steed and rider lie ghastly at the foot of the rampart, the fierce flames of the cannon flashing through the thick smoke around. *Peace* is all spaciousness, serenity, blessedness. The unfathomable blue of the sky, the broad, smiling ocean, the wide sweeps of sunny sward, these are themselves magnificent in conception, as a contrast to the walled up darkness of war. Then there is the bright grass over the sea; the lamb crops the green blade that has grown in the mouth of the rusty cannon; a few glad children sport in front; and there is no question to agitate the mind, more serious than the solution of the thread-puzzle on the child's hands.

Smith. Shall we pretend to have had a conversation upon the aspects of Art in Great Britain, yet pass by William Mallord Turner? I have so far shaken off my despicable bashfulness, that I shall venture to say a word or two of that great artist, and with them let this desultory chat, which to me at least has been pleasant, come to a close.

A complete or final idea of the character and achievements of Turner's genius I cannot profess to have formed. But I have had somewhat uncommon opportunities of observing his pictures, and have examined innumerable engravings from his works. I can say with decision, that I have discerned certain lineaments, vague yet unmistakable, of a gigantic mind, great in its simplicity, in its massiveness, in its sweep of comprehension, in its concentration of energy. Turner had none of your perked and paltry originalities about him. His power of plagiarism was as magnificent as Shakspeare's, Goethe's, or Carlyle's. His real originality was no more doubtful than theirs. "He who has really caught the mantle of the prophet, is the last man to imitate his walk:" and he who catches the mantle, without imitating the gait, is the true original. Turner was the most earnest of scholars; he reminds you continually of other painters; but what he found brick, he left marble. As a realist, his grasp was irresistible, and will not now be questioned. But it is my deliberate opinion that as a poet he was more wonderful than as a realist. He rendered mountains and skies, forests and streams, as they had never previously been rendered. Every bone in the frames of the reclining giants whose weight steadies the earth, every wrinkle on their brows, every gleam of light upon their craggy foreheads, he brought out with solitary power. The springing also of the bough and the sinewy strength of the stem, the wayward grace of the river and boiling torrent foam, the hot haze, swooning over the distances of mid-summer, the scenery of the upper heavens, the lurid or fiery red of stormy sunset, all were Turner's own. But if he surpassed other painters in these and other provinces of pure realism, he surpassed them still more, as I said, in strictly poetic, in creative might. Who could select like Turner? You know that city and the scenery in which it is embosomed: but did you ever see it in that grandour of attitude, could any other painter have showed you it *so?* You would say cities and mountains were proud to sit to their great portrait-painter, since none could perceive like him their characteristic points, none could so elicit and combine their distinctive and contrasted beauties, none could let them so well be seen. Yet selection is by no means the only power of Turner. Taste might go far to impart or regulate a power of selection, but the sovereign imagination alone could give the deepest poetry that dwells in Turner's pictures. He seems, by life-long observation and musing, to have detected nature's secrets of effect, her modes of contrast, her suggestions of thought: and his imagination struck out more grandly that at which she aimed. The strength and stateliness of the precipice, the majesty of mountain shadow, the exulting magnificence of broad streaming light, the mysterious suggestion of infinitude, by the steep and soaring line of mountain side lost in the hanging clouds that seem to vail immensity, are all as it were vocal in a picture by Turner. The mountains are no longer dumb; Turner caught their inarticulate accents; and when he made them speak, all could understand them. This is not an easy thing to explain in words; but the universal sentiment as to prints from Turner proves that I am not alone in finding in his works the most poetic renderings of nature's deepest expressions. A critic, whose literary immortality is, I think, as secure as that of Sporus or King Colley, is severe upon Mr. Ruskin for demanding thought in pictures. The thoughts that are built up in the mountains may be to him a great mystery. But if you ask me where you will find thought, poetry, invention, in landscape painting, I refer you to any volume of engravings after Turner.

I cannot fix upon any picture to illustrate all the characteristics of Turner's genius, and to more than one picture, I must not now refer. Let me take one almost indiscriminately. In Lord Ellesmere's Gallery, there is a large picture by Turner, painted evidently after the great Vandervelde in the same collection. I shall briefly compare the two.

The Vandervelde contains a considerable number of vessels. In front is a Dutch packet-ship, a gleam of color on its sail from the dreary sunlight to windward. It mounts a broken sea, dipping into its foam, which dashes up over the bows. To leeward is a ship with sails clewed up, facing the wind. The sky has two great banks of cloud, one of them again dividing into three tower-like masses, through which is shed a faint illumination of stormy sunlight. The sea in front is broken, yeasty, racing before the wind with fearful velocity. Look now to the Turner.

One vast bank of cloud, piled mountain after mountain, comes darkening over the waves, "cramming all the blast before it." Its rounded tops are steeped in the sombre light which appears in the Vandervelde. A gleam of the same rests on the sail in front. The whole under-part of the great bank of cloud is black and thundery; beneath, the white waves are seen mysteriously rising and writhing. In the distance, a tall, three-masted ship has furled all sail and looks towards the blast. In front, two small vessels are lifted into prominence, running foul of each other, the one with canvas down, the other with bellying sail attempting to hold up to the wind. A sea strikes them both, dashing in wild foam over the bow of that one which has its sail spread. The waves in the foreground roll in one or two huge, angry ridges, the trough of the sea being filled with seething foam.

It is known that the picture by Turner is a companion to that by Vandervelde, and was a direct attempt either to imitate or to grapple with it. But mark how the conception, or rather conceptions, of Vandervelde, gain from the touch of Turner. The forms of the Dutchman's picture seem to have been dissolved or sent apart, and again brought together, into grander, simpler masses, at the word of a mightier imagination. Vandervelde's sea is covered with ships. Only one or two break the loneliness and gloom of Turner's. The sea of Vandervelde is chopping and gusty, a broad plain of countless equal waves. One or two mighty ridges, with millions of wavelets in their hollows, occupy the front of Turner's. But the alteration in which the master mind and hand are most signally displayed is that passed upon the clouds. These all come together in Turner's picture; no division breaks the unity of the simple, overpowering mass; it rolls on there, dark, heavy, towering, majestic, in the grandeur and terror of tempest.

It could, I think, be distinctly proved, that a change, similar to that observable in Turner's treatment of Vandervelde's subject, was effected by him in all that he made, by earnest study, his own. The conceptions of other artists I compare to the many hills, interesting, varied, beautiful, of the newer geological formations. They may be the picturesque crags of the limestone, they may even be the jagged crests of the metamorphic hills; but they are comparatively low and comparatively many: the imagination of Turner, working from lower deeps and with mightier power, upheaved the central ridge, the primary mountain chain, rising above all the rest, unapproached in height, and unbroken and alone in majesty. Composition becomes, with him, vital artistic unity; prettiness becomes noble symmetry and proportion; beauty becomes sublimity. I think I can admire the grace and elegance, the liquid sky and limpid water, the ordered pillars and dignified fronts, of Claude. But my perception of the fact that a precipice is more majestic than a palace gable, is hardly more distinct than my perception of a greatness and majesty in the forms of Turner totally absent from those of Claude. The latter is to the former as Pope was to Homer. And this I say while aware of the historical fact that Turner studied Claude with tears of despairing admiration in his eyes.

And so, farewell.

V.

RUSKIN AND HIS CRITICS.

Our good friends the artists must not be too hard upon us. It would be pleasant, if one only could, to school our ideas exactly to their standard: to watch their cunning pencils, as they bring out lines and hues, too exquisite for our exoteric capacities; to follow their clever pens, as they set down artistic rules, according to which alone we ignoble vulgar must be pleased or displeased; to admire nothing but what they tell us is admirable; to believe nothing but what they tell us is credible; and to find vent for our free activity, only in the becoming and ennobling privilege of paying out the cash. If one could but do this, he might be lapped in the music of their most sweet voices, and bask in a sunshine as pure as Claude's. He might even be patted with benignant condescension on the back, pronounced a man of taste and culture, called a judicious critic and a felicitous collector. Then would gradually gather around him that delicate, translucent vail, that misty, mysterious garment, whose qualities precisely reverse those of the shirt of Hercules, for it thrills with exquisite pleasure the whole frame of the wearer, and causes his breast to swell with the sublime consciousness of connoisseurship, and flutters all bosoms in the dove-cots of fashion, and awakens, when it appears, a whisper, instinct with veneration, spirit-stirring, that here is a veritable and most alarming lion, having no relationship to Bully Bottom the weaver. This might, indeed, be delightful; but the conditions of the enjoyment are hard. Admiration, sympathy, pleasure, are precisely the things that will not force: the very consciousness of our human freedom is bound up with them. Great, also, as the studio and the Art-gallery are, the world is, on the whole, neither a studio nor an Art-gallery. Interests manifold and important, religious, social, domestic, will not cease to play their parts there, in remarkable independence of the rules of the studio. Pictures, moveover, are there prepared for us, of a beauty wondrous, inexhaustible, older than those of the oldest masters, old as the mountains and the skies, with which we cannot help being rather impressed, but which we cannot perfectly see or understand, until some one show them unto us. We must not, therefore, consent to the consecration to Art of a little temple, not only apart from the great world, but shut against it; we must forego the proud honor of being connoisseurs; we must content ourselves with distinctions common to mortal men.

Ruskin must not be given up wholly to the artists. True it is, and let the fact be stated with due emphasis, that we believe him to be, in the province of Art, strictly defined, a critic of marvellous accuracy and of no less marvellous comprehensiveness, whose sympathy, universally acknowledged, is not one whit more remarkable than his science. True it is, that we think we hold in our hand the threads of a detailed and indubitable demonstration of this. Yet Ruskin cannot be viewed solely as a critic of what is generally understood as Art. Nay, he cannot be correctly judged of in the capacity of Art-critic, if he is contemplated in that alone. The nature of man is a unity, and no man can engage long or earnestly in any work, without exibiting the essential characteristics which that unity comprehends. We must regard Ruskin in at least three aspects: as a poet of external nature, a revealer of its beauties, a narrator of its facts; as a thinker, impelled by sympathies of extraordinary power, to reflect on the general condition, religious and social, of mankind; and as a critic, who has brought the general capacities of his nature, primarily and systematically, to an examination of the mode in which the nations of Christendom have pursued and embodied the Beautiful, with special reference to that pursuit and embodiment in his own country, in his own time. It is distinctly to be understood that, if he has radically failed in this last department, he cannot be defended. He might have been a Richter to perceive the beauty of nature; he might have cast abroad, like a Luther, the seeds of moral and religious truth: but he came before the world as an Art-critic, and if he failed here, he failed in what he chose and professed as his life-work. But, thus conceding that no excellence in other provinces could have redeemed failure in this, it may be allowed us to add, that an extraordinary power to perceive natural beauty, and a remarkable range and nobleness of human sympathy, *might* promote instead of counteracting ability to treat expressly of Art, nay, if not implying such ability, is indispensable to it. If Art had not a distinct character, — separable both from physical beauty and human excellence, — it would not have a distinct name. But can it be denied that, standing on her own watch-tower, Art casts her eye now towards the world of nature, now towards the world of man, for suggestion, instruction, and inspiration? The connection between Art and nature, be it what it may, is at least intimate and indissoluble; and a knowledge of nature, and a broad and earnest sympathy with human interests, furnish a presumption in favor of the Art-critic. It would surely be unnecessary to argue with any one who did not look upon an enthusiasm in Art, unable to connect itself with enthusiasm in nature and sympathy with men, as either partial, affected, or altogether unsound. The strong sense of humanity will always recognize, in those wider emotions, the best guarantee of excellence in every species of criticism; and in endeavoring to attain a correct understanding of any critical system, to form a sound estimate of the capacities and achievements of any critic, it will not fail to commend itself as the best mode of procedure, to commence with a survey, in relation to each, of such initial feelings. The artists, therefore, and connoisseurs, must for a little stand aside, while we consult, touching the critic they revile, the oracles of nature.

With an explicitness which was a duty, and with that scientific calmness, with which any man may recall and state the impressions of boyhood, Mr. Ruskin has informed us of the emotions, with which, in his earliest years, he looked upon nature. The passage to which we allude, occurring in the third volume of *Modern Painters*, may fearlessly be pronounced one of the most important, as well as interesting and beautiful, in the whole range of biography. We can quote but a part of it. "The first thing," he says, "which I remember, as an event in life, was being taken by my nurse to the brow of Friar's Crag on Derwentwater; the intense joy, mingled with awe, that I had in looking through the hollows in the mossy roots, over the crag into the dark lake, has associated itself more or less with all twining roots of trees ever since. Two other things I remember, as, in a sort, beginnings of life, — crossing Shapfells, being let out of the chaise to run up the hills,

—and going through Glenfarg, near Kinross, in a winter's morning, when the rocks were hung with icicles; these being culminating points in an early life of more travelling than is usually indulged to a child. In such journeyings, whenever they brought me near hills, and in all mountain ground and scenery, I had a pleasure, as early as I can remember, and continuing till I was eighteen or twenty, infinitely greater than any which has been since possible to me in anything; comparable for intensity only to the joy of a lover in being near a noble and kind mistress, but no more explicable or definable than that feeling of love itself. . . . . Although there was no definite religious sentiment mingled with it, there was a continual perception of sanctity in the whole of nature, from the slightest thing to the vastest;—an instinctive awe, mixed with delight; an indefinable thrill, such as we sometimes imagine to indicate the presence of a disembodied spirit. I could only feel this perfectly when I was alone; and then it would often make me shiver from head to foot with the joy and fear of it, when after being some time away from hills, I first got to the shore of a mountain river, where the brown water circled among the pebbles, or when I saw the first swell of distant land against the sunset, or the first low broken wall, covered with mountain moss. I cannot in the least *describe* the feeling; but I do not think this is my fault or that of the English language, for, I am afraid, no feeling is describable. If we had to explain even the sense of bodily hunger to a person who had never felt it, we should be hard put to it for words; and this joy in nature seemed to me to come of a sort of heart hunger, satisfied with the presence of a Great and Holy Spirit. These feelings remained in their full intensity till I was eighteen or twenty, and then, as the reflective and practical power increased, and the 'cares of this world' gained upon me, faded gradually away, in the manner described by Wordsworth in his Intimations of Immortality."

It is of the emotions experienced amid mountain scenery that Mr. Ruskin here more expressly speaks. But the passage reveals a mental and physical organization, generally adapted to derive pleasure from the appearances of nature, altogether peculiar; and of mountains themselves it must be remembered, that every form of scenery, of the highest beauty or grandeur, excepting only the sublime solitude or majestic fury of the central ocean, belongs pre-eminently to them. It is from the mountain that you behold the sky above and the valley below, the cloud on the shoulders of the hill, the torrent thundering in its chasm, the forest climbing among the crags, the lake slumbering around its promontories. That "intense, superstitious, insatiable, and beatific perception" of the grandeur and loveliness of mountain scenery, which characterized Ruskin in childhood and youth, implied a perception of all that is grandest and loveliest in God's earthly creation.

The words in which Ruskin has consciously described his early passion for nature's beauty are brief and unpretentious, marked by a noble and manly modesty. But the attestation of that passion which he soon unconsciously made, the manifestation forced on him by the abounding of the gift, is as imposing as it is conclusive. At an age when most clever young men are bent on distinction in debating societies, or resting on their laurels as prize versifiers, he published the first volume of *Modern Painters*. Had it been the work of a life-time, it would have secured an immortality of renown: and if one or two works, produced at a similar age, have indicated a genius equally rare, it seems open to no dispute that no work ever published by a very young man effected so profound and important a revolution. It at once took a separate and solitary place among works in English prose. In style and in matter, it was unique. It recalled what had passed entirely out of English composition, the stately march and long-drawn cadence of Hooker and Taylor; beside the richness of its descriptive detail, the *Traveller* was bare, the *Lady of the Lake* general and indefinite; while its clearness of conception, its vigor, and business-like tone, belonged distinctively to prose, and, if not distinctively, at least conspicuously, to the nineteenth century. Its matter was equally remarkable and as original. At a consideration of its doctrines, we have not yet arrived, but its principal contents were a series of descriptions of the aspects of nature, and to these the language could show no parallel. Nay, it was, perhaps, in the nature of things impossible, that at any previous time they could have been produced. A great invention is possible only at one period. The fact is proved by the circumstance that the history of invention is a history of controversy, that great discoveries have often, if not uniformly, been made by different minds about the same time. The production of the first volume of *Modern Painters* in the sixteenth century was equally impossible with the discovery of fluxions in the ninth. This assertion means simply that, at the date of the appearance of this volume, certain elements had entered into civilization, certain agencies had come to bear upon the general mind, absent in other centuries, whose presence was indispensable to its suggestion or accomplishment. Proof of this is necessary, but conclusive proof is at hand.

During the eighteenth century, and with accelerated speed during the early part of the present, a great process went on, by which the ideas of men, touching the realm of physical nature, were rectified and defined. The most prominent intellectual characteristic of the epoch is scientific activity. The prospect embraced within the ken of science continued gradually to widen, until, before the middle of this century, it might be said to comprehend the whole sphere of terrestrial existence, and the material aspects of the astral heavens. From the frigid crags of Iceland to the cactus-hedges of the Cape, from the pebble at your foot to the nebula in the outer deeps of space, from the flower of yesterday to the tree-ferns of the carboniferous period, Science had extended her gaze. Fancy and imagination seemed about to be extinguished, or to become the mere eyes of science. No ocean was now supposed to hide Isles of the Blessed; no Atlantis could now rise before the eyes of the voyager. Geology told you the forms of the mountains. Meteorology guessed at the balancing of the clouds. The lightning went faster and further, as the slave of man, than it ever went from its own lone dwelling in the thunder-cloud. The beasts of the forest had been watched and classified; the flowers of the field were named and known; the very rainbows, with which, from time immemorial, the sun had wreathed the mist and foam of Orinoco, could not escape the eye of science.

It is plain that any mind of remarkable power and susceptibility, going through the stages of culture and development in a time thus characterized, could not escape the pervading influence. Ruskin did not escape it: but it is important to note the nature of the impress which his genius received. His capacity was not distinctively scientific. Taking Coleridge's antithesis between science and poetry, it was rather poetic. That emotion which played so important a part in his early history found satisfaction, not in analysis and classification, but in contemplation, reverence, and wonder. So mighty, however, was that feeling, so earnest and perpetual its action, that its result was a knowledge of the external appearances of nature, poetic in its order but scientific in its accuracy: while it cannot be doubted that, at a certain stage of its early manifestation, the expressly scientific influence of the time came in to assist and define it. The first volume of *Modern Painters* reveals both influences. It gives express evidence of scientific knowledge: it is, from first to last, one tissue of evidence of that pure sensibility, which finds delight in simply looking on the face of nature, and which necessitates knowledge. This combination of science with poetry it is, which imparts essential originality to the volume of which we speak; and so closely allied is such a combination, with the general character of the age, that it may be confidently asserted that it could not have existed, as it certainly did not exist, in any other.

The critics have said things about Ruskin which are to us amazing, which only the evidence of sense could render credible. But we have not yet seen it asserted that he is ignorant of nature. Into this arena no critic has ventured deliberately and openly to step. The wildest fury of insolence, the utmost assurance of imbecility, has here confined itself to feeble innuendo or nursery flippancy. And when we contemplate, in all the comprehensiveness of its range, in all the correctness of its science, in all the glory of its poetry, that revelation of nature which he has made, this is perhaps, even considering what critics Ruskin has had, not wonderful. One is apt, as he reads, to imagine that the whole capacities and the whole life of the author had been devoted to the study of that class of natural appearances with which he is at the moment concerned. Listen to Ruskin's description of the sea, and you think he must have spent his days and years, in watching the beauty of its garlanded summer waves, and the tortured writhing of its wintry billows. Follow his eye as it ranges over the broad fields of the sky, and you are impressed with the idea, that it can never have been turned from observing the procession of the clouds across the blue, or tracing the faint streaks of the cirri, lying, like soft maiden's hair, along heaven's azure, or watching the sun as he touches the whole sky with gold and scarlet and vermilion, to be for him a regal tent at eventide. Go with him into the forest, and you believe that he has studied nothing else, but the forms of stem and branch, the arrangement of light and shade in the hollows of the foliage. Enter with him the cathedral of the mountains, mark attentively as he points out "their gates of rock, pavements of cloud, choirs of stream and stone, altars of snow, and vaults of purple traversed by the continual stars," and you conclude that there he must always have worshipped. But when you have passed with him from province to province of nature's beauty, and have found that in each he is a seer and revealer, can you fail to acknowledge the justice and modesty of his claim, not to be accused of arrogance in asserting that he has walked with nature? Can you, moreover, turn from the loveliness and splendor of the successive visions which have risen before you, without knowing nature better, loving her more, and associating with her loftier, purer, mightier emotions, of reverence and wonder, than ever theretofore?

We have said that, in the sphere of simple description of nature's facts, Ruskin has not been directly and deliberately met. But among the many half-amusing, half-offensive exhibitions of tip-toe mediocrity, trying to see up to the height of this original genius, if haply it may discover that it is merely a small mediocrity like itself, set on some sort of stilts, there have not been wanting hints that Ruskin's "word-painting" is an easy matter. The grandiose mediocrity who, rather condescendingly, consented, once and away, to annihilate Ruskin in the *Quarterly*, is of this opinion. The less grandiose mediocrity who reviewed the first Exhibition Pamphlet in the *Art Journal* utters some expressions, conceived to be like Ruskin's, and remarks that it is easy for the latter to write like this, however difficult it might, we suppose, be, to discuss the high matters with which his serene littleness is conversant. The compliment thus paid to Ruskin is really too high. He might rival Shakspeare in describing Dover Cliff, but there is no ground for believing, that he could dramatically body forth a Slender or an Aguecheek. We verily believe him incompetent, by the utmost effort, to write what his small critic comically fancies is in his manner. But we have no difficulty whatever in making, to these and all other critics of Ruskin, the concession, that there is such a thing as vague and empty verbosity, that there may be glowing, brilliant, fluent diction, without value of thought, sentiment, or information. A book may glitter all over with rhetorical ornament, may sparkle with metaphor, may, by alliteration and antithesis, please the ear and fix the attention, yet be worthless. But the descriptions of Ruskin are done in a style, which nothing but an ignorance, too crass and unconscious to be ashamed, or a perception jaundiced by malevolence, could confound with the mere glitter of voluble feebleness. There is a correspondence between all the real gifts of nature. The true gleam, if you only know it, will always lead you to the real gold. Able thinkers have recognized, — among them, in express terms, Coleridge and Carlyle, — that a linguistic capacity of sterling and surpassing excellence is always connected with real mental faculty, intellectual or emotional. And we assert with perfect confidence, that such verbal pictures as are drawn by Ruskin never were drawn, and could not possibly be drawn, without the existence of such real faculty. They are distinguished by one quality which never pertains to false rhetoric: the quality of unity. You may string together fact after fact, and, to make their jingle somewhat more musical, you may put ever so many sounding adjectives between. But in order to place before the eye of the reader the distinct features of a face, nay the exact likeness of a tree, a flower, a snow-flake, so that he will have each plainly within the sphere of his vision, an act of real observation must have been performed, a capacity to see what is distinctive must have been possessed, a certain amount of genuine mental force must have been put in exercise. And if a man sets before you, in all its breadth and clearness, a wide landscape, letting you see its main lines as distinctly as in a surveyor's map, yet covering it with the very colors in which nature has dressed it, it becomes mere stupidity and ignorance to deny the display of real mental power. The easel of a great painter might be covered with brilliant colors, yet the whole would be a daub; the picture he has completed may show every tint on the easel, it may show a great many more, and yet be no daub: in the one case, the colors mean nothing, they are held together by no relation; in the other, every color is in its own place, every tint is vocal, and the voice of the whole is one. Would it not be a poor mistake, to confound the richness and abundance of the picture's color, with the confused brilliancy produced by the many colors of the daub? Yet this is precisely the pitiful and painful mistake of those critics, who, having discovered, by the exercise of their critical genius, that where there is verbiage there must be many words, exclaim, whenever they perceive many words, that there is verbiage. Ruskin's words are used to bring out the minutest facts of nature, the light and shade on a blade of grass, the blending of hue in the rainbow, the melting into each other of the cloud-shadows upon the mountain side; and critics such as now find admission into the *Quarterly*, whose verbal powers, of fair average excellence, are to those of Ruskin, as the pictorial talents of a sign-painter are to those of Noel Paton, sneer at his facile word-painting. To show the flickering dance of sunbeams on forest leaves, to set before us the very spring and prancing of the waves, to word-paint the wreathing of the mist and every caprice and humor of the sky, required rather an abundant supply of words; but the supply at Ruskin's command was a small matter to his power of laying them on, to the exquisite precision with which he applied every vocable. In all that we are now saying, we must, for proof, appeal mainly to our own experience, and refer the reader to Ruskin's own pages. We do not, for our part, recall a single instance, in which he has deliberately set himself to place a scene before our eyes, without enabling us, after a sufficiently close and steady look, to see it in its grand, consistent features. We invite readers to test the matter for themselves. But we shall quote one passage, which exhibits as well as any we can recollect, the so-called verbiage of Ruskin. Our readers shall peruse it, before we make any remarks upon it. It is a description of the Fall of Schaffhausen: — "Stand for an hour beside the Fall of Schaffhausen, on the north side where the rapids are long, and watch how the vault of water first bends, unbroken, in pure polished velocity, over the arching rocks at the brow of the cataract, covering them with a dome of crystal twenty feet thick, so swift that its motion is unseen except when a foam globe from above darts over it like a falling star; and how the trees are lighted above it under all their leaves, at the instant that it breaks into foam; and how all the hollows of that foam burn with green fire like so much shattering chrysoprase; and how, ever and anon, startling you with its white flash, a jet of spray leaps hissing out of the fall, like a rocket, bursting in the wind and driven away in dust, filling the air with light; and how, through the curdling wreaths of the restless crashing abyss below, the blue of the water, paled by the foam in its body, shows purer than the sky through white rain-cloud; while the shuddering iris stoops in tremulous stillness over all, fading and flushing alternately through the choking spray and shattered sunshine, hiding itself at last among the thick golden leaves which toss to and fro in sympathy with the wild water; their dripping masses lifted at intervals, like sheaves of loaded corn, by some stronger gush from the cataract, and bowed again upon the mossy rocks as its roar dies away; the dew gushing from their thick branches through drooping clusters of emerald herbage, and sparkling in white threads along the dark rocks of the shore, feeding the lichens which chase and chequer them with purple and silver."

It is possible that, at first glance, this may appear a mass of gorgeous confusion: and it is certain that a hurried glance will convey but a slight idea of what it contains. In following the long evolution of the sentence, something of fatigue may be experienced, and the description would doubtless have been more generally and readily appreciated, had the mind been rested by one or two stops skilfully inserted. But it may be questioned whether the impression of concentrated power, of mass, of urgent, irresistible haste, could have been so well conveyed by a succession of sentences. The point to be peculiarly noted, however, is the nature of the "verbiage," abundant enough no doubt, of the passage. Let the reader, amid all its plenitude of adjective, set his finger, if he can, upon an epithet that could be dispensed with, a word which does not state some fact or define some quality. Had the same space been filled with ejaculations about the grandeur and sublimity of the scene — had we heard only of Titanic power, and inexpressible beauty, and tremendous velocity — there would have been an example of verbiage. But examine the passage clause by clause, and you find that its richness of expression is not by any means so remarkable as its condensation. The significance of the adjective "polished," applied to the velocity of the vaulted water, might be expanded into pages. You are told, in one word, that the rocks at the brow of the cataract are arched; you see the light breaking up from the foam under the leaves; you are led from sight to sight, until you know the tints of the lichens on the wetted rocks, and mark the foam paling the water under its surface; and from first to last there is not an indefinite touch, a superfluous word. To attempt to detail what is in the passage is found to be impossible: you cannot say *what* Ruskin has told you in so few words as he has told it.

But masterly as this description is, it can rank only with the less remarkable among Ruskin's pictures of external nature. The subject to be described was comparatively circumscribed, and there was little assistance rendered to the associative imagination, in connecting its bare facts with human sympathy. But in descriptions too numerous to be referred to here, — in such pictures as that of the Campagna of Rome under evening light, and that of Turner's Slave Ship, — not only are the grand lines of fact put strongly in, but that idealizing power is displayed, which, on whatever occasion, or in whatever form exhibited, whether in the poetry of a Shakspeare or Byron, in the prose of a Carlyle, a Richter, a Ruskin, in the colors of a Titian or Turner, seems to be radically the same, and marks the highest genius. If any single example of Ruskin's display of this power were to be regarded as more than an indication, a faint suggestion, of what he has done, the error would be complete: but if the reader can appreciate a very small part in its bearing upon the whole, and thinks it important, as we do, that, in every form of criticism, at least an opportunity should be afforded of comparing the writer's words with his allegations, he may not deem it inappropriate that we subjoin two passages, which, if not in Ruskin's very highest style, yet appear to us to display, along with the unfailing realism, the scientific accuracy, of which so much has been said, traces of that higher power which is characteristic of consummate genius. The first is from the second volume of *The Stones of Venice*, the second from the third volume of *Modern Painters.*

BIRD'S-EYE VIEW OF THE SCENERY OF EUROPE, IN ITS CORRESPONDENCE WITH NATIONAL CHARACTER.

"The charts of the world which have been drawn up by modern science have thrown into a narrow space the expression of a vast amount of knowledge, but I have never yet seen any one pictorial enough to enable the spectator to imagine the kind of contrast in physical character which exists between northern and southern countries. We know the differences in detail, but we have not that broad glance and grasp which would enable us to feel them in their fulness. We know that gentians grow on the Alps, and olives on the Apennines; but we do not enough conceive for ourselves that variegated mosaic of the world's surface which a bird sees in its migration,—that difference between the district of the gentian and of the olive, which the stork and the swallow see far off, as they lean upon the sirocco wind. Let us for a moment try to raise ourselves even above the level of their flight, and imagine the Mediterranean lying beneath us like an irregular lake, and all its ancient promontories sleeping in the sun: here and there an angry spot of thunder, a gray stain of storm, moving upon the burning field; and here and there a fixed wreath of white volcano smoke, surrounded by its circle of ashes; but for the most part a great peacefulness of light, Syria and Greece, Italy and Spain, laid like pieces of golden pavement into the sea-blue, chased, as we stoop nearer to them, with bossy beaten-work of mountain chains, and glowing softly with terraced gardens, and flowers heavy with frankincense, mixed among masses of laurel, and orange, and plumy palm, that abate with their gray-green shadows the burning of the marble rocks, and of the ledges of porphyry sloping under lucent sand. Then let us pass further towards the north, until we see the orient colors change gradually into a vast belt of rainy green, where the pastures of Switzerland, and poplar valleys of France, and dark forests of the Danube and Carpathians, stretch from the mouths of the Loire to those of the Volga, seen through clefts in gray swirls of rain-cloud and flaky veils of the mist of the brooks, spreading low along the pasture lands: and then, further north still, to see the earth heave into mighty masses of leaden rock and heathy moor, bordering with a broad waste of gloomy purple that belt of field and wood, and splintering into irregular and grisly islands, amidst the northern seas, beaten by storm, and chilled by ice-drift, and tormented by furious pulses of contending tide, until the roots of the last forests fail from among the hill ravines, and the hunger of the north wind bites the peaks into barrenness; and, at last, the wall of ice, durable like iron, sets, death-like, its white teeth against us out of the polar twilight. And having once traversed in thought this gradation of the zoned iris of the earth in all its material vastness, let us go down nearer to it, and watch the parallel change in the belt of animal life: the multitudes of swift and brilliant creatures that glance in the air and sea, or tread the sands of the southern zone; striped zebras and spotted leopards, glistering serpents and birds arrayed in purple and scarlet. Let us contrast their delicacy and brilliancy of color and swiftness of motion, with the frost-cramped strength, and shaggy covering, and dusky plumage of the northern tribes; contrast the Arabian horse with the Shetland, the tiger and leopard with the wolf and bear, the antelope with the elk, the bird of Paradise with the osprey; and then, submissively acknowledging the great laws by which the earth and all that it bears are ruled throughout their being, let us not condemn, but rejoice in the expression by man of his own rest in the statutes of the land which gave him birth. Let us watch him with reverence as he sets side by side the burning gems, and smoothes with soft sculpture the jasper pillars, that are to reflect a ceaseless sunshine, and rise into a cloudless sky: but not with less reverence let us stand by him, when, with rough strength and hurried stroke, he smites an uncouth animation out of the rocks which he has torn from among the moss of the moorland, and heaves into the darkened air the pile of iron buttress and rugged wall, instinct with work of an imagination as wild and wayward as the northern sea; creations of ungainly shape and rigid limb, but full of wolfish life; fierce as the winds that beat, and changeful as the clouds that shade them."

THE GREAT MOUNTAINS.

"Inferior hills ordinarily interrupt, in some degree, the richness of the valleys at their feet; the gray downs of southern England, and treeless coteaux of central France, and gray swells of Scottish moor, whatever peculiar charm they may possess in themselves, are at least destitute of those which belong to the woods and fields of the Lowlands. But the great mountains *lift* the lowlands *on their sides.* Let the reader imagine, first, the appearance of the most varied plain of some richly cultivated country; let him imagine it dark with graceful woods, and soft with deepest pastures; let him fill the space of it, to the utmost horizon, with innumerable and changeful incidents of scenery and life; leading pleasant streamlets through its meadows, strewing clusters of cottages beside their banks, tracing sweet footpaths through its avenues, and animating its fields with happy flocks, and slow wandering spots of cattle; and when he has wearied himself with endless imagining, and left no space without some loveliness of its own, let him conceive all this great plain, with its infinite treasures of natural beauty and happy human life, gathered up in God's hands from one edge of the horizon to the other, like a woven garment; and shaken into deep falling folds, as the robes droop from a king's shoulders; all its bright rivers leaping into cataracts along the hollows of its fall, and all its forests rearing themselves aslant against its slopes, as a rider rears himself back when his horse plunges; and all its villages nestling themselves into the new windings of its glens; and all its pastures thrown into steep waves of greensward, dashed with dew along the edges of their folds, and sweeping down into endless slopes, with a cloud here and there lying quietly, half on the grass, half in the air; and he will have as yet, in all this lifted world, only the foundation of one of the great Alps. And whatever is lovely in the lowland scenery becomes lovelier in this change: the trees which grew heavily and stiffly from the level line of plain assume strange curves of strength and grace as they bend themselves against the mountain side; they breathe more freely, and toss their branches more carelessly as each climbs higher, looking to the clear light above the topmost leaves of its brother tree; the flowers which on the arable plain fell before the plough, now find out for themselves unapproachable places, where year by year they gather into happier fellowship, and fear no evil; and the streams which in the level land crept in dark eddies by unwholesome banks, now move in showers of silver, and are clothed with rainbows, and bring health and life wherever the glance of their waves can reach."

We have said that if Ruskin has erred in his express Art-criticism, he cannot be defended from the charge of having radically mistaken his duty, and failed in what he selected as the business of his life. This remark we do not in any sense qualify. We beg leave, also, to observe, that for artists and their art, we entertain a deep respect. Painters in general are certainly raised above the ordinary run of men, by the delicacy of their tastes and by their devotion to beauty: painting is an art which may afford the purest delight, and ennoble while it pleases. But we must maintain that, however erroneous Ruskin's Art-theories might be proved, the revelations of nature which he has made would entitle him to separate and lofty honor; and that, when artists, believing they demonstrate his errors in matters connected solely with Art, imagine that they altogether disentitle him to regard, — prove him a man of small capacity or achievement, — they wholly misconceive their powers, and the attitude in which both they and Ruskin stand to the public. They and he, looked at in one important aspect, stand between us and nature. If Ruskin's word-paintings show us more of nature than their color-paintings, we shall not permit the *manner* of their representation to prejudice us against him and in favor of them. Art may be difficult to know and understand: but nature is not so easy. Custom has cast over her face its obscuring veil; we require to be awakened to pierce it, we require to have it drawn aside that we may see the features beneath. It seems to be an ordinance of Providence in this world — and it is a benign and beautiful ordinance — that everything, excepting, and that perhaps not always, the influence of the Divine Spirit on the mind, possessed and enjoyed by man, shall come to him through the instrumentality of his fellows. The truth perceived first by one becomes the property of millions; the delight, first felt in a single breast, is communicated by sympathy, and thrills through a thousand bosoms. A great man lends a voice to the hills and adds a music to the streams: he looks on the sea, and it becomes more calmly beautiful, on the clouds and they are more radiantly touched: he becomes a priest of the mysteries, a dispenser of the charities, of nature, and men call him poet. Ruskin stands among a select and honored few, who have thus interpreted nature's meaning, and conveyed her bounty to mankind. He has spoken with a voice of power, of those pictures, which ever change yet are ever new, which are old yet not dimmed or defaced, of the beauty of which all Art is an acknowledgment, of the admiration of which all Art is the result, but which, having hung in our view since childhood, we are apt to pass lightly by. He has reminded us that Morning, rosy-fingered as in the days of Homer, has yet a new and distinct smile at each arising, and that, as she steps along the ocean, its foam is always wreathed into new broideries of gold and roses. He has shown us, by evidence which none can resist, that no true lover ever trysted with Spring, by her own fountains or in her own woods, without seeing some beauty never seen before. At his bidding, we awake to a new consciousness of the beauty and grandeur of the world. We have more distinct ideas as to what it is; we know better how to look for it. Summer has for us a new opulence and pride; Autumn, which is Summer meeting death with a smile, a new solemnity and a more noble sadness. Even to Winter we learn to look for his part in nature's pageantry, in nature's orchestral beauty; we find a new music in his storms, a new majesty in his cataracts, a more exquisite pencilling in his frost-work. Artists and artist-critics may rail at Ruskin as they please; but in order to prove his word-painting a small matter, they must prove that Richter's most wonderful passages are mean achievements, that Shelley and Wordsworth, in their moments of richest inspiration, wrote what was "more easy than is supposed," and that those descriptive passages which are the masterpieces of Byron are of small account. We do not call Ruskin a poet. The name, we hold, cannot be claimed unless the distinctive form of poetry, the metrical, has been adhered to. But in the elements of descriptive power, which underlie the garb, either of prose or verse, we have no hesitation in declaring that, with the exception of one or two of Byron's highest efforts, such as his description of the storm in the Alps, the boasted and magnificent descriptions of that poet are decidedly inferior to those of Ruskin. Such a *series* of descriptions, indeed, as Ruskin's, does not, in prose or verse, exist in the English language, or, we are assured, in any other. The value of Ruskin's Art-criticism, we have yet to determine: but it at least must be conceded, that he who has added to our knowledge of nature, to an extent which would have given him high standing as a man of science, and who has irradiated nature by his imaginative power, in a manner which entitles him, in all but the form of his works, to take rank with the greatest descriptive poets that ever lived, is a man of rare and precious genius.

But it is time that we left this wider field, and addressed ourselves to the strict inquiry, how the marvellous natural sensibility of Ruskin has availed him in treating of the theory and practice of Art. We shall confine ourselves, almost entirely, to an investigation of his opinions on painting.

There are two points of view, by taking which successively, it will be possible to obtain a fair and dispassionate idea of Ruskin's opinions on pictorial Art. The first is by considering his great work, *Modern Painters;* the second, by glancing generally at the way he has applied his principles to the criticism of individual artists and schools.

It is of importance, particularly in view of the assaults which have been made upon Ruskin as an Art-critic, that we exhibit his fundamental ideas, as little as may be in our words, and as much as our limits permit in his.

In the very outset of Ruskin's first volume, we find him speaking thus: —

"Painting, or Art generally, as such, with all its technicalities, difficulties, and particular ends, is nothing but a noble and expressive language, invaluable as the vehicle of thought, but by itself nothing. He who has learned what is commonly considered the whole art of painting, that is, the art of representing any natural object faithfully, has as yet only learned the language by which his thoughts are to be expressed. He has done just as much towards being that which we ought to respect as a great painter, as a man who has learned how to express himself grammatically and melodiously has towards being a great poet. The language is, indeed, more difficult of acquirement in the one case than in the other, and possesses more power of delighting the sense, while it speaks to the intellect; but it is, nevertheless, nothing more than language, and all those excellences which are peculiar to the painter as such, are merely what rhythm, melody, precision, and force are in the words of the orator and the poet, necessary to their greatness, but not the tests of their greatness. It is not by the mode of representing and saying, but by what is represented and said, that the respective greatness either of the painter or the writer is to be finally determined."

The nature of Ruskin's system of criticism will manifestly depend upon the meaning he attaches to the "thought" and the "language" here spoken of. It is indispensable, therefore, to ascertain that meaning with certainty and precision. The illustration by which the author explains the passage is first of all worthy of attention.

"Take, for instance, one of the most perfect poems or pictures (I use the word as synonymous) which modern times have seen:—the 'Old Shepherd's Chief-mourner.' Here the exquisite execution of the glossy and crisp hair of the dog, the bright sharp touching of the green bough beside it, the clear painting of the wood of the coffin and the folds of the blanket, are language—language clear and expressive in the highest degree. But the close pressure of the dog's breast against the wood, the convulsive clinging of the paws, which has dragged the blanket off the trestle, the total powerlessness of the head laid close and motionless, upon its folds, the fixed and tearful fall of the eye in its utter hopelessness, the rigidity of repose which marks that there has been no motion nor change in the trance of agony since the last blow was struck on the coffin lid, the quietness and gloom of the chamber, the spectacles marking the place where the Bible was last closed, indicating how lonely has been the life — how unwatched the departure, of him who is now laid solitary in his sleep; — these are all thoughts, — thoughts by which the picture is separated at once from hundreds of equal merit, as far as mere painting goes, by which it ranks as a work of high art, and stamps its author, not as the neat imitator of the texture of a skin, or the fold of a drapery, but as the Man of Mind."

It is just possible that one might be so ignorant of the nature and philosophy of language, as to mistake the meaning of this explicit and satisfactory passage. There may be men, and they may even write in the *Quarterly*, who can find something to bewilder them in the description of the "wood of the coffin and of the folds of the blanket" as "language — language clear and expressive in the highest degree," and who can evince their astonishment by inquiring "what, after all, does such painting express, but hair, wood, and wool?" But it is not necessary to suppose men in general unable to perceive, that it is just this fact of their being hair, wood, and wool, in visible, pictorial representation, and not the alphabetical characters which are used to express these things, by cultivated reviewers, that makes them a language. Were the daguerreotype to be perfected so as to give the color as well as the form of nature, it would render nature's language perfectly. It could not, of course, do so, without giving nature's meaning too, whether deep and solemn, as in mountain scenery, commonplace, as in a street, or trivial, as in a heap of rubbish or a Dutch kitchen. But only in its application by mind, in its application to nature's scenes of exceeding grandeur, or to passages of human history of pathos and significance, could it produce pictures really great, full of meaning and thought. A perfect daguerreotype would render a barber's shop or haystack, as well as a mountain gorge lit by its cataract, or an army reposing under the sinking sun after a hard-fought day. The language in each of these cases would be alike faultless; and if an erudite critic were to slip into the assertion that the language of painting "is in itself *everything*," he would have slipped into the declaration that the two former pictures would be as noble as the two latter. Even with your perfect daguerreotype you must know how to apply it before you have valuable pictures; and even its best application would not give the highest Art; nay, the mind of a great painter will do, without a daguerreotype, what a man of no genius could never do with it.

But there is another point which this illustration makes clear. If it were the duty of a critic, professing to stand between the public and an author, and to declare plainly and honestly what the latter means, to fix upon a word, and attempt, with it, to nail his author down to a certain meaning or no-meaning, there might be defence set up for one who, settling on the word "thought," in the first of the passages just quoted, should "glance at the different fields of thought — moral, speculative, theoretic, poetic, epigrammatic," * and so lead himself and his readers a

* Quarterly Review. March, 1856.

ludicrous wild-goose chase in quest of the meaning of Ruskin. But if the duty of one who comes between the public and an author is precisely the reverse of this, how can any apology be offered for the man who, so coming, should put aside the simple and intentional explanation of Ruskin's meaning in the use of the word, which his illustration affords. The thoughts pointed out by him in Landseer's picture might be called facts, truths, touches of sentiment, proofs of observation or reflection, and so on. It is at least plain that if you inquire only after what precisely occupies "the thinking faculty," you will be led unpardonably as well as hopelessly astray. In the very quotation in which the word "thought" occurs, as that of which the painter's language is the vehicle, the expression "what is represented and said," is used as precisely equivalent. What if a critic seized the former and refused to look at the latter?

But there is more still to be said on this point. Ruskin is a somewhat voluminous writer, and it might be fair, always supposing that you did not wish to gratify a pitiable malignity but to perform a duty to the public, to proceed beyond one or two of his pages, and endeavor to discover whether subsequent declarations do not cast light upon those previously made. The previous quotations are important to an intelligence of Ruskin's meaning, but the following, and one or two others, are also of essential moment. He thus defines greatness in pictures: —

"The greatest picture is that which conveys to the mind of the spectator the greatest number of the greatest ideas." This expression is met with in the same important initiatory chapter from which we made the former quotations. It is difficult to imagine a mistake as to the identity of meaning between the words "thought" in the one case, and "ideas" in the other. And if the author had first categorically stated what the ideas which he looked for in pictures were, and then devoted two volumes to the detailed illustration and exposition of them, would not a distinguished reviewer look very foolishly pompous, in taking that sublime "glance at the different fields of thought — moral, speculative, theoretic, poetic, epigrammatic," when, all the time, the information needed lay at his feet? The distinguished reviewer, endangering the stars with his sublime head, would, we imagine, have fallen into a well! The question is one of simple fact. If what we state can be proved in Ruskin's words, surely the reviewer's position is somewhat ridiculous, surely his academic robes are somewhat draggled.

What, then, are the ideas which Mr. Ruskin looks for in Art? It is perhaps unfortunate that he has used the word "number" in precisely the connection in which it appears; for it affords a color, if no more, to quibbling. Candid criticism, however, will take it for granted, that the ideas he desiderates, however numerous, must, in his view, combine in one unity. Where unity is secured, where the ideas own the sway of one imperial thought, it is most true that the greater their number, the greater the picture is.

Mr. Ruskin proceeds to classify his Ideas as follows: we invite readers to consider whether the sentences, with which he introduces the classification, are calculated to mislead a candid critic, or to remove any misconception which might have been already formed.

"The definition of Art," these are his words, "which I have just given requires me to determine what kinds of ideas can be received from works of Art, and which of these are the greatest, before proceeding to any practical application of the test.

"I think that all the sources of pleasure, or of any other

good, to be derived from works of Art, may be referred to five distinct heads.

"I. Ideas of Power.—The perception or conception of the mental or bodily powers by which the work has been produced.

"II. Ideas of Imitation.—The perception that the thing produced resembles something else.

"III. Ideas of Truth.—The perception of faithfulness in a statement of facts by the thing produced.

"IV. Ideas of Beauty.—The perception of beauty, either in the thing produced, or in what it suggests or resembles.

"V. Ideas of Relation.—The perception of intellectual relations in the thing produced, or in what it suggests or resembles."

It may be maintained that certain of these classes might be merged in each other, and a different mode of statement might by some be desired. But we think that if any one deliberately and carefully peruses the volumes, in which Mr. Ruskin has, so far, explained and illustrated the category, he can hardly fail to acknowledge that it is radically correct, and that it furnishes the groundwork of a complete system of Art-criticism. The first class is one with which all are familiar, who have the slightest acquaintance with critical opinion, or who have at all reflected on the mode in which the efforts of man are pleasing to his fellows. The second and third classes might not, perhaps, have been kept asunder, but represented as differing rather in relation of degree, in inferiority or superiority, than in essential nature. The difference, however, as Mr. Ruskin explains it, is by no means shadowy, the delight in imitation being confined to the mere pleasant illusion of the senses, while the delight in truth can extend to the most sublime facts, both of physical nature and of human feeling. To the discussion of the Ideas of Beauty, the whole of the second volume of *Modern Painters* is, more or less directly, devoted. The Ideas of Relation comprehend "all those conveyable by Art, which are the subjects of distinct intellectual perception and action, and which are therefore worthy of the name of thoughts." "Under this head," we are informed further, "must be arranged everything productive of expression, sentiment, and character, whether in figures or landscapes," and it especially includes the highest human interest.

It must be carefully noticed that the part of the whole work, *Modern Painters*, in which the Ideas of Relation would have come to be discussed and illustrated, has not yet appeared, and may perhaps never appear. After a comparatively brief investigation of the Ideas of Power and of Imitation, the whole of the first volume was devoted to the Ideas of Truth. In this portion of the work was displayed that marvellous acquaintance with the facts of nature, of which we have already spoken. After the Ideas of Truth came the Ideas of Beauty, constituting Part III., and theoretically treated of in the second volume. In it is drawn out that noble theory, which affirms, of all inherent beauty, that it is typical of the Divine attributes; a theory of which the metaphysical profundity may be found to be as remarkable, as the celestial purity of religious feeling, and the mellow splendor of eloquence, with which it is explained. Then there was a pause The symmetrical completion of the work required either that the manifestation of the Ideas of Beauty, in Art and in nature, should be traced, with a fullness corresponding to that with which the Ideas of Truth had been exhibited, —a proceeding, we suspect, anticipated in the first volume,

—or that the Ideas of Relation should be at once taken up. But volume third, consummate as was the power it displayed, proved, in relation to the outlined scheme of the book, an episode. It took up "many things," not expressly the Ideas of Relation. Nor has the fourth volume returned to the subject. It treats of "Mountain Beauty," which might, in great measure, be styled Mountain Truth, and a remark about "changes" which have been permitted "in the arrangement of the book," though breaking the "symmetrical continuation" of the previous volumes, renders one apprehensive that the original plan has been lost sight of, and that the Ideas of Relation will never be expressly taken up.

We confess that this seems to us matter for regret. In the first place, Mr. Ruskin himself distinctly declares these ideas to be the most important with which Art can be conversant. If he neglects their formal treatment, it may be very plausibly urged that he has condemned himself. In the next place, a thorough discussion of these ideas, and the accordance of a due prominence to the human interest with which they are conspicuously allied, might remove a charge which even able and candid critics may bring against Mr. Ruskin. After the pretentious feebleness of the *Quarterly*, the insolence of the *Edinburgh*, and the baseness of *Blackwood*, the critique of Ruskin which appeared in the *National Review* was refreshing and delightful. The writer perceived one half of Ruskin's greatness. He acknowledged his unequalled acquaintance with nature. But he denied him a due, or at least a correspondent measure of human sympathy. He honestly conceived him to love trees and mountains better than men. The mistake, indeed, even in the present state of Ruskin's works, could hardly have failed to yield to a sufficiently careful examination. The chapter on the functions of the Workman in Art in *The Stones of Venice*, the chapter on Vital Beauty in man, and that on Mountain Gloom, both in *Modern Painters*, much of the criticism in the Exhibition Pamphlets, and the whole tenor, indicated in a thousand expressions, of his works, conclusively evince that his heart beats with human sympathy as powerfully, as his senses are acute in the perception of beauty. Had Ruskin's energies been early directed into a different channel, he might have been a profound and sagacious writer on political or social subjects. But such a critic as the National reviewer could not have fallen into the mistake of supposing him open only to impressions of natural beauty, if, in the discussion of Ideas of Relation, he had balanced his treatment of natural beauty by a proportionate investigation of the human element in Art.

We are prevented by the narrowness of our limits, from following Mr. Ruskin in the detailed treatment of the various ideas of Art. It is hardly necessary that we should do so. All we have already said of his descriptions of natural appearance may be taken as declarative of what he has done in discussing the Ideas of Truth. His theory of Beauty, That, so far as it is inherent, it is typical of the Divine attributes, and, so far as it is not inherent, it consists in felicitous performance of vital functions, would require a separate critique. How the first half of the theory can be rejected we hardly see, except to suit an atheistic scheme of things. But whether the elements of the Beautiful do, or do not, typify the Divine attributes, it is at least true that suggestion of infinity, that unity, repose, symmetry, purity, and moderation are characteristics of beauty in Art. However, therefore, you may choose to apply it, the classification of these characteristics is neither vague, fanciful, nor devoid of strict practical value.

Though not professing to subscribe to every one of Ruskin's theoretic opinions, we yet believe him, and think we have at least indicated grounds for believing him, a comprehensive and scientific theorist in Art. But all theories are in some sense but moulds into which the metal of fact is run; and it is an evidence of the preciousness of this metal, that it can be melted from its old appearance and run into new dyes, yet retain its inherent value. Mr. Ruskin was gifted with the power of seeing new truth in nature, and if he has given us that truth he has done a substantial work. His theories may go, his facts cannot. Believing his theories to stand, in the substance of them, stably on facts, we are satisfied that they too will endure. But we have still to glance at him, engaged in the work of practical criticism, when, his theories aside, he brings his living force to solve the artistic problems, to judge the artistic phenomena, of his time. Do we find soundness or unsoundness, consistency or inconsistency, here?

Within the compass of that classification which we have quoted, there was range enough for diversity, both in degree, and nature, of power. Between the ideas of imitation and the ideas of highest truth and relation, there was room for drudging accuracy and for poetic invention. In his treatment of schools and artists, Mr. Ruskin has acted in accordance with a theory thus all-embracing. He has recognized the smallest molehill of real worth: he has ascended to the Himalayas of colossal power. Since, however, many men, who feel angry if you did not count them clever, can perceive consistency in the straightness of a lamp-post, but not in the strong stem, dividing branches, and delicate foliage of a living tree, there have been critics without end to pronounce Ruskin inconsistent.

Ruskin's practical criticism, in its true nature and essential consistency, can be amply and pointedly illustrated, by a single antithetic illustration: his opinion of Turner in contrast or coincidence with his opinion of the pre-Raphaelites.

Within the first thirty pages which Ruskin ever gave to the world, marked applause was accorded to a piece of pure idealization, a touch of highest poetry, from the pencil of Turner. In the fourth volume of *Modern Painters*, large space is devoted to a consideration of the distinctively poetic, the creative, imagination, of that painter. The imaginative power, which summons before the eye of its possessor, as if in vision or dream, forms and colors having no actual existence, but combining in a beauty higher than that of external nature, is there distinctly contemplated; an attempt even is made, — no one but Ruskin could have dared it, — to enter, if we may so speak, the chambers of Turner's mind, and to watch his conceptions coming together. Explicit acknowledgment is thus made, of the reality of the highest imaginative exertion, and it is set in the seat of supreme artistic honor. You must state facts very minutely in order to meet such critics as Ruskin's; else why should we make these references at all? Is not Ruskin most of all distinguished as the expositor and eulogist of Turner, and is not Turner the greatest landscape *poet* that ever used a brush? No painter ever so daringly magnified nature's forms, none ever arranged them anew so superbly in novel combinations, as Turner. It is evident, therefore, that Ruskin acknowledges, and with emphasis, that highest excellence in Art, which we may variously designate as the poetic, the ideal, the creative.

Shortly after the appearance of the first volume of *Modern Painters*, there began to attract attention a remarkable and original school of painting. It obtained the name of the pre-Raphaelite school, from professing the belief, that a pernicious conventionalism in Art dated from the time of Raphael. On its banner, it inscribed the word, Nature. The most conspicuous characteristic of its handling was a daring, uncompromising realism, and the most relentless of its realists was Everard Millais. The newspaper wits were in a state of excitement and commotion. The young painters were pronounced a set of miserable imitators, who could do nothing better than trace cracks in brick walls, make you believe you saw a bundle of hay within a picture frame, and perform despicable little bits of trickery with feathers and hairs. The general public was offended and repelled. The broad and distant horizon, the free sunlight, the pleasing sweeps of cloud, the balanced masses of foliage, the regulated harmony of color, all of which had been confidently looked for in a picture, were, in the pre-Raphaelite paintings, looked for in vain. The brethren would give you only what they could see, so closely and so continuously, that they could paint it line by line and tint by tint. No flowing cloud, no undulating horizon, no breadth of woodland, had you here. You were compelled to cramp yourself into the corner of a room, to concentrate your attention on briars and twining roots in the smallest nook of the dell, to be happy if you got a bit of garden wall with the least possible modicum, straight, level, uninteresting, of cloud. All this was intolerable. But one thing seemed clear:— Ruskin, the unbounded admirer of Turner, the exultant defender of him who gave more of sky and horizon than any painter known to Art, would join the public and the connoisseurs, in scourging these presumptuous youths into summary oblivion. Such, as we trust it is not unbecoming to state, were precisely our own first impressions as to the relation which must subsist between Ruskin and the pre-Raphaelites. We were fresh from *Modern Painters*, and the intense gratification the work had afforded to our love of nature had inspired us with ardor in the study of Art. With its exaltation of poetic thought over skilful execution, we had heartily sympathized. Cordially, if not very intelligently, had we agreed that the Flemish school might be "left in peace to count the spicula of haystacks and the hairs of donkeys." With unfeigned astonishment and perplexity, we heard that Ruskin defended the pre-Raphaelites. We were at fault. If Ruskin admired bareness, narrowness, ugliness, we thought we must have strangely misapprehended his words. The simple and honest course to pursue was, to read Mr. Ruskin's own pamphlet on the subject. We did so: and had not proceeded far when we perceived, that our perplexity originated in partial knowledge of Ruskin, and in still more partial knowledge of the pre-Raphaelites. All that particularly offended us in the pictures of the latter was, in itself, displeasing to Ruskin. For narrowness, littleness, ugliness, in themselves, he had no defence. But beneath all these, he discerned a devotion, not selfish, not conceited, but pure and manly, to nature. He saw that the dexterities of the pre-Raphaelites were not performed for their own sakes, but in determined adherence to fact. He saw that the brothers were on the right *way*, and he proclaimed it. He met our every objection in a manner more precise and explicit than we could have pointed out, by bringing together and comparing Turner and Millais. In the one, there was the eye of an eagle and the soul of a poet; the other had an eye like a microscope and cultivated unflinching realism: but both, as students of Art, sat at the feet of Nature. The pre-Raphaelites, Ruskin distinctly asserted, were yet but scholars. They were parted from Turner by a lifetime of study, such as few men ever had passed through, and by possession of genius, such as appears once in ages: but where Turner had learned his highest lessons, they had also gone to learn. It was plain that Ruskin was perfectly consistent; and a more accurate acquaintance with pre-Raphaelite *principles*, aided by a more careful consideration of Ruskin's words, could hardly have failed, even without his own explanation, to exhibit that consistency. For, in the first volume of *Modern Painters*, occurred the following passage. As one peruses it he cannot help asking in amazement, why, whenever Ruskin addresses *young* painters, young whether in years or in faculty, he is assailed as if he were addressing old, and why, whenever he praises the works of genius fully developed, he is accused of inconsistency for not *similarly* praising the works of beginners.

"From young artists," said Ruskin long ago, "nothing ought to be tolerated but simple *bona fide imitation* of nature. They have no business to ape the execution of masters; to utter weak and disjointed repetitions of other men's words, and mimic the gestures of the preacher, without understanding his meaning or sharing in his emotions. We do not want their crude ideas of composition, their unformed conceptions of the Beautiful, their unsystematized experiments upon the sublime. We scorn their velocity; for it is without direction: we reject their decision; for it is without grounds: we contemn their composition; for it is without materials: we reprobate their choice; for it is without comparison. Their duty is neither to choose, nor compose, nor imagine, nor experimentalize; but to be humble and earnest in following the steps of nature, and tracing the finger of God. Nothing is so bad a symptom, in the work of young artists, as too much dexterity of handling; for it is a sign that they are satisfied with their work, and have tried to do nothing more than they were able to do. Their work should be full of failures; for these are the signs of efforts. They should keep to quiet colors, grays and browns; and, making the earlier works of Turner their example, as his latest are to be their object and emulation, should go to nature with all singleness of heart, and walk with her laboriously and trustingly, having no other thoughts but how best to penetrate her meaning, and remember her instruction; rejecting nothing, selecting nothing, and scorning nothing; believing all things to be right and good, and rejoicing always in the truth. Then, when their memories are stored, and their imaginations fed, and their hands firm, let them take up the scarlet and the gold, give the reins to their fancy, and show us what their heads are made of. We will follow them wherever they choose to lead; we will check at nothing; they are then our masters, and are fit to be so. They have placed themselves above our criticism, and we will listen to their words in all faith and humility; but not unless they themselves have before bowed, in the same submission, to a higher Authority and Master."

The man who thus recognizes every order of excellence, from Turnerism to pre-Raphaelitism, must be substantially sound as a critic of Art. As we listen to his commendations of realism, we have only to inquire whether, as an Art-*education*, nature ought to be paramount or not? It need scarcely be added, that, though Ruskin denounces artistic slavery to any master, his whole exposition and vindication of Turner evince that he can joyfully learn from all masters, so far as they are interpreters of nature, or exhibit true thought and emotion. He will gladly take the hand of

Raphael to lead him to those fields of study where Raphael learned to be what he was; he will earnestly strive to enter into the moods of mind in which Raphael conceived or executed: but he will not stand close up to the canvas of Raphael, letting it shut out the light of heaven and the loveliness of earth, and *steal* from him the thoughts and facts which nature gave to him alone.

Has Ruskin's criticism of individual artists, pre-Raphaelite or other, corresponded with the view we have just taken, the facts we have just adduced? Has he neglected to inform the pre-Raphaelites of their failings, to shake them out of their crotchets? Has he shunned to make such a remark as that the painting of truthful ugliness is the "Nemesis of pre-Raphaelitism," indefensible in itself, though to be laid at the door of those who goaded the pre-Raphaelites into fractiousness? Has he refused to acknowledge diverse excellence, to turn from the crystal transparency, and outline sharp as a knife-edge, of John Lewis, to the pouring skies and matted herbage of David Cox, bestowing words of ardent commendation on both? Has he overlooked the tender feeling hiding behind imperfect execution in the pictures of Hook, because he prizes the rugged facts of Millais? He does not praise now as he praised Turner: he waits until a Turner rise.

The Dutch school may deserve one other word. Mr. Ruskin's willingness to consign all its productions to an *auto da fe* looks at first singular. Were the expressions he has used regarding it unqualified by the context and by the rest of his works, they might admit of no defence. The Dutch painters deserve deep respect as accurate narrators of fact, and as honestly representative of a national character. But considered in connection with the whole aim and development of Art, the Dutch school is without hesitation to be condemned. With all his admiration for artistic truth, Ruskin's Art-instinct is far too sound to permit him to forget that the end of Art is beauty, that her eye is ever upwards. The Dutch artists, with the exceptions he expressly makes, Rubens, Vandyke, Rembrandt, *rested* in their work. They did not press up and up, until the light of common day paled in the higher imaginative radiance never seen on sea or shore. The tendency of a devoted study of their works might be to prevent artists from thus perpetually going on. They were a pre-Raphaelite school struck, at a certain point, with blindness. Had Ruskin wholly approved them, his admiration of pre-Raphaelitism would have been a sanction of its crudities, not a hope for its perfection, and his praise of Turner, not the pinnacle of a symmetrical building, but a contradiction. Thus, as is always the case, a real consistency is most triumphantly vindicated in and through an apparent inconsistency.

One thing Ruskin has always condemned without qualification, and, besides of course, pure falsehood and slovenliness, it alone: The *manufacture* of poetry in form and color, the production of great pictures by conventional rules. No attempt to ape genius can either escape or propitiate him: a thousand academies, chanting the praises of cultured and pretentious mediocrity, would not daunt him in his assault upon it.

It has been objected to Ruskin, and, not perhaps so inappropriately as may appear, by one who proclaims that in the application of his intellectual powers there is "not one single great moral quality," that he forces upon Art a moral responsibility. An unbiassed consideration of Mr. Ruskin's own words shows that he demands of landscape Art what he finds in nature, a tendency, namely, to awaken certain great and elevating ideas. A man of religion, a Christian, finds that all such ideas lead him up towards his Father in heaven, and Ruskin, being thus led in nature, has to deplore the twofold fact, that ancient Art does not so lead him, and that Art in general has hitherto exhibited no power of so leading men. He demands, in Art, earnestness, simplicity, truthfulness, humility, knowing that, when the heart is rightly strung, it will, by these, be turned in the direction of Him who is the source of all such good gifts. The idea of turning all Art into allegory, or of contriving landscapes to suggest ethical doctrines or moral maxims, would be to him as abhorrent, as the idea of graving wise saws on the rocks, or pasting the trees with good advice from the copy books. Yet we should omit a characteristic, without a consideration of which it is impossible to form a comprehension of Ruskin's mind and writings, if we did not take into account his religious earnestness, his Christian piety. Of this he cannot divest himself: if Art required him to divest himself of it, he would abandon Art. Whether the reality and depth of his Christianity have affected the soundness of his artistic views, the reader must now judge for himself. There was no reason why they should have done so and they have not. On the other hand, they have led him into regions of pure and beautiful thought, little known to critics; they have cast over his whole works a softened yet steady-beaming glory, a benign and tranquil splendor; they have caused to break out, ever and anon, as it were tones of music, which waft you gently upwards, leaving material beauty for spiritual, the things of earth for the things of heaven. He has, as we saw, shown that Poetry and Science, though different, are Sisters; and as he shows them they are looking towards God for his light to fall upon both. Therefore it is that the works of Ruskin stand apart from all that has ever been written on Art. They connect themselves with what is greatest and holiest in human duty and devotion, with what is most solemn and benign in the ways of God to man. The following passage may illustrate these remarks. The author has been considering the characteristic of repose in works of Art. In accordance with his uniform method of broadly human treatment, he traces the nobleness of the quality in its highest manifestations:—

"But that which in lifeless things ennobles them by seeming to indicate life, ennobles higher creatures by indicating the exaltation of their earthly vitality into a Divine vitality; and raising the life of sense into the life of faith: faith, whether we receive it in the sense of adherence to resolution, obedience to law, regardfulness of promise, in which from all time it has been the test, as the shield of the true being and life of man; or in the still higher sense of trustfulness in the presence, kindness, and word of God, in which form it has been exhibited under the Christian dispensation; for, whether in one or other form — whether the faithfulness of men whose path is chosen and portion fixed, in the following and receiving of that path and portion, as in the Thermopylæ camp, or the happier faithfulness of children in the good giving of their Father, and of subjects in the conduct of their King, as in the 'Stand still and see the salvation of God' of the Red Sea shore — there is rest and peacefulness, the 'standing still' in both, the quietness of action determined, of spirit unalarmed, of expectation unimpatient: beautiful even when based only, as of old, on the self-command and self-possession, the persistent dignity or the uncalculating love of the creature; but more beautiful yet, when the rest is one of humility, instead of pride, and the trust no more in the resolution we have taken, but in the hand we hold."

Mr. Ruskin's writings afford three or four instances of slips in reasoning, so manifest and so avoidable, that they seem intentionally thrown in the way of those critics who will always insist upon forming the estimate of a field of wheat from its half-dozen bad ears. Thus, in one place, an appeal on behalf of the decaying monuments of architectural Art is founded on an analogy between wasting one's own time and wasting that of one's ancestors. This is an argument which one cares not to answer. Logic is unnecessary in the case;—formal logic, indeed, as Mr. Macaulay, and we suppose multitudes before Mr. Macaulay, remarked long ago, is not used in the thinking operations of any man;—the intuitive sense of every one simply rejects it. If, however, it had to be explicitly shown to be unsound, the task could be performed in a moment. You do not waste your own time, first, because it may be turned to account by yourself, because it is of value to you, second, because you are responsible for it. But a dead man has had all the value out of his time that he can have: and death has forever closed his account of responsibility. A man's fame may be filched from him after his death; but would you call destroying a man's renown synonymous with wasting his time? Whether there is any conceivable sense in which a living man can waste a dead man's time is doubtful, or rather not doubtful; but no human reason, unless nodding, will recognize a parallel between wasting your own time when alive, and wasting your father's when he is dead. With the object in furtherance of which Mr. Ruskin adduced this strange argument, we cordially sympathize. Again, in a volume very recently published, Mr. Ruskin declares his preference for drawing, as a part of the education of children, to writing. No one, he argues, can draw without benefitting himself and his fellows; few can write, without doing no good,—if we remember correctly his language is even stronger,—to either. Of the extreme usefulness of drawing, considered educationally, we are convinced. But to compare it with that art by which human feeling is, in absence, all communicated, and which must be regarded, side by side with reading, as one of those great pillars on which all education rests, and to which all education is secondary, is to propound an obvious paradox. Next, and here a better show of defence can be made, Mr. Ruskin, immediately after declaring it "probable" that "the critical and executive faculties are in great part independent of each other," allows himself to assert, that "a certain power of drawing is *indispensable* to the critic of Art." Had any word but "indispensable" been here used, it might have passed. But this word puts in peril the vital principle involved in the very nature of Art, and without the clear acknowledgment of which we believe dilettantism can never be destroyed or even met, that its effect is totally independent of its methods of production. It is not an easy thing to be able to form a correct judgment on works of Art. The power is in proportion to the accuracy and width of knowledge, possessed of man and nature; and such knowledge, if we inquire, is seldom either accurate or wide. To give precision to observations made by the senses, the power of drawing cannot perhaps be exaggerated. But it is only by enabling one to know nature, that drawing assists him in judging of Art. If the faculty of observation is naturally so acute, and has been so heedfully exercised, that it cannot be deceived as to the form or hue of clouds or foliage, as to the aspects of passion or the lines of thought, it qualifies its possessor to be a critic in Art. Do you require to know the mysterious properties by which the sunbeams and the metal produced the likeness, in order to say whether the daguerreotype has succeeded in rendering the features of your friend? To say that one must be able to draw in order to judge of Painting is to say that, in order to judge of Poetry, one must not only be able to read, must not only have the power of placing its visions before his eyes, but must be able to versify. A fourth instance of inadvertency is found in Mr. Ruskin's sharp attack upon Macaulay, for having, in his essay upon Moore's Life of Byron, spoken in a sneering tone of the pictures of Paradise in old Bibles. The point which cannot fail to strike every reader is, that Mr. Macaulay did not consider these pictures at all in their symbolic significance, that he contrasted them, as delineations of an actual Paradise, with delineations true to nature, and that, so contrasting them, he pronounced them, as Mr. Ruskin doubtless would, absurd. The circumstance that Macaulay spoke of the sets of pictures solely in illustration, both made it legitimate for him to place them in any opposition he chose, and put it out of the question that he should contemplate the deliberate condemnation of either. You may say that a bishop's mitre, considered as a mere covering for the head, is absurd in comparison with a wide-awake; but you would not therefore speak disrespectfully of the mitre. Once more, Mr. Ruskin has assailed, with a violence the less defensible that it is incidental, "metaphysicians and philosophers." These "are, on the whole, the greatest troubles the world has got to deal with." The metaphysician or philosopher is specially defined to be "an affected Thinker, who supposes his thinking of any other importance than as it tends to work." If Mr. Ruskin will accept a definition of work in accordance with his own noble doctrine of utility, laid down in the commencement of the second volume of *Modern Painters*, we shall agree with him in denouncing all such persons as these. But we have yet to learn that Kant was a less practical thinker than Plato, or that Plato was less a metaphysician than Kant; while we look in vain for affected thinkers among the Fichtes and Hamiltons of recent times. If Mr. Ruskin had given the names of those whom he advises prudent people to brush out of their way "like spiders," we might have agreed with him or we might not. But his words will be understood as, on the whole, deprecating the study of metaphysics, and as such we regret them. It would of course be absurd to enter here upon a eulogium or defence of the most sublime studies, theology excepted, in which the intellect of man can be engaged: but why should Mr. Ruskin thus gratuitously strive to alienate that audience, which, of all others, is most fitted to learn of him, and of which it is the highest compliment that we can pay him to say that he is worthy to be the teacher?

A few more instances of unwariness or inaccuracy might be culled from Mr. Ruskin's works. But considering the voluminousness of his writings, it is altogether absurd to view them in any other light than that in which we regard the noddings of Homer, or the grammatical and geographical slips of Shakspeare. They are, for one thing, utterly insufficient to furnish an excuse for the manner in which critics have treated Ruskin. We deliberately assert that several of these have earned the just indignation of Ruskin's audience, that is, of the educated world. The writer in the *Quarterly* whose absolute blindness to the whole meaning of Ruskin in his system of criticism, we think we have already shown, and who is understood to be no less imposing a personage than Sir Charles Eastlake, not only says that his intellectual qualities are guided by no moral principle whatever, that the truth of his conclusions is to him "no object in the process of reasoning," but adds that "his writings have all the qualities of premature old age — its coldness, callousness, and contraction." It is our firm belief that there is not, in the whole range of literature, an expression more amazing, more incomprehensible, than this last. We do not answer it: certainly not. We only request readers, first to read any volume or any page of Ruskin's, and then to ponder, one by one, the words, — coldness, — callousness, — contraction, — as a description of the author's spirit. But the charge of want of controlling principle, of regardlessness of truth in conclusions, amounts to a charge of utter falsity; if our verdict is affirmative, we convict Mr. Ruskin of being, not only a scoundrel, but a scoundrel of the deepest dye, at once false and hypocritical. If all Mr. Ruskin has ever alleged against living artists were concentrated into one thunderbolt, it would fall like a rocket compared with this. To make such an accusation without ample and indubitable proof was surely to run the risk of being excluded from all honorable society. And what is Sir Charles's proof? Why, in the first place, we hear of Ruskin's "revilings of all that is most sacred in the past, and his insults to all who are most sensitive in the present." This about reviling the sacred past is, let us plainly say, insufferable drivel. Ruskin feels, and has expressly said, that the dead can be pained by no criticism; and it is an insult to common sense, to call in question a man's moral integrity, because he rubs the gilt from ancient names. As for insults to the living, the reference is, no doubt, chiefly to the pamphlets on the Academy Exhibitions. It so happens that we agree with nearly every word of the first of these, which alone could be charged with severity, and with no word of it more cordially, according to our humble capacity, than that which condemns Sir Charles Eastlake's insipid and mawkish Beatrice. There is nothing in the pamphlet which a gentleman might not have written, and which gentlemen might not accept. It may perhaps be, that artists in general will not thank the president, for leading us to believe, that they all take to whimpering, when Ruskin, never casting a shadow of reflection on their moral qualities, points boldly and bluntly out their artistic shortcomings. But there is another department of proof, by which Sir Charles would establish Mr. Ruskin's complete moral worthlessness. He quotes several of those expressions in which the latter reflects on the want of faith exhibited, as he believes, at the present time, in the inanity of fashionable amusements, and such things, and we are to take these expressions as satisfactory evidence of "malice, bitterness, and uncharitableness." Readers must refer to pp. 405, 406, vol. 196, of the *Quarterly Review* for this extraordinary passage. It is Sir Charles's last daring attempt to set reason, sense, and even credibility, at defiance. We shall not ask whether there may be reasons for attacking the faithless, frivolous and selfish, besides malice, bitterness and uncharitableness. Nor is it worth while to ask the honorable Sir Charles why he has not seen fit to quote, say, the appeals made by Ruskin on behalf of the Swiss peasants, as well as the attacks on the follies of London. But is it not delightful to figure the indignation of this virtuous president, against two such moral monsters as Mr. Carlyle and Mr. Thackeray? By bringing so grave and definite a charge against Mr. Ruskin, and supporting it as he has done, Sir Charles Eastlake puts himself in a position which few men would like to occupy!

The pert, penny-a-lining flippancy, with which the *Edinburgh Review* attacked Ruskin might best be treated with silent contempt. But there is one point in its article, to which allusion may be made. The reviewer notices that autobiographical passage to which we had occasion to refer; and his mode of noticing it is a passing sneer. Now it admits of no doubt whatever, that the question as to how a critic's system is connected with his natural endowment, is always of importance; and the question is in the case of Ruskin of more express and essential moment than in any other. When you clear away all else, you find that the grand, central affirmation, which he makes in the face of the world, is, that he has brought into view a certain number of the facts of nature. From this, all his teaching branches out: on this, all his theories are, in one sense or other, based. Take from him the circumstance of having made a truthful interpretation, an authentic revelation, of nature, and you take from him everything: leave him this, and it is, as we said, impossible, on any hypothesis, that his system can be destroyed, save in the way in which a sterling currency is destroyed when it is re-stamped. This being so, it was of the last importance for the world to know that he had been pre-eminently fitted, by original endowment, for making observations upon natural appearance; and to have turned aside, when it came directly in his way to give information on the point, would have been to display an unmanly and effeminate sensitiveness. In the sneer of the Edinburgh reviewer, therefore, there was a twofold insult: to the nation, whom he pretended to instruct: to the man, whom he pretended to understand.

But perhaps neither Sir Charles Eastlake's downright accusation of malice, uncharitableness, and regardlessness of truth, in one word, of total reprobacy and worthlessness, nor the piteous frivolity of the last-mentioned imbecile, can be pronounced, on the whole, so base and beggarly, as one of the attacks, occurring incidentally in a rambling kind of article, made upon Ruskin in *Blackwood*. The writer of course discovers indubitable inconsistency in Ruskin's works. Since, in order to know whether a system is consistent or not, you must be of sufficient mental compass to embrace it, as a whole, within your sphere of intellectual vision, we should probably have to make important modifications in the view we have presented of Ruskin and his system, if critics of a certain order did *not* find both inconsistent. Having discovered his inconsistency, the critic proceeds to account for it. Here imitation, and the finish resulting only in imitation, and both the finish and the imitation that end only in themselves, are decried; there truth is exalted, and the finish subservient to truth is praised. Over this remarkable contradiction, the expert critic brings his little lamp. He has found it! Ruskin wanted to praise when he liked and blame when he liked, according as whim or malice prompted, and so he put in two different rules, that he might use the one at one time and the other at another. The fear and dread of such terrible critics as this small ebon dwarf lay upon Ruskin, and so he contrived an elaborate trick, he uttered a deliberate lie, that he might have a weapon against them in the day of battle. We hope it was not Professor Aytoun who propounded this theory. The writers in *Blackwood* toady him so pitiably, that neither general rumor, nor internal evidence, can make you perfectly certain that an article is by him and not an imitation. By discovering what a man finds in the character or system of another, one is led with peculiar accuracy to the truth concerning the essential nature of himself. We should experience a feeling of strange and painful repulsion from the man, in whose breast there dwelt a sympathy, casting so foul and dingy a light as this. We should really not like to be capable of making this discovery in connection with Ruskin. We should fear that there was some baseness, dark, deep-lying, insidious, nestling about our heart and polluting all its streams. Such a perception of moral taint has surely in it something of *recognition!* Professor Aytoun is indeed no poet, except so far as is implied in a certain command over that mechanical part of poetry, which Milton, speaking of Dryden, distinguished as versification ; and his character and poetry seem on the whole a very pertinent exemplification of what greatness is *not.* But he has one quality, both real and precious, which, we shall hope, rendered it impossible for him to find, in all the enthusiasm of feeling and glory of description, exhibited in the works of Ruskin, simply the paraphernalia of a small, nasty lie. Professor Aytoun possesses a talent of genial banter, all his own. It is playful yet manly, brilliant yet full of warm humor. If the vein is not so deep as Thackeray's, we suspect it is more rare. Thackeray has done nothing like *The Raid of t' Pherson.* The perception and appreciation of the two aspects of Highland character, that of this piece and that of the Cavalier ballads, shows a dramatic pliancy and amplitude of mind really fine. Professor Aytoun's banter could not be at present spared from British literature ; it is unique, and we could not supply its place. We shall hope it was not he who arrived at this theory touching Ruskin.

The whole phenomenon of the author of *Modern Painters* and his critical assailants, the mode in which they attack him and the relation in which they stand to him, is singular and anomalous. About two hundred years ago, the London theatres were ringing with the applause of the dramatists of the Restoration. Pit, boxes, gallery, coffee-house, court, echoed their renown. Meanwhile, in obloquy and obscurity, John Milton was dictating *Paradise Lost.* Deafened by the shouts in their ears, dazzled by the glare of lamps and tinsel, the Congreves and Wycherlys knew nothing of him. The dramas of the Restoration are fast settling into that abyss of darkness, which swallows the meteors of the night and the glimmering exhalations of the fen. *Paradise Lost* is rising higher and higher above the mountain-tops of the world, still in the morning of its fame. Confident in the applause of Academies, strong in the renown of Reviews, blatant mediocrity attempts to cry down Ruskin. But he has told the world new truth, and the world will do him justice if he bide his time. Mediocrity may have it for years, but not for ages.

And he has not been without his reward. He has extended a magnificent patronage to those artists who reviled him. That is a reward which *he* can appreciate. Was not Actæon hunted by the base hounds he fed, and that because he, too, caught a glimpse of the Beautiful? But there are artists who can appreciate Ruskin; and the pre-Raphaelite School, if not his express intellectual progeny, at least conforms to his rules. A critic in the *National Review*, very different from those we have noticed, has recognized the supremacy of his knowledge of nature, and may, by more full consideration, learn that it is the accidental manifestation, rather than the real character, of his mind, which is one-sided. It has been acknowledged in the *Times* that, let artists say what they will, he first made the public really aware what a painter they had in Turner. Best of all, the young intellect of Great Britain has heard his voice, the great heart of the nation has owned the might of his genius. The clouds of conventionalism, which have brooded over Europe for centuries, have been touched by his shafts of light and must gradually disappear. He has been a reconciler between Art and mankind, leading Art into the lowly paths of life, setting Art by the household fire, and astonishing men by the information, that the smile on her face is actually warm and human. Let him not hear the critics! Let him not be baited into indignation; let him not permit his sympathies to be chilled by the companionship of contempt! Let him reveal those visions which God has given him only to see among the hills; let him tell us, as he only can, of the streams that run among the valleys; and let him leave to those who have candidly read him, that small vent for their gratitude, which they may find in answering his critics.

VI.

HUGH MILLER.

There is a great deal in this rough-hewn, boisterous, not very exquisitely mannered century, from which the whole class of dilettants and fine gentlemen turn aside. There has been no age in the world, and, until man radically alters there will be none, in which the guinea's stamp has not more or less drawn away men's eyes from the real gold. The nineteenth century has its own sycophancies and idolatries, its own Sir John Pauls and Barnums. But set fairly in comparison with other times, our epoch seems to be incontrovertibly distinguished by the scope it affords to real human faculty, and the willingness with which it recognizes a man when it sees him. He has now a poor chance who places his reliance upon ribands and parchment. He puts himself in an unenviable position who would now presume himself, on the strength of heraldic distinctions and well-filled purse, in a position to do honor, by the expression of his approval, or the bestowal of his company, to the man of genius who has forced his way from the ranks. Even within sixty years, a considerable advance has been made in this respect within the British Islands. There was something of the luxury of a haughty condescension, not unmingled with self-applause, in the reception of Burns by Edinburgh grandiosity at the close of last century. There was a serene complacency in the smiling, as if it were peculiarly beautiful and praiseworthy in people so fine and lofty to encourage the really entertaining and talented ploughman. With rather an effort of kindness, they patronized their king! Alexander Smith, his birth as humble as that of Burns, and coming some sixty years after him, finds a strong figure in the loathing with which he would spurn a rich man's dole, whether, doubtless, of patronage or of pay. Tennyson, the poet of the most refined culture, sees that feudalism with all its apportionment of honor, has become a joke:—

> "Trust me, Clara Vere de Vere,
> From yon blue heaven above us bent,
> The grand old gardener and his wife
> Smile at the claims of long descent."

The duke who would come to confer distinction on Hugh Miller, by taking his hand and showing him a little countenance, would get himself simply covered with derision. A man stands now more solely and independently on the pedestal of his individuality, than was ever the case before. And no man is in this more strikingly representative of his time than he of whom we here speak. What Hugh Miller is and has, he owes entirely to himself. In the firm, deliberate planting of his heavy step, in the quiet, wide-open determination of his eye, in the unagitated, unaffected, self-relying dignity of his whole gait and deportment, you behold the man who feels that, whatever his origin, he may, without pride or presumption, measure himself by the standard of his manhood, and so look every man, of what station soever, in the face.

Hugh Miller's education may also be pronounced if not distinctive of the nineteenth century, yet highly characteristic of it. Theoretic education, the education of letters, is in his case rather peculiarly blended with the education of practice. He is one of the strong men who, amid the sternest toil of mechanical employment, have become acquainted, and that not cursorily and superficially but systematically and profoundly, with those stores of book-knowledge now open to all, if only they have learned to read and have natural force not to be daunted by difficulty: yet his character has derived its brawn and sinew from practice, from the rough jostling and wrestling of life. He has all along been a man of action. Born of a wild, strong, determined kindred, who seem from of old to have lived a life of "sturb and strife," and in a rank of life just sufficiently high to save him from knowing the pangs of want, the world-oyster was to him very firmly closed, but he was the kind of man to open it. Roughing it in the quarry or barrack, seizing the brief intervals of labor to heap up knowledge which a tenacious memory never lost, losing no opportunity, ever ready to strike occasion in its flight, he suddenly emerged into public view, an expert literary workman, and with store of scientific information, the fruit of original discovery, sufficient to secure him a place among the first physical philosophers of his time. Too long a stone-mason to be ever sleeked down into the smooth drawing-room gentleman, rugged, shaggy, burly, like a rough-hewn statue of old red sandstone, he was yet possessed of a very high intellectual culture, familiar with the discussions which have agitated philosophical schools, intimately acquainted with his country's poetry, and master of a style which reminded one of Addison.

His school education was meagre. Through life, he has learned more by the eye than by the ear, and he did not find much to interest him in the instructions of the village pedagogue. He commenced Latin. But he found nothing to attract him in the rudiments of the language. They were exceedingly dry, and he saw no prospect of their becoming alive or useful. He felt his eyes bandaged, and he would not open his mouth to receive the necessary though unpalatable fare. He experienced precisely such a craving for the tangible and practical, as made Arnold, when a boy, refuse to master quantities and accents, and turn from "words" to "things." But Arnold regretted his early refusal, and Miller has still more reason to lament his boyish aversion to Latin. We may remark in passing, that though it ought to be the aim of every teacher to cast, by his skill, an interest over the barest matters, it is an indubitable principle in early education, that the pupil should receive much blindfold, without either liking or understanding it. Both for the culture of faculty, and in order to prepare a man for the many cases in life, in which he will have to proceed unfaltering, when, for a time, the interest flags, and the result is obscure or uncertain, this is a principle of capital importance.

The fact, however, was so, that Hugh Miller left school without gaining even an initial acquaintance with the ancient languages. It is in perfect consistence with all which can be urged in honor of the present and the practical, to avow a feeling of regret on account of this circumstance. True it is, that there exists a vast and noble modern literature, and that the man who knows modern history and a few modern languages, has undergone a very valuable intellectual training. Yet it is a fact, at no time to be forgotten, that every man is "heir of all the ages" behind him, that, in virtue of his intellect, imagination, and sympathy, he may connect himself with earliest times, that he may enrich and exercise his mind by a sympathizing acquaintance with every form of national and individual life, and every masterpiece of mind, which the centuries behind him can show. The past may be compared to a great, ever-ascending pyramid, to which each generation has added a layer or stratum, and from the top of which each generation, as it emerges into the light of the present, may see further than its predecessor. Education is in every age more difficult than in the preceding. But the reward increases in exact proportion to the labor: the higher the pyramid to be ascended, the wider the prospect to be obtained. And it is precisely the strong man, the man endowed with great powers of intellectual vision, who will profit most largely by the extension of the horizon. Hugh Miller, with his fine, scholarly memory, and calm comprehensiveness of glance, is just the man we should like to have seen standing on the pyramid of the past.

It may seem strange, but we must confess that our regret that Hugh Miller did not at an early period acquaint himself with the languages of antiquity is confirmed rather than removed by a consideration of his style. That style we have already alluded to in terms of commendation; and it were not easy to confer on it too high praise. Dr. Buckland did not scruple to inform the world, that he "would give his left hand to possess such powers of description" as Hugh Miller. Recollecting the staid and prosaic habits of professors, we cannot but feel that Dr. Buckland must have been very much struck indeed. The style in question is one of very rare excellence. Easy, fluent, clear, and expressive, it adapts itself, like a silken shawl, to every swell, and motion, and curve of a subject. It is graphic yet not extravagant, strong without vociferation, measured without formality, classically chaste yet pleasingly adorned. It has the soft flow and easy cadence which marked the best distinctive styles of the eighteenth century, stubborned with something of the sterner music of the nineteenth. Such a style belongs only to men of genius. Rich, lucid, pictorial, it casts fascination over the old armor of the pterichthys, or shows a whole geographical district at one view, the physiognomic features strongly brought out, and the whole robed in a beauty at once poetic and scientific.

Yet, we repeat, it seems to us matter for regret, in a linguistic point of view, that Hugh Miller turned away from the portals of antiquity. The almost universally received canon of English style, that it ought to be extremely Saxon, we venture to call in question. It appears rather to be the case that Saxon may be generally trusted to take care of itself, and that mass, majesty, power, and deep, rhythmic cadence, are best secured by an infusion of the Latin element. The grandest prose styles in the language are cased in the Roman armor. The "cathedral music" of Milton was toned by the classic tongues. Johnson went, no doubt, to an unnatural excess, yet the power exercised by his style when he used it must not be overlooked. Burke was a classical scholar. So, with emphasis, was Gibbon. De Quincey, Carlyle, Ruskin, and Macaulay, the most wonderful stylists of our day, are all familiar with the ancient languages. It were, perhaps, bold to assert that this element is absolutely necessary to an English style of the highest order. But the instances cited, together with the fact that very important component parts of our language — parts which embrace more than mere words, and must have influenced the very idiom of the tongue—are derived from antiquity, may sufficiently vindicate the declaration, that Hugh Miller's style would have gained in stateliness and range, had he become, in his earlier days, a thorough classical scholar. In the treatment of a vast majority of subjects, a simple Saxon style, of the Bunyan or Goldsmith type, will suffice; a good Saxon style is as superior to a bad Latin style, as that of Goldsmith was to that of Johnson; but in the highest flights of an author—and Hugh Miller has thought to sustain him in the loftiest linguistic flights —one floats best on the broad pinions of Latin.

But if the classic tongues are an important accession to a literary education, there are other parts, still less easily dispensed with, and in regard to these Hugh Miller furnishes no subject for complaint. With quick faculty and open sympathy, he mastered all the English books that came in his way. He commenced to read at about six years of age, and set about forming a little library for himself. It began with our invaluable nursery literature, rich in adventure, abounding with heroes,—the epic Jack, the travelled Sinbad, the interesting, neat-footed Cinderella, the shifty and politic Puss, knowing how to turn boots to advantage; and the rest. Pope's heroes, in his metamorphosis of Homer's *Iliad*, came next. The author of *Eothen* testifies how the heart of every noble boy is stirred by the fierce and fine-spoken valor of the Popian warriors, set as it is in a melody, clear and ringing as the clang of arms. The *Pilgrim's Progress*, that book for the nursery, the home, the shop, the study, the deathbed, followed. At ten, he fell in with blind Harry's *Wallace*, and some time after, with Barbour's *Bruce*, and was forthwith a patriot and Scotchman to the finger-tips. During all this time, he was under the full influence of Presbyterian opinions and prepossessions. And thus his days passed, until he reached the threshold of manhood, and adopted a profession.

The life of Hugh Miller as an apprentice and journeyman mason may be with sufficient accuracy imagined. It was one of continual toil, and, now and then, of severe hardship. He lived in various localities through the country, generally in bothies or barracks, where several workmen put up together. But for a habit of taciturnity, and a tendency to musing and poetry, there was no difference discernible between him and any other mason. Of subsequent elevation, he never dreamed. His accent was rude, and his appearance gave no hint of intellectual culture. With a leathern apron before him, foul with mud and dust, his hands, it might be, bleeding with his work among the wet stones, none would have recognized him for a man of peculiar and exquisite endowment, who had even then acquired that easy and graceful mastery over the English language, which was to charm a large audience of the most cultivated intellects of the age, and woke the admiring despair of men staggering under their load of erudition. We cannot refrain from taking one look at Hugh Miller during his life as a journeyman mason. The passage by means of which we do so, and which occurs in his autobiography, insists upon associating itself in our minds with that in which Milton so sublimely represents the student of his time as outwatching the bear in converse with the spirit of Plato:—

"There was no one in the barrack with whom I cared much to converse, or who, in turn, cared much to converse with me; and so I learned, on the occasions when the company got dull and broke up into groups, to retire to the hay-loft where I slept, and pass there whole hours seated on my chest. The loft was a vast apartment, some fifty or sixty feet in length, with its naked rafters raised little more than a man's height over the floor; but in the starlit nights, when the openings in the wall assumed the character of square patches of darkness-visible stamped upon utter darkness, it looked quite as well as any other unlighted place that could not be seen, and in nights brightened by the moon, the pale beams, which found access at openings and crevices, rendered its wide area quite picturesque enough for ghosts to walk in. But I never saw any; and the only sounds I heard were those made by the horses in the stable below, champing and snorting over their food. They were, I doubt not, happy enough in their dark stalls, because they were horses, and had plenty to eat, and I was at times quite happy enough in the dark loft above, because I was a man, and could think and imagine. It is, I believe, Addison who remarks, that if all the thoughts which pass through men's minds were to be made public, the great difference which seems to exist between the thinking of the wise and of the unwise would be a good deal reduced; seeing that it is a difference which does not consist in their not having the same weak thoughts in common, but merely in the prudence through which the wise suppress their foolish ones. I still possess notes of the cogitations of these solitary evenings, ample enough to show that they were extraordinary combinations of the false and the true; but I at the same time hold them sufficiently in memory to remember, that I scarce, if at all, distinguished between what was false and true in them at the time. The literature of almost every people has a corresponding early stage, in which fresh thinking is mingled with little conceits, and in which the taste is usually false, but the feeling true."

For a protracted period, Hugh Miller worked for his daily bread, pick or trowel in hand. He, then, for a short time, acted as accountant in a bank in his native town of Cromarty. He had become slightly known in the literary world by the publication of a volume of poems, and contributed to certain periodical works. A volume of tales and legends, now very well known, brought him still further into notice. But the famous non-intrusion controversy was then agitating Scotland. Hugh Miller, strong in his Presbyterian leanings, and keenly alive to the evils of lay patronage, addressed a letter to Lord Brougham, publishing the piece in form of a pamphlet. It awakened a wide interest, and was complimented in no measured terms by O'Connell and Mr. Gladstone. Dr. Candlish, then busied, in co-operation with the other leaders of the evangelical party, about setting on foot a newspaper to advocate the views of the non-intrusionists, had perused the letter in manuscript, and at once pronounced its author the fitting man to conduct the paper. So, in 1840, Hugh Miller became editor of the *Witness* newspaper, and a very brief period elapsed ere he was one of the most influential men in his country.

The "able editor," if we may be permitted to interpose a semi-pilosophical reflection, seems to us something of an interim phenomenon. He marks a state of transition from a state of information and intelligence gone past, to a state of general intellectual culture not yet arrived. It is not indeed necessary to suppose that he will himself pass away; such a supposition would, on the contrary, be highly absurd: but he may gradually undermine the ground he himself stands on, and there are not wanting indications in the present day, that he is being overtaken by the general intelligence. In the olden time, in the days, for instance, of our old friend Abbot Samson, of St. Edmundsbury monastery in the twelfth century, men were led blindfold by some one man who had his eyes open. The chief saw for the vassal, and led him along unknowing whither he went. The priest saw for the flock, told it what he chose, and was implicitly believed. It was, in Fichte's phraseology, the period of unquestioning submission to authority. We are now in progress — we may at least hope or suppose — toward that intellectual state which Fichte defined as "freedom in consistence with reason." Meanwhile, the time is characterized by partial submission and partial freedom. The mass of men judge more, know more, are more free and self-established, than the retainer or monk of the middle ages. The newspaper editor still does much of the thinking for men in general, and people submit, so far, their thoughts to him. But, by the action of the press, you obtain, on the one hand, a greater amount of freedom than ever distinguished the mass before, and, on the other, a higher average of information, a more general exercise of thought, than, were men unassisted by newspapers, would subsist. Mr. Carlyle must not sneer too bitterly against the able editor. The matter perhaps most to be regretted in connection with the profession is, that men, often of great reach and sagacity, should spend their strength in the continual day drudgery of editorial toil. One can sympathize with Hugh Miller when he makes use of these words:— "I remembered that I was a *writer;* that it was my *business* to write,— to cast, day after day, shavings from off my mind (the figure is Cowper's) — that went rolling away, crisp and dry, among the vast heap already on the floor, and were never more heard of," &c. It must not, however, be forgotten, that it is every man's duty to lay so much of his heart's blood on the altar of his time, to speak to and guide his own generation, though other generations hear him not. Now, more than heretofore, we must be content to see a man spreading over twenty years, in weekly dispensings, that teaching which, if condensed into one work, — the result of twenty years' endeavor — might live for twenty centuries. The harvests of the present are not lost, though they are swiftly gathered off the ground and make room for others. Hugh Miller has not been thrown away as a newspaper editor. His teachings have sunk deep into the heart of Scotland, and work at the roots of the national life. More than any layman he contributed to the founding of the Free Church.

But we must view Miller somewhat more particularly in his capacity of man of science. In the commencement of *The Old Red Sandstone*, there occurs the following passage. His life as a stone-mason had begun on the previous day: —

"All the workmen rested at midday, and I went to enjoy my half-hour alone on a mossy knoll in the neighboring wood, which commands through the trees a wide prospect of the bay and the opposite shore. There was not a wrinkle on the water, nor a cloud in the sky, and the branches were as moveless in the calm as if they had been traced on canvas. From a wooded promontory that stretched half-way across the Frith, there ascended a thin column of smoke. It rose straight as the line of a plummet for more than a thousand yards, and then, on reaching a thinner stratum of air, spread out equally on every side like the foliage of a stately tree. Ben Wyvis rose to the west, white with the yet unwasted snows of winter, and as sharply defined in the clear atmosphere, as if all its sunny slopes and blue retiring hollows had been chiselled in marble. A line of snow ran along the opposite hills; all above was white, and all below was purple. They reminded me of the pretty French story, in which an old artist is described as tasking the ingenuity of his future son-in-law, by giving him as a subject for his pencil a flower-piece composed of only white flowers, of which the one half were to bear their proper color, the other half a deep purple hue, and yet all be perfectly natural; and how the young man resolved the riddle and gained his mistress, by introducing a transparent purple vase into the picture, and making the light pass through it on the flowers that were drooping over the edge. I returned to the quarry, convinced that a very exquisite pleasure may be a very cheap one, and that the busiest employments may afford leisure enough to enjoy it. The gunpowder had loosened a large mass in one of the inferior strata, and our first employment, on resuming our labors, was to raise it from its bed. I assisted the other workmen in placing it on edge, and was much struck by the appearance of the platform on which it had rested. The entire surface was ridged and furrowed like a bank of sand that had been left by the tide an hour before. I could trace every bend and curvature, every cross hollow and counter ridge of the corresponding phenomenon; for the resemblance was no half resemblance—it was the thing itself, and I had observed it a hundred and a hundred times when sailing my little schooner in the shallows left by the ebb. But what had become of the waves that had thus fretted the solid rock, or of what element had they been composed? I felt as completely at fault as Robinson Crusoe did on his discovering the print of a man's foot on the sand. The evening furnished me with still further cause of wonder. We raised another block in a different part of the quarry, and found that the area of a circular depression in the stratum below was broken and flawed in every direction, as if it had been the bottom of a pool recently dried up, which had shrunk and split in the hardening. Several large stones came rolling down from the diluvium in the course of the afternoon. They were of different qualities from the sandstone below, and from one another, and, what was more wonderful still, they were all rounded and water-worn, as if they had been tossed about in the sea, or the bed of a river, for hundreds of years. There could not, surely, be a more conclusive proof that the bank which had enclosed them so long, could not have been created on the rock on which it rested. No workman ever manufactures a half-worn article, and the stones were all half-worn! And, if not the bank, why, then, the sandstone underneath? I was lost in conjecture, and found that I had food enough for thought that evening without once thinking of the unhappiness of a life of labor."

That company of quarrymen on the banks of the Cromarty Frith, on that fine spring morning, had been a sight worth seeing. Nothing, probably, would have struck us as we marked the group going out in the morning. Nothing would have arrested our attention in the somewhat lank, bushy-headed, quiet-looking lad, who worked hard, but seemed somewhat of a novice, as we watched them at their toil. But, when we observed, at the hour of noon, that while the others went to lounge, or smoke, or doze, this young man found his rest and pleasure in gazing upon that sublime panorama, where, in the west, Wyvis presides among the mountains, and the glassy Frith lies lake-like at his feet, reminding one of the fine lines in which an American poet describes a great mountain, looking down in the pride of a monarch,

> "While far below the lake in bridal rest
> Sleeps with his glorious picture on her breast;"

when we observed that his eye brightened with the glow of pure delight, and continued to rest on the scene until every feature was pencilled out and hung in the hall of memory; we might have begun to suspect that there was something unusual in this mason. We might have begun to surmise, that nature had twined around his heart some of those finer threads of sympathy which draw her favored child away from the crowd to her own breast. We might have ventured to predict, that the man before us would not die in his present capacity. And then, when we returned with him to the quarry, and noted that, while the others who toiled with him, as they turned up stone after stone, found no sermons therein for them, and felt no questionings arise in their minds, his eye kindled with the quick piercing gleam of curiosity, and he could not resist the impulse to question, and examine, and infer; we might again have ventured to affirm, that nature had here a son who would one day know her well, and perhaps reveal her to men.

We should not have erred in our surmisings. The inquisitive look and cautious glance of that quarryman were signs of the presence of one of the finest observational capacities of the age. The training of the faculty had begun in early youth; its exercise was the solace of years of toil, and the ultimate guide to a brilliant and world-wide reputation. By the shores of the Friths of Cromarty and Moray, under the direction of Uncle Sandy, young Hugh had learned to watch the habits of the crab and the lobster, to admire the tints of the sea-moss, to wonder at the organization of the sea-hare and cuttle-fish. His life as a mason furnished admirable opportunities for the gratification of his curiosity, and the exercise of his observational powers. He was, he tells us, "an explorer of caves and ravines — a loiterer along sea-shores — a climber among rocks." Surrounded by the deep silence of a workman's life, in the seclusion of tastes unshared, of powers unknown, of ambition unawakened, he pursued, calmly, steadily, accurately, his course of observation. Living a life in reality apart, strengthening and expanding his general powers by the study of philosophy and poetry he did not permit his observation to degenerate into a childish storing up of isolated facts. He combined a generalizing power of a high order, with that of minute, unfailing observation. He learned to unite the broad glance of the geographer, with the microscopic inspection of the mineralogist. He could chronicle every tint of hue, every line of form, in the scale embedded in the rock; while by wide philosophic induction, he could ascertain precisely what contribution was made by that scale to the geological history of the planet.

Traversing Scotland from the German Ocean to the Atlantic, from Pentland Frith to the Cheviots, living now among the craggy valleys of Argyllshire, now upon the sandy flats of Moray, his eye became accustomed to every form of landscape. He came speedily to know his country with that profound knowledge, which recognizes the anatomy under the form, and which can predict the form from the anatomy. Possessing also that delicate sensibility to beauty, and that familiar acquaintance with the descriptive stores of English poetry, to which we have already alluded, he was able to cast exquisite lights of fancy over those landscapes which science first revealed to him in their rugged and literal truth. His descriptions of nature were of a kind not merely to instruct and delight the man of science, but to afford intense gratification to the artist, and whoever had a soul open to the enjoyment of nature's beauty. We refer at present to a quality of description deeper than mere style. It relates to the exhibition of nature's facts, which must first be known, and that in a peculiar manner, before the effect can be produced. Miller's descriptions of natural scenes may be compared with those of Ruskin.

He, as well as the great pictorial critic, produces pictures, clear, definite, visible, which one can hang up in the chambers of his mind, and gaze on with unsated pleasure. Hugh Miller and Ruskin started from different points. The latter set out from beauty. He looked over nature for the Beautiful. Had scientific accuracy proved inconsistent with beauty, he would have discarded scientific accuracy, and wrapped himself in a garb of fantasy. But as he looked over nature through the glass of beauty, he discerned, as he believed, that the loveliness of truth was greater than the loveliness of fantasy. So science became for him the handmaid of beauty; his imagination smiled most brightly beside the homely fires of fact. Hugh Miller started from the side of science. He sought for, he described, bare truth. He desired to know and show what the world was, making no postulate in favor of beauty. He opened his eyes and looked. He followed the lines, and imitated the colors, of reality. He held up the page, and lo! the result was beauty. Ruskin set out with poetry, and met science: Hugh Miller set out with science, and met poetry.

A parallel might be instituted, also, between Ruskin and Miller in this, That each attracted to his particular subject of study, a large audience of those previously repelled. Ruskin, by expounding Art on broader principles and in a more eloquent manner than had been formerly done, by freeing it of encumbering technicalities and allying it to general human sympathy, drew a vast miscellaneous audience to listen to essentially profound and accurate artistic teaching. Miller, by arraying science in that garb of beauty which belongs to all the visible forms of nature, allured a similar audience to receive scientific instruction of a kind correspondingly deep and exact.

As a geologist, Hugh Miller stands in the highest of all

orders, if in that order he does not occupy one of the first stations. He is in the order of original discoverers. His place is among the honored few, who have added to the domain of human knowledge. He accurately mapped out, as represented in his own country, one of the most interesting and least known of geographical formations, the Old Red Sandstone. He made express additions to the number of its classified organisms. His views of the science as a whole are comprehensive and philosophical, but it is on this distinctively that his fame as a geologist will repose.

In the cottage of Hugh Miller's boyhood, was that "one Book, wherein for several thousands of years the spirit of man has found light, and an interpreting response to whatever is deepest in him," and which is still the Word of God, whatever the author of these words may think. In Hugh Miller's education, the most important agent of all had been the Bible. For many years, the influence of early instruction had seemed to have passed away, but before the time at which he quitted manual labor, he had reflected deeply on religious subjects, had accepted Christianity as a living faith, and owned the gravitating power of that "Divine Man" whom he saw to be "the sole gravitating point of a system which owes to Him all its coherence, and which would be but a chaos were He away." This leads us to one of the most important aspects in which Hugh Miller can be viewed — that great practical aspect, namely, in which he unites the theologian and the man of science. We shall introduce our remarks upon him in this capacity by a quotation from the remarkable chapter which closes his "Footprints of the Creator:"—

"The first idea of every religion on earth which has arisen out of what may be termed the spiritual instinct of man's nature, is that of a future state; the second idea is, that in this state men shall exist in two separate classes — the one in advance of their present condition, the other far in the rear of it. It is on these two great beliefs that conscience everywhere finds the fulcrum from which it acts upon the conduct; and it is wholly inoperative as a force without them. And in that one religion among men that, instead of retiring, like the pale ghosts of the others, before the light of civilization, brightens and expands in its beams, and in favor of whose claim as a revelation from God the highest philosophy has declared, we find these two master ideas occupying a still more prominent place than in any of those merely indigenous religions that spring up in the human mind of themselves. . . . . There is not in all revelation a single doctrine which we find oftener, or more clearly enforced, than that there shall continue to exist, through the endless cycles of the future, a race of degraded men and of degraded angels. Now it is truly wonderful how thoroughly, in its general scope, the revealed pieces on to the geologic record. We know, as geologists, that the dynasty of the fish was succeeded by that of the reptile — that the dynasty of the reptile was succeeded by that of the mammiferous quadruped — and that the dynasty of the mammiferous quadruped was succeeded by that of man, as man now exists — a creature of mixed character, and subject, in all conditions, to wide alternations of enjoyment and suffering. We know, further — so far, at least, as we have yet succeeded in deciphering the record — that the several dynasties were introduced, not in their lower, but in their higher forms; that, in short, in the imposing programme of creation it was arranged, as a general rule, that in each of the great divisions of the procession the magnates should walk first. We recognize yet further the fact of degradation specially exemplified in the fish and the reptile. And then, passing on to the revealed record, we learn that the dynasty of man in the mixed state and character is not the final one, but that there is to be yet another creation, or, more properly, *re*-creation, known theologically as the Resurrection, which shall be connected in its physical components, by bonds of mysterious paternity, with the dynasty which now reigns, and be bound to it mentally by the chain of identity, conscious and actual; but which, in all that constitutes superiority, shall be as vastly its superior, as the dynasty of responsible man is superior to even the lowest of the preliminary dynasties. We are further taught, that at the commencement of this last of the dynasties there will be a re-creation of not only elevated, but also of degraded beings — a re-creation of the *lost*. We are taught yet further, that though the present dynasty be that of a lapsed race, which at their first introduction were placed on higher ground than that on which they now stand, and sank by their own act, it was yet part of the original design, from the beginning of all things, that they should occupy the existing platform; and that Redemption is thus no after-thought, rendered necessary by the Fall, but, on the contrary, part of a general scheme, for which provision had been made from the beginning; so that the Divine Man, through whom the work of restoration has been effected, was in reality, in reference to the purposes of the Eternal, what he is designated in the remarkable text, '*the Lamb slain from the foundations of the world.*' Slain from the foundations of the world! Could the assertors of the stony science ask for language more express? By piecing the two records together — that revealed in Scripture, and that revealed in the rocks — records which, however widely geologists may mistake the one, or commentators misunderstand the other, have emanated from the same great Author—we learn that in slow and solemn majesty has period succeeded period, each in succession ushering in a higher and yet higher scene of existence; that fish, reptiles, mammiferous quadrupeds, have reigned in turn; that responsible man, 'made in the image of God,' and with dominion over all creatures, ultimately entered into a world ripened for his reception: but, further, that this passing scene, in which he forms the prominent figure, is not the final one in the long series, but merely the last of the *preliminary* scenes; and that that period to which the by-gone ages, incalculable in amount, with all their well proportioned gradations of being, form the imposing vestibule, shall have perfection for its occupant, and eternity for its duration. I know not how it may appear to others; but, for my own part, I cannot avoid thinking that there would be a lack of proportion in the series of being, were the period of perfect and glorified humanity abruptly connected, without the introduction of an intermediate creation of *responsible* imperfection, with that of the dying irresponsible brute. That scene of things in which God became Man, and suffered, *seems*, as it no doubt *is*, a necessary link in the chain."

The theologian of the nineteenth century will have to know and ponder such passages as this, to scrutinize carefully the intimations they read him, to follow conscientiously the clue they put into his hand. The seventeenth century is known among the centuries as that in which the written Word of God was explored, so to speak, to its inmost recess. We say not the work was finished; but, of all ages, the most strictly biblical, that which seemed to live in and upon the simple and separate Bible, was the seventeenth. One great task of the nineteenth century seems to be, to search into and know the works of God. It stands distinguished as the age of physical science. There was a certain danger that theologians should forget that God made the world, and that therefore it was holy. The gaze of hallowed ecstacy with which David had looked from the battlements of Zion, upon the palm-crowned mountains that stood around, as he seized his harp, and burst into a song of praise to God the Maker, seemed to have darkened and narrowed into a cold, critical, peering look, that searched for flaws in creeds, and glanced rather timorously towards the mountains, as if it might turn out that God had not made them after all. As must ever and universally be the case, partiality was error. A certain littleness was imparted to the views of the physical world, as a piece of God's workmanship; a certain glory was taken away from the Word of God, as the oracle of the moral world; by the absence of that light which they were fitted to cast on each other. Such men as Thomas Chalmers, Hugh Miller, John Pye Smith, and others, have essayed to show the inter-reflection of light and glory between the two, and the day will come when the work they have commenced will be fully accomplished. Its even partial accomplishment will mark our century. As it is, the theologian who accepts the facts of God's workmanship as not to be disputed, as facts which, if once well proved, it were irreverent, nay blasphemous, to deny, may already, we think, obtain dim but glorious glimpses into far regions of spiritual truth — into the destinies of man, into the essentials of judgment, into the meaning of death — which the lamp of science faintly indicates when hung over the Word of God. But much has yet to be done, and much must be acknowledged to lie yet unrevealed. Meanwhile the two grand perils are, on the one hand, ignoble fear, and, on the other, presumption. The man who looks over the moral world, and discerns that it is an inexplicable chaos, a standardless battle, a sick and fevered dream, unless God has spoken in the Bible, may surely have such manlike trust in God that he can fearlessly examine every story of the physical dwelling He has made for him, although, for the present, God does not reveal to him how its apparent discrepancies with the moral fabric He has let down from heaven are to be harmonized. Surely, on the other hand, the man, who talks in the fashionable pagan language of the day of "the gods," and who yet must see these gods preparing this earth for man, with much fuss and commotion, and then sitting, like a set of fools, to see the great game of blind-man's-buff which their children play, and laugh at the gropings and mistakes,—the man, who, if he is honest, and bold, and unhesitating in discrowning God and his religion, must accept as the correct and unexaggerated scheme of world-history, that ghastly poem of Poe's, in which, with perfect honesty from his point of view, he portrays man, since his arrival here, as running after phantoms, of which the central phantom is merely the most phantasmal of all, and which very appropriately concludes in these words,

> "The play is the tragedy Man,
> And the hero the conqueror Worm:"

this man, we say, might surely pause ere he declares that the scientific information of yesterday contradicts the alone explaining theory of man's existence. Let the Christian have faith in God's word: let the infidel tumble his moral world in ruins; there is not the slightest fear of his tumbling *the* moral world into ruins. Both infidels and Christians are always thinking God is such an one as themselves. The one party thinks it has got the Sun of the moral universe fairly out. The other takes to trembling and vociferating, and holding up supplementary rush-lights, as if it feared the Sun was going out. Meanwhile the ages roll on, and the mist rolls off, and the Sun is there still. From every new elevation of science, fear it not, there will be a wider prospect of truth. Just now we may be in the valley, and the ocean may be shut out which we saw clearly from the lower hill behind. But onwards! When we reach the top of this other hill before us, the ocean of truth, and the Sun that clothes it all in gold, will be seen spreading further than ever before. Hugh Miller's clear, strong intellect, fine poetic discernment of nature's all-pervading analogies, and manly piety, fit him well to pioneer the scientific, cosmical theology of the latter time.

We have not spoken expressly of Hugh Miller's poetry, and it is unnecessary to do so. His finest poetry is, we presume, his prose. He would, we feel assured, agree in this himself. We go on to mention a characteristic which harmonizes finely with the general strength of his nature, and which seems the result of this in combination with the kindness of his heart: we mean his humor. This is not one of the most important or engrossing of his qualities, but, as far as it goes, it is genuine, and remarkably pleasing. It is a perception of the laughable in nature; of those weaknesses which are not sins, those incongruities which do not hurt, those self-revelations which oscillate amusingly between the egotism that is offensive and the vanity that is despicable; of all those things which were manifestly intended to be kept in check by no ruder weapon than laughter, and which are not checked absolutely, because laughter is good for men in its time. Hugh Miller's laugh is always quiet and kindly; never, to our knowledge, cynical and contemptuous, save when some real iniquity is to be mocked into air. He has no feeling of contempt for the "young lady passenger of forty or thereabouts," who took her seat in the same railway carriage with him, and who "had a bloom of red in her cheeks that seemed to have been just a little assisted by art, and a bloom of red in her nose that seemed not to have been assisted by art at all." It is merely a smile of hearty geniality which lights his features as he encounters two of Shenstone's nymphs on his visit to the Leasowes:—

"I had read Shenstone early enough to wonder what sort of looking people his Delias and Cecilias were; and now, ere plunging into the richly wooded Leasowes, I had got hold of the right idea. The two naileresses were really very pretty. Cecilia, a ruddy blonde, was fabricating tackets; Delia, a bright-eyed brunette, engaged in heading a double-double."

Even when he visits St. Paul's, and speaks thus, he is in the best humor, for all the slyness of his laugh:—

"It is comfortable to have only twopence to pay for leave to walk over the area of so noble a pile, and to have to pay the twopence, too, to such grave, clerical looking men as the officials at the receipt of custom. It reminds one of the blessings of a religious establishment in a place where otherwise they might possibly be overlooked; no private company could afford to build such a pile as St. Paul's, and then show it for twopences."

But perhaps, of all we can say in praise of Hugh Miller, the highest compliment, all things considered, is the last we are to pay him. It is, that he is, in the best sense, a gentleman; that he is truly and strictly polite. We intend, by this, very high praise indeed; true politeness is one of the rarest things. The word has been variously defined. We have heard it indicated as being a knowledge of the little usages of society, such as not pouring tea into a saucer, not speaking in company without an introduction, and such like, and the habit of strictly and naturally conforming to such. This requires no refutation: its very utterance, on the principle that in speaking of a thing you set in the foreground your main idea regarding it, implies hopeless ignorance of the nature of politeness:—

> "The churl in spirit, howe'er he vail
> His want in forms for fashion's sake,
> Will let his coltish nature break
> At seasons through the gilded pale."

True politeness may be met in the hut of the Arab, in the courtyard of the Turk, in the cottage of the Irishman, and is excessively rare in ball-rooms. It is independent of accent and of form, it is one of the constant and universal noble attributes of man, wherever and howsoever developed. It has been defined again, "perfect ease, without vulgarity or affectation." Here manifestly a great advance is made; one half of politeness is correctly defined. Yet we think there is overlooked that part of politeness which refers to others besides one's self; and politeness, as it consists wholly in a certain dealing of man with man, must include both parties in its reference. The truly polite man is not merely at ease, but always sets you at ease. We venture to define it thus: Politeness is natural, genial, manly *deference*, with a natural delicacy in dealing with the feelings of others, and without hypocrisy, sycophancy, or obtrusion. This, we think, is at once sufficiently inclusive and exclusive. It excludes a great many. We cannot agree that Johnson was polite; that is, if politeness is to be distinguished from nobleness, courage, and even kindness of heart; in a word, from everything but itself. Burns was polite, when jewelled duchesses were charmed with his ways; Arnold was polite, when the poor woman felt that he treated her as if she were a lady; Chalmers was polite, when every old woman in Morningside was elated and delighted with his courteous salute. But Johnson, who shut a civil man's mouth with, "Sir, I perceive you are a vile Whig," who ate like an Esquimaux, who deferred so far to his friends, that they could differ with him only in a round-robin, was not polite. Politeness is the last touch, the finishing perfection, of a noble character. It is the gold on the spire, the sunlight on the corn field, the smile on the lip of the noble knight lowering his sword point to his ladye-love. It results only from the truest balance and harmony of soul. We assert Hugh Miller to possess it. A duke in speaking to him would know he was speaking to a man as independent as himself; a boy, in expressing to him an opinion, would feel unabashed and easy, from his genial and unostentatious deference. He has been accused of egotism. The charge is a serious one; fatal, if it can be substantiated in any offensive degree, to politeness. And let it be fairly admitted that he knows his name is Hugh Miller, and that he has a colossal head, and that he once was a mason; his foible is probably that which caused Napoleon, in a company of kings, to commence an anecdote with "When I was a lieutenant in the regiment of La Fere." But we cannot think it more than a very slight foible; a manly self-consciousness somewhat in excess. His autobiography has been blamed as egotistic; we think without cause. The sketches appear to us much the reverse. They are almost entirely what he has seen; what he has done or been is nowise protruded. And shall we blame a man with the eye and the memory of Hugh Miller, for leading us through the many scenes of Scottish life, which he knows better than any man, because he does so in a very natural and orderly way? Wherever he is egotistic, he is not so in conversation—the great test of the polite man. Years in the quarry have not dimmed in Hugh Miller that finishing gleam of genial light which plays over the framework of character, and is politeness. Not only did he require honest manliness for this; gentleness was also necessary. He had both, and has retained them; and so merits fairly

> "The grand old name of gentleman."

It is now 1857; and with all the hopes and forebodings of a new year, there mingles, in my breast, the recollection of a kindness no more to be experienced, of a condescending genial helpfulness no longer to instruct, of a steadfast nobleness whose living presence will no longer animate and cheer, of a great and godly man who has passed away. In the last days of 1856, Hugh Miller died: a self-sacrificed martyr to science. At the great work which was to complete his service to his country and mankind, he toiled on with indomitable resolution, amid the paroxysms of fearful disease. His powerful brain, wearied with the sustained tension of twenty years, recoiled from its work, and, as it were, groaned and struggled for rest. But that adamantine will knew no flinching. Ever, as the paroxysm passed by, and the soft glow of the old genius spread itself again along the mind, the most intense and unremitted exertion was compelled. The light burnt nightly in his chamber, long after the midnight hour, as Hugh Miller continued to write, the body failing, the nerves fluttering, the brain held to its work only by that indomitable will. He feared madness might dash the pen from his hand, before the last line was traced. But the work was finished. On the last day of his life, Hugh Miller said it was done. Madness and the grave could not at least deprive him of that. Then, as might have been expected, despite consultation with a physician, the paroxysm returned with redoubled fury: ere it again subsided, Hugh Miller was no more. Let science honor her too devoted son! For her he worked on undaunted under the thunder-cloud; the lightnings of madness flashing ever and anon around him. He finished his work; closed the book; and looked up as if defiant of the lightning. But it came down and smote him; and he died, may we not say, the greatest of the martyrs of science.

VII

THE MODERN NOVEL.

DICKENS—BULWER—THACKERAY.

"LITERATURE," says so distinguished a novelist as Sir Edward Bulwer Lytton, "commences with poetical fiction, and usually terminates with prose fiction. It was so in the ancient world—it will be so with England and France. The harvest of novels is, I fear, a sign of the approaching exhaustion of the soil." Of whatever the harvest spoken of is a sign, there can be no doubt of its own exuberance. The novel has gone far to supersede all other forms of literature; and where it does not supersede, it has an influence. Philosophy has receded into the background. Poetry, if in itself of rare perfection, occupies no such place in public estimation as it did in the days of Byron. History is specially commended as being equally pleasant reading with fiction. We have dukes and earls patronizing mechanics' institutes and public libraries; we have platform speeches of the sweetest eloquence, setting forth the way in which science and philosophy are to be used in the self-culture of readers; we have the shelves well filled with metaphysical, historical, and scientific treatises. In eighteen months we revisit the institution, and inspect the books. The philosophers, the men of science, the historians, have enjoyed, like kings and queens at their country-seats, an honorable seclusion: the novels are dog's-eared, crumpled, soiled, from the effects of affectionate familiarity. The attraction by which the young aspirant to literary distinction is at present drawn towards fictitious composition seems, at first sight, overpowering. Who would not enlist in an army in which the discipline is lax, the fighting not severe, and the prizes dazzling, rather than in one in which the discipline is the rigid restraint of truth, the fighting a stern struggle up the rugged crags of fact, and the prizes comparatively poor? With all our enlightened support of literature, a young man who would at present determine to devote himself, with energies untrammelled by any other profession, with zeal undivided with any other pursuit, to philosophy, theology, social science, or history, trusting thereto for his daily bread, would do so at the risk of his life. We know an instance of a young literary man in London, of distinguished ability and high aims, who pursued studies of an important nature, but was compelled, at intervals, in order to secure subsistence, to write novels. There is a gentleman, now in Edinburgh, whose name is known in every part of the island, and whose works, in philosophy, political economy, and apologetics, are of high standing, who yet, we are confident, has derived no pecuniary profit whatever from the main labor of his life, and finds his talents of pecuniary avail, only in such off-hand work as occasional lecturing and contributions to the journals. Is not the temptation strong for such a man, to ungird the armor of the legionary, and bind on the light arms which are so effective? Why should the youthful poet keep gazing into the face of the Beautiful, why should the young philosopher dig sedulously in the mines of thought for the True, if literary tinsel will best exchange for current coin, and men prefer the flowers that grow on the surface to the metal that is hidden below?

These remarks may seem logically to require an unqualified denunciation of novels. But, for many reasons, we should deem this an unwise proceeding.

In the first place, he who would engage in the highest literature must always so do with somewhat of the spirit of a martyr. It has ever been the way to reward the most severe and noble efforts of mind in a manner which in itself seems paltry. Milton got five pounds for *Paradise Lost*. We cannot too often recall the remarkable fact. If every generation of mankind, succeeding the appearance of that poem, had raised to its author a new statue of solid gold, they would have made no approach to paying him. The Dantes, the Keplers, the Pascals, and such as they, are not so paid for their mental labors. It is a manifest appointment of nature that they should not be: and, let us say, it is a right appointment, benign, beautiful, and, for the men who seem passed over, an appropriate and sublime honor. By their capacity for such work, they afford a reasonable presumption that they can rightly estimate and duly contemn material payment. It is in celestial coin that they receive their wages. If they know not what this is, if they scorn it, let them descend to lower grades of intellectual labor; let them deal in goods known and wanted in the market, and they will have the success of ordinary traders. But the general law is open to no doubt: the highest spiritual employments are not distinguished by yielding large material rewards. The fact is exemplified in the case of whole professions. Ministers of the gospel will always be paid, on an average, at a rate in no degree correspondent to the abilities they possess or the functions they perform. To men of learning, to professors of erudition and philosophy, the same rule applies. No spectacle appears to us more truly despicable than that of any one who pretends to communicate to men the higher kinds of knowledge, complaining that he is not paid like successful confectioners or ballet dancers, and sending round his hat for coppers. The man who makes it his sole object to amuse, and has talents of extraordinary power, be he novelist or play actor, will be more handsomely remunerated, in the way he can value, than the man whose ambition it is to elevate and improve his fellows. The novelist himself who aims high, both in means and end, must submit to see his gains small in proportion. The public, however, let us add in a corner, has the option of doing that for men of lofty aspirations, which it is not becoming, which in some sense it is not possible, for them to do for themselves!

But it may be questioned, in the next place, whether the facts with which we set out, — facts of which, in themselves, there cannot be any doubt, — do not indicate chiefly a change in the proportion borne by one set of literary works to another, and not solely, if at all, a diminution either in the production or the perusal of those of the higher orders. It may be that though more novels are produced than treatises in history or science, though more fiction is read than philosophy or poetry, the reading public has been so much increased by the influence of novels, that the condition of higher literature is really improved. And to this consideration we may add the hope, that novels may in future do still more to promote this end, awakening the frivolous and indifferent to some sort of mental exertion, and handing them on to nobler studies. Still further it may be here urged, that there are not wanting, at present, novels, which themselves convey wholesome instruction, and which can hardly exercise an enervating influence. Such novels as those of Currer Bell, Kingsley, and Thackeray, are not to be confounded with the productions of the Minerva Press.

After all, the most pertinent remark which cân be made as to this unexampled efflorescence of fictitious literature seems to be that it is a fact, and that it may be pronounced unalterable. This alone makes it worthy of consideration. It were very strange, too, if a phenomenon so vast in extent and so powerful in influence, had no real meaning and could be turned to no account. It may be that, by looking into the matter somewhat closely, we may discover some principle by which the man, who is conscientiously and resolutely bent upon a self-culture as complete as his faculties admit and his time affords, may safely and profitably undertake an incursion into fictitious literature.

What is a novel? The question seems exceedingly easy, and may be so. But it is well to have precise ideas as to its answer, for when you know accurately what a thing is, you have got, in germ, all that it is most important to know concerning it. What, then, we repeat, is a novel?

In every production of Art there are two principal elements, whose unity gives the result. The one is the original type presented in nature, the other the modification — the curtailment, addition, or transformation — effected by the free will and imaginative energy of the artist. Thus, in the art of painting, the type from which the artist sets out is some natural appearance, a landscape, a building, a face. If he is only a daguerreotypist, he records merely the literal facts of nature in their real localities. If he is a true artist, the daguerreotype can do no more than furnish him with studies, and only when he has combined these as he chooses and breathed into them the spirit of his own genius, has he produced a picture. In all Art this distinction holds good.

It is not difficult to discover the original type on which the novel is founded. If we consider, we shall find something not unlike it in life, though by no means the same. The direction in which to turn is manifestly that of history; the first thing that strikes us in a novel is its narrative. It may be profitable to look for a moment at history. If he has a true sense of his Art, the historian will find himself, in certain important respects, resembling the novelist. We do not allude to his depicting manners, or adopting a picturesque style. The similarity lies deeper; in the very materials with which he works. In the life of nations, as well as in that of individuals, are found circumstances corresponding to those which afford the novelist his coloring, and suggest to him his plot. These may serve the historical artist none the worse that the laws by which he works are those of stern realism. Incidents more stirring than imagination ever dreamed, characters more strange and puzzling than novelist ever portrayed, plot more dark and mysterious than ever artist devised, may be already provided him. He may lead us, in earnest curiosity, along the path of Providence, not blunting, by any anachronism of anticipation or disclosure, the feelings of wonder and admiration, with which, at the right moment, we behold the curtain rise. And, be it remarked, the more completely he thus imitates the recognized method of the novelist, the more emphatically does he bring before us the great lessons which it is his duty to teach. In the warlike contendings or peaceful labors of nations, in their growth and decline, in their birth, glory, and destruction, certain grand monitions are providentially addressed to us, constituting one principal portion of that system of education, practical or theoretic, by which nature is pervaded. We all acknowledge that the office of the historian is august and important. But the slightest reflection will make it plain, both that the sphere of the historian is not precisely that of the novelist, and that there is a sphere in which the latter may convey instruction of a value equal to that conveyed by the former. The historian does not and cannot descend into domestic life. Nations in their national capacity and in their national doings are his theme; with battles, sieges, treaties, senates, cities, he deals. He may paint manners; but only in the mass. He may give details of private life; but only to exhibit the hidden strings which guide the men who guide nations. But domestic life has also its instructive lessons. Here, too, Providence teaches. In the festal assemblage and by the household hearth, beside her who is wreathed with orange flower and by the deathbed, the footsteps of Providence may be traced, the voice of Providence may be heard. Warnings, examples, encouragements, intimations, which, if known, prized, and used, would be more precious than rubies, are being ever presented in the common course of life. If it is right to strengthen and widen our powers of intellectual vision, by watching the dealings of God with nations, it is assuredly right, also, to have an accurate and extensive knowledge of domestic life, to gain a wider acquaintance, than our own circle affords, with the perils which beset our private walk, with the modes in which the problems of individual and family life have already been solved. To occupy a field thus rich and thus distinctly marked off, the biographer steps forward. And it will not be called in question that, in the biography, the original type of the novel is found. There is, however, in the circumstances of the case, a reason for fictitious biography, which does not exist for fictitious history. The most interesting and instructive series of incidents may occur in private life, yet cause appear why the actors should be vailed in secresy. The fictitious form provides the vail. In some such series of incidents as we have supposed, lies the realistic groundwork on which the novel should be constructed. By this it is connected with the world of fact. This is to it as the knowledge of the features of a locality, its leading geological lines, its distinctive botanical products, is to the artist who paints a landscape. If the novelist proceeds without such realistic basis, his work is sure to be worthless. The wing of imagination flaps at once in a vacuum. Weak sentimentality takes the place of manly feeling, faded commonplace is offered instead of fresh truth, the whole wears a flabby, sickly aspect, if only the novelist ignores fact and trusts solely to fancy. We do not know any instance of imaginative power on which we would more willingly rely, which we could more absolutely trust, than that of Dickens. Yet when he leaves the alleys of St. Giles and the office in Bow Street, which he has seen, and sets himself to depict what he merely imagines to exist, how strange is the work he produces! Literature does not contain a more false, foolish, preposterous character than Mrs. Clennam. Mr. Dickens fancied this must be what evangelical religion was; and if he had informed us that a Fakir or other Indian devotee swung himself daily in the air, by a hook attached to the top of Nelson's monument, he would not have committed a greater absurdity. We are quite sure there are as many persons in England who believe they will go to heaven by swinging by the foot, as there are who propose to compass that end by abstaining from their usual allowance of oysters. But if the necessity of a realistic basis is distinctly recognized, the function of the novelist is vindicated from all assault, the novel is worthy of respect and attention. The nominally fictitious author becomes the recorder of Providence in domestic life, the historian of the fireside, the philosopher of the family circle. The recognition of this necessity has of late been more express than formerly. The temper of the time sets strongly towards rugged truth and away from smooth, painted falsehood. But no recognition of it could be too emphatic. On its practical acknowledgment we must hang our hope for the production of a literature, in name and form, for obvious and weighty reasons, fictitious, but in reality true, and an honor and blessing to the nation.

But the novel is a work of Art. There is more in it than bare reality. Of this fact the whole history of fictitious composition is a proof, and if the fact has been so, its theoretic vindication or the reverse is of comparatively slight importance. Fact, however, and theory agree. The novel is unquestionably a work of Art, and, being so, it must exhibit some element, for which we can find no precise equivalent, though there may be suggestion or analogue, in nature.

The novel, as we saw, differs broadly from the history. Its theme is always domestic life, however the domestic incidents with which it deals may be affected by public events; just as history is always national, though the destinies of nations may be influenced by domestic circumstances. But not even in the biography is there the precise counterpart of the novel. The biography is spread over the whole period of life. Its incidents derive their relative importance from the illustration they afford of character.

But in the novel a particular period of life is selected, the incidents are grouped round one centralizing interest, and the narrative stops short at life's grand climacteric. What is this interest? What this climacteric? It is love. We must consider it a little.

> "'Love, the soul of soul, within the soul,
> Evolving it sublimely. First, God's love.'

'And next,' he smiled, 'the love of wedded souls,
Which still presents that mystery's counterpart.
Sweet shadow-rose, upon the water of life,
Of such a mystic substance, Sharon gave
A name to! human, vital, fructuous rose,
Whose calyx holds the multitude of leaves,—
Loves filial, loves fraternal, neighbor-loves,
And civic, * * * all fair petals, all good scents,
All reddened, sweetened, from one central Heart!'"

Thus writes Mrs. Barrett Browning in her latest poem. If the first poem ever composed were still before us, should we not find it some lilt, of joyfulness and tears, sung by primeval lover beside the trysting tree? There are feelings of a purely spiritual nature, connecting themselves with man's celestial relations and eternal destiny, which transcend all that pertain to earth. But of those which belong distinctively to the world of living men, whose dwelling is the heart that beats for threescore years and ten, whose sphere of operation is between the silent graves and the silent stars, the greatest, the mightiest, is love. The scale of human emotion, through all its changes of gladness and sorrow, lies between the silver treble of love and the deep bass of death. The fountain of life rises sunward, and the light that falls on its white foam at the highest point is love. The hill of life is climbed in the dewy morning: in the light of noon, on the green, unclouded summit, the loved one is met; as evening steals on, and the dew begins again to fall, the descent is slowly made towards the grave at the foot. Sometimes death starts up on the top, and chills the heart of love at its fullest throbbing: the might of the anguish is then measured by the intensity of the joy.

However we may represent this fact, even though we may be moved to a smile, a fact it is, and one of chief importance. In the Scriptural view of man, it is explicitly attested. The emotion, of which, if we may so speak, the final end is marriage, is expressly appointed to the supremacy among the feelings by which one human being can be attracted towards or linked to another; and the arrangement of the social system, as exhibited in history, corresponds with the original appointment. Innumerable as are the interests which there circle, various as are the orbits there occupied, they all, directly or indirectly, own the regulating power of love.

Turning from life to literature, using the word in its most comprehensive sense, the same fact meets us in broad and clear reflexion. Love was the main theme of epic poetry, and may be called the sole theme of the lyre. Around love Tragedy and Comedy alike arranged their parts. Here, the lovers sat upon the dais, crimson broidered with gold, and from their happy faces gleamed out a light on all around. Comedy arranged the lights, placed the surrounding groups in the most effective positions, appointed the music and the dancing, and showered her smiles upon the happy pair. There, the blue of love's heaven shone pure and serene, above the summer ocean and the balmy isle: but suddenly the blissful calm was swallowed in black, firelit tornado, and, arrayed in the trailing draperies of storm, Tragedy swept by. Take love out of literature, and all of it which is not strictly scientific, — the simple statement of fact and law, — all of it that lies within the province of the imagination, falls into incoherence and disruption. It becomes a system of which the gravitating centre has been unfixed. But while love remains, however the form may change, the radical characteristics of the old imaginative literature will survive. Amid the multitudinous activity, and wild, free life of modern times, the drama and the epic of antiquity may be said to have been shaken from their unities and proprieties, and finally dashed into fragments. But the joys and sorrows of love with which they were concerned emerged from the ruin, and commenced, in fresh and buoyant youth, a new epoch of literary representation in "*the modern novel.*"

The novel, therefore, is scientifically definable as a domestic history, in which the whole interest and all the facts are made to combine in the evolution of a tale of love. A biographic strain of which the key note is love. The application of terms may vary to any extent, but we are convinced that any inquiry into the nature of the novel, bearing reference at once to the laws of Art and to the facts of history, will conduct to a conclusion essentially the one with this.

It would appear to be irrefragably established that the love story is no mere conventional appendage of the modern novel, but bound up in its essence. The passion of love has been indissolubly connected with all imaginative literature. It will not, on a deliberate survey, be questioned by any, that the fictitious literature of modern times is, to at least a large extent, the more formal imaginative literature of antiquity, accommodated to a wider audience and engaged in by a larger class of authors. It were surely too bold to affix the name of conventionalism to what has been an unfailing characteristic of the most popular class of literary works, and which we found correspondent to an important fact in life.

Have we not found a clue at once to the cause of the supreme popularity of the novel with readers, and to the means by which the novelist secures this popularity ? That ancient theme, to which the hearts of the old Greeks thrilled at the Olympic Games, and which fired the Arab eye at the poetical contest in the desert, before the days of Mahomet, has been scrambled for in modern times, by romance poets and novelists, and the novelists have been very successful in the appropriation. They have possessed themselves of the irresistible fascination: they wield the spell which was never yet broken. The sympathetic imagination, evoked by the novelist, enables his reader to enjoy the happiness of the hero and heroine. No one is so stupid as to be unable to live in a land of reverie; the difficult thing is, amid the buffeting of the waves, to keep the foot firm, as on a rock, on the present; therefore the novelist dispenses joy to the widest class. But no one is so wise as to resist the charm. The philosopher succumbs to it as fast as to the toothache, time out of mind the sage's vanquisher. He laughs and weeps with the lover just as other men.

He weeps.—Yes; but may not this give us pause? The luxury of sorrow, about the existence of which there is not a whit more doubt than about that of the luxury of joy, has a puzzling look, which may justify us in turning aside for a moment to consider it. The pathos which wrings your heart, and bathes your cheek in tears, holds you enchained as powerfully as the gladness which makes you laugh for joy. Sympathetic participation is here out of the question. You rejoice *with* Shirley and Moore, when they at last beat out the music of their lives; but you cannot rejoice *with* Nancy when Sykes murders her. Yet the pleasure of tragedy, while of a more august and solemn, seems to be also of a more profound character than that of comedy. We venture upon an explanation of the fact. *All* mighty emotion is in itself pleasurable. This looks like, but is not, a contradiction in terms. Distress, it is true, cannot be delightful; but the weeping by which it is relieved, the overflow of the emotion, is pleasurable. The fire itself burns and scathes the heart: but the streaming of the lava through its tear-channels bears away the woe, and produces, in so doing, a sensation of delight. So far there can be no dispute; the psychological fact is perfectly well known. But may it not be applied to the explanation of that singular pleasure with which we are concerned? Does not the secret of all the joy of tragedy and pathos lie in the skillful opening of the sluices, by which the surcharged fountains of the heart empty themselves in tears? Is not the flow of the emotion secured, without the suffering of the pain? The cause is brought into operation by imagination; the emotion naturally follows: but the surge of emotion and its cause are precisely proportioned to each other, and the former bears the latter fairly out of the heart. The difference between the distress occasioned by literal fact, and that evoked by the tragic artist, may be clearly perceived, by a glance at the scene to which reference has been already made, the murder of Nancy in *Oliver Twist.* Let one, after perusing the description given by Dickens, reflect for a moment on the possibility that such an incident may have occurred in actual life. He instantly experiences a thrill of regret and dismay. But it is very different from that felt while he listened to Mr. Dickens. A new condition affects the case. The sorrow is anchored in the heart by fact. To weep, it is true, gives relief: weeping, as distinguished from not weeping, sorrow relieved as distinguished from sorrow unrelieved, is pleasurable: but the knowledge that such girls have actually been killed can be washed out by no tears; it remains there, demanding a fresh flow, nay, demanding, to relieve the grating pain, that active effort be engaged in, to put such catastrophes beyond the limits of possibility. Imagination in the one case, lulls reason asleep, and produces an emotion powerful while it lasts; when reason awakens, the man declares he has forgotten himself, and the cause and the emotion pass from the mind together. In all cases, whether of real belief or factitious, the emotion in itself is pleasurable: in each case, whether it overflows in weeping or no, it relieves the heart: but in the one case, the pain it assuages is deeply fixed in the heart, and the distress remains long, withstanding the alleviation: in the other, the emotion bears away all the pain, and reason closes behind sorrow the gates of the heart.

But besides this joy of sympathetic participation in happiness, and the other joy of deep and active emotion, though of the kind occasioned by distress, there is another which it is in the power of the novelist to confer upon his readers, and which, as representing one of those large classes not to be omitted in even a partial view of the subject, it will be well to notice. Like his ancient brethren, the epic and dramatic poets, the novelist calls into active operation the sympathies of approbation and disapprobation. He has at his disposal the princeliest rewards and the most severe punishments; love and death are in his hands. These he dispenses with what is not inappropriately styled poetic justice. It is customary to rail considerably at this idea of poetic justice, and to remark that life is sometimes not quite so just as poetry. Yet it lies deep in the nature of man, modified as it is by the circumstances of his present existence, to find in poetic justice an intense pleasure. Virtue consists in holding to the Good and the True in the face of opposition; in defying temptation; in buffeting circumstance; in smiling up, patient, courageous, thankful, through the drizzle of every day existence. There is a notion deep in the hearts of all of us, that we should be what we ought, were circumstances modified to suit us, were we not the victims of a luckless destiny. With Becky Sharp, we think we could be good, if we had five thousand a year. If we have the five thousand, we would be virtuous upon five-and-twenty thousand. We should cultivate all sweet and generous emotions on a sunny bank in Eden. We might take a place in the church triumphant, but the church militant is left to its own battle. In one word, there is beside every man in life, a spectre, more dire than that old black spectre, Care, which restrains his generous impulses; the spectre Selfishness. Remove this phantom, and we would, as a rule, obey the nobler instinct. In literary representation, it is removed. We do not recognize ourselves in nature's mirror. Our instincts, unleashed by selfishness, fly fiercely at us, as dogs may fly at their master when bathing, and when, from his being undressed, they do not know him. Approbation, therefore, is readily accorded to such persons, in a drama or novel, as deserve it. And approbation is always pleasurable. The indignation accompanying disapprobation is to some extent the same; and partly it acts in the manner which we endeavored to define, in considering the luxury of distress. Along both with the approbation and the disapprobation comes an insinuating side wind of self-applause, conveying a portion of all the approbation felt on him that feels it, and casting conscience into pleasant slumber.

The modes of pleasing his readers which we have hitherto discovered to belong to the novelist, pertain primarily to that element in the novel, which is contributed by Art, in the exercise of her inalienable right to mould nature to suit her purposes, to deck her out in what new fascinations, to inspire her with what new thought, the artist chooses. But the delineation of reality itself is a source of real and potent pleasure. Of the enjoyment derived from what is strictly called imitation in pictorial Art—from momentarily mistaking one thing for another—we do not now speak. We allude to the satisfaction experienced when literary description sets vividly before us any scene, face, or incident, which, in actual existence, would not in any measure arrest us. Mr. Dickens interests us in the description of a threadbare coat, on which our glance would not have lingered for a moment. Mr. Thackeray keeps us pleasantly entertained, in the presence of persons, whom, in actual life, we should find insufferably tedious. "A touch of nature makes the whole world kin." When we recognize accurate description of fact in any literary work, we are apt to forget all other qualities in our abounding delight. No doubt this pleasure depends partly, if not entirely, on sympathy with the exertion of human power; but the fact is sufficient for us, and we shall not tarry to discuss its theory.

We have already ventured to hint a rule, to enunciate a principle, by which the novel may be tested, its dross discovered and rejected, its sterling metal discerned and appropriated. We have found it made up of a real and an ideal element. To investigate the connection between the two would lead us into deep and protracted discussion. But so much is known of the relation borne by the one to the other, that strength of realism is the surest pledge of strength in the exercise of the pure imagination. Let the demand made of novels therefore be, life, life, and again, life; truth in the delineation of character, truth in portraying passion, truth in the direction given to the reader's sympathies. The novelist may dispose his personages as he will, but, once he has disposed them, they must act in accordance with human nature and the facts of life. Our space forbids any attempt to draw all the distinctions which it might be useful here to lay down. But the practical test we offer will be found not to fail. It is possible, indeed, that the novelist may accurately narrate facts, yet select such facts as ought not to be brought forward into observation. In some instances, these may come under the head of gross immorality, in which case they must be simply condemned and scorned. In others, they may be of an abnormal and exceptional sort, beyond the legitimate province of Art.* Of such we cannot speak here; but nothing we could discover regarding them would lead us to doubt the general principle, that truthful delineation of life implies power in the writer and wholesomeness for the reader. With this in his hand, discreetly borne, any one may venture into the domain of fictitious literature.

We say the novelist may adjust the relations of his characters as he pleases. He is of course bound down by certain laws of probability and natural fitness; but, on the whole, he may modify circumstances to his mind, if he correctly and correspondingly modifies the actings of his personages. It is a poor error, to be turned from essential truth by the thin veil of fictitious form. Whether such a man as Othello lived or no is of little consequence; that is, it matters little whether his name was Othello, whether he was by birth a Moor, whether he served the Venetians. Wherever a warm, impulsive, passionate nature, noble and generous to the core, is subdued by love and maddened by jealousy, the Othello of Shakspeare will appear. Romeo and Juliet may never have trod the streets of Verona; but wherever love exerts its strange, transforming power, there will be Romeos and Juliets. The intense burning of Shakspeare's truth forces its way, and shines out clear upon us, through geographical mistakes, anachronisms, and the

* See the Essay on Ellis, Acton, and Currer Bell.

wildest play of the imagination. Prospero is none the less a man, that he dwells in an enchanted island and has dealings with Ariel and Caliban. The angelic love and pity which unite in the smile and the tear of Cordelia are most true. The fiendish malignity in the eye and on the brow of Iago is also, alas! true. Lear is as a great ship, tossing in a mighty wind, but in such a tempest precisely so would such a ship rock and strain.

This matter of truth in the delineation of character, is of first rate importance in estimating the value of any work of fiction. It may be of use to name a few of the more common errors fallen into in this department. In the first place, men are apt to be converted into mere embodiments of single passions. Life is represented as a wild hurly-burly of passionate excitement. No allowance, or insufficient allowance, is made for the continual small rain of custom and habit, which so cools the heated brain in every day existence. Next, there is a peculiar liability to failure, in what might be called the right depicting of silence. Men, it is well known, when they feel most deeply are not apt to be loud in the communication of their feelings. If they are men of action, they are still less likely to be loquacious. But how is the poor novelist to get on without his noisy dialogue and sounding soliloquy? Again, we meet with mere oafs and oddities, fit inmates of Bedlam, or such as inhabit travelling caravans. It cannot be doubted that these are almost entirely beyond the legitimate province of the novelist. Last of all, an error, precisely the reverse of that with which we set out, is often committed. An exclusively intellectual nature, a superhuman superiority to, or inhuman absence of, passion, is imputed to the supposititious characters.

All these errors, variously combined and modified, are

abundantly represented in the novels of the Minerva Press. That this class of novels still exists is too evident: but it does not now occupy any seat of honor, and no Monk Lewis will arise to rescue it from merited disdain. If we consider it well, we shall find that its absurdities are, on the whole, traceable to an absence of that sound, basing realism, which we have praised so highly. It exhibited, on a grand scale, the sickliness, the foolish vagaries, of an imagination not walking constantly with life. It rendered an invaluable service to criticism, by furnishing an incomparable example of those false sources of popularity, those exaggerated descriptions of passion, those morbid excitements, those modish ideals, — of honor, of beauty, of picturesqueness, of sublimity, — which may, for a time, secure unbounded success, but which, having no root in nature, are fleeting as the whims they pamper. No critic can henceforward be at a loss for specimens of sentimentality, theatricality, fustian, and the mock sublime.

Since nature alone affords inexhaustible variety, the Minerva Press novel becomes soon recognizable, by the recurring circle of its plots and characters. The book opens with an atrocious murder. A body is found in some pond, or river, or dungeon, or in the mysterious glade of some haunted wood. The reader must be particularly on his guard here against jugglery. Unless he is genuine Yorkshire, a man whom he believed dead will surely arise to his discomfiture in after days, heading some band of robbers, and performing all manner of truculent work. The reader must insist upon seeing the coffin nailed down and committed to the grave; if the death has been hanging, he must watch by the fatal tree, at least three hours, to certify himself that injured innocence is not cut down before life is extinct; he must inspect the throat, to see that no iron ring has been inserted to cheat the hangman. However, be it agreed that there is a murder, and a mysterious one. The guilt of it somehow casts a dark shadow around some sweet Adeline or Angelina, who is either accused while innocent, or defrauded by cruel relatives who have done the deed. In process of time, some good-looking, gallant, mustachioed Herbert, or Lionel, or Clifford, rights the oppressed, sets all in train about the murder, talks the highest sentiment, and marries Angelina. This instructive narrative is, of course, enlivened by a due allotment of night attacks, tapers twinkling in ruins in lone woods, rapturous ejaculations, superhuman devotions, and valiant deaths. The novelist amends nature, but not in a cunning or admirable manner; not in accordance with the deeper laws of nature itself, with which it is well for Art always to consort, but in accordance with the requirements of mode, in subservience to the trick o' the time. He improves men in the manner of the applauded French dramatist, who made men of the old Romans, by putting them in court dresses and presenting them at Versailles. To this class of novels appears to belong the whole series bearing the title of Mysteries, whether of Paris, of London, or Udolpho. *Requiescant!*

The three greatest living novelists are Mr. Dickens, Sir Edward Lytton Bulwer, and Mr. Thackeray.

We cannot undertake to say how much of the popularity of Mr. Dickens is owing to that exertion of his genius which is in itself highest, and how much to that large class of cases, in which, as must appear to a sound criticism, he has, if not subjected his genius to dishonor, at least permitted it to indulge in child's play. It is not for him to depend on the delineation of those personal eccentricities, which Sterne called hobby-horses, Jonson humors and which Mr.

Macaulay has so finely characterized in his essay on Fanny Burney. The Minerva Press itself might be challenged to produce, from a like number of volumes, a number of oafs, deformed persons, idiots, and monomaniacs, equal to that which can be collected from the works of Mr. Dickens. Consider the fat boy in *Pickwick.* What an exquisite observation was required, in order to discriminate from his fellows that delicately marked character; what a fine touch was necessary to set distinctly on the canvas that instructive and charming personage! Tupman is simply a man of "humor" in Ben Jonson's sense. So is Winkle. Turning to the author's later works, the same characteristic is presented. Skimpole, in *Bleak House*, is an oddity. Richard is a nonentity, with a foible or two which might have cost him his freedom and secured him lodging in a lunatic asylum. The little mad woman, the repulsive being who is destroyed by spontaneous combustion, the brutalized old miser, and so on, all belong to the same class. Boythorn must have a canary to perch about his person. Jarndyce must have idiosyncrasies about the growlery and the east wind. Surely Mr. Dickens does not confer the highest honor upon his genius, when he sets it to such tickling of the fancy as this.

And his genius is worthy of honor. No writer could be named on whom the indefinable gift has been more manifestly conferred. His early works are all aglow with genius. The supreme potency with which he commands it, is shown in the total absence of effort, in the classic chasteness and limpid flow, of thought, fancy, and diction. You are in a meadow just after dawn; the flowers are fresh as if they had awakened from slumber, and the dew is on them all. A word, an idea, a glimpse of beauty, is always at hand; the writer never tarries a moment; yet there is no display, no profusion, of opulence. You do not see him waving the wand; the tear or the smile is on your cheek before you are aware.

The distinctive power of Dickens lies, we think, in a sympathy of extraordinary range, exquisite delicacy, and marvellous truth. He does not so much look, with steady, unparticipating gaze, until he knows and remembers the exact features of life: he feels. With all human sorrow he could weep; with all human mirth he could laugh; and when he came to write, every emotion he aimed at exciting was made sure, by being first experienced in his own breast. It was not with the individual man, in the wholeness of his life, in the depths of his identity, that he naturally concerned himself. It was kindness, rather than the one kind man, that he saw. It was mirth, rather than the whole character which is modified by humor. Qualities, capacities, characteristics, rather than complete men, glassed themselves in the mirror of his clear and open soul. 'With all his accuracy in detailed portraiture, it is a superficial perception of the order of his genius, which does not see that its power rested naturally less on realism, than on a peculiar, delicate, and most captivating idealization. Pickwick, at least in the whole earlier part of his history, is an impossible personage. He belongs to broad farce. But we laugh at his impossible conversation with the cabman. We laugh at his impossible credulity as he listens to Jingle. We laugh at his impossible simplicity at the review. The far-famed Sam Weller, too, corresponds to no reality. The Londoner born and bred is apt to be the driest and most uninteresting of beings. All things lost for him the gloss of novelty when he was fifteen years old. He would suit the museum of a *nil admirari* philosopher, as a specimen, shrivelled and adust, of the ultimate result of his principle.

But Dickens collected more jokes than all the cabmen in London would utter in a year, and bestowed the whole treasure upon Sam. His eye was far too acute for the comical to let it rest on any one funny man. In the case of those of his characters whom we are simply to admire and love, the same distinctive mode of treatment is exhibited. Rose Maylie and Esther Summerson are breathing epitomes of the tendernesses, the sweetnesses, the beauties, of life. Oliver Twist concentrates the single good qualities of a hundred children. The kind-hearted man, Dickens's stock character, be his name Pickwick, Jarndyce, or Clennam, seems always radically the same, and corresponds well enough with our theory. Perhaps it is essential deficiency in the highest power of individualization, which drives Mr. Dickens, it may be unconsciously, to affix, by way of labels, to the personages of his story, those insignificant peculiarities which all can perceive.

Amid the tumult and distracting blaze of his fame, one is by no means safe from the blunder of overlooking the kernel of genuine and precious humanity, of honest kindliness, of tender yet expansive benignity, which is in the centre of Dickens's being. His nature must originally have been most sweetly tuned. He must from the first have abounded in those qualities, which are so beautiful and winning when combined with manly character and vigorous powers; a cheerful gentleness, a loving hopefulness, a willingness to take all things and men for the best, an eye for the loveable; such a disposition as one finds in Goldsmith, a passionate admiration of happy human faces, a delight in the sports and laughter of children. He has always, too, been earnestly desirous to promote the welfare of men, to remove abuses, to do practical good. In the conduct of *Household Words*, it is easy to see, he has ever had his eye on the practical, coming down heartily now on one social wrong or absurdity, now on another, the manner perhaps not always unexceptionable, the spirit always right.

His stepping forward to aid the Administrative Reform Association was very characteristic, and strikingly indicated the practicality and nobleness of his nature. That miserable association could expose the evils of maladministration only as the Helot could expose the evils of drunkenness. But Dickens could not sit apart in the approved literary fashion. When men arose visibly, and declared it their wish and endeavor to bring talent into the councils of the nation, they could not, of course, look for any aid from him who had been preaching hero-worship and the importance of finding talent for the nation all his days. Mr. Carlyle was quiet. Mr. Maurice published a weak and windy pamphlet, to the effect, of course, that you both should and should not support Administrative Reform. Dickens simply attempted to render some practical assistance. Thus he has ever acted. A pure white flame of ambition to do practical good has ever burned steadily in his breast, and no blustering applause, no favoring fortune, could dim its brightness. It is a consideration of this fact, associated with that of his warm and generous sympathy with every emotion he believes at once noble and sincere, which makes it so mournful that Dickens has never really in any sense known what true evangelical Christianity is. The most earnest and exalted feeling that dwells in the human breast is to him strange and inconceivable. He has had no glimpse of the beauty and joy of holiness. The zeal which has sent hundreds from the luxuries and adulations of civilization, to die, with wasted cheek and burning brow, on the sterile sands of moral and physical desolation, is to him a delusion and absurdity. The delight that can be found in the sabbatic calm of devotion, the solace and blissful rest of worship, are to him hypocritical affectations or wholly unknown. He has indeed felt his heart drawn out in sympathy towards the perfect humanity of the Saviour, towards His tender compassion and infinite self-sacrificing love: but of the religion of Jesus in its truest form now extant he knows only a painful and revolting caricature.

Sir Edward Bulwer Lytton seems to have been adapted by nature to succeed as a novelist; and he has succeeded. The characteristic of his mind is diffused and comprehensive energy. Neither emotionally nor intellectually, is Sir Edward's mind determined, with overwhelming force, in one direction. The result has been that neither in the province of pure imagination, nor in that of pure intellect, has he attained the highest degree of excellence. As a thinker, men will not accept him for a guide; as a poet, he has failed. The novel is in some respects a debatable region, between the spheres of the philosophic thinker and the poet. In the department of the novel he has accordingly won very distinguished honor. The creations of his fertile mind, decked out in the fairest colors, float between the domains of unimaginative prose and truly imaginative poetry. The rhythmic melody, the heaven-kindled enthusiasm, the deep, unfeigned faith, which pervade the prose of Milton are absent from his works; the penetrating logic of Butler, the determined inquisition of Foster, are alike foreign to him; but his prose holds in solution about as much poetry as prose can, and his novels contain about as much thought as readers will endure.

The special ability of Bulwer appears to lie in the delineation of that passion with which the novel is so deeply concerned, the passion of love. All true and manly passions, let it be said, are honored and illustrated in his pages. But he stands alone among novelists of his sex in the portraiture of love, and specially of love in the female breast. The heroism, the perfect trust the strength in death, are painted by him with a sympathetic truth for which we know not where to seek a parallel. The effect of Eugene Aram's speech at his trial, upon Madeline, his betrothed,—the calm, beautiful, satisfied smile, which lit up her wan features,—is a golden letter from the very handwriting of nature. Then, where, out of Shakspeare, can we find such a series of female portraits as those in *Rienzi?* One scarce knows to which of the masterly delineations to accord the palm. There is the weak, womanly Adeline, strong only in love, able to die beautifully, but not to live well. In Irene, there is love's complete, ineradicable devotion, all-subduing, spontaneous, self-sacrificing. In Nina, proud love gazes, self-reliant, and self-satisfied, on all the world around, but sinks in womanly tenderness on the breast of the loved one. Adeline is the soft, flower-like woman, growing fair in the calm summer radiance, but withering in the wintry blast. Irene is the human angel, of whom poets have so long sung. Nina is the queen, ready to live with, or die for, her husband-king. Rienzi himself is nobly imagined, endeavoring to tread the surges and engulfed.

Mr. Thackeray is, as a novelist, so pointed and unmistakable a contrast to Mr. Dickens, that it is interesting to find them writing at the same time. Thackeray is as little of an idealizer as it seems possible to be, if you write novels at all. He cuts into conventionalism so daringly, that you fear sometimes, as when he gives you a novel without a hero, that he goes too far, and puts in peril the essence of his Art. If he does idealize, it is not in the manner of Dickens, but in one strikingly different. He selects characters as Dickens selects characteristics. But he depends for success not on the power of his personages to evoke sympathy, negative or positive, but on their strict correspondence with fact. It cannot, perhaps, be said that he, any more than Mr. Dickens, reaches the Shakspearean substratum of character. His eye is that of an artist. It has been trained to take in the whole aspect of the outer man, not only in the minutiæ of his dress, but in the whole monotonous circumstance of his every day life. His popularity is the most powerful evidence to which one could easily point, of the capacity residing in the exhibition of bare, or even repulsive fact, to interest mankind. It is said that Thackeray abandoned the career of an artist, because, according to his own avowal, he could only caricature. He felt the absence of the higher idealizing power. His novels exhibit the radical qualities which would have distinguished his pictures. It is not emotionally that we regard them. They call forth no glow of admiration, no warm, loving sympathy, no wonder, no reverence. He makes his appeal to sterner, colder powers, to reflection, to the cynic's philosophy, to contempt. It may be better, higher, more noble and self-denying, in him, to do so; but the fact is patent. And its inevitable consequence has been and will be, a popularity not so wide, a command over the heart not so great, as those of men who permit fancy to lay on color, and imagination to heighten life. The non-existent Pickwick will always be more deeply loved than the actual Dobbin. The positive folly and knavishness of Job and Jingle will always interest more than the dismally negative stupidity of Jos. The metallic heartlessness, the machine-like selfishness, of Becky, marvellous, inimitable, as that portrait is, will neutralize all her cleverness in attempting to awaken so warm an interest as Rose Maylie, Nancy, or Esther Summerson. Facts of perfect notoriety bear out this view. Thackeray owes his popularity in great measure to reviewers. The men who were not in the way of experiencing emotion recognized his power. The clever young fellows of a satirical cast, laboring under the misfortune, painfully conscious to themselves, of being before their age, were all on his side. Currer Bell, with woman's vehemence and woman's cordiality, made up her mind that he was a great teacher, come with some profound and important message for his generation; and, having made up her mind, she emphatically announced it. Of truth, whether intellectual or ethical, the works of Thackeray contain, demonstrably and indubitably, but a superficial film. But the voice of Currer Bell was heard, and the trumpetings of reviewers, the applause of knowing young men, and other causes, gradually brought him into notice. Thackeray became the fashion. Dickens owed as little of his popularity to reviewers as the Great Unknown or the Oxford Graduate. It must not be, from this, inferred that Mr. Dickens is to be set before Mr. Thackeray. The reverse might, indeed, be argued, although we do not intend to argue either. Mr. Thackeray succeeded, without any aid, in obtaining an audience, select it is true, but so cultivated and influential, that, somewhat as in the case of Wordsworth, the nation at large was forced to acknowledge him. Those who could find satisfaction in the uncompromising recital of nature's facts thronged around him.

If it were asked what one aspect of life Mr. Thackeray has distinctively exhibited, the answer could be given in one word, — the trivial aspect. The characters he draws are neither the best of men nor the worst. But the atmosphere of triviality which envelopes them all was never before so plainly perceivable. He paints the world as a great Vanity Fair, and none has done that so well.

The realism of Thackeray can hardly fail to have a good effect in fictitious literature. It represents the extreme point of reaction against the false idealism of the Minerva Press. It is a pre-Raphaelite school of novel writing. And as pre-Raphaelitism is not to be valued in itself, so much as in being the passage to a new and nobler ideal, the stern realism of Thackeray may lead the way to something better than itself.

We found that the novel occupies a distinct and legitimate place among the forms of human exertion, and we cannot but deem it a crude and shallow error to pronounce upon it a sentence of indiscriminating condemnation. The man who looks resolutely for truth, and bids away from him any feeble desire to be merely amused, may derive important information as to his time, and valuable knowledge of human nature, by a heedful and limited study of modern novels. But, on the whole, our decision would be that the more limited this study is the better. Converse with rugged fact, whether of history or science, is what, beyond question, most effectually braces and nourishes the mind. If the tendency of the time were to strike its roots into the rock, and not to seek the soft sunshine above, one might freely advise indulgence in light reading. But since the tendency on this side is by no means likely to run to excess, and since the studious facilitation of mental exercise, and the habitual use of intellectual stimulants, are exceedingly apt to enervate and destroy the mind, our final counsel is to lay, as much as may be, the novel on the shelf.

VIII.

ELLIS, ACTON, AND CURRER BELL.

EVEN while the heart of the British nation is filled to overflowing by one great anguish and one great hope, we cannot doubt that a thrill of real sorrow will pass to every corner of the land with the tidings that Mrs. Nicholls, formerly Charlotte Bronte, and known to all the world as Currer Bell, is no more. But a few months ago, we heard of her marriage. It became known, with a smile of happy surprise, that the merciless derider of weak and insipid suitors had found a lord and master, that the hand which drew the three worshipful ecclesiastics, Malone, Donne, and Sweeting, had been locked at the altar in that of a curate. And already the smile fades away in the sound of her funeral knell, leaving us to reflect, that all of fruit and flower which time might have matured in the garden of her genius has been nipped by the frost of death. There is something which strikes us as peculiarly touching in the death of Currer Bell. She seemed so full of animation, of vigor; life danced like wine in her veins: all she said was so fresh and stirring; the child-look, taking this for a grand world, worth living in, no place for whining, was still on her face. The brave little woman! — in whose works you could not point to a slovenly line, to an obscure or tarrying idea. One thought of her as combining the iron will of her little Jane, with the peerless nature of her Shirley, the beautiful pantheress, the forest-born. She could have stood out under the lightning, to trace, with firm pencil, its zig-zags of crackling fire. And now she too is but a few handfuls of white dust! Her step will never more be upon the loved wolds of Yorkshire and the broad moors which she made classic by her genius.

> "Her part in all the pomp that fills
> The circuit of the summer hills
> Is that her grave is green."

It is a trite, yet ever a suggestive remark, that the variety of nature is infinite. You have been watching the sun, when, as if in love's changefulness, he smiled from behind April clouds on the awakening earth. Those evanescent lights on lawn and lea, those bright gleams on the distant river, that fantastic sport of the sunlight, kindling its broad and silvery illumination, burst after burst, amid the mountain mist, will never be seen again. Every effect of nature is solitary. Each star has its own twinkle, every lily of the field its peculiar and unshared beauty. The Hand whose touch is perfection repeats not its strokes. But, without inquiring what specifically is that mystic thing called genius, it is universally conceded, that it is of its essential nature to be, in a peculiar sense, unexampled and alone. Whether it be a positive addition to the ordinary complement of human faculty, or whether it be some new and cunning harmony, some delicate balancing, some exquisite sharpening, of the ordinary mental powers, it is at least agreed that, from the eye in which men discern genius, there falls over the world a light whose very novelty urges to the term. It has been said by Coleridge, that the effect of genius on its possessor is to perpetuate, in mature age, the wakeful curiosity, the fresh enjoyment, the loving surprise, with which healthful childhood gazes on the new world; to enable a man to see, in the clear, strong light of intellectual noontide, the same fairness and freshness over the earth as when it lay under the dewy dawn. Be this as it may, the fact is beyond question, that there is a difference between the perceptions of such an one and those of the throng. Into recesses of the human heart, whither, erewhile, we could not penetrate, this new light guides our steps. Secret and ravishing glimpses of beauty, to which we never before thrilled, are now revealed to us. Passions which lay dormant in our breasts have been awakened ere we were aware, to overflow in tears or flash in fire. Truths which were altogether unknown, or, through custom, faded and powerless, have beamed forth with startling or alluring clearness. And when here, too, death asserts his iron rule, it is no figure of speech, but a simple statement of fact, that tones have died away which we can never hear again from the universal harp of nature, that "a light has passed from the revolving year," and that Providence has again worked out, in all it involves of responsibility and monition, those high intents for which there was sent among us an original mind. The mind of Currer Bell was assuredly original; and when we add, that the genius by which it was characterized was accompanied by an earnestness which might be called religious, and turned, by a strong human sympathy, upon the general aspects and salient points of the age, it becomes a matter of serious moment to sum up the work she has done, and estimate the lesson she has taught us. The office of criticism is twofold; it has one duty to perform for behoof of the author and another to the reader. From that point of view which every honest and individual, though nowise remarkably powerful, mind occupies, lights of guidance or suggestion may be discerned, of value to the highest; honest criticism of living authors is therefore beyond question to be approved. But this task, and whatever of even apparent acerbity it may entail, ceases with the life of the author. As we received from the dying hand the gift to which there will be no addition, however it may be required of us to define its value, we may at least permit to criticism the tone of affection and respect. It is singularly so in the case of Currer Bell. Whatever estimate we may form of the net result of positive instruction — the actual amount of such sound available thought as will pave the highways of the world — to be found in her works, we cannot but think with tender emotion on the darkness which has so soon swallowed the brief and meteoric splendor of her career; while we should deem that reader of perceptions strangely blunted, who has never discerned that, with all her vigor and sternness, it was deep and womanly love which filled the inmost fountains of her heart. It is well, too, to remember, that it were an important mistake to test the value of any work, or series of works, by the mere logical truth they contain. The true, the beautiful, and the good, are inalienably allied. In the immeasurable system of education which nature has constructed around us in this world, their conscious or unconscious influences are perpetually blended. He who came to unfold celestial and unattainable truth, deemed not His teaching complete, until He turned the eyes of His disciples on the loveliness of the lily and the gay carelessness of the birds. Every tone of true pathos, every revealing glance by which a new aspect of nature's loveliness opens on our eyes — all that tends, in what way soever, to make us nobler, gentler, better — must be reckoned in the account of what an author has conferred upon us.

The name of Currer Bell has constantly been associated with those of her two sisters, Emily and Anne, known in the literary world as Ellis and Acton Bell. The three were the daughters of a clergyman of the Church of England, who, as we learn from the newspapers, still "at Haworth, near Keighley, in Yorkshire," survives his wife and all his children. Genius, as has not unfrequently happened, was, in the case of the three sisters, associated with the seeds of fatal disease. Perhaps our whole literary annals will show no more touching episode than that on which the leaf has just been turned by the death of Currer Bell. It is our present purpose to treat chiefly of the works of this last, but we shall be pardoned for making allusion to her sisters.

Emily Bronte, author of *Wuthering Heights*, was, we have no hesitation in saying, one of the most extraordinary women that ever lived. We have felt strongly impelled to pronounce her genius more powerful, her promise more rich, than those of her gifted sister, Charlotte. For accepting this avowal, the reader will be somewhat prepared, by perusing the following sentences, from the biographic notice, brief, but of thrilling interest, of her two sisters, given to the world by Currer Bell:—"My sister Emily first declined. The details of her illness are deep-branded in my memory; but to dwell on them, either in thought or narrative, is not in my power. Never in all her life had she lingered over any task that lay before her, and she did not linger now. She sank rapidly. She made haste to leave us. Yet, while physically she perished, mentally she grew stronger than we had yet known her. Day by day, when I saw with what a front she met suffering, I looked on her with an anguish of wonder and love. I have seen nothing like it; but, indeed, I have never seen her parallel in anything. Stronger than a man, simpler than a child, her nature stood alone. The awful point was, that, while full of ruth for others, on herself she had no pity; the spirit was inexorable to the flesh; from the trembling hand, the unnerved limbs, the faded eyes, the same service was exacted as they had rendered in health."

The picture thus vividly drawn of a frail form standing up undaunted in the scowl of death, should be kept before us as we turn to the work left us by Ellis Bell. It were a strange and surely a distempered criticism which hesitated to pass sentence of condemnation on *Wuthering Heights*. We have no such hesitation. Canons of art sound and imperative, true tastes and natural instincts, of which these canons are the expression, unite in pronouncing it unquestionably and irremediably monstrous. If there is any truth or indication of truth in all that the most artistic of nations alleged concerning the line of beauty, if it is true that in every work of art, however displayed, we must meet the proofs of moderation, of calmness, of tempered and mastered power; if it is a reasonable demand that the instances of nature's abortion, from which we would turn away in the street, objects and incidents which awake no higher emotion than abhorrent disgust, be honored with no embalming rites, but left to be taken out of our sight, like dead dogs and carrion, by that nature which never perpetuates what is gross or noisome; this work must be condemned. On the dark brow and iron cheek of Heathcliff, there are touches of the Miltonic fiend; but we shrink in mere loathing, in "unequivocal contempt," from the base wretch who can use his cruelty as the tool of his greed, and whose cruelty itself is so unredeemed by any resistance or stimulant, as to expend itself on a dying son or a girl's poodle. There are things which the pen of history cannot be required to do more than touch on and pass by. We desire not admittance into the recesses of the palace of Sujah Dowlah, we will not penetrate the privacy of the Cæsars. If the historic artist must at times show us the darkest evil, that we may avoid it, or sweep it from the earth, neither his nor any other art can altogether forego the glorious privilege of washing its creations in pure water, and shunning, at least, the foul and offensive. The whole atmosphere, too, of this fiction is distempered, disturbed, and unnatural. Fever and malaria are in the air. The emotions and the crimes are on the scale of madness; and, as if earthly beings, and feelings called terrestrial, were not of potency sufficient to carry on the exciting drama, there are dangerous, very ghostly personages, of the spectral order, introduced, and communings held with the spirit world which would go far to prove Yorkshire the original locality of spirit-rapping. All this is true, and no reader of the book will deem our mode of expressing it severe. Yet we have perfect confidence in pointing to *Wuthering Heights*, as a work containing evidence of powers it were perhaps impossible to estimate, and mental wealth which we might vainly attempt to compute. A host of Titans would make wild work, if directed by a child to overturn the mountains; a host of dwarfs would do little good or harm in any case; but bring your Titans under due command, set over them a judgment that can discern and command, and hill will rise swiftly over hill, till the pyramid is scaling the sky. The powers manifested in this strange book seem to us comparable to a Titan host; and we know no task beyond their might, had they been ruled by a severe taste and discriminating judgment. The mere ability to conceive and depict, with strength so unwavering and clearness so vivid, that wild group of characters, the unmeasured distance into which recedes all that is conventional, customary, or sentimental, the tremendous strength and maturity of the style, would be enough to justify our words. The very absurdities and exaggerations of the construction lend their testimony here. Not for a moment, with such materials, could the aim of art have been attained, could belief, in some sense and for some space, have been produced, save by commanding powers. It may be the wild and haggard pageantry of a dream at which we gaze, but it is a dream we can never forget. Though the dissent and denial of our reason are, when we pause, explicit, we no sooner resign ourselves to the spell of the magician, than we feel powerless to disbelieve. In the strength of the assertion, we overlook its absurdity. Touching the character of Heathcliff, moreover, and, with less expressness, of that of Cathy Earnshaw, we have a remark to make, which will extend to certain of the characters of Currer Bell, and which might, we think, go far to point out a psychological defence, to be urged with some plausibility, of much that is extravagant and revolting in either case. The power over the mind of what Mr. Carlyle calls "fixed idea," is well known; the possession of the whole soul by one belief or aim produces strange and unaccountable effects, commingling strength and weakness, kindness and cruelty, and seeming, at first sight, to compromise the very unity of nature. Ellis Bell, in *Wuthering Heights*, deals with a kindred, though somewhat different phenomenon. She has not to do with intellect, but emotion. She paints the effects of one overmastering feeling, the maniac actings of him who has quaffed one draught of maddening passion. The passion she has chosen is love. There is still a gleam of nobleness, of natural human affection, in the heart of Heathcliff in the days of his early love for Cathy, when he rushes manfully at the bull-dog which has seized her, and sets himself, after she is safe in Thrushcross Grange, on the window ledge, to watch how matters go on, "because," says he, "if Catherine had wished to return, I intended shattering their great glass panes to a million fragments, unless they let her out." But we watch that boyish heart, until, in the furnace of hopeless and agonizing passion, it becomes as insensible to any tender emotion, to any emotion save one, as a mass of glowing iron to trickling dew. Heathcliff's original nature is seen only in the outgoing of his love towards Cathy; there he is human, if he is frenzied; in all other cases, he is a devil. As his nature was never good, as there were always in it the hidden elements of the sneak and the butcher, the whole of that semi-vital life which he retains towards the rest of the world is ignoble and revolting. His sorrow has been to him moral death. With truly diabolic uniformity, every exercise of power possible to him upon any creature, rational or irrational, Cathy, of course, excepted, is made for its torment. He seems in one half of his nature to have lost all sensibility, to be unconscious that human beings suffer pain. The great agony of passion has burned out of his bosom the chords of sympathy which linked him to his kind, and left him in that ghastly and fiendish solitude, which it is awful to dream of as a possible element in the punishment of hell. However frightful the love-scenes in the death chamber of Cathy — and we suppose there is nothing at all similar to these in the range of literature — we feel that we are in the presence of a man. When we think on his early roamings with his lost and dying love on the wild moors, we can even perceive, stealing over the heart, a faint breath of sympathy. But when he leaves the world of his real existence — the world of his love for

Cathy, whether as a breathing woman, or as the wraith which he still loves on — we shrink from him as from a corpse, made more ghastly by the hideous movements of galvanism. Somewhat different is the effect of the same passion upon Cathy. Hers was originally a brave, beautiful, essentially noble nature; through all her waywardness, we love her still; and though her passion for Heathcliff costs her her life, it never scathes and sears her soul into a calcined crag like his. To the last, her heart and imagination can bear her to the wild flowers she used to gather amid the heath; strange and wraith-like as she grows in the storm of that resistless passion, we know full well that no mean, or cruel, or unwomanly thought could enter her breast. Viewed as a psychological study of this sort, a defence might, we say, be set up for the choice of these two characters; and when thus confessedly morbid, their handling will be allowed to be masterly. Nor can it be alleged that instances of similar passion, attended by like results, are not to be met with in real life. Madness, idiocy, and death, are acknowledged to follow misguided or hopeless affection. In the case both of Cathy and Heathcliff, there was unquestionably a degree of the first. But the defence can at best be partial, for, we submit, bedlam is no legitimate sphere of art. Of one thing, however, there can be no doubt. The girl's hand which drew Heathcliff and Cathy, which never shook as it brought out those lines of agony on cheek and brow, which never for a moment lost its strength and sweep in flourish or bravura, was such as has seldom wielded either pen or pencil.

We might descant at great length on the variety of power displayed in this extraordinary book; but we should leave it without conveying an idea, even partially correct, of its general character, if we omitted to notice those touches of nature's softest beauty, those tones of nature's softest melody, which are blended, so cunningly as to excite no sense of discord, with its general excitement and gloom. We cannot forbear quoting here a passage which seems to us deeply suggestive; the speaker is a young girl, and he of whom she speaks a boy about her own age: —

"One time, however, we were near quarrelling. He said the pleasantest manner of spending a hot July day was lying from morning till evening on a bank of heath in the middle of the moors, with the bees humming dreamily about among the bloom, and the larks singing high up overhead, and the blue sky and bright sun shining steadily and cloudlessly. That was his perfect idea of heaven's happiness. Mine was, rocking in a rustling green tree, with a west wind blowing, and bright, white clouds flitting rapidly above; and not only larks, but throstles, and blackbirds, and linnets, and cuckoos, pouring out music on every side, and the moors seen at a distance, broken into cool, dusky dells; but close by great swells of long grass undulating in waves to the breeze; and woods, and sounding water, and the whole world awake and wild with joy. He wanted all to lie in an ecstacy of peace; I wanted all to sparkle and dance in a glorious jubilee."

Does this not bear witness to much? No sympathy but that of a green heart could have won access to that child's heaven. None but a free, and elastic, and loving nature could thus, with the inimitable touch of truth and reality, have heard, through the ear of that glad girl, in the joy-toned anthem of bird, and water, and rustling branch, the very music of heaven. The faithfulness of the picture, the perfect and effortless realization of the whole summer scene, so that we hear that west wind, and see those bright white clouds — the cumulous clouds which the summer long, are the flocks of the west wind — and scent that bloom of the warm, waving heather, is demonstration absolutely sufficient of that inborn love of nature's joy and beauty which never yet dwelt in a narrow or unworthy breast. This short extract, too, is sufficient to prove maturity and excellence of style. There is a free, strong, graceful force in every line; there is no dallying, no second touch; the little scene groups itself gracefully together as if to that summer music.

We make no more than an allusion to Ellis Bell's poetry. It is characterized by strength and freshness, and by that original cadence, that power of melody, which, be it wild, or tender, or even harsh, was never heard before, and comes at first hand from nature, as her sign of the born poet. We have compared the poetry of the three sisters; and in spite of a prevailing opinion to the contrary, we scruple not to declare, that the clear result of our examination is the conclusion that Ellis Bell's is beyond measure the best.

But, after all, we must pronounce what has been left us by this wonderful woman, unhealthy, immature, and worthy of being avoided. *Wuthering Heights*, we repeat, belongs to the horror school of fiction, and is involved in its unequivocal and unexcepting condemnation. We say not that a mind, inured to the task, cannot, by careful scrutiny and severe discrimination, derive valuable hints and important exercise from such works. You may trace and emulate strength of touch and richness of color, while you detest the subject. You may listen to snatches of woodland music, and thrill to tints of woodland beauty, in the neighborhood of the hyena's den. But we do not for this recall our condemnation. At the foot of the gallows, touches of nature's tenderness may be marked: in the pallid face of the criminal you may note workings of emotion not to be seen elsewhere. Anatomy might be studied, with both novelty and force of instruction, in the quivering of the muscles and wrenching of the forehead of one who lay on the wheel. But it admits not of question, that the general effect of such spectacles is brutalizing, and we would therefore without hesitation terminate their publicity. On exactly the same grounds, would we bid our readers avoid works of distempered excitement. Even when such are of the highest excellence in their class, as those of Ellis Bell and Edgar Poe, we would deliberately sentence them to oblivion. Their general effect is to produce a mental state alien to the calm energy and quiet homely feelings of real life; to make the soul the slave of stimulants, and those of the fiercest kind; and, whatever morbid irritability may for the time be fostered, to shrivel and dry up those sympathies which are the most tender, delicate, and precious. Works like those of Edgar Poe and this *Wuthering Heights* must be plainly declared to blunt, to brutalize, and to enervate the mind. Of the poetry, also, of Ellis Bell, it must be said that it is not healthful. Its beauty is allied to that wild loveliness which may gleam on the hectic cheek, or move while it startles, as we listen to maniac ravings. And wherefore this unchanging wail, whence this perpetual and inexpressible melancholy, in the poems of one so young? What destiny is it with which this young heart so vainly struggles, and by which it is overcome? Is it possible that, under the sunny azure of an English sky, and while the foot is on English moors, so utter a sadness may descend on a girl, whom we expect to find "a metaphor of spring, and mirth, and gladness," the sister of the fawn and the linnet? The spectacle is deeply touching, and, alas! the explanation is at hand; an explanation which, while it leaves untouched the assertion that the beauty of these poems is that of the blighted flower, changes every feeling with which we might momentarily regard their author into pitying sorrow. Her genius was yoked with death. It never freed itself from the dire companionship, never rose into freedom and clearness. As in the old Platonic chariot, her soul, borne by her winged genius, rose strong and daring towards the empyrean; but ere it breathed the pure serene, that black steed, which was also yoked indissolubly to the car, dragged her downwards even to the grave. Her poetry, whatever tones of true and joyful lyric music it may at intervals afford, is, as a whole, but the wild wailing melody to which was fought the battle between genius and death.

Of Anne Bronte, known as Acton Bell, we have scarce a remark to make. In her life, too, sadness was the reigning element, but she possessed no such strong genius as her sister. "Anne's character," says Currer Bell, "was more subdued; she wanted the power, the fire, the originality of her sister, but was well endowed with quiet virtues of her own. Long-suffering, self-denying, reflective, and intelligent, a constitutional reserve and taciturnity placed and kept her in the shade, and covered her mind, and especially her feelings, with a sort of nun-like veil, which was rarely lifted." Her death is thus recorded by the same authority: — "She (Ellis) was not buried ere Anne fell ill. She had not been committed to the grave a fortnight, before we received distinct intimation that it was necessary to prepare our minds to see the younger sister go after the elder. Accordingly, she followed in the same path, with slower step, and with a patience that equalled the other's fortitude. I have said that she was religious, and it was by leaning on those Christian doctrines in which she firmly believed, that she found support through her most painful journey. I witnessed their efficacy in her latest hour and greatest trial, and must bear testimony to the calm triumph with which they brought her through." She died May 28, 1849. The last lines written by Acton Bell are so full of pathos, awaken a sorrow so holy and ennobling, and breathe a faith so strong and tranquil, that we cannot pass them by:—

"I hoped, that with the brave and strong,
My portion'd task might lie;
To toil amid the busy throng,
With purpose pure and high.

But God has fix'd another part,
And he has fix'd it well:
I said so with my bleeding heart,
When first the anguish fell.

Thou, God, hast taken our delight,
Our treasured hope away:
Thou bidd'st us now weep through the night,
And sorrow through the day.

These weary hours will not be lost,
These days of misery,
These nights of darkness, anguish-tost,
Can I but turn to thee:

With secret labor to sustain
In humble patience every blow;
To gather fortitude from pain,
And hope and holiness from woe.

Thus let me serve thee from my heart,
Whate'er may be my written fate;
Whether thus early to depart,
Or yet awhile to wait.

If thou should'st bring me back to life,
More humbled I should be;
More wise—more strengthen'd for the strife,
More apt to lean on thee.

Should death be standing at the gate,
Thus should I keep my vow;
But, Lord! whatever be my fate,
Oh, let me serve thee now!"

"These lines written," adds Currer Bell, "the desk was closed, the pen laid aside, forever."

It may well be doubted whether any more than a faint and mournful reminiscence of Ellis and Acton Bell will survive the generation now passing away. But the case is widely different with the eldest of the sisters. Currer Bell has won for herself a place in our literature from which she cannot be deposed. Her influence will long be felt, as a strong plastic energy, in the literature of Britain and the world. The language of England will retain a trace of her genius. We have no intention, at present, to subject her works to a detailed criticism; we purpose merely to notice a few of her leading characteristics, and, listening to her words as those of one who scrupled not to assume the tone of a censor of her age, and considered every word she penned matter of conscientious regard, to endeavor to define, briefly but articulately, the worth of her teaching. Currer Bell professed to be no idle entertainer. She did not, indeed, tag on a moral to the end of her book, — else it had been little worth, — or even blazon it on its surface. But she professed to write truly, to show living men and women, meeting the exigencies, grappling with the problems of real life, to point out how the battle goes in private circles, between pretension and reality, between falsehood and truth. If we were content to listen to her as a historian, she relinquished with a smile the laurel of the romancer. She was the professed foe of conventionality, and the whole tone of her writings evinces her desire to fling off its trammels. To what extent she succeeded we may learn as we proceed.

The style of Currer Bell is one which will reward study for its own sake. Its character is directness, clearness, force. We could point to no style which appears to us more genuinely and nobly English. Prompt and business-like, perfectly free of obscurity, refining, or involution, it seems the native garment of honest passion and clear thought, the natural dialect of men that can work and will. It reminds one of a good highway among English hills: leading straight to its destination, and turning aside for no rare glimpse of landscape, yet bordered by dewy fields, and woods, and crags, with a mountain stream here rolling beneath it, and a thin cascade here whitening the face of the rock by its side: utility embosomed in beauty. Perhaps its tone is somewhat too uniform, its balance and cadence too unvaried. Perhaps, also, there is too much of the abruptness of passion. We should certainly set it far below many styles in richness, delicacy, calmness, and grace. But there is no writer whose style can be pronounced a universal model; and for simple narrative, for the relation of what one would hear with all speed, yet with a spice of accompanying pleasure, this style is a model as nearly perfect as we can conceive. And its beauty is so genuine and honest! You are at first at a loss to account for the charm which breathes around, filling the air as with the fragrance of roses after showers; but the secret cannot long remain hidden from the poor critic, doomed to know how he is pleased. It lies in the perfect honesty, combined with the perfect accuracy, of the sympathy with nature's beauty which dwelt in the breast of the author; in the fact that she ever loved the dew-drop, the daisy, the mountain bird, the vernal branch. Uncalled for and to her unconsciously, at the smile of sympathy, the flowers and the dew-drops come to soften and adorn her page.

Of Currer Bell's love of nature we wish we had space to speak at some length: we can offer merely one or two remarks. There is nothing so commonly mimicked, and there are few things so rarely displayed, as genuine love and accurate knowledge of nature. The truth is, nature is somewhat difficult to know: we think not of noting the tints in a picture which has hung in our eyes since childhood. And whatever may be said of universal beauty, we have become perfectly assured of this, that he who sets himself really to watch nature will find the beauty of her general aspect merely the contrast by which she illustrates her moods and moments — the every day dress by which she sets off her jewelry: and that few indications can be surer of a want of delicate appreciation of the loveliness of sky, and cloud, and mountain, than the commonplace prating about all being beautiful which we behold. Currer Bell, like her sister Ellis, gives us such pictures of nature, so detailed, so definite, so unmistakable, so fresh, that they rise before us like a reminiscence, or give us an assurance as of eyesight. We could quote, in illustration of these remarks, passage after passage of perfect truth, not in any measure the less true that the scenes described have been seen by the eye of an original imagination, or that an exquisite fancy has at times flung a pearl-wreath round the dove's neck, where nature's touches of azure and gold were already gleaming. Among the more ordinary but most easily appreciable of such passages, is that careless passing description in the third volume of *Shirley*, of the general effect of an east wind in a cloudless August sky, and the sudden change to the west: — "It was the close of August: the weather was fine — that is to say, it was very dry and very dusty, for an arid wind had been blowing from the east this month past: very cloudless, too, though a pale haze, stationary in the atmosphere, seemed to rob of all depth of tone the blue of heaven, of all freshness the verdure of earth, and of all glow the light of day. . . . . But there came a day when the wind ceased to sob at the eastern gable of the rectory, and at the oriel window of the church. A little cloud like a man's hand arose in the west; gusts from the same quarter drove it on, and spread it wide; wet and tempest prevailed awhile. When that was over, the sun broke out genially, heaven regained its azure, and earth its green: the livid cholera-tint had vanished from the face of nature; the hills rose clear round the horizon, absolved from that pale malaria-haze." Not more true, but more rare, is the following bit of woodland painting, which, we humbly submit, is worthy of Wordsworth: — "I know all the pleasantest spots: I know where we could get nuts in nutting-time; I know where wild strawberries abound; I know certain lonely, quite untrodden glades, carpeted with strange mosses, some yellow as if gilded, some a sober gray, some gem-green. I know groups of trees, that ravish the eye with their perfect, picture-like effects: rude oak, delicate birch, glossy beech, clustered in contrast; and ash-trees stately as Saul, standing isolated, and superannuated wood-giants clad in bright shrouds of ivy." The reader of these works will know we could quote similar sketches from every chapter.

Allied with this power of original and loving observation of nature, and here naturally claiming our attention, the imaginative faculty of Currer Bell was altogether new and remarkable. It would lead us very far to discuss and determine the relations and distinctions between the powers of perception, of imagination, and of thought. We lean to the belief, that a definite line cannot be drawn between them; that it is not possible in every case to distinguish between the piercing glance which perceives, and the imaginative gaze which bestows; between the strong memory which retains, and the clear conception which recalls. We doubt not that the imagination of Currer Bell was concerned in every embracing look she cast over nature; and we should deem it a vain assay to disentangle the complexity of faculty by which so fair a variety of beauty was lured to her page. But there are effects of imagination which are unmistakably its own, where no scene or form of nature is recalled, but where, from her tints and her lines, a chosen number are selected, and the whole arranged anew by a power which we must name creative. We may falter in defining the precise faculty which enables us to paint perfectly the waving corn or the glowing garden. But we own the magic of imagination at once, when, in the midst of her gardens, or surrounded by swarthy reapers and crowned with the yellow sheaf, the Flora or the Ceres stands before us. It is to efforts of the imaginative faculty thus unmistakable, that we direct attention in the case before us. There are pieces of poetic creation in the prose works of Currer Bell, distinct, not only from the general texture of her composition, but, so far as we know, from anything in the English language. They are not of great number, but so distinct are they and striking, that every one of them could, after a single perusal of her works, be pointed out. The three pictures selected by Rochester from Jane's portfolio, the Mermaid and Nereides in *Shirley*, and a few such, complete the list. We shall select one as an example, perhaps the finest, yet closely resembling in all important particulars the others. It is the personification of nature in the second volume of *Shirley*: —

"The gray church, and grayer tombs, look divine with this crimson gleam on them. Nature is now at her evening prayers; she is kneeling before those red hills. I see her prostrate on the great steps of her altar, praying for a fair night for mariners at sea, for travellers in deserts, for lambs in moors, and unfledged birds in woods. . . . . I saw — I now see — a woman-Titan: her robe of blue air spreads to the outskirts of the heath, where yonder flock is grazing; a veil, white as an avalanche, sweeps from her head to her feet, and arabesques of lightning flame on its borders. Under her breast I see her zone, purple like that horizon; through its blush shines the star of evening. Her steady eyes I cannot picture—they are clear, they are deep as lakes, they are lifted and full of worship, they tremble with the softness of love and the lustre of prayer. Her forehead has the expanse of a cloud, and is paler than the early moon, risen long before dark gathers; she reclines her bosom on the ridge of Stilbro' Moor, her mighty hands are joined beneath it. So kneeling, face to face she speaks with God."

We have nothing in the poetry of Currer Bell to compare with this. There seems to us a grandeur of conception, a strength and sweep of line, a calm and beautiful glow of color, a Grecian harmony and finish, in the whole creation, which would render no epithet of applause extravagant. It has the unity of poetry. Had it been wrapped in a garment of metrical harmony, it would have been recognized as one of the most powerful and beautiful personifications in the range of our poetic literature. We might speak in similar terms of her pictures of the Mermaid and the Nereides. By the wizard and plastic might of her imagination, the sea-woman of the North is once more informed with life, and glares appalling from the ridge of the wave. By the same original energy, the poetic dream of the old Greek mind is rescued from enveloping oblivion, and the daughters of Nereus, filmy as the foam amid which they glide, rise spectral before us, as they might to the eyes of the young bard of Hellas, wandering belated by the moonlit surge of the Ægean. Passages of solitary brilliancy are of frequent occurrence in all our more imaginative prose writers. Apostrophic bursts and long elaborate similes are abundantly to be met with. But the clear and separate creation of poetry, the group or the figure, fairly chiselled from the flawless marble and left forever in the loneliness of their beauty, we know not to have been ever formally introduced into English prose, save by Currer Bell.

The peculiar strength of Currer Bell as a novelist can be pointed out in a single word. It is that to which allusion was made in speaking of *Wuthering Heights;* the delineation of one relentless and tyrannizing passion. In hope, in ardor, in joy, with proud, entrancing emotion, such as might have filled the breast of him who bore away the fire of Jove, love is wooed to the breast. But a storm as of fate awakens: the blue sky is broken into lightnings, and hope smitten dead; and now the love which formerly was a dove of Eden is changed into a vulture, to gnaw the heart, retained in its power by bands of adamant. As the victim lies on his rock, the whole aspect of the world changes to his eye. Ordinary pleasures and ordinary pains are impotent to engage the attention, to assuage the torment. No dance of the nymphs of ocean attracts the wan eye, or for a moment turns the vulture aside. Such a passion is the love of Rochester for Jane, perhaps in a somewhat less degree, that of Jane for Rochester; such, slightly changed in aspect, is the passion beneath which

Caroline pines away, and that which convulses the brave bosom of Shirley. With steady and daring hand, Currer Bell depicts this agony in all its stages; we may weep and tremble, but we feel that her nerves do not quiver, that her eye is unfilmed. So perfect is the verisimilitude, nay the truth, of the delineation, that you cannot for a moment doubt that living hearts have actually throbbed with like passion. It is matter, we believe, of universal assent, that Currer Bell here stands almost alone among the female novelists of Britain, and we doubt whether, however they surpass her in the variety of their delineations, there is any novelist of the other sex who, in this department, has exhibited greater power.

What positive lesson, we ask finally, moral or intellectual, did Currer Bell read to her age? The question can be simply and briefly answered. In her works, there is a universal assertion of rights and emotions stamped by the seal-royal of nature, against the usurpations of avarice and mode. The passion which is kindled really by nature, though the hearts in which it glows may be far asunder, shall burn its way, through station, through prejudice, through all obstacles that can oppose it, until the fires unite, and rise upwards in one white flame. The true love of Rochester for the governess he employs, the true love of the rich and brilliant Shirley for her tutor, must finally triumph: Nature and Custom contend, and the "anarch old" goes down. It is always so; the sympathy with nature's strength and reality is unchanging. Poltroonery, too, of all sorts, baseness, feeble pretension, and falsehood, are crowned with their rightful scorn. Valor, fortitude, strength of will, and all the stalwart virtues that bear the world before them, are honored and illustrated. The great duty of submission, without fainting or murmuring, to the decrees of Providence, is proclaimed with overwhelming power, and indeed with an iteration which makes us at times fain to cry out, that this is Currer Bell's one lecture, which we may expect at any moment to be held by the button-hole to hear. "I disapprove everything utopian. Look life in its iron face, stare reality out of its brassy countenance:" this is the gist of all her moralizing. The lesson, however, belongs to the stern and practical ethics of life, not easily rendered trite, and we deem worthy of special remark a particular instance in which we have it, or one nearly allied to it, is enforced; in all the fiction we ever read, we could point to no case of instruction, at once so practical, so impressive, and so precious. It is a particular touch in the delineation of the triumph of resolution and principle in the breast of Jane Eyre. The conflict is at its height. Reason and conscience falter, and will give no clear decision; they seem inclined rather to regard surrender as a less evil than the possible suicide of Rochester. Then it is that the epic heroism of little Jane, while it reaches the climax of its grandeur, reaches also the height of its practical value. "I had no solace from self-approbation: not even from self-respect. I had injured — wounded — left my master. I was hateful in my own eyes. Still, I could not turn, nor retrace one step. God must have led me on. As to my own will or conscience, impassioned grief had trampled one, and stifled the other." The same phase of her agony had been presented shortly before, and perhaps with still greater force. We believe this no mere imaginary picture. There are situations in life when blackness is overhead and desolation within, and not anything remains but an indestructible, unaccountable, scarce conscious instinct of duty; when the soul may be likened to one who clings to a rope in a swoon, while a great billow goes over him, and his only chance is, that the *senseless* hand still holds spasmodically on. In the hour of sorest need, the figure of that invincible girl may rise, with a look of real and potent encouragement, to steel many a heart to defy the devil to the last.

The assertion of what we may call the sacredness of natural emotion, in its natural modes of action, made by Currer Bell, merits an attention altogether peculiar. There are few subjects on which we would speak with greater emphasis. It relates to a part of the system of natural ethics which Christians are most apt to neglect, but of which the neglect is as pernicious as it is indefensible. Has it not a somewhat singular sound, to talk of the Christian duty of permitting in the formation of the nuptial tie (nay, of enjoining and insisting on) the free play of the natural affections? Is it not widely customary, for men and women, ready to die in defence of Christian principle, anxiously and prayerfully shaping their lives by the teaching of the New Testament, either themselves to marry, or to lend their sanction to marriages, in which it is well known and deliberately contemplated, that no feeling of intense attachment, no love, exists in the breast of either party? Men whom it would be hard not to call excellent, clergymen especially, regard entrance upon the married state as a part of the formal and mechanical business of life. At a certain age, the duties of the parish are entered upon, the manse is furnished, and then, for various reasons, of comfort, of economy, of respectability, a wife is "taken." Young persons of the other sex are, so far as we can judge, equally apt to look upon marriage with no sense of the fact that affection is here one with duty, and its absence a sin. Parents, again, as will occur to every one, though of sincere and habitual piety, though desirous of promoting the best interests of their children, and while deeply concerned that their daughters are wedded to men of position and means, of integrity and ability, nay, of religion, will pass over, or lightly shuffle by, all questions touching capacity of affection or sympathy of nature. Yet one would think a single look beneath the outermost vail of appearance might convince all that, with the answers practically rendered to such questions as these, is vitally and indissolubly connected the real happiness, or the bitter misery, of after life. One would imagine, too, that it required no very penetrating inquisition into the laws of things, to discover that, on the original settlement of such questions, depend unnumbered influences, of the most intimate and inevitable kind, affecting the moral and religious condition of the community. One would think, last of all, that it required a studious and habitual opposition to the plainest teaching of the gospel, or a blindness wholly marvellous to the nature of that teaching, to persist in meeting with a direct negative the Christian view of marriage. The teachings of nature and of Christianity are here in the strictest and most beautiful accordance. Nature and experience testify, for their part, that a lifetime of cohabitation, where there is no natural, mutual, overpowering attraction, no love, is not only a lifetime of chronic suffering, an imprisonment in "polar ice," but a condition in which each noble and genial emotion is met by a subtle poison, pervading the moral atmosphere, by a biting frost-wind, where it ought to have found the balmiest sunshine, by chilling and withering sleet, where nature would have prepared for it gentle, fostering rain. Looking beyond the individual victims of such a rebellion against nature, to those to whom they are related as parents, the aspects of the case, holding still by the light of mere experience and common sense, are, if possible, still more obvious and impressive. The education of the family circle, no one will dispute, is the most important of all. It may not be a matter of so common reflection, that the part of this education, which consists in express precepts and oral instruction, is of trivial importance compared with the silent, practical education of parental life, from the responsibility of which the parent never escapes for a moment, and of which the influence, searching and perpetual, can be counteracted by no set words, however earnest and well studied! If the parents are not united by a love which, in its fervid intensity, sets them apart from the rest of the world, and causes every other earthly feeling to revolve in an orbit comparatively remote, the unity of the family circle is broken. A fatal element insinuates itself into the affection with which the children are regarded. They are taught by the presence of no mighty and beautiful emotion in those to whom they look up, to know the happiness of pure affection, to admire it, to aspire after it. For the first few years of life, the parent is to the child, with hardly any qualification, in the place of God. The home is the first temple in which man worships. The parent is the impersonation of perfection. And if, in striving after that perfection, as the child will do almost before he can speak, he is guided by no melodious harmony of parental love, embracing his parents and uniting in himself, his whole nature, intellectual as well as moral, may from the first be stunted. The influences of which we speak are not such as can be minutely defined: could they be so, they would be slight. But it is impossible, on fair consideration, to deny their supreme power. It is the enactment of nature, visible in every department of the physical universe, that the life of the parent, in its substance and its form, be, so to speak, stamped upon the offspring. No discordance can enter into parental existence, without marking itself in the character and life of the child. The assumptions of mode and affectation may fall away, but the deepest nature will be transmitted. The face may be unmoved before the world, the breast may lie, sternly placid, over the beating, burning heart, but a drop of the internal agony, with all its power to paralyze emotion and embitter life, will find its way into the bosom of the offspring. And if all this belongs to the most practical and homely truth of nature, Christianity is not less but more explicit. It is strange and anomalous that ideas, so poor and dishonoring, of the formation of the nuptial relationship should prevail, considering the august and peculiar place accorded to that relationship by Scripture. The family relations are those habitually chosen to illustrate the most sublime conceptions which are brought by Scripture before the mind of man, — the relations between the Persons of the Trinity and the Saviour and his church. St. Paul does not scruple to make the love entertained by Christ for his redeemed the model and measure of connubial affection. The Creator in Paradise gave this feeling the express pre-eminence over all others: the Saviour affirmed his words. It is impossible to reflect earnestly on the deep-lying and wonderful threads of connection, which run through Scripture and human history, through Christianity and nature, without perceiving that the emotion, crowned by the Creator in Paradise, signally honored by the Saviour, and measured by Paul by an infinite standard, is that which plays, in the natural world, so strange and prominent a part; grouping around itself all comedy and tragedy, the life of literature and art, the source of half the nobleness and half the crime of human history, unique in its nature and irresistible in its influence, undefinable by any but in some way conceived of by all, and known distinctively by the name of love. It admits of no doubt that the existence of this emotion is the sign appointed by God in nature for the formation of the nuptial tie, that this is one of the great correspondences which pervade the system of things, as that of reason to truth, that of conscience to rectitude, that of vision to the objects of perception, that of climate to natural productions. Without this affection the nuptial unity is impossible; marriage, in the sense of nature and Scripture, cannot be. And yet the Christian world very generally, if not very explicitly, coincides with the idea of Johnson that marriages might be well enough arranged by the chancellor! That the rest of the world is, in all practical points, as much to blame here as that calling itself distinctively Christian, is probably the fact. But it is to books not belonging to strictly Christian literature, that one would point, for the most emphatic assertion of theoretic truth in the matter. In the conclusion of his essay on Mirabeau, Mr. Carlyle takes occasion, from certain circumstances in the history of his hero, to set his fiery finger on this great social commandment. And we concentrate in brief compass a critique on the writings of Currer Bell, when we say that their central doctrine for the reconstitution of social ethics, their one remedy for the cure of social ills, is the permission of free play to the passion of love, and the abolition of its counterfeits.

There being, therefore, much of what is stirring and healthful in the works of Currer Bell, can we close with a declaration that the region in which her characters move is the highest and purest, and that she has solved, or hinted how we may solve, the social problems which at present confront the earnest and practical mind? We cannot. We must record our distinct and unalterable negative in either case. The truth she proclaims is one sided. Her scheme of life is too narrow. The pleasures and sufferings of existence do not all depend on one emotion though it be that of love, on one passion though itself be right. Her works are the ovation of passion. It may be true, it may be noble, it may be allied with principle, but Passion is ever the conqueror and king. The joys of existence which have any real point, the sorrows which have any real bitterness, are alike in the dispensation of Passion. Is more than a word necessary to make this assertion good? Who sees not more to be desired in the very anguish of the love of Caroline or Shirley, than in the blanched existence of Miss Ainley? Do we not mark St. John Rivers go away, joyless and marble-cold, on his high mission, while Passion welcomes back Jane to his burning, bliss-giving arms? Where Passion appears, all becomes real and alive: where Passion is not, the widest philanthropy, the holiest devotion, are powerless to confer happiness. And shall we thus crown Passion, and bend the knee before him? By no means. Passion, when alone, is essentially and ignobly selfish. Despite a barren kindness of heart, the existence of Rochester is utterly selfish. *His* luckless marriage, *his* impure loves, *his* interesting sorrows, have eaten up the substance of his life. One would say, were he a sound example, that a man was linked by no duties to his fellows, that, in a world like this, a man, without being coward or caitiff, could be occupied solely by self. "Love thy neighbor as thyself:" know thyself a unit among millions: perform the duties God has assigned thee towards thyself, but value not that self beyond any other of a million units. How thorough the reversal of the whole manner of Mr. Rochester's existence, which would have been wrought by the simple adoption, as its leading principle, of this divine motto of Christian philanthropy, in which is bound up the regeneration of the world! There *must* be a love higher than that of mere passion. There must be joys, moral, intellectual, spiritual, whose pure oil can make the lamp of life burn as clearly and cheerfully as the flame of passion, and far more beautifully. To say otherwise, were to utter a libel upon nature, to impugn the justice and love of God. Of a love, pure and lofty, allying us to God and man, illumining the universe around us with the mingled lights of heaven and home, Currer Bell gives no representation, nay, she gives a caricature, which, while wondrous in execution, is utterly false. St. John had no affection for Jane which could be named love. It is to be regretted that she did not think of cutting short all his fine speeches, by simply pointing him to the measure allotted to connubial affection by Paul, and telling him that, unless he felt within him the power to love her as his own soul, nay, with an unutterable force of affection to be compared with the infinite love of Christ for his own body, his own church, he committed a *sin* in asking her to become his wife. There is an altar on which terrestrial and celestial love can blend their fires. If passion is the whole of love, it must debase and not ennoble.

When we speak of those practical problems, on which Currer Bell has touched, but which she has not solved, we refer specially to the dreary pictures she draws in *Shirley* of the social standing of woman. Marriage, we are told, is the one hope of the great majority of England's daughters, a hope destined in countless cases to be never realized. A youth of scheming inanity, deriving a faint animation from this hope, must fade into a blighted and solitary age. The authority of a lady may be taken as conclusive of the state of the case here; but when we assent to her allegations, and paragraph after paragraph has impressed them on our minds, we have no more, by way of remedy, than a sentence of general and valueless exhortation to fathers to cultivate the minds of their daughters. There is nothing in the works of Currer Bell to assure us that any amount of cultivation will produce fresh and satisfying happiness, unless that one wish which she points to is gratified. She indicates no fields of pleasure accessible to all. She exhibits not the means of the cultivation she commends, and leaves us to guess the connection between culture and enjoyment. The hand of this gifted woman had power, we think, to paint a daughter of England gladdening and beautifying her existence, though the light of passion never rose upon her path. But this she has not done.

The publication of Mrs. Gaskell's most interesting and valuable biography of Currer Bell might seem to require the addition of certain qualifying remarks to the preceding. Not the slightest modification, however, has been felt to be necessary in the view given of the genius and aims of the authoress. But there are two circumstances brought to light in this biography, which have, in themselves, an interest and importance justifying particular observation. The first is, that the artistic instinct of Currer Bell was, in one chief instance, more piercing and accurate, more strictly in accordance with the verities of life and nature, than that general mode of thought which ruled her habitual and practised opinions. The central doctrine of her works was found to be the sacredness of the natural affections in the formation of the marriage relationship — the necessity of the existence of a distinctive feeling, called love, in every such case. It is impossible to imagine that, in those works, this necessity is asserted in reference to the man, but not in reference to the woman. All the power of the authoress is exerted to set in strong colors the sense which Shirley has of the dishonor done to her and to himself by Robert Moore, when he proposes to marry her without loving her: and all that is claimed for woman in what Currer Bell wrote would be at once given up, by the concession, that it would have been right and natural in Shirley to marry Moore, while feeling towards him as he felt towards her. But when Currer Bell became Charlotte Bronte, when she ceased to be the artist and became the woman, she made this concession. In so many words, she declared that "respect," entertained by a woman for a man, was a feeling which could justify her in marrying him. Moore respected Shirley very deeply; and Currer Bell pours out on him in full measure the burning fountains of her scorn, for having, in that state of feeling, proposed marriage; but the heart of Shirley was not so sacred or precious a gift, but that it might have been given with a cold hand; not love but respect would have justified *her* in blending her being with another. But Charlotte Bronte shall not prevail against Currer Bell: this commonplace surrender to the dreariest working of social mechanism shall not invalidate the magnificent protests of genius. The second circumstance revealed by the biography of Currer Bell which demands a word of notice, is antithetically contrasted with the first. In the one, the woman was less true than the authoress: in the other, the authoress is less true than the woman. In words clear and forcible as those which it was her habit to use, Charlotte Bronte expressed her conviction, that a noble and every way admirable life could be led by a woman, with no aid from passion, with no thought of marriage. And with this opinion for every day practice, the portrait given in her works of one leading such a life is Miss Ainlie, and the place accorded to passion in the dispensation of happiness such as was seen.

END OF FIRST SERIES.

VALUABLE

LITERARY AND SCIENTIFIC WORKS,

PUBLISHED BY

GOULD AND LINCOLN,

59 WASHINGTON STREET, BOSTON.

ANNUAL OF SCIENTIFIC DISCOVERY FOR 1859; or, Year-Book of Facts in Science and Art, exhibiting the most important Discoveries and Improvements in Mechanics, Useful Arts, Natural Philosophy, Chemistry, Astronomy, Meteorology, Zoology, Botany, Mineralogy, Geology, Geography, Antiquities, &c., together with a list of recent Scientific Publications; a classified list of Patents; Obituaries of eminent Scientific Men; an Index of Important Papers in Scientific Journals, Reports, &c. Edited by DAVID A. WELLS, A. M. With a Portrait of Prof. O. M. Mitchell. 12mo, cloth, $1.25.

VOLUMES OF THE SAME WORK for years 1850 to 1858 inclusive. With Portraits of Professors Agassiz, Silliman, Henry, Bache, Maury, Hitchcock, Richard M. Hoe, Profs. Jeffries Wyman, and H. D. Rogers. Nine volumes, 12mo, cloth, $1.25 per vol.

This work, issued annually, contains all important facts discovered or announced during the year.

☞ Each volume is distinct in itself, and contains *entirely new matter.*

INFLUENCE OF THE HISTORY OF SCIENCE UPON INTELLECTUAL EDUCATION. By WILLIAM WHEWELL, D. D., of Trinity College, Eng., and the alleged author of "Plurality of Worlds." 12mo, cloth, 25 cts.

THE NATURAL HISTORY OF THE HUMAN SPECIES; Its Typical Forms and Primeval Distribution. By CHARLES HAMILTON SMITH. With an Introduction containing an Abstract of the views of Blumenbach, Prichard, Bachman, Agassiz, and other writers of repute. By SAMUEL KNEELAND, Jr., M. D. With elegant Illustrations. 12mo, cloth, $1.25.

"The marks of practical good sense, careful observation, and deep research, are displayed in every page. The introductory essay of some seventy or eighty pages forms a valuable addition to the work. It comprises an abstract of the opinions advocated by the most eminent writers on this subject. The statements are made with strict impartiality, and, without a comment, left to the judgment of the reader." — *Sartain's Magazine.*

KNOWLEDGE IS POWER. A View of the Productive Forces of Modern Society, and the Results of Labor, Capital, and Skill. By CHARLES KNIGHT. With numerous Illustrations. American Edition. Revised, with Additions, by DAVID A. WELLS, Editor of the "Annual of Scientific Discovery." 12mo, cloth, $1.25.

☞ This is emphatically *a book for the people.* It contains an immense amount of important information, which everybody ought to be in possession of; and the volume should be placed in every family, and in every School and Public Library in the land. The facts and illustrations are drawn from almost every branch of skilful industry, and it is a work which the mechanic and artisan of every description will be sure to read with a RELISH.

WORKS OF HUGH MILLER.

THE OLD RED SANDSTONE; or, New Walks in an Old Field. Illustrated with Plates and Geological Sections. New Edition, Revised and much Enlarged, by the addition of new matter and new Illustrations, etc. 12mo, cloth, $1.25.

This edition contains over *one hundred pages of entirely new matter*, from the pen of Hugh Miller. It contains, also, several additional new plates and cuts, the old plates re-engraved and improved, and an Appendix of new Notes.

"It is withal one of the most beautiful specimens of English composition to be found, conveying information on a most difficult and profound science, in a style at once novel, pleasing, and elegant." — Dr. Sprague — *Albany Spectator.*

THE FOOT-PRINTS OF THE CREATOR; or, the Asterolepis of Stromness, with numerous Illustrations. With a Memoir of the Author, by Louis Agassiz. 12mo, cloth, $1.00.

Dr. Buckland *said he would give his left hand to possess such power of description as this man.*

TESTIMONY OF THE ROCKS; or, Geology in its Bearings on the two Theologies, Natural and Revealed. "Thou shalt be in league with the stones of the field." — *Job.* With numerous elegant Illustrations. One volume, royal 12mo, cloth, $1.25.

This is the largest and most comprehensive Geological Work that the distinguished author has yet published. It exhibits the profound learning, the felicitous style, and the scientific perception, which characterize his former works, while it embraces the latest results of geological discovery. But the great charm of the book lies in those passages of glowing eloquence, in which, having spread out his facts, the author proceeds to make deductions from them of the most striking and exciting character. The work is profusely illustrated by engravings executed at Paris, in the highest style of French art.

THE CRUISE OF THE BETSEY; or, a Summer Ramble among the Fossiliferous Deposits of the Hebrides. With Rambles of a Geologist; or, Ten Thousand Miles over the Fossiliferous Deposits of Scotland. 12mo, cloth, $1.25.

Nothing need be said of it save that it possesses the same fascination for the reader that characterizes the author's other works.

MY SCHOOLS AND SCHOOLMASTERS; or, the Story of my Education. An Autobiography. With a full-length Portrait of the Author. 12mo, cloth, $1.25.

This is a personal narrative, of a deeply interesting and instructive character, concerning one of the most remarkable men of the age.

MY FIRST IMPRESSIONS OF ENGLAND AND ITS PEOPLE. With a fine Engraving of the author. 12mo, cloth, $1.00.

☞ A very instructive book of travels, presenting the most perfectly life-like views of England and its people to be found in any language.

☞ *The above six volumes are furnished in sets, printed and bound in uniform style:* viz.,

HUGH MILLER'S WORKS, Six Volumes. Elegant embossed cloth, $7.00; library sheep, $8.00; half calf, $12.00; antique, $12.00.

MACAULAY ON SCOTLAND. A Critique, from the "Witness." 16mo, flexible cloth, 25 cts.

IMPORTANT NEW WORKS.

CYCLOPÆDIA OF ANECDOTES OF LITERATURE AND THE FINE ARTS. Containing a copious and choice Selection of Anecdotes of the various forms of Literature, of the Arts, of Architecture, Engravings, Music, Poetry, Painting, and Sculpture, and of the most celebrated Literary Characters and Artists of different Countries and Ages, &c. By KAZLITT ARVINE, A. M., author of "Cyclopædia of Moral and Religious Anecdotes." With numerous Illustrations. 725 pp. octavo. Cloth, $3.00 ; sheep, $3.50 ; cloth, gilt, $4.00 ; half calf, $4.00.

This is unquestionably the choicest collection of *Anecdotes* ever published. It contains *three thousand and forty Anecdotes*, and such is the wonderful variety, that it will be found an almost inexhaustible fund of interest for every class of readers. The elaborate classification and Indexes must commend it especially to public speakers, to the various classes of *literary and scientific men*, to *artists*, *mechanics*, and *others*, as a DICTIONARY *for reference*, in relation to facts on the numberless subjects and characters introduced. There are also more than *one hundred and fifty fine Illustrations.*

THE LIFE OF JOHN MILTON, Narrated in Connection with the POLITICAL, ECCLESIASTICAL, and LITERARY HISTORY OF HIS TIME. By DAVID MASSON, M.A., Professor of English Literature, University College, London. Vol. I., embracing the period from 1608 to 1639. With Portraits, and specimens of his handwriting at different periods. Royal octavo, cloth, $0.00.

This important work will embrace three royal octavo volumes. By special arrangement with Prof. Masson, the author, G. & L. are permitted to print from advance sheets furnished them, as the authorized American publishers of this magnificent and eagerly looked for work. Volumes *two* and *three* will follow in due time ; but, as each volume covers a definite period of time, and also embraces distinct topics of discussion or history, they will be published and sold independent of each other, or furnished in sets when the three volumes are completed.

THE GREYSON LETTERS. Selections from the Correspondence of R. E. H. GREYSON, Esq. Edited by HENRY ROGERS, author of "Eclipse of Faith." 12mo, cloth, $1.25.

"Mr. Greyson and Mr. Rogers are one and the same person. The whole work is from his pen, and every letter is radiant with the genius of the author. It discusses a wide range of subjects, in the most attractive manner. It abounds in the keenest wit and humor, satire and logic. It fairly entitles Mr. Rogers to rank with Sydney Smith and Charles Lamb as a wit and humorist, and with Bishop Butler as a reasoner. Mr. Rogers' name will share with those of Butler and Pascal, in the gratitude and veneration of posterity." — *London Quarterly.*

"A book not for one hour, but for all hours ; not for one mood, but for every mood ; to think over, to dream over, to laugh over." — *Boston Journal.*

"The Letters are intellectual gems, radiant with beauty, happily intermingling the grave and the gay. — *Christian Observer.*

ESSAYS IN BIOGRAPHY AND CRITICISM. By PETER BAYNE, M. A., author of "The Christian Life, Social and Individual." Arranged in two Series, or Parts. 12mo, cloth, each, $1.25.

These volumes have been prepared by the author exclusively for his American publishers, and are now published in uniform style. They include nineteen articles, viz. :

FIRST SERIES : — Thomas De Quincy. — Tennyson and his Teachers. — Mrs. Barrett Browning. — Recent Aspects of British Art. — John Ruskin. — Hugh Miller. — The Modern Novel ; Dickens, &c. — Ellis, Acton, and Currer Bell.

SECOND SERIES : — Charles Kingsley. — S. T. Coleridge. — T. B. Macaulay. — Alison. — Wellington. — Napoleon. — Plato. — Characteristics of Christian Civilization. — The Modern University. — The Pulpit and the Press. — Testimony of the Rocks : a Defence.

VISITS TO EUROPEAN CELEBRITIES. By the Rev. WILLIAM B. SPRAGUE, D. D. 12mo, cloth, $1.00 ; cloth, gilt, $1.50.

A series of graphic and life-like Personal Sketches of many of the most distinguished men and women of Europe, portrayed as the Author saw them in their own homes, and under the most advantageous circumstances. Besides these "pen and ink" sketches, the work contains the novel attraction of a *fac-simile of the signature* of each of the persons introduced.

VALUABLE TEXT-BOOKS.

THE LECTURES OF SIR WILLIAM HAMILTON, BART., late Professor of Logic and Metaphysics, University of Edinburgh; embracing the METAPHYSICAL and LOGICAL COURSES; with Notes, from Original Materials, and an Appendix, containing the Author's Latest Development of his New Logical Theory. Edited by Rev. HENRY LONGUEVILLE MANSEL, B. D., Prof. of Moral and Metaphysical Philosophy in Magdalen College, Oxford, and JOHN VEITCH, M. A., of Edinburgh. In two royal octavo volumes, viz.,

I. METAPHYSICAL LECTURES (*now ready*). Royal octavo, cloth.

II. LOGICAL LECTURES (*in preparation*).

☞ G. & L., by a special arrangement with the family of the late Sir William Hamilton, are the Authorized American Publishers of this distinguished author's *matchless* LECTURES ON METAPHYSICS AND LOGIC, and they are permitted to print the same from advance sheets furnished them by the English publishers.

MENTAL PHILOSOPHY; Including the Intellect, the Sensibilities, and the Will. By JOSEPH HAVEN, Prof. of Intellectual and Moral Philosophy, Amherst College. Royal 12mo, cloth, embossed, $1.50.

It is believed this work will be found pre-eminently distinguished.

1. The COMPLETENESS with which it presents the whole subject. Text-books generally treat of only *one class* of faculties; this work includes the *whole*. 2. It is strictly and thoroughly SCIENTIFIC. 3. It presents a careful analysis of the mind, as a whole. 4. The history and literature of each topic. 5. The latest results of the science. 6. The chaste, yet attractive style. 7. The remarkable condensation of thought.

Prof. PARK, of Andover, says: "It is DISTINGUISHED for its clearness of style, perspicuity of method, candor of spirit, acumen and comprehensiveness of thought."

The work, though so recently published, has met with most remarkable success; having been already introduced into a large number of the leading colleges and schools in various parts of the country, and bids fair to take the place of every other work on the subject now before the public.

THESAURUS OF ENGLISH WORDS AND PHRASES, so classified and arranged as to facilitate the expression of ideas, and assist in literary composition. New and Improved Edition. By PETER MARK ROGET, late Secretary of the Royal Society, London, &c. Revised and edited, with a List of Foreign Words defined in English, and other additions, by BARNAS SEARS, D. D., President of Brown University. A NEW AMERICAN Edition, with ADDITIONS AND IMPROVEMENTS. 12mo, cloth, $1.50.

This edition is based on the London edition, recently issued. The first American Edition having been prepared by Dr. Sears for *strictly educational purposes*, those words and phrases properly termed "vulgar," incorporated in the original work, were omitted. These expurgated portions have, in the present edition, been *restored*, but by such an arrangement of the matter as not to interfere with the educational purposes of the American editor. Besides this, it contains important additions of words and phrases not in the English edition, making it in *all respects more full and perfect than the author's edition*. The work has already become one of standard authority, both in this country and in Great Britain.

PALEY'S NATURAL THEOLOGY. Illustrated by forty Plates, with Selections from the Notes of Dr. Paxton, and Additional Notes, Original and Selected, with a Vocabulary of Scientific Terms. Edited by JOHN WARE, M. D. Improved edition, with elegant newly engraved plates. 12mo, cloth, embossed, $1.25.

This work is very generally introduced into our best Schools and Colleges throughout the country. An entirely new and beautiful set of Illustrations has recently been procured, which, with other improvements, render it the best and most complete work of the kind extant.

VALUABLE WORKS.

THE PURITANS; or the Court, Church, and Parliament of England, during the reigns of Edward VI. and Elizabeth. By SAMUEL HOPKINS, author of "Lessons at the Cross," etc. In 3 vols. Vol. I. *now ready*. Octavo, cloth, per vol., $2.50.
VOL. II. READY IN FEBRUARY, " " " " $2.50.

It will be found the most interesting and reliable History of the Puritans yet published, narrating in a dramatic style many facts hitherto unknown.

LIMITS OF RELIGIOUS THOUGHT EXAMINED, in Eight Lectures delivered in the Oxford University Pulpit, in the year 1858, on the "Bampton Foundation." By Rev. H. LONGUEVILLE MANSEL, B. D., Reader in Moral and Metaphysical Philosophy at Magdalen College, Oxford, and Editor of Sir William Hamilton's Lectures. With the Copious NOTES TRANSLATED for the American Ed. 12mo, cloth, $1.00.

This volume is destined to create a profounder sensation in this country than any philosophical or religious work of this century. It is a defence of revealed religion, equal in ability to the "Analogy" of Bishop Butler, and meets the scepticism of our age as effectually as that great work in an earlier day. The Pantheism and Parkerism infused into our popular literature will here find an antidote. The Lectures excited the highest enthusiasm at Oxford, and the Volume has already reached a *third* edition in England. The copious "Notes" of the author having been translated for the American edition by an accomplished scholar, adds greatly to its value.

THE HISTORICAL EVIDENCES OF THE TRUTH OF THE SCRIPTURE RECORDS, STATED ANEW, with Special Reference to the Doubts and Discoveries of Modern Times. In Eight Lectures, delivered in the Oxford University pulpit, at the Bampton Lecture for 1859. By GEO. RAWLINSON, M.A., Editor of the Histories of Herodotus. With the Copious NOTES TRANSLATED for the *American Edition* by an accomplished scholar. 12mo, cloth, $1.00.

SIR WILLIAM HAMILTON'S LECTURES ON LOGIC. With Notes from Original Materials, and an Appendix containing the Latest Development of his New Logical Theory. Edited by Prof. H. LONGUEVILLE MANSEL, Oxford, and JOHN VEITCH, M. A., Edinburgh. Royal octavo, cloth, $3.00. *(In press.)*

MORAL PHILOSOPHY, including Theoretical and Practical Ethics. By JOSEPH HAVEN, D. D., late Professor of Moral and Intellectual Philosophy in Amherst College; author of "Mental Philosophy." Royal 12mo, cloth, embossed, $1.25.

It is eminently scientific in method, and thorough in discussion, and its views on unsettled questions in morals are discriminating and sound. It treats largely of Political Ethics — a department of morals of great importance to American youth, but generally overlooked in text-books. In the history of ethical opinions it is unusually rich and elaborate.

POPULAR GEOLOGY; With Descriptive Sketches from a Geologist's Portfolio. By HUGH MILLER. With a Resume of the Progress of Geological Science during the last two years. By MRS. MILLER. 12mo, cloth, $1.25.

This work is likely to prove the most popular of Hugh Miller's writings, and to attain the widest circulation. It is written in his best style, and makes the mysteries of Geology intelligible to the common mind. As an architect explains the structure of a house from cellar to attic, so this accomplished geologist takes the globe to pieces, and explains the manner in which all its strata have been formed, from the granite foundation to the alluvial surface. It supplies just the information which many readers have been longing for, but unable to find. Also,

HUGH MILLER'S WORKS. Seven volumes, uniform style, in an elegant box, embossed cloth, $8.25; library sheep, $10.00; half calf, $14.00; antique, $14.00.

MANSEL'S MISCELLANIES; including "Prolegomina Logica," "Metaphysics," "Limits of Demonstrative Evidence," "Philosophy of Kant," etc. 12mo, cloth, *(In press.)*

IMPORTANT WORKS.

LIFE AND CORRESPONDENCE OF REV. DANIEL WILSON, D. D., late Bishop of Calcutta. By Rev. JOSIAH BATEMAN, M. A., Rector of North Cray, Kent. With Portraits, Map, and numerous Illustrations. One Volume, Royal octavo, cloth, $3.00.

BRITISH NOVELISTS AND THEIR STYLES. Being a Critical Sketch of the History of British Prose Fiction. By DAVID MASSON, M. A., Author of "The Life and Times of John Milton," etc. etc. 16mo, cloth, 75 cts.

This charming volume will find its way to many American homes, and win for its author a place by the side of the masters of English Fiction, of whom he discourses so pleasantly.

THE LEADERS OF THE REFORMATION. LUTHER, CALVIN, LATIMER and KNOX, the Representative Men of Germany, France, England, and Scotland. By J. TULLOCH, D. D., Author of "Theism," etc. 12mo, cloth, $1.00.

A portrait gallery of sturdy reformers, drawn by a keen eye and a strong hand. Dr. Tulloch discriminates clearly the personal qualities of each Reformer, and commends and criticises with equal frankness.

LESSONS AT THE CROSS; or, Spiritual Truths Familiarly Exhibited in their Relations to Christ. By SAMUEL HOPKINS, author of "The Puritans." With an Introduction by Rev. GEORGE W. BLAGDEN, D. D. New Edition. 16mo, cloth, 75 cts.

THE CRUCIBLE; or Tests of a Regenerate State; designed to bring to light suppressed hopes, expose false ones, and confirm the true. By Rev. J. A. GOODHUE, A. M. With an Introduction by Rev. E. N. KIRK, D. D. 12mo, cloth, $1.00.

A volume of peculiar originality and power. It presents novel, original and startling views. It places within the Christian fold many who claim no place there; cuts off from it many who consider themselves entitled to all its privileges, and applies tests of spiritual character, which are vitally distinct from those which are current in the popular religion of the day. It is one of the books to be read, marked and inwardly digested.

GOTTHOLD'S EMBLEMS; or, Invisible Things Understood by Things that are Made. By CHRISTIAN SCRIVER, Minister of Magdeburg in 1671. Translated from the Twenty-eighth German Edition by the Rev. ROBERT MENZIES. 8vo, cloth, $1.00; cloth, bevelled boards, $1.25; cloth, bevelled boards, red edges, $1.25. FINE EDITION, TINTED PAPER, royal 8vo, cloth, $1.50; cloth gilt, $2.00; half Turkey morocco, $4.00; Turkey morocco, $5.00.

Its singular merits will soon make it a favorite in American households; for all readers will pronounce it the most fascinating of devotional books. It teaches how to find God *everywhere*, and to carry devotion into the humblest duties of daily life. Its juicy thoughts and rich suggestions have an equal charm for the scholar and the unlearned.

THE GREAT CONCERN; or, Man's Relation to God and a Future State. By NEHEMIAH ADAMS, D. D. 12mo, cloth, 85 cts.

Pungent and affectionate, reaching the intellect, conscience, and feelings; admirably fitted to awaken, guide, and instruct. The book is just the thing for wide distribution in our congregations. — *N. Y. Observer*.

EVENINGS WITH THE DOCTRINES. By Rev. NEHEMIAH ADAMS, D.D. 12mo, cloth. (*In preparation.*)

THE STILL HOUR; or, Communion with God. By Prof. AUSTIN PHELPS, D.D., of Andover Theological Seminary. 16mo, cloth, 50 cts.

CHRIST IN HISTORY. By ROBERT TURNBULL, D. D. A New and Enlarged Edition. 12mo, cloth, $1.25.

THESAURUS OF ENGLISH WORDS AND PHRASES.

So Classified and Arranged as to Facilitate the Expression of Ideas, and Assist in Literary Composition. By PETER MARK ROGET, late Secretary of the Royal Society, and author of the "Bridgewater Treatise," etc. Revised and Enlarged; with a LIST OF FOREIGN WORDS AND EXPRESSIONS most frequently occurring in works of general Literature, Defined in English, by BARNAS SEARS, D. D., Secretary of the Massachusetts Board of Education, assisted by several Literary Gentlemen. 12mo., cloth. $1.50.

☞ A work of great merit, admirably adapted as a text-book for schools and colleges, and of high importance to every American scholar. Among the numerous commendations received from the press, in all directions, the publishers would call attention to the following:

We are glad to see the Thesaurus of English Words republished in this country. It is a most valuable work, giving the results of many years' labor, in an attempt to classify and arrange the words of the English tongue, so as to facilitate the practice of composition. The purpose of an ordinary dictionary is to explain the meaning of words, while the object of this Thesaurus is to collate all the words by which any given idea may be expressed. — *Putnam's Monthly.*

This volume offers the student of English composition the results of great labor in the form of a rich and copious vocabulary. We would commend the work to those who have charge of academies and high schools, and to all students. — *Christian Observer.*

This is a novel publication, and is the first and only one of the kind ever issued in which words and phrases of our language are classified, not according to the sound of their orthography, but strictly according to their signification. It will become an invaluable aid in the communication of our thoughts, whether spoken or written, and hence, as a means of improvement, we can recommend it as a work of rare and excellent qualities. — *Scientific American.*

A work of great utility. It will give a writer the word he wants, when that word is on the tip of his tongue, but altogether beyond his reach. — *N. Y. Times.*

It is more complete than the English work, which has attained a just celebrity. It is intended to supply, with respect to the English language, a desideratum hitherto unsupplied in any language, namely, a collection of the words it contains, and of the idiomatic combinations peculiar to it, arranged, not in *alphabetical* order, as they are in a dictionary, but according to the *ideas* which they express. The purpose of a dictionary is simply to explain the meaning of words — the word being given, to find its signification, or the idea it is intended to convey. The object aimed at *here* is exactly the converse of this: the idea being given, to find the word or words by which that idea may be mostly fitly and aptly expressed. For this purpose, the words and phrases of the language are here classed, not according to their sound or their orthography, but strictly according to their signification. — *New York Evening Mirror.*

An invaluable companion to persons engaged in literary labors. To persons who are not familiar with foreign tongues, the catalogue of foreign words and phrases most current in modern literature, which the American editor has appended, will be very useful. —*Presbyterian.*

It casts the whole English language into groups of words and terms, arranged in such a manner that the student of English composition, when embarrassed by the poverty of his vocabulary, may supply himself immediately, on consulting it, with the precise term for which he has occasion. — *New York Evening Post.*

This is a work not merely of extraordinary, but of peculiar value. We would gladly praise it, if any thing could add to the consideration held out by the title page. No one who speaks or writes for the public need be urged to study Roget's Thesaurus. — *Star of the West.*

Every writer and speaker ought to possess himself at once of this manual. It is far from being a mere dull, dead string of synonymes, but it is enlivened and vivified by the classifying and crystallizing power of genuine philosophy. We have put it on our table as a permanent fixture, as near our left hand as the Bible is to our right. — *Congregationalist.*

This book is one of the most valuable we ever examined. It supplies a want long acknowledged by the best writers, and supplies it completely. — *Portland Advertiser.*

One of the most efficient aids to composition that research, industry, and scholarship have ever produced. Its object is to supply the writer or speaker with the most felicitous terms for expressing an idea that may be vaguely floating on his mind; and, indeed, through the peculiar manner of arrangement, ideas themselves may be expanded or modified by reference to Mr. Roget's elucidations. — *Albion, N. Y.*

IMPORTANT NEW WORKS.

THE CHRISTIAN LIFE: Social and Individual. By PETER BAYNE, A. M. 12mo. Cloth. $1.25.

Contents. — PART I. STATEMENT. I. The Individual Life. II. The Social Life. PART II. EXPOSITION AND ILLUSTRATION. *Book I. Christianity the Basis of Social Life.* I. First Principles. II. Howard; and the rise of Philanthropy. III. Wilberforce; and the development of Philanthropy. IV. Budgett; the Christian Freeman. V. The social problem of the age, and one or two hints towards its solution. *Book II. Christianity the Basis of Individual Character.* I. Introductory: a few Words on Modern Doubt. II. John Foster. III. Thomas Arnold. IV. Thomas Chalmers. PART III. OUTLOOK. I. The Positive Philosophy. II. Pantheistic Spiritualism. III. General Conclusion.

PARTICULAR attention is invited to this work. In Scotland, its publication, during the last winter, produced a great sensation. Hugh Miller made it the subject of an elaborate review in his paper, the Edinburgh *Witness*, and gave his readers to understand that it was an extraordinary work. The "*News of the Churches*," the monthly organ of the Scottish Free Church, was equally emphatic in its praise, pronouncing it "the religious book of the season." Strikingly original in plan and brilliant in execution, it far surpasses the expectations raised by the somewhat familiar title. It is, in truth, a bold onslaught (and the first of the kind) upon the Pantheism of Carlyle, Fichte, etc., by an ardent admirer of Carlyle; and at the same time an exhibition of the Christian Life, in its inner principle, and as illustrated in the lives of Howard, Wilberforce, Budgett, Foster, Chalmers, etc. The brilliancy and vigor of the author's style are remarkable.

PATRIARCHY; or, the Family, its Constitution and Proba[tion]. By JOHN HARRIS, D. D., President of "New College," London, and author of "The Great Teacher," "Mammon," "Pre-Adamite Earth," "Man Primeval," etc. 12mo. Cloth. $1.25. ☞ A new work of great interest.

This is the third and last of a series, by the same author, entitled "Contributions to Theological Science." The plan of this series is highly original, and has been most successfully executed. Of the two first in the series, "Pre-Adamite Earth" and "Man Primeval," we have already issued four and five editions, and the demand still continues. The immense sale of all Dr. Harris's works attest their intrinsic worth. This volume contains most important information and instruction touching the family — its nature and order, parental instruction, parental authority and government, parental responsibility, &c. It contains, in fact, such a fund of valuable information as no pastor, or head of a family, can afford to dispense with.

GOD REVEALED IN NATURE AND IN CHRIST: Including a Refutation of the Development Theory contained in the "Vestiges of the Natural History of Creation." By the Author of "THE PHILOSOPHY OF THE PLAN OF SALVATION." 12mo. Cloth. $1.00.

THE author of that remarkable book, "The Philosophy of the Plan of Salvation," has devoted several years of incessant labor to the preparation of this work. Without being specifically controversial, its aim is to overthrow several of the popular errors of the day, by establishing the antagonist truth upon an impregnable basis of reason and logic. In opposition to the doctrine of a mere subjective revelation, now so plausibly inculcated by certain eminent writers, it demonstrates the necessity of an external, objective revelation. Especially, it furnishes a new, and as it is conceived, a conclusive argument against the "*development theory*" so ingeniously maintained in the "Vestiges of the Natural History of Creation." As this author does not publish except when he has something to say, there is good reason to anticipate that the work will be one of unusual interest and value. His former book has met with the most signal success in both hemispheres, having passed through numerous editions in England and Scotland, and been translated into four of the European languages besides. It is also about to be translated into the Hindoostanee tongue. (III)

AMOS LAWRENCE.

DIARY AND CORRESPONDENCE OF THE LATE AMOS LAWRENCE; with a brief account of some Incidents in his Life. Edited by his son, WILLIAM R. LAWRENCE, M. D. With fine steel Portraits of AMOS and ABBOTT LAWRENCE, an Engraving of their Birth-place, a Fac-simile page of Mr. Lawrence's Hand-writing, and a copious Index. Octavo edition, cloth, $1.50. Royal duodecimo edition, $1.00.

This work was first published in an elegant octavo volume, and sold at the unusually low price of $1.50. At the solicitation of numerous benevolent individuals who were desirous of circulating the work—so remarkably adapted to do good, especially to young men—*gratuitously*, and of giving those of moderate means, of every class, an opportunity of possessing it, the royal duodecimo, or "*cheap edition*," was issued, varying from the other edition, only in a reduction in the size (allowing less margin), and the *thickness* of the paper.

Within six months after the first publication of this work, *twenty-two thousand* copies had been sold. This extraordinary sale is to be accounted for by the character of the man and the merits of the book. It is the memoir of a Boston merchant, who became distinguished for his great wealth, but more distinguished for the manner in which he used it. It is the memoir of a man, who, commencing business with only $20, gave away in public and private charities, *during his lifetime* more, probably, than any other person in America. It is substantially an *autobiography*, containing a full account of Mr. Lawrence's career as a merchant, of his various multiplied charities, and of his domestic life.

"We have by us another work, the 'Life of Amos Lawrence.' We heard it once said in the pulpit, 'There is no work of art like a noble life,' and for that reason he who has achieved one, takes rank with the great artists and becomes the world's property. WE ARE PROUD OF THIS BOOK. WE ARE WILLING TO LET IT GO FORTH TO OTHER LANDS AS A SPECIMEN OF WHAT AMERICA CAN PRODUCE. In the old world, reviewers have called Barnum THE characteristic American man. We are willing enough to admit that he is A characteristic American man; he is ONE fruit of our soil, but Amos Lawrence is another. Let our country have credit for him also. THE GOOD EFFECT WHICH THIS LIFE MAY HAVE IN DETERMINING THE COURSE OF YOUNG MEN TO HONOR AND VIRTUE IS INCALCULABLE."—MRS. STOWE, IN N. Y. INDEPENDENT.

"We are glad to know that our large business houses are purchasing copies of this work for each of their numerous clerks. Its influence on young men cannot be otherwise than highly salutary. As a business man, Mr. Lawrence was a pattern for the young clerk."—BOSTON TRAVELLER.

"We are thankful for the volume before us. It carries us back to the farm-house of Mr. Lawrence's birth, and the village store of his first apprenticeship. It exhibits a charity noble and active, while the young merchant was still poor. And above all, it reveals to us a beautiful cluster of sister graces, a keen sense of honor, integrity which never knew the shadow of suspicion, candor in the estimate of character, filial piety, rigid fidelity in every domestic relation, and all these connected with and flowing from steadfast religious principle, profound sentiments of devotion, and a vivid realization of spiritual truth."—NORTH AMERICAN REVIEW.

"We are glad that American Biography has been enriched by such a contribution to its treasures. In all that composes the career of 'the good man,' and the practical Christian, we have read few memoirs more full of instruction, or richer in lessons of wisdom and virtue. We cordially unite in the opinion that the publication of this memoir was a duty owed to society."—NATIONAL INTELLIGENCER.

"With the intention of placing it within the reach of a large number, the mere cost price is charged, and a more beautifully printed volume, or one calculated to do more good, has not been issued from the press of late years."—EVENING GAZETTE.

"This book, besides being of a different class from most biographies, has another peculiar charm. It shows the inside life of the man. You have, as it were, a peep behind the curtain, and see Mr. Lawrence as he went in and out among business men, as he appeared on 'change, as he received his friends, as he poured out, 'with liberal hand and generous heart,' his wealth for the benefit of others, as he received the greetings and salutations of children, and as he appeared in the bosom of his family at his own hearth stone."—BRUNSWICK TELEGRAPH.

"It is printed on new type, the best paper, and is illustrated by four beautiful plates. How it can be sold for the price named is a marvel."—NORFOLK CO. JOURNAL.

"It was first privately printed, and a limited number of copies were distributed among the relatives and near friends of the deceased. This volume was read with the deepest interest by those who were so favored as to obtain a copy, and it passed from friend to friend as rapidly as it could be read. Dr. Lawrence has yielded to the general wish and made public the volume. It will now be widely circulated, will certainly prove a standard work, and be read over and over again."—BOSTON DAILY ADVERTISER.

(p)

www.ingramcontent.com/pod-product-compliance
Lightning Source LLC
LaVergne TN
LVHW021148110826
845150LV00005B/1155

* 9 7 8 1 4 2 5 5 4 6 8 5 4 *